FLAMMARION ICONOGRAPHIC GUIDES

GODS AND HEROES
OF CLASSICAL ANTIQUITY

D1009118

FLAMMARION ICONOGRAPHIC GUIDES

GODS AND HEROES OF CLASSICAL ANTIQUITY

IRÈNE AGHION
CLAIRE BARBILLON
FRANÇOIS LISSARRAGUE

Flammarion

Paris - New York

Designed and typeset by Yves Raynaud

English translation by Leonard N. Amico

Copy-editing by Kate Swainson

Proof-reading by Scott Steedman

Origination by Welcrome, Paris
Printed and bound by Canale, Turin

Flammarion
26 rue Racine
75006 Paris

200 Park Avenue South, Suite 1406
New York
NY 10003

Original title: *Héros et Dieux de l'Antiquité* Copyright © Flammarion 1994.

For the English translation:
Copyright © Flammarion 1996. All rights reserved. No part of this publication may be reproduced in any form or by any means, electronic, photocopy, infor-mation retrieval system, or otherwise without written permission from Flammarion.

Library of Congress Catalog Card Number: 96-86005

ISBN: 2-08013-581-3 (HB)
ISBN: 2-08013-580-5 (PB)

Numéro d'édition: 1183 (HB); 1227 (PB)
Dépôt légal: October 1996

Printed in Italy

INTRODUCTION

This guide is intended for readers who love art as well as for those who are simply curious about it. Its purpose is to provide ready access to the narrative content of many works that readers are likely to come across in museums or books. It is true that paintings are more than simple illustrations, that they are above all, as Maurice Denis said, "orderly arrangements of color and form." Nevertheless, because an image essentially shows something, it often narrates or alludes to a myth or legend that has formed the basis of Western culture but whose meaning now escapes us. This is why we have made a concise collection of the tales that have inspired artists throughout the centuries.

It seemed best to arrange the tales alphabetically to help those readers looking for particular information. Like most catalogues and museum monographs, we use the Latin spelling for ancient heroes and gods and try to be consistent in the text for each entry. Nevertheless, we retain certain Greek names when doing otherwise would make the commentaries absurd; it was, after all, Athena, not Minerva, who lent her name to Athens; likewise, Hermaphroditus was more the son of Hermes and Aphrodite than of Mercury and Venus. When Greek names differ from Latin ones, as in Athena and Minerva or Dionysus and Bacchus, cross-references are made to the Latin. We also provide a translation of these names in the principal European languages so that readers can get their bearings when faced with foreign-language titles.

Where legends consist of more than one episode and introduce many characters, we treat each episode separately under headings reserved for minor characters. This makes information about minor characters more easily accessible. Thus, Adonis appears separately from Venus, and although Jupiter's lovers are mentioned in the entry on this god, they are discussed in greater detail under their own name: Antiope, Danaë, Europa, and Ganymede, for example. Some entries are not about heroes or gods but instead explain a Latin quotation (*Quos ego*) or group related themes (hunting or metamorphosis, for example) and then refer the reader to individual entries for more detailed information.

Each character entry opens with a brief account of the historical or mythological tradition, highlighting the important features that clarify the meaning of the works of art. Next, the ways in which the myth or legend is represented are discussed, with distinctions made between ancient and modern representations. Broadly speaking, all artistic production from the Renaissance to the present is classed as modern. Consequently, all mythical characters—gods, heroes, or mere mortals—are studied from two perspectives. In contrast, historical figures often have no ancient iconography and many were not portrayed before the early Middle Ages, by which time they had become moralizing heroes with exemplary virtues.

When necessary, the entries end with a list of attributes, cross-references to other entries, sources, and a concise bibliography. Defining an attribute is difficult. The term traditionally refers to the precise iconographic element that distinguishes one character from another, such as Mercury's caduceus or Apollo's lyre. In contrast to saints in Christian iconography, however, ancient characters were not systematically endowed with attributes, so this aspect of the guide is far from consistent. Ancient iconography, for all that has been said of it, was not so mechanical: except for some gods whose attributes indicate their sphere of activity, in ancient art there are hardly any attributes in the strict sense of the term.

In the section on sources, we note the texts from which modern works of art derive—when such texts exist—rather than all the texts that allude to a specific character and which the reader will find in specialized encyclopedias. Here again the problem is complex, for ancient and modern images do not work according to the same logic. The question is not *whether* images illustrate texts, but rather *when* they do. Achilles, for example, appears in many ancient works of art that do not follow to the letter what is for us the fundamental account of Achilles' adventures—*The Iliad*. Indeed, ancient craftsmen knew more about this hero than we do, and they accordingly followed their own inspiration to narrate his feats visually. Since the Renaissance, however, access to ancient culture has been filtered through a system of learning that is largely dependent on philology and a close reading of the relevant texts. The result is that, since the Renaissance, painters have made reference to *The Iliad* for Achilles much more explicitly than their Greek or Roman predecessors did. Moreover, the original written accounts of these ancient tales and legends were often reworked by modern authors in their efforts to reassemble them into books for easier reading. Ultimately, works such as Boccaccio's *Genealogy of the Gods* (1472) or Chompré's *Concise Dictionary of Fable* (1759)—to cite only two—were republished so often that they became like bibles for artists and poets from the fifteenth through nineteenth centuries. This explains why bringing together ancient and modern images, as we have here, permits the reader to assess the influence of a mythological theme as well as to appreciate the variety of interpretations such a theme inspired.

At the end of an entry, we sometimes cite books or articles that treat the iconography of a specific character in greater depth. Nevertheless, the principal iconographic repertories are found in the general bibliography.

The format of this guide limited both the number and length of entries, and a concern for brevity led to some works of art being left out of the sections analyzing representations. We did not seek to be exhaustive and instead of discussing general considerations preferred to cite particular works, specifying their date and location, citing sometimes the best known and sometimes the rarest. The same applies to our choice of illustrations, for which we sought to mix ancient with modern and rare with familiar.

The goal of the book, then, is both modest and practical. It shows how artists interpret mythology and ancient history, but is neither a history of mythology nor a treatise on the nature of mythology. Instead, it more simply intends to guide the footsteps, open the eyes, and assist in looking.

AN EXAMPLE: MANTEGNA'S *PARNASSUS*

Clearly, understanding a painting does not end with identifying its subject, and an iconographic analysis, while indispensable, falls far short of doing justice to the richness of a work of art. Mantegna's *Parnassus*, painted for Isabella d'Este in 1497 and now in the Louvre, readily exemplifies this. At first glance, the painting is about a group of

Parnassus.
Andrea Mantegna, 1497.
Paris, Louvre.

ancient gods. Mars and Venus stand side by side on an arch of rock in front of a bed, dominating the composition. A cupid shoots his blow-pipe at the god Vulcan, seen at left in his forge. In the right fore-ground, Mercury accompanies Pegasus. In the center of the painting, the nine Muses dance at the divine couple's feet to the sound of the lyre played by Apollo, who is seated on a tree stump. Such a scene, although portraying only ancient gods, has no parallel in antiquity. The grouping of Mars, Venus, Vulcan, Mercury, Apollo, and the Muses instead reflects a specific historical context: the fifteenth century, the city of Mantua, and the court of the Gonzagas.

Gian Francesco Gonzaga's wife, Isabella d'Este, commissioned the painting from Mantegna to decorate her *studiolo*, a special room reserved for meditation and study in the tradition of those found, for instance, at Ferrara and Urbino. One principle behind such rooms, which sometimes contained collections of precious objects and anti-quities, was to strike a certain thematic harmony not only between the room and its decoration but also between its collection and the identity of its owner. Isabella d'Este's *studiolo*, as the 1975 study by Sylvie Beguin beautifully demonstrates, was a model of its kind. To better understand Mantegna's work, one must as far as possible imagine it in its original context, with its patron and her collection of antiquities as well as with the entire figurative program of which this painting is but one element.

Isabella would certainly have chosen a mythological theme as she was an impassioned intellectual, reader of Latin, and patron of music and dance. Her collection comprised ancient reliefs—including a sarcophagus representing Pluto, Proserpine, Mercury, and Cerberus—as well as bronze miniatures of the monumental sculptures, such as the *Apollo Belvedere*, that were once the glory of ancient Rome. She therefore chose paintings inspired by classical antiquity to accompany these objects.

Mantegna's painting, in which Mars and Venus triumph, is actually an allegory of the Mantuan court, celebrating the marriage of

7

Isabella d'Este and Gian Francesco Gonzaga. As a great military leader, Gonzaga appropriately appears here in the guise of Mars; this makes his wife Venus, but a virtuous and celestial Venus who acts as protectress of the arts, as the Muses dancing at the couple's feet suggest. Any notion of marital discord is effaced by relegating to the background Vulcan, the blacksmith whom Love rejected, making Mars and Venus appear the parents of Harmony. Highly symbolic fruits and flowers surround the couple: myrtle (Venus's flower), quince and lemons (fruits associated with marriage), and laurel (befitting the Muses and victory). But there is more. The colors of the sheets on the couple's bed—blue, red, and white—are those of the planets Venus, Mars, and Mercury, as well those of the d'Este and Gonzaga families. The presence of Mercury and Pegasus in the foreground might appear strange but is explicable as an allusion to the planet and constellation that presided over the couple's marriage. Thus, more than just a courtly allegory that portrays princes as gods, the painting makes an appeal to several systems of reference that, while operating individually through a color code, a plant code, and an astrological code, function in parallel and generally serve to identify the couple and the circumstances celebrated in the painting.

If we now take into account the other paintings commissioned for the *studiolo*, a similar spirit involving the allegorical use of mythology becomes evident. The original ensemble comprised seven paintings, each of which entered the Louvre by different routes. Besides this *Parnassus*, Mantegna painted a pendant, *Pallas Expelling the Vices from the Grove of Virtue*, in which Isabella is now likened to the goddess of wisdom. Perugino provided *The Battle of Love and Chastity*. A *Reign of Comus*, a subject drawn from the *Dionysiaca* of Nonnus, was begun by Mantegna and completed by Costa, who also executed a *Coronation*, a kind of allegory of Isabella's court. Two canvases by Correggio were later added: an *Allegory of the Virtues* and an *Allegory of the Vices*. Mythology impregnates the entire group and portrays Isabella in the dual role of Venus and Minerva, a spiritual and moral goddess. Each painting would have reinforced the allegorical value of those around it, using mythology to uphold a view of the world and its governing princes rather than to relate legendary events. Thus mythology can serve as a repertory of themes from which the artist may draw inspiration at will and which can be freely enriched by playing on seemingly inexhaustible associations and combinations.

Finally, we note that the title usually given to Mantegna's painting, *Parnassus*, dates from the nineteenth century and that Parnassus is most unlikely to be the subject. The presence of Pegasus, who caused the Hippocrene spring, where the Muses quench their thirst, to gush forth with a kick of his hoof, could have encouraged identification with Parnassus. However, his presence may be explained otherwise, as we have noted. The presence of the nine dancing Muses is insufficient to place the work among the many other depictions of Parnassus where Apollo reigns. In its turn, the title that Mantegna's painting bears today modifies our perception of the work.

This brief exercise cannot be repeated systematically, and any analysis must first define the limits of its conceptual framework. Nevertheless, each work of art should be placed in the original context or epoch of its patrons and viewers. As Gombrich amusingly reminds one of his interlocutors, "everything is always more complicated."

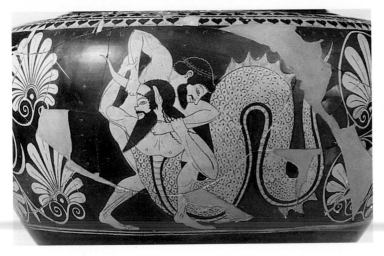

Achelous and Hercules Wrestling.
Attic red-figure stamnos by Oltos, c. 500 B.C.
London, British Museum.

ACHELOUS

Gk. and Ger. Acheloos; Lat. and Sp. Achelous; It. Acheloo; Fr. Achéloos.
River god.

HISTORY/MYTHOLOGY

This river god is known largely for his fight with Hercules over the affections of Deianira, daughter of King Oeneus of Calydon. Despite his many metamorphoses, including a serpent, a bull, and a sea monster, Hercules finally wrestled him down and tore off one of his horns.

REPRESENTATIONS

The head of Achelous—with its long beard and mustache, animal horns, and ears—is found as a decorative element on Etruscan metalwork of the fifth and fourth centuries B.C. It is engraved on the bronze bases of some Etruscan mirrors and in low relief on many handle braces for bronze vases, on pendants for gold necklaces, and, more modestly, on small terracotta ornaments.

In the same period, Achelous's profile is found on a variety of Greek marble reliefs (notably in Athens, Acropolis Museum). He rarely appears as an isolated figure in Greek ceramics; some examples show him wrestling with Hercules (Attic, black-figure vases, late sixth–early fifth centuries B.C.). Hercules also appears on a particularly important example of Attic red-figure ceramics, painted by Oltos, in which Achelous, who has a human face and the body of an animal, is shown having one of his horns torn off by Hercules (c. 500 B.C., London, British Museum).

Achelous also figures in numerous intaglios, as well as on Sicilian (Gela) and southern Italian coins from the late sixth to the third centuries B.C.

Modern representations, other than sixteenth- through eighteenth-century Italian ones, are rare. Notable from the Italian works are a painting by Guido Reni in which Achelous takes on human form (*Hercules Fighting with Achelous*, 1620–21, Paris, Louvre) and the lost

9

painting by Giovanni Antonio da Pordenone (1483–1539) which once decorated the gallery of the Palais Royal in Paris.

Attributes: Beard and long mustache. Body of an animal (bull, sea serpent). Human face with horns and ears of an animal.

Cross-references: Deianira. Hercules.

Sources: Ovid, *Metamorphoses* IX, 1–97.

Bibliography: H. P. Isler, *Acheloos*, Berne, 1970.

ACHILLES

Gk. Achilleus; Lat. Achilles; It. and Fr. Achille; Sp. Aquiles; Ger. Achiles.
Greek hero and a central character in *The Iliad*.

HISTORY/MYTHOLOGY

Ajax Carrying the Body of Achilles. Detail from an Attic krater, c. 570 B.C. Florence, Museo Archeologico.

Achilles, the "best of the Achaeans," was the son of a goddess, Thetis, and a mortal, Peleus. His mother dipped him into the river Styx to make him invulnerable but held him by one heel, which became his only weak spot; according to other versions of the legend, she dipped him into fire. Frightened, Peleus took the child away from his mother and entrusted him to the centaur Chiron, who taught him music and the art of hunting. According to *The Iliad*, Ulysses, Nestor, and Patroclus urged Achilles to join their expedition against Troy as leader of the Myrmidons. It was then that Thetis warned her son that he must choose between a life that would be brief but filled with glory and one that would be long but buried in obscurity; Achilles chose glory.

A later variant of the legend claims that, after an oracle predicted that Achilles would die at Troy, his parents dressed him as a girl and sent him to Lycomedes, king of Scyros, who raised him with his daughters. When the soothsayer Calchas warned Ulysses that Troy could not be taken without Achilles, however, Ulysses came up with a scheme. He disguised himself as a merchant selling cloth and embroideries, and paid a visit to the court of Lycomedes; hidden among the goods he offered for sale were weapons, and Achilles, unable to resist, revealed his true nature by reaching for them.

The Iliad is not about the war with Troy, but rather about an episode from the tenth year of the siege: the wrath of Achilles. The Greeks had abducted Chryseis, the daughter of Apollo's priest, during a raid, and she was awarded to Agamemnon when the spoils were divided up. When a plague broke out afterward in the Greek camp, however, the soothsayer Calchas explained that it was sent by Apollo to avenge Chryseis's father, whereupon Achilles compelled Agamemnon to restore the maiden to her father. Agamemnon demanded in return the share of spoils that had been awarded to Achilles: the beautiful Briseïs. Outraged, Achilles retired to his tent and refused to take his place in combat. The Greeks consequently resisted Trojan attacks with difficulty, until their camp was threatened. Despite pleas from Agamemnon and ambassadors from Ulysses, nothing could shake Achilles from his wrath. At Achilles' darkest hour, his loyal friend Patroclus got him to agree to loan him his armor. Patroclus, now disguised as Achilles, succeeded in upsetting the Trojans, and disaster was averted, but not without a heavy price, for Patroclus was killed by Hector, who stripped him of his armor. Grief-stricken, Achilles called for help from his mother, Thetis, who

The Education of Achilles.
Giovanni Battista Rosso,
c. 1534–37.
Galerie François I,
Fontainebleau,
Château de Fontainebleau.

went to Hephaestus and ordered a new suit of armor. He then
became reconciled with Agamemnon, returned to battle, drove back
the Trojans, and avenged Patroclus by killing Hector, whose corpse
he insulted by dragging it behind his chariot seven times around Troy.
He organized a funeral for Patroclus and at first refused to surrender
Hector's body to his parents, but when the gods became outraged, he
conceded by exchanging Hector's corpse for an enormous ransom:
Priam himself.

Other accounts depict the battle which Achilles fought with the
Amazons, who sided with the Trojans, and how he fell in love with
Penthesilea at the very moment of killing her with his sword. Achilles
himself was in turn killed by Paris with an arrow to the heel, his only
weak spot. During the fall of Troy, the young Polyxena, Priam's
daughter, was sacrificed on Achilles' tomb.

REPRESENTATIONS

Ancient representations of Achilles, the Greek hero par excellence,
are abundant and depict the whole of his life. Some late works form
complete cycles; these include the marble coping of the Capitoline
(fourth century A.D., Rome) and—with no fewer than seven scenes
devoted to Achilles' childhood and education—the silver plate of
Kaiseraugst (mid-fourth century B.C., August).

The bath in the Styx is depicted in a mosaic from Xanthos (fifth
century B.C., Museum of Antalya). Achilles entrusted to Chiron is a
frequent subject in Attic ceramics (amphora, c. 520 B.C., Boulogne-sur-
Mer, Musée). In Pompeian painting, Chiron is seen teaching Achilles
to play the lyre. Achilles unmasking himself at the court of Lycomedes
is the subject of several Roman monuments. In such works, Achilles
usually leaps into the foreground and grabs a shield from the goods
brought by Ulysses; he may be dressed as a girl (sarcophagus, c. A.D.
200, Naples, Museo Archeologico), or appear as a heroic nude (sarcophagus, second quarter of the third century A.D., Paris, Louvre). The
arming of Achilles is depicted on many ancient vases, whether it be
the arming that took place when Achilles left Phthia, in which case
Thetis is accompanied by Nereids who carry a complete outfit (hydria,
c. 550 B.C., Paris, Louvre), or the one that took place later, when

Thetis replaced the armor that Hector stripped off Patroclus (amphora by Amasis Painter, c. 540 B.C., Boston, Museum of Fine Arts).

Two episodes from the life of Achilles hold an important place in ceramic iconography. One is the hunt for the young Troilus, Priam's youngest son, for which illustrations of the following sequences occur equally frequently: Achilles waits in ambush behind the fountain where Troilus has brought his horse to drink (Laconian dinos, c. 560 B.C., Paris, Louvre); Achilles chases the young horseman and his sister Polyxena, who lets her hydria fall (hydria from the Leagros Group, c. 520 B.C., London, British Museum); Achilles gets ready to kill Troilus, who has sought sanctuary on Apollo's altar (Tyrrhenian amphora, c. 560 B.C., Florence, Museo Archeologico). The second episode is Achilles playing dice with Ajax (amphora by Exekias, c. 540 B.C., Rome, Musei Vaticani).

Episodes corresponding to those described in *The Iliad*—the wrath of Achilles—are also represented. During his quarrel with Agamemnon, Achilles draws his sword while Thetis tries to restrain him (lost Pompeian fresco). In Ulysses' mission to Achilles, as depicted by the Kleophrades Painter, the hero is completely enveloped in his cloak, lowers his head, and refuses to speak (hydria, c. 480 B.C., Munich, Antikensammlungen). In another work by the same artist, Patroclus leaves Achilles to join the battle after receiving his armor (stamnos, c. 480 B.C., Rome, Villa Giulia). Often represented is the duel between Achilles and Hector, which takes place in the presence of gods; in an example by the Berlin Painter, Athena encourages Achilles while Apollo encourages Hector (krater, c. 490 B.C., London, British Museum). Even more popular among vase painters, however, was Achilles insulting Hector's corpse by dragging it behind his chariot; the avenged soul of Patroclus hovers above the chariot (hydria from the Leagros Group, c. 510 B.C., Boston, Museum of Fine Arts). That scene also appears on Roman sarcophagi, on lamps, and on a silver vessel (oenochoe from Berthouville, first century A.D., Paris, Bibliothèque Nationale, Cabinet des Médailles). In the context of Hector's ransom, vase painters depicted Priam coming to plead with

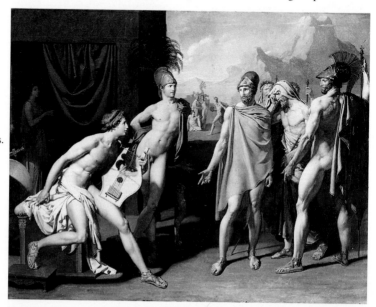

The Envoys from Agamemnon Sent to Achilles to Urge Him to Fight, Find Him in His Tent with Patroclus, Singing of the Feats of the Heroes.
Jean-Auguste-Dominique Ingres, 1801.
Paris,
École des Beaux-Arts.

Achilles, who is in the middle of eating while Hector's body lies on his bed (skyphos by the Brygos Painter, c. 490 B.C., Vienna, Kunsthistorisches Museum). In Roman representations of the ransom, Achilles is seated and Priam kneels before him in barbarian costume (sarcophagus, third century A.D., Paris, Louvre; stucco relief, c. A.D. 160, Rome, Via Latina).

Artists also illustrated the post-Homeric additions to the Achilles legend, including his battle with Penthesilea and his battle with Memnon, the goddess Aurora's son. In the case of the second subject, the heroes' divine mothers are present and sometimes beg Jupiter to save their sons; Jupiter then has Mercury weigh each hero's destiny on a scale (psychostasia: cup by Epictetus, c. 510 B.C., Rome, Villa Giulia). Achilles being killed by Paris with an arrow to the heel is represented very early, but the subject is rare (Protocorinthian aryballos, c. 680 B.C., Athens, National Museum); more frequently represented is Ajax carrying the dead body of Achilles on his back (shield band, c. 560 B.C., Olympia; krater by Kleitias, c. 570 B.C., Florence, Museo Archeologico).

The entire life of Achilles has sometimes been painted in modern times as a cycle. The most important example was provided by Rubens and actually consists of a series of sketches and paintings for tapestries (c. 1631, seven of the eight sketches are in Rotterdam, Museum Boymans-van Beuningen; of the paintings, three are in Madrid, Prado, and two are in Pau, Musée des Beaux-Arts). The division of sequences adopted by Rubens corresponds to the most frequently represented themes in the pictorial tradition.

The earliest episode, that of Thetis dipping Achilles into the Styx, is attested by a drawing attributed to Giulio Romano, but often found in the context of complete cycles, such as the one by Donato Creti (1671–1749, Bologna, Pinacoteca).

The education of Achilles is a much more frequent subject. It was depicted at Fontainebleau (Rosso, c. 1534–37, Galerie François I) and in a series of four panels by Jean-Baptiste de Champaigne (1666–71, two in the Louvre, two in the Château de Maison-Laffitte). In each of those examples as well as in a painting by Giuseppe Maria Crespi (c. 1695, Vienna, Kunsthistorisches Museum), the subject serves to evoke the ideal of a princely education in the arts of the hunt, war, and music.

The subject of Ulysses trying to tempt Achilles, disguised as a girl, away from the court of Lycomedes appears on a cassone by Niccolo Giolfino (1476–1555, Verona, Museo). It was a popular theme in baroque painting, for the sumptuous display of Ulysses' cloth and jewels allowed artists to combine the richness of still-life painting with a play of facial expressions and sexual ambiguity, as exemplified in a work by Carlo Cicagni, in which Achilles is about to unsheathe a sword (1628–1719, Kassel, Gemäldegalerie). Poussin depicted the subject several times: the king's daughters are grouped around a chest while Achilles, at right and wearing a helmet, either contemplates his new image in a mirror (1656, Richmond, Museum of Fine Arts) or grabs a sword (c. 1651, Boston, Museum of Fine Arts).

A rarer subject is Achilles about to stab Agamemnon with his sword while Minerva tries to control his anger (fresco by Tiepolo, 1757, Vicenza, Villa Valmarana, Salla de Iliade). The degradation of Hector's corpse is also depicted by David in *The Obsequies of Patroclus*, a work in which Achilles is seen presenting Hector's corpse to that of Patroclus (1779, Dublin, National Gallery of Ireland).

Attributes: Arms. Chariot. Dice.

Cross-references: Agamemnon. Ajax the Greater. Amazons. Chiron. Hector. Memnon. Paris. Patroclus. Penthesilea. Polyxena. Thetis. Ulysses.

Sources: Homer, *The Iliad*. Statius, *Achilleide*.

Bibliography: E. Haverkamp-Begemann, *The Achilles Series, Corpus Rubenianum Ludvig Burchard*, vol. 10, London, 1975. D. Kemp-Lindemann, *Darstellungen des Achilleus in greichischen und römischen Kunst*, Frankfurt, 1975.

ACIS *See* Galatea.

ACTAEON

Gk. and Ger. Aktaion; Lat. Actaeon; It. Atteone; Sp. Acteon; Fr. Actéon.
Young prince from Greek mythology.

HISTORY/MYTHOLOGY

Actaeon was the son of Aristaeus and Cadmus's daughter, Autonoe, but he was raised by the centaur Chiron, who taught him how to hunt. He unwittingly surprised the goddess Diana while she was bathing nude in a spring with her companions the nymphs. Offended, Diana changed him into a stag, whereupon he was devoured by his own dogs.

REPRESENTATIONS

The moment chosen in antiquity is Actaeon's death. Young, beardless, and dressed as a hunter, he defends himself with a club against a pack of attacking dogs. No metamorphosis is visible; instead, the dogs simply fail to recognize their master and mistake him for wild game. Actaeon is shown with an animal skin tied around his shoulders in a metope from Selinunte (c. 465 B.C., Palermo, Museo Nazionale). He is shown

Actaeon Devoured by His Dogs. Metope from the Temple of Selinunte, c. 465 B.C. Palermo, Museo Nazionale.

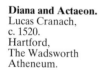

Diana and Actaeon. Lucas Cranach, c. 1520. Hartford, The Wadsworth Atheneum.

falling backward on one knee in most Attic vases. The Pan Painter provided two versions of the subject: in one Actaeon is a simple hunter (480 B.C. krater in Boston, Museum of Fine Arts); in another he is entirely clothed in an animal skin (c. 470 B.C., fragmentary krater from Athens, National Museum). From the fourth century onward, Italiot vase painters, followed by Pompeian painters, depict Actaeon's metamorphosis: on a head that is still human are stag horns.

Actaeon has been a frequent subject in modern art since the beginning of the fifteenth century, especially in Italian art (Cesari, *Diana and Actaeon*, c. 1600, Paris, Louvre). Titian painted two separate episodes: the frightened Actaeon discovering Diana and her companions (c. 1556–59, Edinburgh, National Gallery of Scotland), and Actaeon devoured by his dogs while the goddess pursues him (after 1559, Harewood House). Albani (1578–1660) created two versions of the *Metamorphosis of Actaeon into a Stag* in which the metamorphosis has barely begun. In general, painters focused on the moment when Actaeon surprises Diana while she bathes; under the pretext of celebrating the goddess's modesty, the subject allowed artists to illustrate the theme of the voyeur and, at the same time, to make the painting's spectator an unpunished voyeur. Two different scenes from the legend are often combined: the goddess and her companions bathing, and the same group being frightened by the intruder, as demonstrated in the many versions by Cavaliere d'Arpino (c. 1600, seven versions, one of which is in the Louvre). In the eighteenth century, the focus is on the play between transgression and voyeurism: painters add a more explicitly erotic dimension to their works, and Diana seems less cruel. One example of this is de Troy's painting *Diana Surprised by Actaeon* (1734, Basel, Kunstmuseum), in which the goddess seems to watch with remorse as Actaeon turns into a stag and retreats from the group of nymphs.

Attributes: Horns (of a stag). Hunting costume.

Cross-references: Chiron. Diana.

Sources: Ovid, *Metamorphoses* III, 131–252.

Bibliography: E. W. Leach, "Metamorphoses of the Actaeon Myth in Campanian Painting," *Mitteilungen des deutschen Archäologisches Instituts* 88 (1981): 307–27; S. Z. Levine, "To See or Not to See, the Myth of Diana and Actaeon in the Eighteenth Century," *The Loves of the Gods*, ex. cat., Fort Worth, 1992, pp. 73–95.

ADMETA *See Alcestis.*

ADONIS

Gk., Lat., Sp., Fr., and Ger. Adonis; It. Adone.
Divinity with Semitic origins.

HISTORY/MYTHOLOGY

Adonis was the offspring of an incestuous union brought about by Venus. His mother, Myrrha, had offended Venus by not worshiping her, and for this reason was made to fall in love with her own father, King Cinyras of Paphos, who then slept with Myrrha without recognizing her. When Cinyras became aware of what had happened, he tried

Venus and Adonis.
Fresco from Pompeii,
first century B.C.
Naples, Museo Nazionale.

Adonis at the Hunt and the Death of Adonis. Sarcophagus, second century A.D. Paris, Louvre.

to kill Myrrha, who fled and was turned into a myrrh tree by the gods. It is from this tree that Adonis was born. Sheltered by the nymphs and as beautiful as love itself, Adonis seduced even Venus, who followed him while he hunted and also advised him on the dangerous animals to avoid. He was nevertheless killed by a wild boar. Venus wept over him, then founded a cult in his honor and, from a mixture of his blood and nectar, created a new flower: the anemone. Another version of the myth has Jupiter entrust Adonis to Persephone for a portion of the year and to Venus for the remainder.

REPRESENTATIONS

Adonis is shown surrounded by Venus, cupids, and nymphs on several ancient vases from the end of the fifth century B.C. Dating from the same period is a small series of vases with representations of "gardens of Adonis," a festival celebrated by women in the dead hero's honor. The sharing of Adonis by Venus and Persephone is a subject found on an Apulian pelike: the two goddesses stand on either side of Zeus, who is enthroned, with Adonis stretched out on a bed in the lower register (middle of the fourth century B.C., Naples, Museo Archeologico).

In Roman art, both the birth and death of Adonis appear in Pompeian painting (A.D. 63, House of the Dioscuri, and A.D. 68–79, House of Adonis, respectively). Several ancient Roman sarcophagi narrate the whole story of the young hunter: Adonis bids farewell to Venus before leaving for the hunt; Adonis is wounded by the wild boar; Venus tends to the wounded Adonis; and Venus mourns Adonis (second century A.D., an example in Paris, Louvre).

The subject of Venus and Adonis has been very popular in modern times, and representations are accordingly numerous. The birth of Adonis appears from the end of the fifteenth century, when it was depicted by Giorgione (lost, cited by Ridolfi in 1648); it also appears in baroque painting, as exemplified by Guerchino (Dresden) and Franceschini (1648–1729, three versions in Genoa, Vienna, and Dresden). A drawing by Poussin, created for Lord Marin, who dedicated a poem to this subject, demonstrates this artist's interest in the myth (1623, Windsor), which Boucher also depicted (c. 1760, painting known through engravings). In such works, Myrrha is shown transformed into a tree and surrounded by nymphs, who assist her during childbirth; Diana herself is sometimes seen holding the newborn.

The scene most often represented is Venus trying to prevent Adonis from leaving for the hunt while cupids restrain the young hero's dogs. The play between glances and touches is the major focus of such works, whose model apparently derives from a painting by Titian (1553–54, Madrid, Prado, variants in Rome, Galleria Nazionale

Achilles Grasps at the Shade of Patroclus.
Henry Fuseli, 1803.
Zurich, Kunsthaus.

Alexander's Victory over Darius.
Albrecht Altdorfer, 1529.
Munich, Alte Pinakothek.

The Death of Adonis.
Engraving by Pierre
Louis de Surugue after
Boucher,
eighteenth century.
Paris, Bibliothèque
Nationale de France,
Cabinet des Estampes.

and London, National Gallery). The same subject appears in the work
of many painters, including Veronese (several versions, one in Madrid,
Prado, c. 1580), Cornelisz van Haarlem (several versions, one in New
York, Metropolitan Museum of Art, and Poussin (c. 1625, Rhode
Island). That tradition was continued in French painting in works by
Nicolas Mignard (c. 1650, Minneapolis), Louis de Boullogne (1668,
Versailles) and François Lemoyne (1729, Stockholm).

The death of Adonis, with Venus discovering her lover lying on
the ground, is less frequently depicted. It appears in Poussin's *The
Kingdom of Flora*, in which Venus causes the anemone to spring from
Adonis's blood (1631, Dresden). In a fresco by Rosso at
Fontainebleau, Venus is seen tearing her hair as she descends from
heaven in her chariot; three winged graces lift the body of Adonis (c.
1536, Galerie François I). Veronese's version is less dramatic and at
the same time more moving: a cupid supports the head of Adonis
while Venus takes his hand (*Venus with the Dying Adonis and
Amorini*, c. 1580, Stockholm, Nationalmuseum). Poussin depicted
Venus in tears and kneeling beside the corpse (c. 1627, Caen, Musée
des Beaux-Arts). The birth of the anemone is clearly indicated in
Lépicié's pendant for another floral myth, the story of Narcissus (1769,
Versailles, Petit Trianon).

Attributes: Boar. Bow. Hunting dogs. Tree.

Cross-references: Venus.

Sources: Ovid, *Metamorphoses* X, 298–518 (Myrrha) and 708–39 (Adonis). Apollodorus, III, 14, 3 gives a different version. Bion of Smyrna, *Lament for Adonis.*

Bibliography: W. Atallah, *Adonis dans la littérature et l'art grec*, Paris, 1966. *The Loves of the Gods*, ex. cat., Fort Worth, 1992, pp. 262–7, 492.

ADRASTUS *See* Amphiaraus.

AEGEUS

Gk. and Ger. Aigeus; Lat. Ægeus; It. Egeo; Sp. Egeo; Fr. Égée.
Legendary Athenian king.

HISTORY/MYTHOLOGY

Aegeus, an Athenian king, was the father of Theseus. Nevertheless, on Theseus's return to Athens after a long absence, Aegeus did not immediately recognize his son. Meanwhile Medea, whom Aegeus had married during Theseus's absence, tried to poison her stepson. Theseus was saved only after Aegeus identified him by the sword he carried.

REPRESENTATIONS

Representations of Aegeus are rare and almost exclusively limited to ancient art. The king is seen consulting Thetis at Delphi, probably, as Petrarch tells us, to discover whether or not he will have a descendant, on an Attic cup attributed to the Codrus Painter (c. 440 B.C., Berlin, Antikensmuseum). Aegeus also appears as a secondary figure at his son's confrontation with the Marathon bull (krater from the Polygnotus Group, c. 440 B.C., New York, Metropolitan Museum of Art). Finally, Aegeus is shown with other Attic heroes at the birth of Erichtonius on a cup by the Codrus Painter (c. 440 B.C., Berlin, Antikensmuseum).

Theseus Recognized by His Father.
Hippolyte Flandrin, 1832.
Paris,
École des Beaux-Arts.

Aegeus welcomes his son in Paolo Uccello's painting of the adventures of Theseus (c. 1460, Seattle Art Museum). The subject for the 1832 Prix de Rome competition, won by Hippolyte Flandrin, was "Theseus Recognized by His Father" (Paris, École des Beaux-Arts).

Attributes: Scepter.

Cross-references: Theseus.

Sources: Plutarch, *Life of Theseus* III, 5. Ovid, *Metamorphoses* VII, 404–24.

AEGISTHUS *See* Agamemnon.

AENEAS

Gk. and Ger. Aineias; Lat. Æneas; It. Enea; Sp. Eneas; Fr. Énée. Trojan hero.

HISTORY/MYTHOLOGY

Aeneas, a Trojan leader, was the son of Venus and Anchises, and husband of Creusa, the daughter of Priam, king of Troy. He accompanied Paris to Sparta in search of Helen and confronted the principal Greek heroes during the Trojan War. When Troy fell, he fled with his father (Anchises), his son (Ascanius), and the city's penates, which earned him the name Aeneas the Pious. He set sail for Italy with a group of Trojans and, after a long voyage, which included a stay in Carthage with its queen, Dido, he landed at Latium, where he married Lavinia. He fought Turnus, king of the Rutulians, and subsequently founded Latium. He disappeared during a storm.

REPRESENTATIONS

The Sacrifice of Aeneas.
9 B.C.
Rome, Ara Pacis.

Aeneas appears frequently as a subject in both Greek and Roman art. He appears beside Paris during the abduction of Helen on an Attic vase (skyphos by Makron, c. 490 B.C., Boston, Museum of Fine Arts) and fights Achilles on Homeric basins (150–125 B.C., Athens, National Museum). In an important series of vases, Aeneas flees Troy with Anchises on his back (oenochoe, c. 510 B.C., Paris, Louvre). He is also depicted on gems and in Pompeian painting, including caricatures (Herculaneum); on some Greek coins from the city of Aieneia, which considered Aeneas its founder (Chalicidan, fifth century B.C.); and on some Roman coins, starting from the reign of Caesar, who, as a member of the Julian *gens Julia*, traced his ancestry to Aeneas. This iconography, as found on various coins from the Imperial period, implied allegiance to Rome.

The encounter with Dido at Carthage, as well as the hunt during which Dido seduces Aeneas, is found in mosaics and on sarcophagi (sarcophagus, c. A.D. 150, Rome, Museo Nazionale Romano). The discovery of an extraordinary sow, which was interpreted as an augur for the prosperity of Aeneas's descendants, and the ensuing sacrifice of the animal, appears on several reliefs, notably reliefs from the Ara Pacis, or the Altar of Peace, which Augustus consecrated (9 B.C., Rome). Virgil's *Aeneid* ensured the popularity of the Aeneas myth and fixed its components, particularly through illustrated versions of

Dido with Aeneas Recounting the Misfortunes of Troy.
Pierre-Narcisse Guérin, 1815. Paris, Louvre.

all Aeneas's adventures, beginning with his battle against Turnus (fifth century A.D., manuscript in Rome, Vatican).

Modern artists have largely focused on Virgil's tale of Dido and Aeneas. Representations of this subject are often in the form of a series of paintings or frescoes (paintings by Niccolò dell'Abbate, before 1552, Modena, Galleria Estense; frescoes by Ludovico Carracci, 1584, Bologna, Palazzo Fava). A series of seven paintings by Antoine Coypel for the Regent corresponds to the following episodes: Aeneas appearing to Dido; Aeneas carrying Anchises; the death of Dido; the descent of Aeneas into Hades; Jupiter appearing to Aeneas; Evander mourning the death of his son Pallas; Turnus slain by Aeneas (1716–17, now in Paris, Louvre, in Montpellier, and in Arras).

The subject of Aeneas carrying Anchises on his shoulders became emblematic of filial piety (Alciati, 1602 edition, emblem 194) and occurs frequently in painting. Adam Elsheimer provided a dramatic, nocturnal version that is set against a background of fire (c. 1600, Munich, Alte Pinakothek), whereas Lionello Spada focused on the family, including Aeneas, Anchises, Creusa, and Ascanius (c. 1600, Paris, Louvre). This subject also occurs in sculpture (Bernini, c. 1619, Rome, Galleria Borghese; Lepautre, 1696–1716, Paris, Tuileries). A rarer subject is the battle with the Harpies, the mythical creatures who befouled the dinner of Aeneas's companions (François Perrier, c. 1646, Paris, Louvre). More frequent subjects are: Aeneas and Dido taking refuge from a storm in a grotto, where they make love (Gaspard Dughet, seventeenth century, London, National Gallery) and the descent into Hades under the Sibyl's guidance. In Giuseppe Maria Crespi's painting of the latter, Charon is in the foreground and the Sibyl takes Aeneas by the hand (1665–1747, Vienna, Kunsthistorisches Museum). Other artists preferred to represent this subject in the context of a sweeping landscape that is set either in the Elysian Fields (Sebastiano Conca, 1680–1764, Florence, Galleria Feroni) or on the shores of Lake Avernus, where Aeneas plucked the golden bough that gave him access to the Underworld (Turner, *Aeneas and the Sibyl, Lake Avernus*, 1798, London, Tate Gallery).

Venus visiting Vulcan's forge to ask for arms for Aeneas is a very frequent subject (Giulio Romano, 1525, Mantua, Palazzo Ducale; Le

Nain, 1641, Reims, Musée Saint-Denis). The presence of cupids beside the goddess, who visits her official husband, distinguishes this scene from another that is rare and shows Thetis asking for arms for Achilles. The erotic rapport between Venus and Vulcan is as explicit in a work by Boucher (1732, Paris, Louvre) as it is in another by Nantoir (1734, Montpellier, Musée Fabre). Poussin depicted the next scene, in which Venus directs Aeneas's attention to the weapons and armor, positioned like booty at the foot of a tree (1639, Rouen, Musée des Beaux-Arts).

Finally, in representations of the apotheosis of Aeneas, the hero is shown bathing in the river Numicius while Venus anoints him with immortalizing ambrosia. Compositions of this subject often resemble pagan baptisms, as exemplified in works by Charles de la Fosse (c. 1690–1700, Nantes, Musée des Beaux-Arts) and Restout (1749, Strasbourg). Tiepolo treated the same subject as an ascension (1764, Madrid, Palacio Real, ceiling in the Guard Room).

Cross-references: Anchises. Dido. Sibyl. Venus.

Sources: Virgil, *Aeneid*.

Bibliography: E. Rosenthal, *The Illuminations of the Vergilius Vaticanus*, 1972. *The Loves of the Gods*, ex. cat., Fort Worth, 1992, nos. 4, 5, 35, 38, 43.

AEOLUS

Gk. and Ger. Aiolos; Lat. Æolus; It. and Sp. Eolo; Fr. Éole.
Master of the winds.

HISTORY/MYTHOLOGY

Aeolus, the son of Neptune, mastered the winds. He welcomed Ulysses with hospitality when that hero landed on the island of Aeolia and gave him a wineskin containing all the winds except Zephyr, who was to lead Ulysses back to Ithaca. Ulysses' companions, however, opened the skin while he slept, thinking that there was wine in it, and unleashed a storm.

Aeolus Loosing the Winds Which Cover the Mountains with Snow.
Detail from Jean-Jacques Lagrenée, *L'Hiver*, 1775. Paris, Louvre.

REPRESENTATIONS

In several gems, a companion of Ulysses is seen leaning over a wineskin. This sometimes alludes to the preparation of the wine that was to intoxicate the Cyclops, but when incisions suggest wind, or when a head with inflated cheeks emerges from the wineskin, the representation alludes to the winds that Aeolus imprisoned (Etruscan scarab, Paris, Bibliothèque Nationale, Cabinet des Médailles).

Aeolus exercising his power was depicted by Jean-Jacques Lagrenée on the ceiling of the Gallery of Apollo in the Louvre: on orders from Juno, who tried to prevent Aeneas from reaching the right port, Aeolus frees the winds that later cause Aeneas to run aground at Carthage (1775, Paris, Louvre). In a painting by Albani, Aeolus is addressed by Juno, who is shown in her chariot in the sky accompanied by Iris. He opens a door to free puff-cheeked children (1578–1660, Turin, Galleria dell'Accademia Albertini).

Attributes: Child with puffed cheeks. Wineskin.

Cross-references: Ulysses.

Sources: Homer, *The Odyssey* X, 1–79. Virgil, *Aeneid* I, 50–86.

AESCULAPIUS

Gk. and Ger. Asklepios; Lat. Asclepius; It. and Sp. Esculapio; Fr. Esculape.
God of medicine.

HISTORY/MYTHOLOGY

Aesculapius was the son of Apollo and a princess named Coronis who, while carrying Apollo's child, preferred the love of a mortal. Apollo became jealous, killed Coronis, and entrusted the care of Aesculapius to the centaur Chiron, who raised him and taught him the art of medicine. Aesculapius later proved himself so skillful that he restored Hippolytus to life. Jupiter put an end to this disorder, however, by striking Aesculapius dead with a thunderbolt, whereupon Apollo avenged his son's death by killing the Cyclops.

REPRESENTATIONS

Aesculapius.
Engraving after
a first-century B.C.
bronze.
Herculaneum.

In ancient votive reliefs consecrated to Aesculapius, the god of medicine is shown accompanied by his daughter Hygea (Health). He often holds a snake-entwined staff.

Aesculapius appears in a fresco by Niccolò dell'Abbate (1551–56, Fontainebleau, Salle de Bal). In an engraving by Goltzius, Apollo entrusts Chiron with his son's education (c. 1590, London, British Museum). In a painting by Luca Giordano, Aesculapius receives Roman messengers who have come to ask for his help during an epidemic (1655–60, Brunswick, Herzog Anton Ulrich-Museum).

Michel Corneille drew the death of Aesculapius's mother, Coronis, who was denounced to Apollo by a raven (1641–1708, Paris, Louvre). The death of Coronis is the subject of a painting by Domenichino: she is seen lying on the ground after Apollo releases one of his arrows from the sky (1616–18, London, National Gallery).

Attributes: Snake.

Cross-references: Apollo. Chiron. Cyclops.

Sources: Ovid, *Metamorphoses* II, 600–34 (death of Coronis); XV, 626–744.

AESON *See* Jason.

AGAMEMNON

Gk., Lat., Sp., Fr., and Ger. Agamemnon; It. Agamemnone.
Legendary king of Mycenae.

HISTORY/MYTHOLOGY

Agamemnon, the son of Atreus, was the brother of Menelaus. He reigned over Mycenae with his wife Clytemnestra, with whom he had three children: Iphigenia, Electra, and Orestes. He played an important role in the Trojan War as king of kings, or leader of the entire Greek expedition. When the fleets were about to set sail from Aulis, Diana, who was incensed at Agamemnon for killing a sacred doe during a hunt, held back the winds and demanded the sacrifice of Iphigenia. Agamemnon slew his daughter, causing Clytemnestra to hate him.

During the ninth year of the war, he came into conflict with Achilles. The Greeks had captured Chryseis and Briseïs in an expedition, and awarded Chryseis to Agamemnon and Briseïs to Achilles. When a plague befell the Greeks, however, the oracles claimed it was sent by Apollo as punishment for insulting his priest, Chryseis's father. Agamemnon was consequently forced to give up his captive, and demanded Briseïs from Achilles as compensation. Outraged, Achilles retired to his tent and refused to fight until, when the Trojans were on the verge of taking the Greek camp, Agamemnon yielded and returned Briseïs to him.

Agamemnon returned from Troy with Cassandra after the war, only to be slain upon his arrival in Mycenae by Clytemnestra and her lover, Aegisthus; Cassandra also fell victim to Clytemnestra. Orestes, urged on by his sister Electra, later avenged his father by killing his mother and her lover.

Briseïs Led to Agamemnon.
Giovanni Battista Tiepolo.
Fresco in the Villa Valmarena, Vicenza, 1757.

23

REPRESENTATIONS

Agamemnon is seen holding a scepter and a knife while presiding over the sacrifice of Iphigenia on an Apulian krater (350 B.C., London, British Museum). In a Pompeian fresco, he is represented as a veiled figure turning away from the central scene (first century B.C., House of the Tragic Poet).

Agamemnon appears mainly in two contexts: his dispute with Achilles over Briseïs and his murder by Clytemnestra. He is seen dragging away Briseïs, followed by Talthybius and Diomedes, on a skyphos by Makron, (c. 480 B.C., Paris, Louvre). One side of a krater by the Dokimasia Painter shows Clytemnestra murdering Agamemnon, while on the other side Orestes slays Aegisthus (c. 460 B.C., Boston, Museum of Fine Arts). Agamemnon also appears in Attic ceramics as a secondary character in scenes from the Trojan War, including Ajax's suicide and the theft of the *Palladium*.

The quarrel between Achilles and Agamemnon and the restoration of Briseïs to Achilles are the particular subjects of works by Rubens (designs for a series of tapestries dedicated to the *History of Achilles*, c. 1631, Madrid, Prado). For the first episode, Minerva holds back Achilles by the hair; for the second, Briseïs stands timidly in the middle of the image while Greeks lay presents at Achilles' feet.

In a fresco by Tiepolo in the Villa Valmarana near Vicenza (1757), Agamemnon covers his face to avoid seeing Iphigenia being sacrificed. In a work by Jean Jouvenet, Agamemnon looks imploringly at Diana, but the deer that will be substituted for the young girl is already present, as the goddess points out to the distressed father (*The Sacrifice of Iphigenia*, 1685, Troyes, Musée des Beaux-Arts).

Attributes: Knife. Scepter.

Cross-references: Cassandra. Electra. Iphigenia. Orestes.

Sources: Aeschylus, *Orestes*.

AGAVE *See* Pentheus.

AGLAUROS

Gk., Lat., and Ger. Aglauros; It. Aglauro; Sp. Aglaura; Fr. Aglaure.
Legendary princess.

HISTORY/MYTHOLOGY

Aglauros, the daughter of the Athenian king Cecrops, was the sister of Herse and Pandrosos. She and her sisters, known collectively as the Cecropides, were entrusted by Minerva with the care of a basket containing the young Erichtonius, and were forbidden to open it. Overcome by curiosity, Aglauros disobeyed the goddess. According to Ovid's version, Mercury fell in love with Herse when he saw the Cecropides and asked Aglauros to arrange for them to meet. After Minerva made her jealous, however, Aglauros tried to prevent the meeting and was turned into stone by Mercury.

REPRESENTATIONS

Ancient representations focus on the presence of Aglauros and her sisters at the birth of Erichtonius, as exemplified by a cup by the

Codrus Painter (c. 440 B.C., Berlin, Antikensammlungen). On one side are King Cecrops, Hephaestus, Herse, and Earth, who holds out the infant Erichtonius to Athena; on the underside are Aglauros, Erechtheus, Pandrosos, Aegeus, and Pallas; inscriptions identify all the figures.

In modern iconography, Mercury sees the three sisters from the sky and falls in love with Herse (Jan Boeckhorst, 1605–68, Vienna, Kunsthistorisches Museum); Aglauros jealously spies on Mercury and Herse; Aglauros tries to prevent Mercury from entering Herse's house; Mercury causes Aglauros to fall and, with his caduceus, turns her into stone (Veronese, c. 1580, Cambridge, Fitzwilliam Museum; Pierre, 1763, Paris, Louvre).

Attributes: Basket.

Cross-references: Erichtonius. Mercury.

Sources: Apollodorus, *The Library* III, XIV, 3 and 6. Ovid, *Metamorphoses* II, 552–61 (the curiosity of Aglauros) and 710–835 (her jealousy).

Mercury (Hermes), Herse, and Aglaurus.
Paolo Veronese, c. 1580. Cambridge, Fitzwilliam Museum.

AGRIPPINA *See* Nero.

AJAX THE GREATER

Gk. Aiax; Lat. and Fr. Ajax; It. Aiace; Sp. Ayax; Ger. Aias.
Hero from Greek mythology.

HISTORY/MYTHOLOGY

There are two Ajaxes in Homeric tradition. One, Ajax the Greater, was the son of Telamon who commanded the men of Salamis. The other was the son of Oileus whose iconographic importance is restricted to his role in Cassandra's death. After Achilles, Ajax the Greater was first among the Achaeans. He participated in the mission sent to convince Achilles to resume his position in combat after his dispute with Agamemnon. He fought the most valiant Trojans, most notably Aeneas and Hector. After the death of Achilles, whose body he carried from the battlefield, he entered into rivalry with Ulysses over the dead hero's arms. When the Greeks voted to award them to Ulysses, Ajax became so blind with rage that he mistook a herd of rams for Greeks and slaughtered them. When he came to his senses and took account of his mistake, he killed himself. From Ajax's blood sprang a flower, the lark's foot, whose petals bear two letters that spell out the beginning of his name as well as his cry of grief: AI.

REPRESENTATIONS

Ajax appears frequently in ceramics, especially those from Attica. Thus we are familiar with his great duels against Aeneas (cup by Oltos, c. 510 B.C., Berlin, Charlottenburg) and Hector (amphora by the Kleophrades Painter, c. 480 B.C., Würzburg, Martin von Wagner Museum). The strong bond between Ajax and Achilles is reflected in an important series of works that show the heroes playing dice between battles (amphora by Exekias, c. 540 B.C., Rome, Vatican) and on the François Vase, where Ajax is seen carrying the body of Achilles (c. 570 B.C., Florence, Museo Archeologico). The Greeks voting on who will be awarded Achilles' weapons is a subject found on a cup by Douris (c. 490 B.C., Vienna, Kunsthistorisches Museum). Finally, the suicide of Ajax, who threw himself on his sword, is an ancient subject encountered on the armbands of shields from Olympia (beginning of the sixth century B.C.) and on an amphora by Exekias (c. 540 B.C., Boulogne-sur-Mer, Musée).

Ajax's suicide and the birth of a new flower from his blood appears in Poussin's painting *The Kingdom of Flora* (1631, Dresden, Gemäldegalerie).

Attributes: Arms (of Achilles). Dice. Lark's foot. Sword.

Cross-references: Achilles. Cassandra. Hector. Ulysses.

Sources: Ovid, *Metamorphoses* XIII, 1–398. Sophocles, *Ajax*.

Bibliography: M. Davies, "Ajax at the Bourne of Life," *Eidolopoiia* (colloquium of **Lurmarin [?]**), Rome, 1985, pp. 83–117.

AJAX (SON OF OILEUS)

Gk. Aiax; Lat. and Fr. Ajax; It. Aiace; Sp. Ayax; Ger. Aias.
Hero from Greek mythology.

HISTORY/MYTHOLOGY

Ajax, son of Oileus, was chief of the Locriens in *The Iliad*; he was lesser by far than the other Ajax, son of Telamon, at whose side he often fought. While Troy was being taken, he dragged away Priam's daughter, Cassandra, along with the statue of Athena, the *Palladium*, at whose side she had sought sanctuary. According to other versions of the legend, Ajax raped the young girl. Athena used Nauplius to punish Ajax when the Greeks returned, by inciting him to avenge the death of his son, Palamede, whom the Greeks had stoned: Nauplius lit a fire on the reefs to misguide Ajax's ships, which were smashed to pieces as a result.

The Shipwreck of Ajax.
Giovanni Battista Rosso, 1536.
Galerie François I,
Fontainebleau,
Château de
Fontainebleau.

REPRESENTATIONS

Nearly one hundred Attic vases show Ajax attacking Cassandra while she seeks sanctuary at Athena's statue. In the earliest representations of this subject, the statue brandishes its lance at Ajax as if it were alive, while a miniscule Cassandra runs to its feet. From 500 B.C. onward, Cassandra is usually shown nude in red-figure ceramics, and the eroticism of the scene is made more explicit (hydria by the Kleophrades Painter, c. 490 B.C., Naples, Museo Archeologico). The same scene is found in Pompeian painting, on an Etruscan mirror, and on various cameos.

Ajax, son of Oileus, has rarely been represented in modern times, but two noteworthy works are a painting by Rubens showing Ajax seizing Cassandra (c. 1616, Vaduz, Collection of the Prince of Liechtenstein) and a fresco by Rosso in the Galerie François I at Fontainebleau (1536) depicting the shipwreck, a subject probably chosen as an allusion to the misfortunes of France's king.

Attributes: Shipwreck. Statue (*Palladium*).

Sources: Homer, *The Iliad* II, 527–30.

ALCESTIS

Gk. and Ger. Alkestis; Lat., It., and Fr. Alceste; Sp. Alcestes.
Princess from Greek mythology.

HISTORY/MYTHOLOGY

Alcestis was the only one of King Pelias's daughters not to have had a part in his murder, which was inspired by Medea. She is known mostly for being the wife of Admetus, who obtained her hand by passing a test imposed by Pelias in which he had to yoke a lion with a boar and then lead them. When Admetus was on his deathbed, Alcestis agreed to go to Hades in his place. When Hercules, who was being hosted in the mourning house, learned of Admetus's death, he brought Alcestis back up from Hades to her family. Through this story, Alcestis came to serve as a model of marital devotion, as Euripides represented her in his play, *Alcestis*.

Alcestis.
Apulian loutrophoros,
c. 360 B.C.
Basel,
Musée des Antiquités.

REPRESENTATIONS

Alcestis's marriage preparations are represented on an ancient epinetron (c. 420 B.C., Athens, National Museum); she is seen bidding her children farewell on an Apulian loutrophoros (c. 340 B.C., Basel, Antikensmuseum) and a Roman sarcophagus (Rome, Villa Albani).

The subject of Hercules bringing Alcestis back to Admetus's palace is infrequently represented in modern times, but it is seen in French painting at the end of the seventeenth century by Noël Coypel (Grenoble, Musée de Peinture et Sculpture) and at the beginning of the eighteenth by Antoine Coypel (painting known through a preparatory drawing, as well as through an engraving by Desplaces, 1715). This is also the subject of Louis Galloche's reception painting for the Academy (1711, Paris, École des Beaux-Arts).

Cross-references: Hercules.

Sources: Euripides, *Alcestis*.

**Hercules Returning
Alcestis to Admetus.**
Antoine Coypel,
drawing, c. 1700.
Private Collection.

Alexander.
Cameo, c. 320 B.C.
Paris, Bibliothèque
Nationale de France.

ALCIBIADES *See* Socrates.

ALEXANDER

Gk. and Ger. Alexandros; Lat. Alexander; It. Alessandro;
Sp. Alejandro; Fr. Alexandre.
King of Macedonia (356–323 B.C.).

HISTORY/MYTHOLOGY

Alexander the Great (356–323 B.C.) bequeathed to the history of the Western world a name synonymous with hero, conqueror, and sometimes destroyer. From the age of thirteen—when he began his education under Aristotle—until his death, he amassed accomplishments that are distinguished by military as well as intellectual prowess. The story of his life is told through conquests that followed one upon the other without respite, and which were characterized by a mixture of brutality and clemency. The military campaigns themselves occurred along two main axes: one extending through Asia, which was then under the domination of Darius III, from 334 through 327 B.C., and another extending through India, from 327 through 325 B.C. By this date Alexander had only two years to live, and he spent these in his Persian capitals preparing for a new campaign in Arabia.

What is most striking about this grandiose epic are both Alexander's battles and the symbolic acts he performed as part of a conscious effort to cast himself as a Trojan War hero.

He scored his first victory over the Persians at the Battle of Granica, in spring of 334 B.C. This was followed by the conquest of Greek cities on the southern coasts of Asia Minor, in Lycia, Pamphylia, and Phrygia, where the episode of the Gordian knot—named after the Phrygian city of Gordium—took place. The first formal battle between Persian and Macedonian armies was fought in 333 B.C. at Issus in Cilicia. While Darius returned in defeat to Babylon to reassemble an army, Alexander continued his conquest of coastal cities. He besieged Tyre for six months in 332 B.C. and after that difficult victory triumphantly marched into Egypt, which he occupied and where he founded Alexandria. He next headed east, stole a second victory from Darius at the Battle of Gaugamela (also known as the Battle of Arbela, after a nearby village), and occupied Darius's residences at Babylon, Susa, Persepolis, and Pasagardae.

Alexander pursued Darius, who shored up in Media, but Darius was assassinated by Persian conspirators led by the satrap Bessus. Alexander then posed as Darius's avenger and political inheritor, going so far as to attend to Darius's funeral and to pursue Bessus, whom he had judged and executed in 329 B.C. He adopted Darius's court ceremonies and in 327 B.C. married Roxana, daughter of the noble Bactrian, Oxyartes. Some Macedonians took offense at being treated in the same way as the Persians, but Alexander vigorously suppressed them.

The army set out to conquer India in the spring of 327 B.C. and crossed the Indus a year later. Although some local princes submitted spontaneously and were received by Alexander in audience at Taxila, others refused to recognize Alexander's sovereignty. Among the latter was the Indian king Porus, who fought with three hundred chariots and two hundred elephants in a particularly bloody battle. Although Alexander was the victor, he acknowledged the courage of his adversary, who, when asked how he would like to be treated, replied: "Treat me as a king!"

Eight years of campaigns had by now exhausted Alexander's soldiers, who resisted the conqueror for the first time on the banks of the Hyphasis (Beas) in autumn of 326 B.C. Forced to yield to their demands, Alexander retraced his steps with his army.

The army descended the Indus in the winter of 326 B.C. with a considerable fleet (about one thousand boats, built on-site) and subdued or massacred the native populations it encountered along the way. Then in 325 B.C., Alexander stationed himself at Patala, on the Indus delta, and had his army return to Persia in multiple columns: one by inland routes, a second along the coast of the Persian Gulf, and a third by sea across the Gulf itself. Upon his return to his Persian capitals after that hard journey, Alexander next faced the difficult task of suppressing incipient revolts and conspiracies. He conformed to the Persian custom of polygamy by marrying two Achaemenid princesses in 324 B.C., and was joined in the sumptuous wedding feast by many companions-in-arms who married noble Persians and Medians. This policy of cultural assimilation met with disapproval from some Macedonian soldiers, who felt threatened, but Alexander dispelled their fears and made plans for a campaign in Arabia. Upon arriving in Babylon, however, he was struck down with a fever and died on 13 June 323 B.C. His succession proved a difficult issue: when asked about it on his deathbed, Alexander purportedly replied that he left his kingdom "to the most worthy." Rivalry between his close associates was all the more violent because there was no direct heir other than a simple-minded half-brother and a posthumous child by Roxana. Alexander's body was brought to Alexandria by Ptolemy for burial.

REPRESENTATIONS

Alexander the Great carefully controlled his own iconography by designating official portraitists: Lysippus for sculpture (bronze, Naples, Museo Nazionale), Apelles for painting, and Pyrogeteles for gems (cameo in Paris, Bibliothèque Nationale, Cabinet des Médailles). In the many coins that were struck with his image, he is likened to Jupiter, Ammon, and Hercules, or he wears an elephant hide. Alexander's coinage spread throughout the Mediterranean and to the far reaches of India and Central Asia, and quickly became the most important monetary unit in the entire Greek world.

Alexander the Great's life gave rise to one of the most important iconographic repertoires, one that continually inspired artists from antiquity through the eighteenth century—without interruption in the Middle Ages—and beyond the reaches of the Western world.

Portraits—bust, full-length and equestrian—in all media (medallions, bronzes, gems, marble, etc.) are legion in the Hellenistic world. Those portraits aside, the main themes chosen by artists can be grouped according to epoch and geographic origin. Among the exceptionally rich objects that were discovered in 1977 and 1978 in the royal tombs of Vergina is an ivory-on-wood portrait of the young Alexander (350–325 B.C., Thessalonika, Museum). The small head reflects all the individual features that characterize Alexander the Great: full, round cheeks; powerful neck; somewhat low but prominent and furrowed forehead; aquiline nose; very deeply set eyes; thick lips; small mouth; strong jaw; and, when intact, a shock of hair sprouting from the forehead (marble bust, late third–early second century B.C. from a third-century B.C. prototype, Boston, Museum of Fine Arts).

The Battles

The four most important battles that resulted in Macedonian victories are abundantly represented. Vast compositions that mix weapons and cavalry, these works provide a setting for often complex and grandiose mass representations. The first battle, that of Granica, is identifiable because of the presence of the river after which it was named. In representations of the Battle of Issus, most famously the mosaic found in the House of the Faun at Pompeii, Alexander, shown as a simple horseman, is grouped with Darius, who flees in his chariot. The two protagonists reappear in the Battle of Guagamela (or Arbela) in similar form (the defeat and flight of Darius). The fourth of Alexander's battles to inspire multiple representations is the one waged against Porus in India. Here the vanquished king's elephants are visible and his surrender usually appears in the foreground; also discernable is Alexander's sensitivity to the courageous king's pride. All these battles were abundantly represented in the seventeenth century; they were often rendered as cycles, of which the most famous example is still the one created by Le Brun for Louis XIV, now in the Louvre.

The Great Personal Deeds

A number of other adventures nourished the legend of Alexander; they are represented in the visual arts from Hellenistic times onward. The Macedonian prince exhibited physical courage even in his youth, when he harnessed his horse Bucephalus and when he led his comrades at hunts (the lion hunt with Cratere, third-century B.C. mosaic, Pella, Archeological Museum). Another celebrated subject is the Gordian knot, for which artists capture the moment when Alexander cuts the undoable knot with his sword and represent the knot as either a braided crown (Perino del Vaga, Rome, Castel Sant'Angelo) or a tangle of rope (Berthélémy, 1767, Paris, École des Beaux-Arts). Artists linked Alexander to the world of Homeric heroes through depictions of him worshiping at Achilles' tomb (Dufresnoy, middle of the seventeenth century, Paris, Louvre).

Alexander's interest in contemporary philosophy is another subject that attracted the attention of artists. Some works evoke Alexander's loyal attachment to Aristotle (Jean-Baptiste de Champaigne, *Alexander Having Exotic Animals Brought to Aristotle for Study*, 1673, Musée de Versailles); others evoke his encounter with Diogenes, contrasting the magnificence of Alexander shown at the peak of his glory with the cynic Diogenes's willful destitution. Alexander's dealings with the painter Apelles are also represented, revealing the high esteem in which Alexander held the arts. Alexander's marriage to Roxana provided scope for paintings of lavish interiors, as exemplified by Sodoma's fresco (1512, Rome, Farnesina). Painters were inspired above all by the *Triumphs of Alexander*, a subject that celebrated the prince's military victories and power. One of the most famous works in this category remains the *Triumphal Entry of Alexander into Babylon*, which formed part of Le Brun's cycle and which served as a cartoon for tapestries at Versailles. The triumph theme remained popular until the end of the nineteenth century, as demonstrated by Moreau's painting *The Triumph of Alexander the Great* (c. 1885, Paris, Musée Gustave Moreau).

The Sovereign's Clemency

It became fashionable within European court iconography, particularly in the seventeenth and eighteenth centuries, to glorify ruling princes through analogy to Alexander. Louis XIV provided the most celebrated example while following a tradition that was in fact established by Roman emperors. Although any of the themes alluded to above could be used to glorify a living monarch, the most important ones were those that demonstrated the conqueror's clemency.

In this category are representations of Alexander treating women with nobility after his victories. Thus the conqueror is shown rescuing Timoclea, the Theban heroine who resisted the indecent overtures of a

The Marriage of Alexander and Roxana.
Giovanni Sodoma, 1512.
Rome, Farnesina.

dishonest soldier (Domenichino, *Alexander and Timoclea*, about 1615, Paris, Louvre). The respect that Alexander accorded Darius's family, which is something that actually served his political ambitions, is illustrated in such compositions as *The Family of Darius Before Alexander* (Veronese, c. 1565, London, National Gallery), the *Queens of Persia at the Feet of Alexander* (Mignard, 1669, St. Petersburg, Hermitage; Le Brun, 1660–61, Versailles, Musée), and *The Family of Darius at the Feet of Alexander* (Sodoma, 1512, Rome, Farnesina; Jouvenet, 1680, Paris, Lycée Louis-le-Grand, and so on). The handsome young prince responds to the pleas of suffering women and children with sensitivity and solicitude. In depicting the "supplicants," artists make a modern interpretation—seen particularly in the eighteenth century—of ancient texts that place less stress on this.

Alexander extended his clemency to men as well. They were fallen kings whom he restored to dignity, such as the elderly Abdalonymus, who was pulled from working the fields to appear before the prince (Restout, *Abdalonymus Appearing Before Alexander*, 1738, Orleans, Musée Municipal), or even his doctor, Philip, whom Alexander continued to trust after his entourage accused him of trying to poison the prince (representations of *Alexander and His Doctor Philip* are particularly numerous in the eighteenth century, when they became emblematic of loyalty and friendship in the context of *à l'antique* genre painting).

The Excesses
In sharp contrast to the chorus of works celebrating Alexander's glory, a few exceptions bring into focus less flattering behaviors and deeds. One example illustrates Alexander's consultation with Apollo's oracle, when he proved himself so impatient to master his own destiny that he anticipated the Pythia's response (Lagrenée, *Alexander Consulting Apollo's Oracle*, 1789, Montpellier, Hôtel de Ville). Better still is a torture scene concerning an episode of cruelty in the life of Alexander: Darius's loyal supporter Batis is attached to a chariot to be dragged in punishment for having remained mute despite Alexander's threats (Lagrenée, *The Loyalty of One of Darius's Satraps*, 1787, Aurillac, Musée). In the creative context of the eighteenth century, such a work is nothing less than visual criticism of a despotic monarchy.

Attributes: Gordian knot.

Cross-references: Apelles. Aristotle. Diogenes.

Sources: Arrian, *Anabasis and Indica*; Plutarch, *Life of Alexander*, and numerous ancient texts. Pseudo-Callisthenes, *Alexander-Romance*. Quintus Curtius, *History of Alexander.*

Bibliography: *Alexander the Great, History and Legend in Art*, ex. cat., Thessalonica, Athens, 1980. M. Bieber, "The Portraits of Alexander the Great," *Proceedings of the American Philosophical Society* 95 (5): 373–427. C. Grell and C. Michel, *L'École des princes ou Alexandre disgracié*, Paris, 1988. D.O.A. Klose, *Von Alexander zu Kleopatra. Herrscherporträts der Greichen und Barbaren*, Staatliche Münzsammlung, Munich, 1922. *The Search for Alexander*, ex. cat., Washington, Chicago, Boston, San Francisco, 1980–81.
For Louis XIV compared to Alexander the Great, see O. and P. Rantum, *The Century of Louis XIV*, Toronto, 1972.

ALPHEUS *See* Arethusa.

AMAZONS

Gk., Lat., Fr., and Ger. Amazons; It. Amazzoni; Sp. Amazonas.
Legendary race of female warriors.

HISTORY/MYTHOLOGY

Amazons.
Volute krater
by Euphronius,
c. 510 B.C.
Arezzo, Museo
Archeologico.

The Amazons were a race of female warriors descended from Mars and Harmonia. They lived on the slopes of the Caucasus or in Thrace and Scythia, depending on the version of the legend. No men lived among them; instead they mated with foreigners, kept the female offspring, and killed the male ones.
Different Greek heroes braved the Amazons, including Bellerophon, Hercules—who had to steal the girdle of Hippolyta, queen of the Amazons—and Theseus, who helped Hercules and also abducted Antiope. The Amazons retaliated by invading Attica and installing themselves on the hill of Ares (Areopagus). They came to the aid of the Trojans during the seige of Troy but were repelled by Achilles, who fell passionately in love with Penthesilea as he was killing her.

REPRESENTATIONS

In ancient art, the Amazons are horse-riders whose weapons clearly differ from those of the hoplites: they have bows, arrows, hatchets, and light, crescent-shaped shields that emphasize how different they are. The Amazons are one of the most popular themes in Attic ceramics, where their battles with Hercules and Theseus claim equal attention, and in temple sculpture, where their combats appear in continuous relief (Bassae, Parthenon). In Athenian ideology, the struggle during the Amazon invasion of Attica became a symbol for armed vigilance against barbarian invasions.
The Trojan episode is emphasized in Roman sarcophagi, where the subject is either Achilles lifting the body of Penthesilea or, more rarely, the Amazons' arrival in Troy after Hector's death.
In the Renaissance, Boccacio's poetic account of the struggle between Theseus and the Amazons (*Teseide*) was represented by Carpaccio (1500, Paris, Musée Jacquemart-André). The subject of the

Bacchus.
Leonardo da Vinci, 1511–15.
Paris, Louvre.

Bellerophon Slaying the Chimera.
Peter Paul Rubens, 1635.
Bayonne, Musée Bonnat.

**The Battle
of the Amazons.**
Peter Paul Rubens.
Engraving.

great Amazonian battles reappeared in baroque painting (Rubens, about 1615, Munich, Alte Pinakothek).

Attributes: Arms (bow). Barbarian costume.

Cross-references: Achilles. Hercules. Penthesilea. Theseus.

Sources: Plutarch, *Life of Theseus*, 1, 27.

Bibliography: D. von Bothmer, *Amazons in Greek Art*, Oxford, 1957.

AMPHIARAUS

Gk., Fr., and Ger. Amphiaraos; Lat. Amphiaraus;
It. and Sp. Anfiarao.
Soothsayer from Greek mythology.

HISTORY/MYTHOLOGY

Amphiaraus, a seer and warrior, ruled over Argos. After he and his cousin, Adrastus, quarreled, he married Adrastus's sister, Eriphyle, to effect a reconciliation, and the two men agreed to let her decide any other disagreements. When Adrastus was later engaged to help Polynices recover sovereignty over Thebes from his brother Eteocles, Amphiaraus at first refused to take part in the expedition, knowing it would fail, but changed his mind after Eriphyle, bribed by Polyneices with a necklace, sided with Adrastus. When the expedition of the Seven against Thebes was routed, Amphiaraus and his chariot were swallowed up by the earth. A sanctuary was consecrated to him, and his oracle was consulted there after his death.

Amphiaraus.
Domenico
del Barbiere.
Engraving,
sixteenth century.

REPRESENTATIONS

A subject sometimes seen in Attic vase painting is Eriphyle bribed by the necklace (Attic oenochoe, c. 440 B.C., Paris, Louvre), but more common are the seven chieftains preparing for war, particularly the

33

departure of Amphiaraus's chariot (Attic amphora, c. 520 B.C., Chiusi, Museo Archeologico). Also seen is the chariot swallowed up by the earth (Attic krater, c. 450 B.C., Ferrara, Museo Archeologico), also depicted on Etruscan urns (first century B.C., Volterra). Several reliefs from the sanctuary of Oropos show the hero healing the sick (fourth century B.C., Athens, National Museum).

There are few modern representations of Amphiaraus. The chariot engulfed by the earth is the subject of a School of Fontainebleau engraving by Domenico del Barbiere. Amphiarus's departure is represented in a relief by Crenier (1906, Paris, Musée d'Orsay).

Attributes: Chariot.

Sources: Homer, *The Odyssey* XV, 245–8. Apollodorus, III, 6, 2–3. Philostratus, *Imagines* I, 27.

AMPHION

Gk., Lat., Fr., and Ger. Amphion; It. Anfione; Sp. Anfion.
Legendary character.

HISTORY/MYTHOLOGY

Amphion, the son of Jupiter and Antiope, was the twin of Zethus. He devoted himself to music while Zethus farmed and hunted. Together they avenged their mother, whom King Lycus and his wife Dirce had mistreated, by attaching Dirce to a bull and dragging her over rocks. The brothers subsequently ruled over Thebes; Zethus used his strength to move the stones needed to build the city's walls, while Amphion moved them with his music.

REPRESENTATIONS

The twins, shown face-to-face, are clearly distinguished from each other by a lyre and a hunting dog in a Hadrianic relief (Rome, Palazzo Spada). Circe's punishment is represented in an imposing marble group discovered in Rome in 1545: the two young men subdue the bull to which she will be attached (*Farnese Bull*, beginning of the third century A.D., Naples, Museo Archeologico).

The power of Amphion's music to move stones has been of particular interest to modern painters (Primaticcio, c. 1540, Château de Fontainebleau). Tiepolo associated Amphion with Orpheus and used the story of Amphion constructing Thebes's ramparts for his *Allegory of Eloquence* (1724–25, Venice, Palazzo Sandi). A four-part panel painting, which once decorated the interior of a seventeenth-century Parisian townhouse, groups four gods of music: Pan, Amphion, Musaeus, and Marsyas (Paris, Louvre).

Attributes: Bull. Lyre.

Cross-references: Antiope. Jupiter.

Sources: Homer, *The Odyssey* XI, 260–65. Philostratus, *Imagines* I, 10.

AMPHITRITE

Gk., Lat., Fr., and Ger. Amphitrite; It. and Sp. Anfitrite.
Sea goddess.

HISTORY/MYTHOLOGY

Amphitrite was the daughter of Nereus. She was courted by Neptune and lived with him in the ocean after they married. Ancient poets used her name to personify the sea.

REPRESENTATIONS

Amphitrite sits next to Neptune in Olympian assemblies (cups by Sosias, 510 B.C., Berlin, Charlottenburg and by the Codrus Painter, 440 B.C., London, British Museum). The most frequent subject is the wedding of Neptune and Amphitrite, which is treated as a triumphal procession. The goddess stands next to Neptune in a chariot drawn by sea-horses in a mosaic representation from Constantine (fourth century A.D., Paris, Louvre).

Amphitrite is also grouped with Neptune in modern painting. Amphitrite in her chariot occupies the center of a composition by Poussin (c. 1634, *The Triumph of Neptune and Amphitrite*, Philadelphia, Museum of Art). A canvas by Rubens shows her standing on the crests of waves and supported by Neptune. Amphitrite is particularly adaptable for use on fountains and water basins (Versailles, Basin of Amphitrite).

Attributes: Dolphins. Sea animals.

Cross-references: Neptune. Nereids.

The Triumph of Amphitrite.
Giovanni Battista Tiepolo, 1740. Dresden, Gemäldegalerie.

AMPHITRYON *See Hercules.*

AMPHORA *See Satyrs.*

Neptune and Amymone (detail).
Carle van Loo,
1757.
Nice, Musée
des Beaux-Arts
Jules-Chéret.

AMYMONE

Gk., Lat., and Ger. Amymone; It. and Sp. Amimone; Fr. Amymoné.
Legendary Libyan princess.

HISTORY/MYTHOLOGY

Amymone was one of fifty daughters of Danaüs. When she and her
family arrived at Argos, Neptune, who had inherited the Argolid, caused
a drought. Amymone was sent by her father to look for water and,
after walking for some time, fell asleep only to be awakened by an
ill-intentioned satyr. Neptune arrived and chased off the satyr by
throwing his trident, which caused a spring to gush forth where it landed.
Amymone then yielded to the god and conceived Nauplius as a result.

REPRESENTATIONS

Representations of two episodes occur with equal frequency in ancient
art: Amymone attacked by satyrs (krater by the Dinos Painter, c. 420
B.C., Vienna, Kunsthistorisches Museum) and Amymone's encounter
with Neptune (krater by the Nekyia Painter, c. 450 B.C., Vienna,
Kunsthistorisches Museum). A cupid sometimes flies overhead
(mosaic from Paphos, Cyprus, third century A.D.).

Modern artists have represented Neptune defending Amymone
against the satyr's attack (Boucher, 1764, Versailles, Grand Trianon).

Attributes: Hydria.

Cross-references: Danaïds. Neptune. Satyrs.

Sources: Apollodorus, II, ɪ, 4. Philostratus, *Imagines*, I, 8.

Bibliography: S. Kaempf-Dimitriadou, *Die Liebe der Götter in der atti-schen Kunst*, Bern, 1979, pp. 26–30.

ANCHISES

Gk. and Ger. Anchises; Lat. Anchisa; It. and Fr. Anchise; Sp. Aquises.
Prince from the Trojan legend.

HISTORY/MYTHOLOGY

Anchises was a descendant of Tros and belonged to the dynasty of
Trojan princes. Venus fell in love with him and seduced him by passing
herself off as the mortal daughter of a Phrygian; Aeneas was the offspring of this union. Although Venus warned Anchises not to arouse
Jupiter's wrath by revealing the child's divine origin, Anchises got
drunk one day and boasted of his love affair. As a result, depending
on the version of the story, Jupiter made him either lame or blind. In
his old age he was carried on his son's shoulders from the fallen city of
Troy; according to Virgil, he died at Drepaon in Sicily during Aeneas's
voyage.

Venus and Anchises.
Paulin-Jean-Baptiste
Guérin, 1822.
Nice, Musée
des Beaux-Arts
Jules-Chéret.

REPRESENTATIONS

Anchises is seen being carried by Aeneas, who is preceded by his
wife and son, in a series of Attic vases. An oriental archer sometimes
accompanies the group (Attic oenochoe, c. 510 B.C., Paris, Louvre).

In modern painting, the meeting of Venus and Anchises has
been depicted by Annibale Carracci (c. 1597–1600, Rome, Palazzo
Farnese); the quote from Virgil that accompanies the painting,
"*genus unde latinum*," alludes to the claim that the Latin race
descended from Aeneas. There is a more romantic version of the
same episode by Paulin-Guérin (1822, Nice, Musée des Beaux-Arts
Jules-Chéret).

The flight from Troy, which became emblematic of filial piety, is
the most frequently represented episode: Aeneas, surrounded by
Creusa and Ascanius, carries Anchises. The scene is sometimes set in
a landscape that includes the burning city of Troy (Adam Elsheimer,
c. 1600, Munich, Alte Pinakothek). More often, the composition
focuses on the father and son group (Lionello Spada, 1576–1622,
Paris, Louvre; Carle van Loo, 1729, Paris, Louvre). That composition
is equally frequent in sculpture (Bernini, 1618, Rome, Villa
Borghese; Girardon, before 1715, Troyes, Musée des Beaux-Arts).

Cross-references: Aeneas. Venus.

Sources: Virgil, *Aeneid* III, V and VI.

ANDROMACHE

Gk. and Ger. Andromache; Lat. Andromacha; It. and Sp. Andromaca;
Fr. Andromaque.
Princess from Trojan legend.

HISTORY/MYTHOLOGY

The Trojan princess Andromache was the wife of Hector and the
mother of Astyanax. Her son was executed by the Greeks during the
fall of Troy, and she herself was abducted by Neoptolemus
(Pyrrhus), the son of Achilles, who married her. For these reasons,
Andromache has come to represent the wife and mother who suffers
as a victim of war.

**Andromache
Mourning Hector
(detail).**
Jacques-Louis
David, 1783.
Paris, École
des Beaux-Arts.

REPRESENTATIONS

Some Greek vases depict a warrior bidding farewell to a woman: from inscriptions, the couple is clearly intended to be Hector and Andromache (Chalcidian krater, c. 530 B.C., Würzburg, Mainfränkisches Museum); the child Astyanax is not represented here.

Hector bidding farewell to Andromache, as described in *The Iliad*, is the subject of paintings by Antoine Coypel (1661–1722, Tours, Musée des Beaux-Arts, as well as a cartoon for tapestry, Paris, Louvre), Pompeo Batoni (1761, Northampton, Manor), Angelica Kauffmann (1768, England, Satram Collection), and Joseph-Marie Vien (1786, Paris, Louvre) among others. Astyanax occupies a major position in all these works. David depicted Andromache grieving over Hector's corpse (1793, Paris, École des Beaux-Arts). Finally, Ulysses tearing Astyanax away from his mother is sometimes shown (Louis Silvestre le Jeune, 1708, formerly in Prague, known through an engraving by Jean Audran).

Attributes: Child.

Cross-references: Astyanax. Hector. Ulysses.

Sources: Euripedes, *Andromache*. Homer, *The Iliad* VI, 394–496 (the farewell).

ANDROMEDA *See* Perseus.

ANTAEUS

Gk. and Ger. Anaios; Lat. Anæus; It. and Sp. Anteo; Fr. Antée.
Legendary giant.

HISTORY/MYTHOLOGY

Antaeus, the son of Neptune and Earth (Gaea), was a Giant. He was invincible as a fighter because he regained his strength each time he

**Hercules Wrestling
Antaeus.**
Euphronius, krater,
c. 510 B.C.
Paris, Louvre.

touched earth. Hercules finally defeated him on his way through Libya
by lifting him off the ground and strangling him.

REPRESENTATIONS

Hercules wrestling Antaeus is seen on gems and vases; one noteworthy
example is a krater by Euphronius in which the two wrestlers are locked
together on the ground (c. 510 B.C., Paris, Louvre).

The subject appears in Renaissance in painting (Pollaiuolo,
1433–98, Florence, Uffizi; Hans Baldung Grien, c. 1530, Vienna,
Kunsthistorisches Museum) and sculpture (bronze by Antico, c. 1519,
Vienna, Kunsthistorisches Museum).

Cross-references: Hercules.

Sources: Ovid, *Metamorphoses* IX, 182–3.

**Hercules Strangling
Antaeus.**
Baron Antoine Gros,
drawing,
nineteenth century.
Paris, École
des Beaux-Arts.

ANTINOUS

Gk. and Ger. Antinoos; Lat. Antinous; It. and Sp. Antinoo;
Fr. Antinoüs.
Favorite of the Emperor Hadrian (died A.D. 130).

HISTORY/MYTHOLOGY

Antinous was a young Bithynian slave who became the favorite of
Hadrian; he was worshiped by a cult after his mysterious death (he
drowned in the Nile in A.D. 130). The emperor mourned him and erected statues and temples dedicated to him throughout the Empire. His
name remains synonymous with perfect beauty.

REPRESENTATIONS

Some artists seem to capture the individual personality of the model,
while others idealize him, which is justified by Antinous's deification.

The two most celebrated statues are the Belvedere *Antinous* and
the Capitoline *Antinous* (Rome, Musei Vaticani and Rome, Musei
Capitolini, respectively). In the first, which modern artists have regarded
as a model of anatomical proportion, Antinous is endowed with the
features of an athlete; the second, which was found in Hadrian's Villa,
is subtler in temperament but was equally appreciated in the eighteenth
and nineteenth centuries. In a half-length representation in a monumental relief, Antinous is a youth with two crowns, one on his head,

Antinous.
Relief, c. A.D. 130.
Rome, Villa Albani.

the other in his hand; his features are pure and his expression somber, as in other portraits (Rome, Villa Albani Torlonia). Antinous also appears on medals, including one from Tius, in Bithynia, in which he is seated on a panther and dressed as a hero.

Bibliography: C. Clairmont, *Die Bildnisse des Antinoüs*, Rome, 1966. H. Meyer, *Antinoos*, Rome, 1966.

ANTIOCHOS AND STRATONICA

Lat. Antiochos, Stratonica; Fr. Antiochus, Stratonice; Ger. Antiochos, Stratonike.
King and queen of Syria.

HISTORY/MYTHOLOGY

Antiochos I Soter (281–261 B.C.), the son of Seleucus I Nicator, king of Syria (c. 355–280 B.C.), was near death for love of his stepmother, Stratonica. He tried to hide his forbidden passion, but his doctor, Erasistratus, identified the source of his illness by observing his reaction when the queen entered his presence. Seleucus abandoned his wife to his son, knowing that this was his only salvation; he also accorded him a portion of his kingdom.

Ancient historians found this manifestation of paternal love particularly touching, and Petrarch glorified the triumph of Antiochos's love.

REPRESENTATIONS

From the end of the fifteenth through the nineteenth centuries, Italian and northern European painters frequently represented the bedside scene from the story of Antiochos. In the Sala di Venere of the Palazzo Pitti (c. 1645), Pietro da Cortona combined various elements

Antiochos and Stratonica. Jacques-Louis David, 1774. Paris, École des Beaux-Arts.

of the story while at the same time condensing the sequences. The son remains silent, his eyes full of love; the doctor has a sly expression; the father readily accepts the news.

In a painting by Antonio Bellucci, Stratonica seems to share Antiochos's passion and leans toward the patient as if to give her consent (1654–1726, Kassel, Gemäldegalerie). The subject, which was popular among neoclassical painters, is restricted to Erasistratus's discovery of the cause of Antiochos's illness in canvases by David (Prix de Rome, 1774, Paris, École des Beaux-Arts) and Ingres (1840, Chantilly, Musée Condé). Stratonica, who is present in both paintings, is positioned near the door and with lowered eyes; in David's painting, the doctor points a guilty finger at Stratonica, who seems deeply frightened.

Sources: Lucian, *De dea Syria*. Plutarch, *Life of Demetrius* LII.

Bibliography: W. Stechow, "'The Love of Antiochos with Fair Stratonica' in Art," *The Art Bulletin* 27 (1945): 221–37.

ANTIOPE

Gk., It., Sp., Fr., and Ger. Antiope; Lat. Antiopa.
Legendary character.

HISTORY/MYTHOLOGY

Antiope was the daughter of the river god Asopus or, according to other versions of the legend, the daughter of the hero Nycteus. Her extraordinary beauty seduced Jupiter, who turned himself into a satyr to ravish her. She then fled from her father's house and gave birth to twins, Amphion and Zethus.

REPRESENTATIONS

The subject of Jupiter as a satyr approaching Antiope does not appear in antiquity, but it enjoyed some popularity in Renaissance courts. It went hand in hand with the other metamorphoses of Jupiter, who was

Jupiter and Antiope (detail).
Antoine Watteau, 1715.
Paris, Louvre.

always in search of new love affairs, and gave them an opportunity to represent sexual desire explicity, as exemplified in works by Titian (c. 1535–40, Paris, Louvre) and Rubens (1616–17, London, Buckingham Palace). Most often, the satyr is placed behind the unclothed woman whom he gazes at and exposes to the spectator (Watteau, 1715–16, Paris, Louvre). Jupiter in the form of a satyr is usually identifiable through the more or less discreet presence of one of his attributes, particularly an eagle or a thunderbolt (van Dyck, 1615–16, Ghent, Museum voor Schone Kunsten); in the absence of such attributes, the subject is barely distinguishable from Venus and a satyr, or a nymph and a satyr (Correggio, 1528, Paris, Louvre).

Cross-references: Amphion.

Sources: Ovid, *Metamorphoses* VI, 111.

Bibliography: A. de Mirimonde, *Gazette des Beaux-Arts* 95 (March 1980): 107–20.

ANTIPHILOS *See* Apelles.

ANTONY *See* Cleopatra.

APELLES

Gk., Lat., and Ger. Apelles; It. and Fr. Apelle; Sp. Apeles.
Greek painter (first half of the fourth century B.C.).

HISTORY/MYTHOLOGY

Apelles, the most famous painter from antiquity, lived during the first half of the fourth century B.C. at Sicyon and then in Macedonia, where he was engaged by Philip. He made several portraits of the Macedonian king before becoming the favorite painter of Alexander the Great and his generals. He traveled to various cities after his patron's death and spent time in Ephesus and Alexandria. The events in his life that have traditionally captured attention are more legendary than historically accurate, but they are important for what they reveal about ancient notions of art and artists; at the same time, they inspired works of art that function as small, independent allegories.

The first anecdote about Apelles involves the painter Protogenes. Apelles paid a visit to Protogenes, who was not at home, and drew a line on a plank as a sign that he had called. When Protogenes returned, he crossed Apelles' line with one of his own. Apelles became the victor after a second visit by retracing his line with exceptional finesse—*linea summae tenuitatis*. Although Pliny speaks of the event as a contest, the anecdote actually served as a point of departure for reflection on drawing and its supremacy over other modes of artistic expression in the Renaissance development of a philosophy of aesthetics.

A second story, one about Apelles and a shoemaker, is comical but also inspires serious reflection on art criticism. When the shoemaker found a fault in the sandal worn by a figure Apelles had painted, the artist followed his advice and corrected the detail. When the shoemaker then became so confident that he tried to extend his criticism to other parts of the painting, Apelles cut him short with the

Apelles Paints Campaspe.
Jacques-Louis David,
1819.
Lille,
Musée des Beaux-Arts.

famous line, "*Ne sutor ultra crepidam!*" ("No higher than the sandal, shoemaker!").

Two stories illustrate the personal relationship between Apelles and Alexander. The first reports that Alexander dared comment on aesthetics during a sitting. Apelles interrupted him, saying that his words were making even the slaves brewing his colors laugh.

The second highly celebrated story is about Alexander and his mistress, Campaspe. It is more flattering to the prince: Alexander commissioned a portrait of Campaspe, and then offered her to Apelles when the artist fell in love with his model. Posterity accords a double meaning to the anecdote: the first is social and highlights the intrinsic nobility of art as well as of the artist who, by extension, is elevated to a position of special dignity; the second meaning is allegorical and tends to reassert the notion that beauty belongs to those who devote themselves to it.

Two anecdotes tell about the risks Apelles was exposed to because of the jealousy he aroused. Both took place in Alexandria. In the first, Antiphilos, another painter, was so jealous of the attention King Ptolemy lavished on Apelles that he accused the artist of taking part in a conspiracy. Ptolemy was about to condemn Apelles when one of the conspirators gave testimony that proved him blameless. Now convinced of Apelles' innocence, the king rewarded him with one hundred talents and enslaved Antiphilos. The episode inspired Apelles' painting, *Calumny*. Known through Lucian's description, the painting allegorized Envy, Ignorance, Slander, Calumny, Conspiracy, and Trickery, as well as Repentance and Truth, and staged these figures before one that resembled Ptolemy except for the fact that it had, like Midas, the ears of an ass.

Finally, Pliny tells about an incident that occurred when a storm forced Apelles, who was on bad terms with Ptolemy, to land at Alexandria. A messenger invited the artist to court, but his arrival there threw Ptolemy into a nearly violent rage until Apelles foiled the conspiracy by making a charcoal sketch of the messenger so that he could be identified.

Ancient literature highly praises numerous works by Apelles, including *Calumny* and a nude inspired by the courtesan Phryne, entitled *Venus Andyomene*.

The Calumny of Apelles.
Antoine Caron, drawing, before 1599.
Paris, Louvre.

REPRESENTATIONS

Renaissance artists illustrated all the above episodes, which provided subject matter for works ranging from cycles to individual representations, from murals to easel paintings. Vasari depicted *Alexander Giving Campaspe to Apelles* for a cycle at Arezzo (1540) and illustrated the shoemaker anecdote in his house in Florence.

The *Calumny* episode was particularly popular and allowed Italian Renaissance artists to represent in the guise of ancient myth the rivalries so common among artists attached to the court or to powerful patrons; the two most important examples are a drawing by Raphael in the Louvre and a painting by Botticelli (1495) in the Uffizi, each of which is faithful to Lucian's description of the original work by Apelles.

The subject with the longest-lasting popularity in painting is Apelles and Campaspe, which made Alexander a princely model of emotional control and devotion to the arts. François I adopted that model as his own and commissioned Primaticcio to depict the subject in the Duchesse d'Etampes' bedroom at Fontainebleau (1541–44, now lost). The story of Apelles and Campaspe also inspired many Italian painters through the eighteenth century (Tiepolo, 1725–26, Montreal, Musée des Beaux-Arts).

The same story also provided painters with the very symbol of their art, and allusions to it may appear as a painting within a painting in allegories of painting that were destined for the collection cabinets of early seventeenth-century Flemish amateurs.

Although Cupid often appears alongside Apelles, he is appropriately absent in a celebrated painting by David that is characterized by carefully controlled passion: Campaspe's modesty provokes intense gazes from Alexander and Apelles, each of whom seems more enthralled by Beauty than by the sensuality of the very woman who exudes it.

The School of Apelles is a subject that is sometimes represented without any direct relationship made to specific events in the painter's life: it instead serves as a justification for depicting artists' studios and living models; the artist may be surrounded by numerous students, as in a painting by Jean Broc (1800, Paris, Louvre).

44

Attributes: Drawing. Painting.

Cross-references: Alexander. Phryne.

Sources: Pliny the Elder, *Natural History* XXXV, 86–7. Lucian, *Calumniae non temere credendum.*

Bibliography: P. Georgel and A.-M. Lecoq, *La Peinture dans la peinture*, Paris, 1987, II: "Fables et héros." J.-M. Massing, *La Calomnie d'Apelle*, Strasbourg, 1990.

APHRODITE *Greek name for* Venus.

APOLLO

Gk. Apollon/Phoibos; Lat. Apollon/Phœbus; It. and Ger. Apollo;
Sp. Apolo; Fr. Apollon.
Greek god.

HISTORY/MYTHOLOGY

Apollo, who was Diana's twin and the son of Jupiter and Leto, was born on the island of Delos. He was god of the bow and the lyre, each of which is worked by pulling strings. He could punish by inflicting illness with his arrows, but he could also heal and purify, and he presided over the founding of cities. As a god of music, he was regarded as a master of harmony, a position he shared with his Muses. He also exercised power over the oracles, particularly those of Delphi, which he rid of the snake, Python, before reigning there alternately with Dionysus; Hercules tried in vain to usurp his position. Apollo was sometimes associated with the Sibyls and, as the father of Aesculapius, with medicine.

As the embodiment of all that is rational in Greek thought, Apollo was often contrasted with Dionysus. However, Apollo was also vengeful, sometimes cruel, and even murderous: he slew the giant Tityus with his bow for trying to rape Leto, massacred Niobe's children because their mother insulted his, and killed Marsyas for daring to challenge him to a musical competition.

As his sister became identified with the Moon, so Apollo became identified with Helios, the Sun, and was consequently called Phoebus, the Shining One, the Pure One, the Bright One. It is this guise, which is associated with musical harmony, that dominates the modern tradition. Apollo's beauty, however, did not make his love affairs any happier: Daphne escaped him by turning into a tree; Coronis, Aesculapius's mother, preferred a mortal over him (the god's arrows would punish her); and Hyacinthus, the beautiful *epheboi*, was accidentally killed by him.

REPRESENTATIONS

Apollo is the male youth *par excellence* in archaic Greek art and is accordingly portrayed as a nude, immobile, and long-locked kouros. The most well-known statues are the *Apollo Belvedere*, in which he steps forward with an outstretched arm (installed in the Vatican in 1509, a copy of a fourth-century B.C. original), and the *Apollo Sauroctonus* ("lizard killer"), in which he leans against a tree (Paris, Louvre, Roman copy of an original, fourth-century B.C. bronze by Praxiteles). Apollo often holds a kithara in divine assemblies, and he is frequently surrounded by Artemis and Leto, or is accompanied by

Apollo Belvedere.
Second century A.D.
Rome, Musei Vaticani.

Apollo and Daphne.
Dosso Dossi,
c. 1520–25.
Rome,
Galleria Borghese.

Apollo and Diana (detail).
Lucas Cranach,
c. 1530 .
Brussels,
Musées Royaux
des Beaux-Arts.

the Muses (hydria by the Villa Giulia Painter, c. 460 B.C., Rome, Musei Vaticani). He may appear with a palm tree, an allusion to the tree on Delos that Leto held on to during childbirth, or a tripod, an allusion to an accessory used at divinations and to the offerings made to obtain the god's favor. In addition, Hercules and Apollo fought over a tripod during their quarrel for control of Delphi (pediment on the Siphnian Treasury, c. 525 B.C., Delphi). Apollo often holds a sacrificial cup (phial) and gestures as if to drink. He is crowned with laurel, whose role is important in prophetic inspiration, and grouped with the swan that carried him to the Hyperboreans, and a deer, which alludes to his role as god of the hunt.

In the modern pictorial tradition, Apollo retains the youthful and dazzling appearance of a Greek god, the incarnation of ideal beauty, but loses his darker side. He is also more strongly identified with the Sun, whose chariot he drives (Gallery of Apollo, Palace of Versailles). His connection with the Muses makes him an essential figure in all allegorical representations of the arts and music: in a painting by Maerten de Vos, each Muse holds a different instrument (end of the sixteenth century, Brussels, Musées Royaux des Beaux-Arts). Apollo plays string instruments—the lyre, the kithara, or the violin—as opposed to the flute or syrinx, which are reserved for Pan and satyrs (Dosso Dossi, c. 1520–25, Rome, Galleria Borghese); he reigns over Parnassus, the prototypic symbol of poetic inspiration (Raphael, 1510–11, Rome, Vatican, Stanza della Segnatura; Poussin, c. 1631–33, Madrid, Prado).

In the nineteenth century, Apollo appeared in almost all decorative programs for buildings dedicated to music and dance: examples are Garnier's Opéra (inaugurated in 1875) and the Théâtre des Champs-Élysées (inaugurated in 1913, Maurice Denis's ceiling). This tradition continued into the twentieth century (the decorative sculpture of the Palais Chaillot, the monumental *Apollo* by Bouchard, 1937). In the contemporary period he remains the symbol of art and poetry, and was particularly important to the Symbolists (Redon, *The Chariot of Apollo*, Paris, Musée d'Orsay). Outside the narrative context, he is also the epitome of masculine beauty in the decorative arts.

Attributes: Bow. Chariot. Deer. Hunt. Laurel. Palm tree. Snake. String instruments (lyre, kithara, violin).

Cross-references: Aesculapius. Bacchus. Daphne. Hyacinthus. Leto. Marsyas. Muses. Niobe. Tityus.

Sources: *Homeric Hymn to Apollo.*

Bibliography: M. Fumaroli, *L'inspiration du poète de Pousssin*, Cahiers du Louvre, dossier 36, reprinted in *L'École du silence*, Paris, 1994.

APOTHEOSIS

This term designates the rare moment when a mortal rises to divine status and is welcomed among the gods. It is generally used in connection with Hercules, who was mortal through his mother (Alcmena) but divine through his father (Jupiter), and who was welcomed among the Olympian gods by his protectress Minerva. Aeneas, son of the Trojan Anchises and the goddess Venus, was also deified. Finally, Homer, undoubtedly mortal in origin but divinely inspired as a poet, was also apotheosized.

Cross-references: Aeneas. Hercules. Homer.

APPLE *See* Atalanta. Atlas. Caesar. Graces. Paris. Venus.

ARACHNE

Gk., Lat., and Ger. Arachne; It. and Sp. Aracne; Fr. Arachné.
Legendary character.

HISTORY/MYTHOLOGY

Arachne was a young Lydian maiden so skilled at weaving that people
said she had learned her art from Minerva herself. However, she refused
the goddess's patronage and even challenged her to a contest in which
each wove different motifs. Minerva went first and represented the
Olympian gods and how they punish those who defy them; Arachne
wove the shameful metamorphoses of Jupiter and Neptune, two lovers
of mortals. Embittered by the quality of Arachne's work, Minerva
beat her to the ground with her shuttle. When the maiden hanged herself, the goddess changed her into a spider (*arachne* in Greek), hanging from a web.

REPRESENTATIONS

The subject is rare in antiquity, but a marble relief from the Forum of
Nerva shows Minerva standing before a fallen Arachne (A.D. 97, Rome).
　　In the Villa Farnese at Caprarola (c. 1565, Camera des Fileuses),
Taddeo Zuccari portrayed the punishment of Arachne: Minerva
stands before the shattered loom while the partially metamorphosed
maiden already hangs from the ceiling. Arachne flees Minerva's
wrath in the foreground of a sketch by Rubens (1636–38, Richmond,
Virginia Museum of Fine Arts). Velázquez inserted the subject into
the background of his painting *The Tapestry Weavers* (1657, Madrid,
Prado).

Attributes: Loom. Spider.

Cross-references: Minerva. Neptune.

Sources: Ovid, *Metamorphoses* VI, 5–145.

ARCADIA

Arcadia, which is situated in the middle of the Greek Peloponnese,
was once a mountainous and unspoiled region largely inhabited by
shepherds and traditionally ruled by Pan. It was thought of as a
world both primitive and idyllic. In one painting by Guerchino and
two by Poussin, *The Arcadian Shepherds* (c. 1630, Chatsworth, and
c. 1638, Paris, Louvre), shepherds are shown deciphering the Latin
words *Et in Arcadia ego* inscribed on a tomb. The phrase could be
translated as "Even I lived in Arcadia," although the exact meaning
is "I [death] am here even in Arcadia." It is the latter sense that Sir
Joshua Reynolds understood for his own version of the subject
(1769, Crowe Hall).

Bibliography: E. Panofsky, "Et in Arcadia ego: Poussin and the
Elegiac Tradition," in *Meaning in the Visual Arts*, Harmondsworth,
1970, pp. 340–67.

Et in Arcadia Ego.
Francesco Barbieri,
Il Guerchino, 1618.
Rome, Galleria
Nazionale d'Arte
Antic.

ARCHIMEDES

Gk., Lat., and Ger. Archimedes; It. Archimede; Sp. Arquimedes;
Fr. Archimède.
Mathematician from Syracuse (287–212 B.C.).

HISTORY/MYTHOLOGY

Archimedes, the greatest mathematician in antiquity, was born and
died at Syracuse, a place he hardly ever left except for an early voyage
to Alexandria, where he studied Euclid. During repeated Roman
attacks on Syracuse, he used all his knowledge to defend his country.
When the Roman general Marcellus blockaded the city, one of his
soldiers surprised Archimedes at his home and summoned him to follow.
Archimedes was in the middle of trying to finish a project and,
because he delayed, the soldier killed him with his sword.

Marcellus himself mourned the loss of such a great intellect and
erected a tomb in Archimedes' honor; to conform with Archimedes'
wishes, a sphere was placed on the tomb in a cylinder and inscribed
with numbers that expressed the mathematical relation between the
two objects.

When Cicero was questor in Sicily, he discovered the great man's
tomb, which had been overgrown by bushes.

REPRESENTATIONS

Archimedes often appears alongside other ancient scholars and philosophers in Renaissance portrait galleries and in decorative programs
that glorified antiquity, as exemplified in Perugino's fresco for the

Stanza della Segnatura in the Vatican (1511), or in Carducci's fresco for the library of the Escurial (1592). This representational tradition continued in the seventeenth century, and was perpetuated in nineteenth-century iconographic programs, as can be seen in a cycle by Delacroix, which contrasts the uncivilized and civilized worlds, symbolized by Attila and Orpheus respectively, and in which Archimedes is positioned next to Orpheus.

Two specific episodes are also depicted. One is the death of Archimedes, for which artists contrast the soldier's brutality with the fright of the elderly man, caught buried in his research when the sword strikes. In a painting by Giovanni Battista Langetti, Archimedes is at his work table and gestures broadly as if to protect his manuscripts as much as himself. The second episode is Cicero's discovery of Archimedes' tomb, which provided an edifying subject for historical landscape painting, as evidenced in a work by Valenciennes (1787, Toulouse, Musée des Augustins).

Attributes: Books. Instruments of geometry.

Cross-references: Orpheus.

Sources: Plutarch, *Life of Marcellus*, 14–19.

Bibliography: D.L. Simms, "The Trail for Archimedes' Tomb," *Journal of the Warburg and Courtauld Institutes* 53 (1990): 281–5.

ARES *Greek name for* Mars.

ARETHUSA

Gk., Lat., and Ger. Arethusa; It. and Sp. Aretusa; Fr. Arétuse.
Nymph of the Peloponnese and Sicily.

HISTORY/MYTHOLOGY

Arethusa was one of Diana's nymphs. On one occasion while she was bathing in the waters of the river Alpheus, the offspring of Ocean and Thetis, Alpheus fell in love with the nymph, took on human form, and pursued her. To protect her nymph, Diana changed her into a spring, whereupon Alpheus turned himself back into a river and followed Arethusa from Elis (near Olympia) to Sicily. He re-emerged at Ortygia (Syracuse) and there mixed his waters with those of the spring.

REPRESENTATIONS

The nymph Arethusa's head is surrounded by dolphins as it appears on coins from Syracuse.

Modern artists have represented the subject of Alpheus pursuing Arethusa: Diana, in the heavens, protects the nymph by pulling her away from her pursuer (sketch attributed to Louis Boullogne, 1654–1733, Budapest, priv. coll.). Restout depicted the same subject (1720, Rouen, Musée des Beaux-Arts).

Attributes: Dolphin. Spring.

Cross-references: Diana.

Sources: Ovid, *Metamorphoses* V, 572–641. Pausanias, V, 7, 2.

The Argonauts.
Detail from
an Attic krater
attributed
to the Niobid
Painter, c. 460 B.C.
Paris, Louvre.

ARGONAUTS

Gk. and Ger. Argonauti; Lat. Argonaute; It. Arganauti;
Sp. Argonautas; Fr. Argonautes.
Legendary characters.

HISTORY/MYTHOLOGY

When Jason left on his quest for the Golden Fleece he built a ship called
the *Argo* ("Rapid") whose crew of approximately fifty members, all of
whom were heroes with different degrees of celebrity, were known as
the Argonauts. The list varies, but among the Argonauts were Argos
(the son of Phrixus), Orpheus—the musician whose own song drowned out that of the Sirens—Amphiaraus, Zetes and Calaïs (sons of
Boreas), Castor and Pollux (the Dioscuri), Hercules, and Hylas, to
name only a few.

The legend of the Argonauts is one of the oldest and most
complicated in Greek mythology; Homer does not recount it and it
comes down to us only in its late form through a poem by Apollonius
of Rhodes (third century B.C.).

REPRESENTATIONS

The *Argo*, with Orpheus and the Dioscuri, appears on the metopes of
the Sicyonian Treasury at Delphi (c. 560 B.C.). The subject of an Attic
krater attributed to the Niobid Painter is probably the Argonauts
prior to their departure (c. 460 B.C., Paris, Louvre).

The departure of the Argonauts was illustrated in the
Renaissance by Ercole de' Roberti (late fifteenth century, Padua) and
Dosso Dossi (c. 1520, Washington, National Gallery of Art). Moreau
revived the relatively rare subject of the *Argo* for his *Return of the
Argonauts*, which is dominated by the figure of Jason brandishing the
Golden Fleece (1897, Paris, Musée Gustave Moreau).

Attributes: Ship.

Cross-references: Amphiaraus. Castor and Pollux. Hercules. Hylas.
Jason. Orpheus.

Sources: Apollonius of Rhodes, *Argonautic.*

Bibliography: M. Vojatzi, *Frühe Argonautenbilder*, Würzburg, 1982.

ARGUS

Gk. and Ger. Argos; Lat. and Fr. Argus; It. and Sp. Argo.
Legendary Argian hero.

HISTORY/MYTHOLOGY

Argus was an Argian hero endowed with one, four, or one hundred eyes
(depending on the myth's version) that never closed. Juno entrusted the
indefatigable watchman with keeping watch over Io, whom Jupiter
had transformed into a heifer. Jupiter then assigned Mercury the task of
liberating Io, which he did by putting Argus to sleep and then chopping
off his head. As a memorial to Argus, Juno decorated the tail of her
legendary animal, the peacock, with his eyes.

Argus and Io.
Detail from an
oenochoe,
c. 460 B.C.
Naples,
Museo Nazionale.

Argus and Juno.
Peter Paul
Rubens,
c. 1610–11.
Cologne,
Wallraf-Richartz
Museum.

REPRESENTATIONS

In Greek images, Argus appears as a body covered with eyes (Attic amphora c. 480 B.C., Hamburg, Kunstgeschichte Museum) and as a being with two faces (Attic amphora, c. 540 B.C., London, British Museum). The predominant subject is Mercury putting the shepherd to death.

Although Italian Renaissance painters took up the subject, Flemish baroque painters particularly illustrated the pastoral scene of Mercury lulling Argus to sleep with his music (Jordaens, c. 1620, Lyon, Musée des Beaux-Arts); Fragonard copied a Flemish painting of the first half of the seventeenth century (c. 1760, Paris, Louvre). Rubens depicted Juno placing the dead Argus's eyes on the peacock's tail (1610–11, Cologne, Wallraf-Richartz Museum).

Attributes: Double face. Eyes. Peacock.

Cross-references: Io. Juno. Mercury.

Sources: Ovid, *Metamorphoses* I, 625–723.

ARIADNE

Gk. and Ger. Ariadne; Lat. and Sp. Ariadna; It. Ariauna; Fr. Ariane.
Legendary Cretan princess.

HISTORY/MYTHOLOGY

Ariadne was the daughter of Minos, king of Crete, and Pasiphaë. She was seduced by Theseus when he came to Crete to fight the Minotaur. Ariadne helped the hero escape from the labyrinth by giving him a ball of string, which he unwound at the start of his entry and later followed to find his way out. Ariadne left Crete with Theseus but was abandoned by him during a stopover at Naxos; versions vary as to whether this was simple betrayal or a divine command. The lonely Ariadne was discovered by Dionysus (Bacchus) who formed a constellation by throwing her crown into the heavens and then married her and provided a lavish wedding feast.

REPRESENTATIONS

In ancient art, Ariadne is sometimes seen giving the ball of string to Theseus (Pompeian fresco, c. A.D. 70, Naples, Museo Nazionale). Her abandonment by Theseus is a frequent subject: she sleeps while the hero slips away and Mercury looks on (Attic cup, 480 B.C., Tarquinia). A statue known since 1512 probably represents the sleeping Ariadne (second-century B.C. copy, now in Rome, Vatican). Innumerable Attic vases show Dionysus accompanied by a woman who is sometimes identified by inscription as Ariadne.

Modern painters have rarely depicted the abandonment (Carlo Saraceni, c. 1608, Naples, Galleria di Capodimonte). The scene most often represented instead is the encounter between Bacchus and Ariadne, a tradition that begins with Titian, who was inspired by the texts of Philostratus and Catullus (1522–23, London, National Gallery). In Antoine Coypel's painting, *Bacchus and Ariadne*, Hymen, the god of marriage, acts as a go-between for the two main characters. The triumph of Ariadne is the central subject in Annibale Carracci's ceiling for the Palazzo Farnese (1597–1600, Rome). Giorgio de Chirico often incorporated the sleeping Ariadne into compositions, most notably for *The Silent Statue or Ariadne* (1913, Düsseldorf, Kunstsammlung Nordhein-Westfalen).

Attributes: Ball of string.

Cross-references: Bacchus. Theseus.

Sources: Catullus, LXIV, 50–201 (wedding). Ovid, *Metamorphoses* VIII, 169–82; *Ars Amatoria* I, 529–30, 555–6. Philostratus, *Imagines* I, 15. Plutarch, *Life of Theseus*, 20.

ARION

Gk., Lat., Sp., Fr., and Ger. Arion; It. Arione.
Musician from Lesbos (seventh–sixth centuries B.C.).

HISTORY/MYTHOLOGY

The invention of the dithyramb, a song in honor of Dionysus, is attributed to Arion, a musician from Methymna, on the island of Lesbos. According to Herodotus, Arion was captured by pirates while returning from Tarentum; he asked to sing one last time before being thrown into the sea, and his song attracted dolphins, which carried him to safety.

REPRESENTATIONS

Arion.
Andrea Briosco,
called Riccio,
1507–16.
Paris, Louvre.

A lyre-player straddling a dolphin appears on coins from Methymna. Arion is also found in numerous mosaics.

In modern painting, Arion serves as one of the legendary musicians who are sometimes grouped with Orpheus (Mantegna, Camera degli Sposi, completed in 1474, Mantua, Palazzo Ducale). He occasionally holds a modern instrument, such as a viol, in place of the lyre. Arion continued to be depicted into the nineteenth century (sculpture by Hiolle, 1870, Paris, Musée d'Orsay).

Attributes: Dolphin. Lyre.

Cross-references: Orpheus.

Sources: Herodotus, *The Histories* I, 33–4. Ovid, *Festivals* II, 79–118.

ARISTAEUS *See* Actaeon.

ARISTOTLE

Gk., Lat., Sp. and Ger. Aristoteles, It. Aristotele; Fr. Aristote.
Greek philosopher (Stagirus, Macedonia, 384 B.C. – Chalcis, Euboea, 322 B.C.)

The Lay of Aristotle.
Hans Baldung Grien.
Engraving, 1513.

HISTORY/MYTHOLOGY

Aristotle was born in Macedonia but as a youth went to Athens to study the teachings of Plato and stayed there for about twenty years. He then settled on Lesbos and was called from there by Philip of Macedon to educate the young Alexander. The sovereign purportedly informed him of his son's birth with these celebrated words: "I inform you that I have a son. I thank the gods not so much for this as for making him born in the time of Aristotle." The philosopher devoted approximately twelve years to this memorable education before re-establishing himself in Athens, where he founded a school, the Lyceum, and wrote the major part of his works. Alexander remained faithful to his tutor and even went to the trouble of providing Aristotle with examples of the oriental plants and animals that he came across for his studies in the natural sciences. As a gesture of largesse, Alexander also helped establish a library for the philosopher and his pupils. Aristotle fell victim to the wave of anti-Macedonian hatred that followed Alexander's death, and after the Areopagus condemned him to die, he exiled himself to Chalcis, on the island of Euboea, and died there shortly afterward.

A thirteenth-century *trouvère*, Henri d'Andelys, who was himself inspired by a new Arabian horse, took pleasure in ridiculing Aristotle with an anecdote entitled *The Lay of Aristotle*. According to that tale, Aristotle reproached Alexander for falling so in love with an Indian maiden that he lost all concern for his glory. The reprimand brought the prince to his senses, and he broke with the girl, who then swore revenge against Aristotle. She first flattered him so much that he yielded to her physical charms. Then, to flaunt both her victory and her revenge, she humiliated him by making him indulge in her fantasy of riding him like a horse—saddled, bridled, and crawling on all fours. The anecdote gave rise to an expression used in French parlor games, "*faire le cheval d'Aristote.*"

REPRESENTATIONS

Several ancient texts mention portraits and statues of Aristotle, who is in fact identifiable in about fifteen busts—all Roman copies of a lost

Aristotle with a Bust of Homer.
Rembrandt van Rijn, 1653.
New York, Metropolitan Museum of Art.

Greek original—the best of which is in Vienna (Claudian period, Vienna, Kunsthistorisches Museum).

Representations of philosophers are found in large-scale compositions, such as *The School of Athens* by Raphael or *The Apotheosis of Homer* by Ingres, in which Aristotle flanks Plato, the other great master of Greek philosophy. But the life story of the "prince of philosophers" has hardly inspired painters. At the very most, Aristotle appears in the context of Alexandrian iconography, receiving Asiatic animals from the hands of his illustrious pupil (Jean-Baptiste de Champaigne, *Alexander Having Exotic Animals Brought to Aristotle for Study*, 1673, Versailles, Musée). The remaining representations of Aristotle are intended to inspire reflection, as exemplified by Rembrandt's painting, *Aristotle with a Bust of Homer*, in which the elderly philosopher is deep in thought and poses his hand on top of a bust of Homer (1653, New York, Metropolitan Museum of Art).

The subject of Aristotle humiliated and ridden horseback by a maiden, who is often called Phyllis, is more frequently illustrated, mainly in fifteenth- and sixteenth-century illuminated manuscripts, ivories, drawings, etc.

Attributes: Books. Exotic animals.

Cross-references: Alexander. Homer.

Sources: Henri d'Andelys, *The Lay of Aristotle*.

ARMS

The hero's arms had strong symbolic value and were often given specific iconographic treatment. Their origin was sometimes divine: Vulcan forged arms both for Achilles at the request of Thetis, and for Aeneas, whose mother (Venus) seduced her husband for a full suit of armor. Ajax and Ulysses fought bitterly over the dead Achilles' arms until the Greeks voted to give them to Ulysses, who turned them over to Neoptolemus, Achilles' son. That the transfer of arms from one hero to another signified heroic descent is demonstrated by Hercules, who entrusts Philoctetes with his bow just before dying on the funeral pyre. The relationship between a hero, his identity, and his arms is demonstrated by the return of Ulysses, who passes the test Penelope imposed on her suitors because only he is capable of stringing his own bow.

Cross-references: Achilles. Aeneas. Ajax the Greater. Hercules. Mars. Minerva. Penelope. Penthesilea. Ulysses.

ARRIA AND PAETUS

Historical Roman characters (first century A.D.)

HISTORY/MYTHOLOGY

Paetus, a Roman magistrate who died around A.D. 42, was implicated in Scribonianus's conspiracy against the emperor Claudius and was therefore condemned to die. Paetus's wife, Arria, recognized that there was no way of escaping the verdict and that her husband did not have the courage to comply. She drove a dagger into her own chest, withdrew it, and then held it out to her husband crying, "*Paete, non dolet*," or, "Paetus, it doesn't hurt."

REPRESENTATIONS

In the nineteenth century an ancient sculptural group in the Villa Ludovici was mistaken for Arria and Paetus. The statue was later identified as two Gauls, for, contrary to Roman legend, the male figure plays the main role by heroically taking his own life to escape the enemy immediately after killing his wife.

The moment represented in modern painting and sculpture is when Arria withdraws the dagger from herself and holds it out to Paetus. One can almost hear the famous "Paetus, it doesn't hurt," which is sometimes the title. The courageous heroine's calm face is contrasted with her husband's tortured expression. In sculpture, the couple is generally represented alone (Lepautre, 1691, Paris, Louvre) or accompanied by a horrified servant who supports Arria's body, which bears traces of the wound (Vincent, 1785, Amiens, Musée des Beaux-Arts).

Attributes: Dagger.

Sources: Pliny the Younger, *Letters* III, 16, 6. Dio Cassius, LX, 16, 6.

ARROWS *See* Apollo. Cupid. Hercules.

Artemisia.
Greek sculpture,
fourth century B.C.
London,
British Museum.

ARTEMIS *Greek name for* Diana.

ARTEMISIA

Gk., Lat., It., Sp., and Ger. Artemisia; Fr. Artémise/Artémisie.Queen of Halicarnassus (377–353 B.C.).

HISTORY/MYTHOLOGY

Artemisia, the satrap of Caria from 377 to 353 B.C., was both the sister and wife of Mausolus. She was so grief-stricken by her husband's death that she did not stop seeking to immortalize his memory, and for this imported artists from around the world and commissioned both literary and artistic works. She ultimately had a tomb built, the Mausoleum, whose magnificence made it one of the seven wonders of the world. Her love for Mausolus even drove her to the extraordinary step of making a beverage from his ashes and drinking it. Still inconsolable, she outlived her husband by only two years.

REPRESENTATIONS

The statue of Artemisia originally stood next to one of her husband on the Mausoleum of Halicarnassus (London, British Museum).

She is represented from the sixteenth century onward. Artists have exclusively focused on the episode in which she drinks Mausolus's ashes. In such scenes, she is on the verge of drinking, with the cup in her hand or near her lips. A number of painters, from Salvati (1510–63, Florence, Uffizi) to Subleyras (1699–1749, Bologna, Pinacoteca), depicted this penultimate act of love.

Artemisia occurs as a subject in other media. Cartoons for tapestries by Antoine Caron portray Catherine de Medicis and Henri II as Artemisia and Mausolus (sixteenth century, Paris, Bibliothèque Nationale de France, Cabinet des Estampes). In sculpture, Artemisia is one of the few historical subjects to appear in the gardens of Versailles (by Lefevre and Desjardins, 1687–94).

Attributes: Cup.

Sources: Cicero, *Tusculan Disputations*. Aulus Gellius, X, 18, 3. Valerius Maximus, IV, 6, ext. 1.

ASCLEPIUS *Greek name for* Aesculapius.

ASS *See* Midas (ears of an ass). Priapus. Silenus.

ASTYANAX

Gk., Lat., Fr., and Ger. Astyanax; It. Astianatto; Sp. Astianax.
Prince from the Trojan legend.

HISTORY/MYTHOLOGY

Astyanax, the "Prince of the city," was the son of Hector and Andromache. As heir to Hector, the best of the Achaeans, he constituted a threat to the Greeks who, upon the fall of Troy and at the instigation of Ulysses, decided to do away with the child by throwing him from the city's ramparts.

REPRESENTATIONS

In scenes representing the fall of Troy, or the *Ilioupersis*, the child Astyanax is brutally slaughtered: either Neoptolemus holds him by the foot and flings him at the head of his grandfather, Priam, who takes refuge on the altar of Zeus (cup by the Brygos Painter, c. 480 B.C., Paris, Louvre), or his bleeding body lies beside the altar or on his grandfather's knees (hydria by the Kleophrades Painter, c. 490 B.C., Naples, Museo Archeologico).

In modern painting, beginning especially in the seventeenth century, Astyanax appears in scenes that show Hector and Andromache bidding each other farewell, as seen in the painting by Joseph-Marie Vien (1786, Paris, Louvre). He appears with his mother alongside the body of Hector in a painting by David, *Andromache Mourning Hector* (1783, Paris, École des Beaux-Arts). Finally, Ulysses tearing Astyanax away from his mother has occasionally been depicted (Sébastien Bourdon, 1616–71, known through an engraving by Samuel Bernard, 1615–87).

Attributes: Child.

Cross-references: Andromache. Hector.

Sources: Homer, *The Iliad* VI, 394–496 (farewells). Euripides, *Trojan Women*, 1133–250.

ATALANTA

Gk., Fr., and Ger. Atalante; Lat., It., and Sp. Atalanta.
Greek mythological princess.

Atalanta and Meleager.
Laurent de La Hyre.
Engraving,
eighteenth century.

HISTORY/MYTHOLOGY

Atalanta was the daughter of an Arcadian king who abandoned her at birth; she was raised by hunters and consecrated herself to Diana. She took part in the Calydonian boar hunt, was the first to wound the boar, and was awarded the spoils by Meleager. During one of the Argonauts' expeditions, she defeated Peleus in a wrestling match at the funeral games held in honor of Pelias.

According to Boeotian legend, after an oracle advised her to be wary of marriage, Atalanta, who was an excellent runner, announced that she would marry the man who could beat her in a race, and would kill the man who lost. With help from Venus, however, Hippomenes took up the challenge and won: he dropped golden apples from the goddess on to the track and Atalanta lost speed by picking them up. Once married, Hippomenes neglected to thank Venus, who then punished both him and Atalanta by inciting them to make love in the temple of Cybele, a profanation that resulted in their being turned into lions.

REPRESENTATIONS

The Calydonian boar hunt, with Atalanta and Meleager at the head, is a frequent subject in ancient art and appears in all media: Etruscan mirrors and urns, Greek vases, and Roman mosaics and sarcophagi (sarcophagus from Rome, Musei Capitolini, A.D. 25). In a Pompeian

Atalanta and Hippomenes.
Guido Reni, 1637–9.
Naples, Galleria
di Capodimonte.

fresco, Atalanta is seen reclining with Meleager; the boar's head is posed at Meleager's feet (c. A.D. 40, Naples, Museo Nazionale). The wrestling match between Atalanta and Peleus during the funeral games was depicted in the sixth century B.C. (Chalcidonian Hydra, c. 540 B.C., Munich, Antikensmuseum).

The subject of the hunt is taken up again in baroque art. Forming part of a series of six or seven lost paintings about Meleager that were intended to be woven into tapestries by the Manufacture de Nancy, Le Brun's *The Hunt of Meleager and Atalanta* portrays Atalanta as a young woman who is about to shoot an arrow at a boar, under attack by dogs (c. 1658, Paris, Louvre). The race with the Golden Apples, inspired by Ovid, is also a frequent subject (Rubens, 1637–38, Madrid, Prado; Guido Reni, 1618, Naples, Galleria di Capodimonte).

Attributes: Boar. Golden apples.

Cross-references: Argonauts. Diana. Meleager. Peleus.

Sources: Apollodorus, III, 9, 2. Ovid, *Metamorphoses* X, 560–707.

ATHAMAS *See* Bacchus. Ino.

ATHENA *Greek name for* Minerva.

ATLAS

Gk., Lat., Sp., Fr., and Ger. Atlas; It. Atlante.
Giant from Greek mythology.

HISTORY/MYTHOLOGY

Atlas was the father of the Pleiades and the Hesperides. He was also a Titan and, when his race revolted, was condemned by Jupiter to support the vault of the sky. When Hercules needed to gather the Golden Apples from the garden of the Hesperides, Atlas offered to go look for them provided Hercules would take his place. Upon returning, however, Atlas refused to reshoulder the sky, and Hercules was forced to outsmart him: he asked Atlas to slide a cushion over his shoulders and while the Titan complied, Hercules shifted the burden back on to Atlas.

REPRESENTATIONS

In a composition from a Laconian cup, Atlas carries the sky and faces his brother, Prometheus, who is eaten by an eagle (c. 560 B.C., Rome, Vatican). In one of the metopes from the Temple of Zeus at Olympia, Atlas is seen bringing the Golden Apples to Hercules, who supports the sky with Athena's help (c. 460 B.C., Olympia, Museum). There is also a statue of Atlas in which the Titan buckles under the weight of a globe that is incised with constellations (Naples, Museo Nazionale, Roman copy after a Hellenistic original).

Annibale Carracci depicted Atlas supporting the world (c. 1600, Rome, Palazzo Farnese), while Pierre Puget used the figure of Atlas as a flanking element for the door of the Hôtel de Ville in Toulon (1656–57).

Atlas Bringing Hercules the Golden Apples from the Garden of the Hesperides.
c. 460 B.C.
Olympia,
Museum of Olympia.

Attributes: Globe. Rock.

Cross-references: Hercules. Prometheus.

Sources: Hesiod, *Theogony* 516–18. Ovid, *Metamorphoses* IX, 199.

ATROPOS *See* Fates.

ATTIS

Gk. Atys; Lat., It., and Fr. Attis; Sp. Atis/Atys; Ger. Attis/Attes.
Phrygian god.

HISTORY/MYTHOLOGY

Traditions surrounding the Phrygian god Attis vary. According to Ovid, he was chastely loved by Cybele, who made him guardian of her temple on condition that he remain a virgin. He fell in love with a nymph, however, and was consequently driven so mad by Cybele that he became delirious and castrated himself; from his blood sprang violets.

REPRESENTATIONS

Numerous statuettes in Hellenistic or Roman art show Attis as a young child holding a syrinx, a torch, or a tambourine. He wears a Phrygian cap and a curious barbarian costume consisting of a sort of shirt, buttoned to the collar, and pants that are held by clips but which leave his lower stomach and torso exposed. In some reliefs he is shown reclining (second–third century A.D., Saint-Rémy-de-Provence, Musée.

The subject is rare in modern art. A statue by Donatello, the so-called *Atys-Amorino*, draws inspiration from ancient models but otherwise adds wings to the character while exposing its buttocks.

Attis (detail).
Donatello, c. 1440.
Florence, Bargello.

Attributes: Phrygian cap. Sewn but open garment. Syrinx.

59

Cross-references: Cybele.

Sources: Ovid, *Festivals* IV, 221–44.

Bibliography: M. Vermaseren, *The Legends of Attis in Greek and Roman Art*, Leiden, 1966.

ATYS *Greek name for* Attis.

AUGEAS *See* Hercules.

Augustus.
First century.
Paris, Louvre.

AUGUSTUS

Lat. and Ger. Augustus; It. and Sp. Augusto; Fr. Auguste.
Roman emperor (Rome, 63 B.C. – Nala, A.D. 14).

HISTORY/MYTHOLOGY

Octavius was born in 63 B.C. and was the great-nephew of Julius Caesar, who adopted him. He took the name of Augustus only when he became emperor.

He appointed himself Caesar's political heir after Caesar died. He very soon entered into rivalry with Antony, which resulted in their division of the Roman world: the West went to Octavius and the East to Antony. After Antony allowed Cleopatra to take a strong hold of Roman possessions, however, Octavius, whose popularity in Rome continued to grow, declared war on the Egyptian queen and defeated her and Antony at the Battle of Actium (31 B.C.). After this, Octavius began to assert his exclusive authority. Without radically changing the Republic's institutions, he substituted them with those of the principate, which were founded on the balance of power between the Senate and himself. He radically reformed religious institutions as well as the Empire's administration and politics. Nevertheless, his military campaigns were aimed more at strengthening the Empire's frontiers than fulfilling his personal ambitions, and for this reason ancient authors regarded him as the man who "closed the gates of the Temple of Janus," that is, as a peacemaker. Augustus was moreover a great patron of arts and letters, and ushered in the golden age of Roman classicism, which is customarily called "the Age of Augustus."

REPRESENTATIONS

There are many sculptures of Augustus, both busts and full-length. Some endow him with attributes according to his different functions: he is veiled in his religious role of *Pontifex maximus*, or crowned with shafts of wheat as an allusion to the abundance he brought Rome, or his forehead is encircled by a ribbon decorated with laurel (all three sculptures are in Rome, Museo Nazionale Romano). In addition, Augustus is often represented on medallions or engraved stones.

In modern painting, the most popular subject involving Augustus has been the closing of the Temple of Janus, a symbol of the victory of peace over war. It appears in a fresco in the Palazzo Malavezzi in Bologna (Tibaldi, 1527–97) and in subsequent centuries in paintings by Boullogne (1681) and Carle van Loo (1765), both in Amiens, Musée des Beaux-Arts. Different ancient busts of Augustus inspired Ingres for his

Augustus.
Cameo,
first century A.D.
Paris, Bibliothèque
Nationale de France.

painting *Tu Marcellus eris*, in which Virgil reads the *Aeneid* before the emperor, Livia, and Octavius (1812, three versions, of which the most complete is the Musée des Augustins, Toulouse).

Augustus has sometimes been represented meditating at the tomb of Alexander (Sébastien Bourdon, seventeenth century, Paris, Louvre).

Attributes: Laurel. Wheat (sheaves).

Cross-references: Alexander. Virgil.

Sources: Suetonius, *The Twelve Caesars*, 22.

AURORA

Gk. and Ger. Eos; Lat., It., and Sp. Aurora; Fr. Aurore.

HISTORY/MYTHOLOGY

Aurora, a first-generation Titan, was the sister of Helios (the Sun) and Selene (the Moon). Homer described her as the "rosy-fingered" goddess. When Aurora made love with Mars, Venus grew jealous and punished her by making her keep falling in love for eternity. As a result, Aurora fell in love with the giant Orion, whom she took to Delos, then with Cephalus, whom she pursued in vain (he preferred Procris), and finally with Thonos, for whom she obtained immortality but not eternal youth, which caused Thonos to grown old indefinitely until he shrivelled up. The dew that Aurora scatters was born of the tears she shed over her dead son Memnon, who was killed by Achilles at Troy, when she came to gather up his body.

Aurora and Cephalus.
Pierre-Narcisse
Guérin, 1810.
Paris, Louvre.

REPRESENTATIONS

In Greek ceramics, Aurora is winged; she is seen pursuing or abducting the young hunter Cephalus, the object of her unrequited love (pelike by the Altamura Painter, c. 460 B.C., Paris, Louvre). She may also appear behind her son Memnon, the Ethiopian chief who aided the Trojans, or even gathering up his body after Achilles kills him (cup by Douris, c. 480 B.C., Paris, Louvre).

In the Palazzo Schifanoia in Ferrara (1471), Aurora drives Apollo's chariot (month of May). Aurora appears frequently in baroque painting, especially in ceiling decorations; she is often in a chariot, torch in hand, clearing a path for the Sun and shedding dew (Guido Reni, 1612–14, Rome, Casino Rospigliosi). Rubens portrayed Aurora descending to a reposing Cephalus (c. 1638, London, National Gallery); similarly, Boucher depicted the young hunter on a cloud beside Aurora (1733, Nancy, Musée des Beaux-Arts).

The goddess is often treated as an allegory of morning; she is still represented in the nineteenth century in both painting (Philipp Otto Runge, *The Morning*, 1808, Hamburg, Kunsthalle) and sculpture (Puech, *Aurora*, 1900, Paris, Musée d'Orsay).

Attributes: Chariot. Rose. Torch.

Cross-references: Cephalus. Memnon.

Sources: Ovid, *Metamorphoses* VII, 690–752.

Bibliography: S. Kaempf-Dimitriadou, *Die Liebe der Götter in der attischen Kunst*, Bern, 1979, pp. 16–21. *The Loves of the Gods*, ex. cat., Fort Worth, 1992, nos. 44 and 59.

Bacchante.
After an original
from the fourth
century B.C.
Rome, Palazzo
dei Conservatori.

AUTONOE *See* Actaeon. Cadmus.

AX *See* Tereus.

BACCHANTES or MAENADS

Gk. and Lat. Bacche; It. Baccante; Sp. Baccantes; Fr. Bacchantes; Ger.
Bacchantin.
Companions of the god Bacchus.

HISTORY/MYTHOLOGY

The Bacchantes, or Maenads, were companions of Bacchus. As such,
they were driven by a kind of Dionysian possession (*mania*) that was
largely due to the effects of music and dance, although sex and
drunkenness also contributed. The Bacchantes gathered on mountains
to celebrate the god's mysteries and there played familiarly with wild
animals (lions, panthers, and snakes); they defended themselves, when
necessary, with thyrssi, or long shafts decorated with ivy. They could
in fact be a group of joyous and innocent women but, when seized by
Dionysian frenzy, could become a menacing pack capable of destroying whoever opposed them—for example Pentheus.

REPRESENTATIONS

The Bacchantes are shown dancing in unison to the sound of *auloi*
(flutes), tambourines, and rattles. They are crowned with ivy or grapevines, and wear fawn or panther skins called nebris or pardalide (cup
by the Brygos Painter, c. 480 B.C., Munich, Antikensammlungen). In
the most ancient images Bacchantes embrace and voluntarily submit
to passionately aroused satyrs; however, a very distinct change occurs
around 500 B.C., when they are seen chasing or fleeing from satyrs,

**Sleeping
Bacchante.**
Eugène Delacroix,
1844.
Paris, Louvre.

Bacchanal.
Detail from Titian,
The Andrians,
1518–19.
Madrid, Prado.

who now subdue Bacchantes only when they find them sleeping (hydria by the Kleophrades Painter, c. 500 B.C., Rouen, Musée d'Archéologie).

Bacchantes appear frequently from the Renaissance onward as figures that animate either the processions of Bacchus or the orgiastic rite celebrated in that god's honor—the Bacchanal. Titian provided the iconographic prototype for such representations based on Philostratus's description of a feast held in honor of Dionysus on the Island of Andros (*The Andrians*, 1518–19, Madrid, Prado). As a pagan but paradisical feast during which wine flowed freely, the Bacchanal—the Bacchantes' own festival—became a pretext for celebrating an ancient ideal in a serious (Poussin, *Bacchanalian Revel before a Term*, 1631–33, London, National Gallery) or unabashedly libertine manner (Jacob van Loo, *Bacchic Scene*, 1653, Amsterdam, Rijksmuseum).

Before he placed his dancing Bacchantes on the façade of Garnier's Opéra in Paris, Carpeaux sculpted a circle of Bacchantes whose frenzy shocked the prudish public in Second-Empire France (1869, Paris, Musée d'Orsay).

In the modern tradition, the Bacchantes' violence is sometimes seen being unleashed against Orpheus, whom they, in fact, put to death (Levy, *The Death of Orpheus*, 1863, Paris, Musée d'Orsay).

Attributes: Grapevine. Ivy. Lion. Panther. Skin of fawn or panther. Snake. Tambourine. Thyrsus.

Cross-references: Bacchus. Orpheus. Satyrs.

Sources: Euripides, *Bacchae*. Philostratus, I, 25 (*The Andrians*).

Bibliography: G. Cavalli-Björkmann, ed., *Bacchanals by Titian and Rubens*, Stockholm, 1987.

BACCHUS

Gk. and Ger. Dionysos; Lat. and Fr. Bacchus; It. Bacco; Sp. Baco.

HISTORY/MYTHOLOGY

Bacchus was the son of Jupiter and Semele. After Semele, who was pregnant with him, was struck by thunderbolts emanating from Jupiter's divine countenance, she could not carry her child to term.

Bacchus (detail).
Leonardo da Vinci,
1511–15.
Paris, Louvre.

Jupiter therefore sewed the child into his thigh and later himself gave birth to Bacchus. After Juno's jealousy drove his adoptive parents mad, the young god was first raised by Athamas and Semele's sister Ino, and ultimately entrusted into the care of the nymphs of Nysa.

Accounts of Bacchus's wanderings vary and are even contradictory. After he himself was driven mad by Juno, he went to Phrygia, where Cybele purified him. He next passed through Thrace, where his presence aroused the hostility of King Lycurgus, who locked up the god's companions, the Bacchantes. Lycurgus was then driven mad and, mistaking his son for a grapevine, cut him with a hatchet as if pruning him. Bacchus next led an expedition to India, after which he returned to Greece, where he again encountered difficulties. His arrival at Thebes, for example, provoked the animosity of his cousin, King Pentheus, and he instilled a murderous frenzy in the king's mother, Agave, who was another of Semele's sisters. At some point he traveled incognito across the sea toward Naxos, and was taken hostage by Tyrrhenian pirates; at that point he revealed his divine nature by immobilizing the ship, transforming her mast into a grapevine and the pirates into dolphins. At Naxos, he discovered the sleeping Ariadne, whom Theseus had abandoned, married her, and took her up to Olympus, where he finally found his place.

Bacchus fought on the side of the other gods in their battle against the Giants, using as weapons his attributes of ivy and grapevines, as well as the snakes and large feline animals that normally accompany him.

REPRESENTATIONS

In early ancient art, Dionysus is represented as a long-bearded god who wears a crown of ivy or grapevines and is dressed in a long, almost feminine robe; he also holds a two-handled drinking cup (cantharos). A more youthful type—one that portrays him as a beardless adolescent—appears toward the end of the fifth century B.C.

In Greece, the god was sometimes simply represented as a mask hanging on a pillar, a type of effigy that preceded the development of theater (amphora, c. 520 B.C., Tarquinia, Museum). Comedies and tragedies eventually formed part of festivals honoring Dionysus, and in this way he became associated with the theater.

Bacchus was at first not associated with sexual frenzy and was not represented as drunk until the end of the fifth century B.C., when he is surrounded by drunken satyrs and Maenads who dance, sing, and carry drinking vessels. His retinue is formed of Bacchantes, shown entranced by music and dance, and satyrs who are drunk with wine (amphora by the Kleophrades Painter, c. 500 B.C., Munich).

The subject of the triumph of Bacchus dominated Roman representations, and it is characterized by a procession in which the god, surrounded by satyrs, Bacchantes, and cupids, is led in a chariot drawn by panthers or centaurs (sarcophagus, c. A.D. 140–150, Copenhagen, Ny Carlsberg Glyptothek).

Narrative cycles focus mainly on the childhood of Bacchus (mosaic from Nea Paphos, c. A.D. 325–350, Cyprus), his returning of Hephaestus (Vulcan) to Olympus after intoxicating him (krater by Kleitias, c. 570 B.C., Florence, Museo Archeologico), and, more rarely, his encounter with the Tyrrhenian pirates (cup by Exekias, c. 530 B.C., Munich, Antikensammlungen).

Bacchus and Ariadne have been a popular subject since the Renaissance. During this period, however, Bacchus also appears as the god of drunks and orgies in works that contrast him with Apollo. He appears in this guise until the end of the nineteenth century in many works that, following Titian's lead (*The Andrians*, 1518–19, Madrid,

64

Boreas Abducting Orithyia.
Giovanni Antonio Pellegrini, first half of the eighteenth century.
Paris, Louvre.

The Meeting Between Antony and Cleopatra.
Giovanni Battista Tiepolo, 1747–50.
Fresco, Venice, Palazzo Labia.

**The Indian Triumph
of Bacchus.**
Mosaic,
third century A.D.
Sousse,
Archaeological
Museum.

Prado; *Bacchus and Ariadne*, 1522–23, London, National Gallery),
exploit the subject of the Bacchanal, where he is accompanied by
cupids, satyrs, and Maenads. When Bacchus is contemplated exclusively
as the god of wine (Caravaggio, 1596, Florence, Uffizi), he is often
grouped with Ceres (wheat) and Venus (love) (Rubens, 1612–13, Kassel,
Gemäldegalerie) as part of an allegory of fertility and prosperity.

Attributes: Bull. Cantharos. Drinking horn. Goat. Grapevine. Ivy.
Panther.

Cross-references: Ariadne. Bacchantes. Erigone. Pentheus. Satyrs.
Seasons. Semele. Vulcan.

Sources: *Homeric Hymn to Dionysus* (pirates). Catullus, LXIV
(wedding). Diodorus Siculus, *Library of History* III, 63–4. Nonnus of
Panopolis, *Dionysiac.* Ovid, *Metamorphoses* III, 310–15 (childhood),
597–691 (pirates). Philostratus, *Imagines* I, 15, 19.

Bibliography: T. Carpenter, *Dionysian Imagery in Archaic Greek Art*,
Oxford, 1986. C. Kerényi, *Dionysos*, London, 1976. R. Turcan,
Sarcophages romains à représentations dionysiaques, Paris, 1966.

BANQUET

The banquet held a special place in the social life of the ancients, for
whom hospitality and conviviality were essential values. Although
representations of banquets or feasts of the gods are rare in antiquity
(Attic cup by the Codrus Painter, c. 440 B.C., London, British
Museum), a number of accounts in which the banquet is a central element have been represented in modern times. This is particularly true
for accounts of wedding feasts held in the gods' presence, such as the
wedding of Thetis and Peleus (Rubens, 1636–38, Chicago, Art
Institute) and the marriage of Psyche (Giulio Romano, 1527–28,
Mantua, Palazzo del Tè, Sala di Psiche, in which a formal banquet is
grouped with a simple one).

Ancient artists focused largely on certain debauched banquets,
such as the one in which Achilles dines alone while Hector's corpse

The Banquet of Cupid and Psyche. Giulio Romano, 1527–28. Mantua, Palazzo del Tè.

lies under his bed, or the wedding of Pirithoüs, in which the centaurs try to rape the bride. Also represented are shocking cannibalistic meals, such as when the Cyclopes devour the companions of Ulysses or Tereus unknowingly eats his own son.

In modern times, a few royal and more civilized banquets from the past have served as the base for large-scale compositions, among them the banquet of Dido and Aeneas and the banquet which Cleopatra held for Antony (Tiepolo, 1747–50, Venice, Palazzo Labia).

Cross-references: Achilles. Centaurs. Cleopatra. Cyclops. Psyche. Tereus. Thetis.

BASKET *See* Aglauros. Erichtonius. Fates (basket of spindles).

BAUBO

Character from Eleusinian mythology.

HISTORY/MYTHOLOGY

After her daughter, Proserpine, was abducted by Pluto, Ceres (Demeter) searched for her at Eleusis. The goddess was welcomed there by Dysaules and his wife, Baubo, who momentarily brought the goddess out of her grief by obscenely lifting up her dress and at last getting her to laugh.

REPRESENTATIONS

A woman with uplifted dress and her face where her stomach should be—rather like a painting by Magritte—appears on a series of terracottas from the sanctuary of Demeter at Priene, in Asia Minor.

Cross-references: Ceres.

Sources: Clement of Alexandria, *Protrepticus*, II, 20, 3.

BAUCIS *See* Philemon.

BEAR *See* Callisto.

BEARD *See* Achelous. Bacchus. Boreas. Diogenes. Jupiter. Mercury. Neptune. Nestor. Ocean. Pluto. River.

BELISARIUS

Gk. and Ger. Belisarios; Lat. Belisarius; Sp. and It. Belisario; Fr. Bélisaire.
Byzantine general (Thrace, c. A.D. 490 – Constantinople, 565).

HISTORY/MYTHOLOGY

Belisarius, who was born in A.D. 490 and died in 565, was a general under the Byzantine emperor Justinian I. He brilliantly served Justinian's ambition of uniting the legacies of Constantine and Augustus. Belisarius distinguished himself in a large series of battles against the Persians, drove the Vandals out of Africa (534) and the Goths out of Italy, and triumphantly entered Rome on 9 December 537. Nevertheless, his victories were as precarious as they were brilliant, and barbarian invaders quickly reconquered liberated territories. In addition, he was suspected of disloyalty and incurred the hostility of Justinian, who recalled him to Constantinople, although the Empire continued to call on his sword in times of peril. Nevertheless, Belisarius was ultimately divested of all honors and imprisoned after conspiracies brought his loyalty into question, and he died soon afterward.

Belisarius Recognized by a Soldier Who Served under Him Just When a Woman Gives Him Alms.
Jacques-Louis David, 1781.
Lille,
Musée des Beaux-Arts.

67

The most reliable source for the general's military accomplishment is the *History of the Wars of Justinian*, written by Belisarius's secretary and advisor, Procopius. The legend claiming that Belisarius was blinded by order of Justinian and then reduced to begging on the streets of Constantinople, on the other hand, was circulated by Johannes Tzetes, a twelfth-century Greek monk and compiler; in later versions of the same story, a helmet came to replace the sack as a more noble and moving symbol.

The legend of Belisarius was popular for so long that the "Tower of Belisarius" in Constantinople, where the imprisoned general was supposed to have held out a small sack to collect alms from passersby, continued to be pointed out even in the nineteenth century. It also inspired many literary works, including a novel by Marmontel, which had such a resounding success after its publication in 1763 that Belisarius became popular once more.

REPRESENTATIONS

Owing to the legend's enormous popularity, it overshadowed historical fact in the iconography of Belisarius. In the sixteenth century, the title *Belisarius Begging* was given to an ancient statue in the Borghese (now in the Louvre), a work that has since been identified as Augustus imploring Nemesis. Paintings of Belisarius almost always represent him begging. A work that was long attributed to Van Dyck became widely known in the eighteenth century through an engraving. Here Belisarius, with helmet and shield lying on the ground, is seated and holds a staff while extending his hand toward a young woman who joins others in giving alms; nearby, a cuirassed soldier clasps his hands together in shock and dismay at the sight.

David's celebrated *Belisarius Recognized by a Soldier*, which postdates the book by Marmontel that many painters found inspiring, added to the cast of main characters a child who accompanies the old man and holds out a helmet to collect alms from the woman. Rather than lapsing into sentimentality, however, the painting remains a serious work that heralds the debut of neoclassicism.

Gérard retained the motif of the child-guide while breaking with iconographic tradition: the blind old general walks with the aid of a staff but now carries the child, who has a snake wrapped around his legs and is apparently dying (*Belisarius*, 1800, Munich, Galerie Leuchtenberg). The subject of Belisarius lost its appeal after the French Revolution and the Consulate.

Attributes: Helmet. Staff.

Sources: Procopius, *History of the Wars of Justinian.*

BELLEROPHON

Gk., Lat., and Ger. Belerophon; It. Bellerofonte; Sp. Belerophontes; Fr. Bellérophon.
Legendary character.

HISTORY/MYTHOLOGY

Bellerophon, the son of the Corinthian king Glaucus, lived in exile at Argos in the palace of King Proteus. There the queen fell in love with him and deceived her husband into believing that Bellerophon had tried to seduce her when the youth shunned her advances. To rid himself of Bellerophon without breaking the honored traditions that then governed hospitality, Proteus sent him to Iobates in Lycia with a message asking him to kill the letter-bearer. Iobates then imposed several trials on Bellerophon, one of which was to fight the Chimera, the divine fire-breathing monster that was "lion in front, serpent behind, and goat in the middle." With the help of Pegasus—the winged horse born of Medusa that he himself had tamed at Corinth—Bellerophon triumphed and even married the king's daughter. When he later became so proud, however, that he tried to fly Pegasus up to Mount Olympus, Zeus struck him dead with thunderbolts.

Bellerophon Leading Pegasus to Water. Hellenistic relief, second century A.D. Rome, Palazzo Spada.

REPRESENTATIONS

An Apulian stamnos shows Bellerophon arriving with the deadly letter. (c. 400 B.C., Boston, Museum of Fine Arts). The battle with the Chimera has been represented at least since the Protocorinthian period (aryballos, c. 650 B.C., Boston, Museum of Fine Arts) and also appears on Attic and Italiot ceramics; Pegasus is portrayed without wings on a terracotta relief from Melos (c. 450 B.C., London, British Museum). Bellerophon also figures on Corinthian coins.

Representations of Bellerophon are rare in modern times, but his taming of Pegasus is shown on a small Florentine bronze by Bertoldo di Giovanni (c. 1480, Vienna, Kunsthistorisches Museum). Bellerophon is also seen astride Pegasus and plunging towards a roaring Chimera in a sketch by Rubens (c. 1635, Bayonne, Musée Bonnat).

Attributes: Winged horse.

Cross-references: Pegasus.

Sources: Homer, *The Iliad* VI, 155–205.

Bibliography: J.-M. Moret, "Le départ de Bellérophon sur un cratère campanien de Genève," *Antike Kunst* XV (1972): 95–106.

BIRD *See* Harpies (bodies of). Sirens. Tereus.

BLINDFOLD *See* Fortune. Homer.

BOAR *See* Adonis. Alcestis. Alexander. Atalanta. Hecate (head). Meleager. Peleus.

BOAT *See* Charon.

BOOK *See* Archimedes. Aristotle. Calliope. Cato. Clio. Sappho.

BOREAS

Gk., Lat., Sp., and Ger. Boreas; It. Borea; Fr. Borée.
God of the north wind.

**Boreas Blowing at
the Raft of Ulysses.**
Boeotian skyphos,
c. 440 B.C.
Oxford, Ashmolean
Museum.

HISTORY/MYTHOLOGY

Boreas, the god of the north wind, was the son of Aurora (Eos). The
special bond that existed between Thrace and Athens was based on
the tradition that Boreas, who was believed to have been born in
Thrace, raped Orithyia, the daughter of the Athenian king,
Erechtheus. The Athenians also attributed the destruction of the
Persian fleet to Boreas, and for this reason they established a cult in
his honor in 480 B.C. According to *The Odyssey*, it was Boreas who, at
the command of Jupiter, blew Ulysses off course. Finally, the god's
two sons, Zetes and Calaïs (the Boreads), took part in the expedition
of the Argonauts.

REPRESENTATIONS

Boreas is represented as a winged and bearded god with disheveled
hair. He is seen blowing Ulysses' raft off course on a Boeotian vase
(c. 440 B.C., Oxford, Ashmolean Museum). In several scenes on Attic
ceramics the unkempt god, who sometimes appears in Thracian dress,
pursues Orithyia (krater by the Boreas Painter, c. 470 B.C., Bologna,
Museo Archeologico) or grabs her by the waist (amphora by the
Orithyia Painter, c. 470 B.C., Berlin, Antikensammlungen). Boreas and
Orithyia are also the subject of a sculpted group from Delos (fragments from the acroteria of the Temple of Apollo, known as the
Temple of the Athenians, c. 425 B.C.).

The abduction was also represented by baroque painters, most
notably Annibale Carracci (c. 1600, grisaille in the Palazzo Farnese,
Rome), Rubens (c. 1615, Vienna, Gemäldegalerie), and Francesco
Solimena (1657–1747, three versions, including one in Rome, Galleria
Spada, and one in Vienna; in all these works Boreas is represented as a
winged god who shifts through space. As a winged god, Boreas was
found particularly suitable for ceiling paintings, many of which are
organized along plunging diagonals (Giovanni Pellegrini, 1675–1741,
Paris, Louvre).

Attributes: Beard. Wings.

Cross-references: Argonauts. Aurora.

Sources: Ovid, *Metamorphoses* VI, 681–721.

Bibliography: K. Neuser, *Anemoi*, Rome, 1982.

BOW *See* Adonis. Amazons. Apollo. Cupid. Diana. Paris. Philoctetes. Ulysses.

BOWL *See* Diogenes.

BRASIER *See* Mucius Scaevola.

BRIDGE *See* Horatius Cocles.

BRISEÏS *See* Achilles.

BRUTUS

Lucius Junius Brutus, historical figure (Rome, sixth century B.C.).

HISTORY/MYTHOLOGY

Brutus the Elder (Lucius Junius Brutus) should be distinguished from Caesar's assassin, Brutus the Younger (Marcus Junius Brutus). The former was the nephew of Tarquinius the Great and was partly responsible for the fall of the monarchy and the advent of the Roman Republic. Indeed, according to Livy, Brutus the Elder had protected himself by pretending he was unaware of the renowned cruelty of the Tarquins until he brutally ended that sham by withdrawing the dagger from Lucretia's body. He then spoke out openly against this unjust

The Lictors Bringing Brutus the Bodies of His Sons.
Jacques-Louis David.
1790.
Paris, Louvre.

71

death and used it as a *cause célèbre* to incite revolt and topple the monarchy. He ultimately shared the consulship with Lucretia's husband, Collatinus, when the Republic was founded in 508 B.C. He is equally famous for another episode in the early history of the Republic: as consul he presided over the execution of his own sons, Titus and Tiberius, when they were found guilty of conspiring to restore the monarchy.

REPRESENTATIONS

An imaginary portrait of Brutus appears on a denarius struck in 59 B.C. by his descendant Marcus Junius Brutus, a magistrate of the mint.

Brutus sometimes appears in representations of Lucretia's death as someone who either witnesses her suicide, listens to her last words (a demand for revenge), or holds the bloody dagger. A work by Botticelli highlights the political consequences of the young Lucretia's rape and suicide by having Brutus present her dead body to soldiers in order to provoke their revolt (*The Story of Lucretia*, 1500, Boston, Isabella Stewart Gardner Museum).

The death of Brutus's sons also proved to be an inspiring subject for artists. The very moment of their execution is the subject of a painting by Léthière; set in the Forum, the scene concentrates on the impassivity of Brutus while one son humbles himself and begs pardon as the dead body of the other son is carried away (1812, Paris, Louvre). David's *The Lictors Bringing Brutus the Bodies of His Sons* captures the next moment and adds the grief-stricken figures of Brutus's wife and two daughters (1790, Paris, Louvre). Both paintings evoke *exemplum virtutis* (the model of courage) by highlighting the conflict between paternal love and civic virtue.

Cross-references: Lucretia.

Sources: Livy, I, 59–60.

BUCEPHALUS *See* Alexander.

BULL

The bull occupies a prominent position in mythology. It is the form taken by some river gods, such as Achelous, as well as by Bacchus and even Jupiter, who transformed himself into a bull to abduct Europa and to cross the sea with her. Bulls were often sacrificed to Neptune, who sent a particularly beautiful one to Crete, where it seduced Pasiphaë and resulted in the Minotaur's birth. Bulls could also be ferocious and dangerous: Hercules (on Crete) and Theseus (at Marathon) each fought exceptionally powerful ones.

Cross-references: Achelous. Bacchus. Europa. Hercules. Minotaur. Pasiphaë. Theseus.

BURNING COALS *See* Porcia.

BUSIRIS

Gk., Lat., Sp., Fr., and Ger. Busiris; It. Busiride.
Mythical Greco-Egyptian character.

HISTORY/MYTHOLOGY

Busiris was pharoah during a time when Egypt was struck by drought;
he subjected all foreign visitors to ritual sacrifice in an effort to
remedy the problem. He was about to kill Hercules, who was in Egypt
on his way back from Libya, when the hero broke his chains en route
to the sacrificial altar, killed Busiris, and massacred the Egyptians.

REPRESENTATIONS

The sacrifice scene is represented at the peak of its confusion on a
series of Attic vases: the ritual instruments fall to the ground, Hercules
grabs the Egyptians and uses them as a weapon, and the pharaoh takes
sanctuary on the sacred altar. Epictetus depicted the subject twice
while introducing slight changes in each version (c. 500–510 B.C.,
London, British Museum, and Rome, Villa Giulia).

This episode from the adventures of Hercules appears not to have
been represented in modern art.

Cross-references: Hercules.

Sources: Apollodorus, *The Library* II, 5, 11.

BUTADES

Greek artisan.

HISTORY/MYTHOLOGY

A legend involving the origin of drawing is staged around a young
Corinthian maiden, Dibutades (daughter of Butades), who, knowing
her lover was leaving on a long journey, traced the contour of the shadow he cast by lamplight on to a wall. Dibutades' father, who was a
potter, then used the drawing to create a terracotta relief.

Dibutades.
Detail from Robert
Tournières,
*The Invention
of Drawing*, 1716.
Paris,
École des Beaux-Arts.

REPRESENTATIONS

The legend of Dibutades and her lover has been illustrated only since
the seventeenth century, for the Renaissance preferred a less detailed
legend, which Leonardo expressed in these terms: "The first painting
was the linear contour of a man's shadow projected on to the wall by
the sun." Two works in the Albertina, Vienna, a century apart in date,
testify to the level of interest taken in Pliny's account, and each shows
the young woman drawing her young lover's portrait by lamplight
(Sandrart, 1675, drawing, known through an engraving; Benjamin
Calau, 1724–85, drawing).

Artists in the eighteenth century accentuated the romantic element,
as exemplified in a painting by Robert Tournières, *The Invention of
Drawing*, in which a cupid flying above the characters draws the maiden's
attention to the shadow and guides her hand (1716, Paris, École des
Beaux-Arts).

The legend of Butades was most popular in Europe during the
years 1770–1820, when it led to the common acceptance of the idea
that love was the very source of art.

Attributes: Drawing. Shadow.

Sources: Pliny, *Natural History* XXXV, 151.

Bibliography: P. Georgel and A.M. Lecoq, *La Peinture dans la peinture*, Paris, 1987, pp. 100–103.

BUTES *See* Centaurs.

Hercules
and Cacus.
Etruscan mirror,
fifth century B.C.
London,
British Museum.

CACUS

Lat. and Ger. Cacus; It. Caco; Fr. Cacus.
Mythical Roman monster.

HISTORY/MYTHOLOGY

Vulcan's son Cacus lived in a cave on the Aventine, in Rome, and terrorized the surrounding area. When Hercules paused on the banks of the Tiber after having stolen Geryon's cattle, Cacus himself stole some of the cattle from Hercules. He tried to cover his tracks by making the cattle walk backward, but he was found out and killed by Hercules when one of the animals began to low from within the cave.

REPRESENTATIONS

The subject is rare in Roman art but appears on a medallion of Antoninus Pius (A.D. 140–43) in which the Romans are seen thanking Hercules for rescuing them from Cacus, who lies dead in front of his cave.

Hercules and Cacus have been sculpted together several times by modern artists, including Baccio Bandinelli (marble, 1534, Florence, Piazza della Signoria). The savagery of Cacus is underscored in a painting by Domenichino entitled *Landscape with Hercules Pulling Cacus from His Cave*, which the artist painted as a pendant to his *Landscape with Hercules Battling Achelous in the Form of a Bull* (1621, Paris, Louvre). Poussin also depicted the subject in a landscape (c. 1660, Moscow, Pushkin Museum). The most dramatic representation, however, is by François Le Moyne, in which the violent aspect of Hercules' strength is manifested by juxtaposing the hero with a terrifying portrayal of Cacus vanquished and sprawled out dead on the ground (*Hercules Subduing Cacus*, sketch, 1718, Paris, Louvre; the definitive work, a reception piece for the Académie, is in the École des Beaux-Arts).

Cross-references: Achelous. Geryon. Hercules.

Sources: Ovid, *Festivals* I, 543–78. Virgil *Aeneid*, VIII, 184–279.

CADMUS

Gk. and Ger. Kadmus; Lat. Cadmus; It. and Sp. Cadmo; Fr. Cadmos.
Legendary heroic founder of Thebes.

HISTORY/MYTHOLOGY

Cadmus was the heroic founder of Thebes, in Boeotia. He had gone in search of his sister, Europa, when an oracle advised him to found a city. He first had to rid the area of Mars's son, an enormous snake (or dragon) that had already devoured his companions. Having accomplished this, he was told by Minerva to sow the dragon's teeth. From the sown teeth sprang armed warriors, who proceeded to slay one another until at last only five remained, and it was with these survivors that Cadmus founded Thebes. Cadmus later married Harmonia, the daughter of Venus and Mars, in the presence of the gods; one of Harmonia's gifts was a necklace that would later be given to Amphiarus's wife, Eriphyle. The couple's offspring were Autonoe, Ino, Agave, and Semele.

REPRESENTATIONS

Cadmus.
Paestan krater,
c. 350 B.C.
Paris, Louvre.

Greek ceramists depicted Cadmus fighting the dragon (Paestan krater, c. 350 B.C., Paris, Louvre), as well as the wedding of Cadmus and Harmonia, in which the couple's chariot is led by a team consisting of a boar yoked with a lion (Attic amphora, c. 500 B.C., Paris, Louvre).

In baroque painting, in addition to the battle with the dragon (Cornelisz Van Haarlem, 1562–1638, Vienna Kunsthistorisches Museum), the combat between the warriors that spring from the dragon's teeth is also represented; Minerva is beside Cadmus, who turns to watch the scene (Rubens, 1636, sketch, Norfolk, priv. coll.; painting by Jordaens, 1637–38, Madrid, Prado).

Attributes: Dragon. Snake. Teeth.

Cross-references: Amphiaraus. Europa. Semele.

Sources: Ovid, *Metamorphoses* III, 1–137.

CADUCEUS *See* Iris. Mercury.

CAENEUS

Gk., Ger., and Fr. Kaineus; Lat. Caeneus.
Legendary character.

HISTORY/MYTHOLOGY

Caeneus was a Lapith, one of a race that inhabited Thessaly, in northern Greece. He was originally a maiden named Caenis whom Neptune raped when she visited the seashore, but when the god afterward granted her any wish, she asked to become a man so she would never again be raped, whereupon she became the invulnerable Caeneus. When the centaurs could not kill Caeneus with their weapons in the battle between Lapiths and centaurs at the wedding of Pirithoüs and Hippodamia, they drove him into the ground by piling trees and rocks on top of him.

Caeneus and Neptune.
Engraving after
Bartholomeus Spranger,
1580.

REPRESENTATIONS

In archaic art, Caeneus is shown half-buried and with torso emerging from the ground (Attic hydria, c. 470 B.C., London, British Museum); he sometimes holds two swords as an allusion to his double nature.

Neptune kissing Caeneus has occasionally appeared in art, resembling Neptune and Amymone (Hendrik Golztius, 1649, engraving, London, British Museum).

Cross-references: Centaurs.

75

Sources: Ovid, *Metamorphoses* XII, 189–207, 459–532. Virgil, *Aeneid* VI, 448.

Bibliography: E. Laufer, *Kaineus*, 1985.

CAENIS *See* Caeneus.

CAESAR

Lat. and Ger. Caesar; It. Cesare; Sp. Cesar; Fr. César.
Roman statesman (101–44 B.C.).

HISTORY/MYTHOLOGY

Julius Caesar was born into a patrician family in 101 B.C. but allied himself with the Plebeians. He sided with Marius against Sylla and began his quest for power after the latter's death. He held different magisterial offices, then founded the first Triumvirate with Crassus and Pompey, and obtained a consulship in 59 B.C.

As proconsul in cisalpine Gaul and the Narbonne, Caesar won several famous battles in Gaul (conquered in 51 B.C. after the defeat at Alesia and the surrender of the last Gallic strongholds). He crossed the Rubicon in 50 B.C. and then marched on Rome, triggering a civil war that lasted four years. Pompey fled, but Caesar caught up with him and defeated his supporters in the Battle of Pharsalus. He pursued Pompey into Egypt, but the latter was assassinated by Ptolemy III's men. Caesar punished Pompey's executioners when they brought him his enemy's head, and at the same time crushed the last of Pompey's supporters; he then entrusted the throne of Egypt to Cleopatra. Now master of the Mediterranean world, he celebrated his fifth triumph in Rome. He secured absolute power without ostensibly rendering the Republic's institutions powerless—a contradiction that became less and less tenable—and adopted his great-nephew Octavius to ensure that his powers were perpetuated. To his titles of dictator and censor for life, he attempted to add king and was about to receive it when conspirators assassinated him with daggers during a meeting of the Senate on the Ides of March (15 March) in 44 B.C. Marcus Junius Brutus fatally stabbed him.

REPRESENTATIONS

Ancient busts, statues, and coins are true portraits of Julius Caesar. In a statue on the Capitoline in Rome, he wears a cuirass and the paludamentum, and holds an apple in his right hand. The head added to a colossal marble statue in the Louvre follows this exactly. A bust in the Museo Nazionale in Naples and two others in the Uffizi appear to reflect the physiognomy on coins.

Representations of Caesar in the Middle Ages were usually linked to those of the nine Worthies, of which he was one. Throughout the modern period, Caesar appears in series that portray the Roman emperors. In addition, living rulers up to the time of Napoleon III had themselves portrayed as Caesar, carrying the ancient attributes of toga, laurel, and so on.

In the fifteenth century an important iconography developed whose prototype was Mantegna's *Triumph of Caesar*, a cycle of nine paintings of equal dimensions that formed a frieze in the Palazzo San

Julius Caesar.
Bust.
Naples,
Museo Nazionale.

Sebastiano in Mantua (1486–94, now in London, Hampton Court). In this series, which functions as a general evocation of Roman antiquity, the different characters appear in ceremonial procession.

Certain episodes from Caesar's life were particularly favored by artists. Caesar being brought the head of Pompey, for example, is often represented from the sixteenth through eighteenth centuries. Here Caesar turns away from the horrifying object in a gesture of contempt more for barbaric methods than for the enemy. In a painting by Antonio Zanchi, Caesar gestures with his hand toward the bloody head of his enemy while lifting his eyes toward heaven, as if to call on both as witnesses to a deplorable infamy (late seventeenth–early eighteenth century, Capo d'Istria, Casa Maechesi Gravisi).

Among representations of Caesar's other great deeds, the crossing of the Rubicon inspired its own artistic treatment. The hero is on horseback and meditates on his historic decision in front of a torrent. The subject appears several times in nineteenth-century history painting (Boulanger, Salon of 1857; Chenevard, preparatory designs for the decoration of the Pantheon).

The episode most inspirational for painting, however, was the assassination of Julius Caesar, which has been a popular subject since the end of the fifteenth century (Jacopo del Sellai, panels now in Berlin, Staatliche Museen, showing the preparation and execution of the murder) through the nineteenth century (Rochegrosse, *The Death of Caesar*, 1887, Grenoble, Musée de Peinture et de Sculpture). Some artists, including Gérôme, preferred to represent the moment afterward, when the corpse is abandoned by the conspirators (1867, Baltimore, Walters Art Gallery).

Cross-references: Cleopatra. Worthies.

Sources: Caesar, *The Conquest of Gaul; The Civil War*. Lucan, *Pharsalia*. Plutarch, *Life of Caesar*. Suetonius, *The Twelve Caesars* I.

Bibliography: Michelet, *Roman History* II, pp. 260–307 (campaigns in Gaul).

CALDRON *See* Medea.

CALLIOPE *See* Muses.

CALLISTO

Gk. and Ger. Kallisto; Lat., It., and Fr. Callisto; Sp. Caalisto.
Arcadian nymph.

HISTORY/MYTHOLOGY

Callisto, the daughter of King Lycaon, was a beautiful Arcadian nymph and one of Diana's chaste companions until Jupiter disguised himself as Diana in order to seduce her. She became pregnant by him. This was discovered one day by Diana when they were bathing together, and Diana chased her away. Callisto was changed into a bear by Juno, who was jealous, and then into the constellation Ursa Major by Jupiter, whose child she bore.

Jupiter and Callisto.
Peter Paul Rubens,
1613.
Kassel, Staatliche
Kunstsammlungen.

REPRESENTATIONS

The ancients sometimes depicted Callisto's metamorphosis into a bear (Apulian oenochoe, c. 370 B.C., Malibu, J. Paul Getty Museum).

Modern artists have represented Jupiter, disguised as Diana, seated next to Callisto while he seduces her. Only an eagle or a thunderbolt identify the god (Boucher, 1769, London, Wallace Collection; Fragonard, c. 1753, Angers, Musée des Beaux-Arts). This particular metamorphosis of Jupiter provided painters, particularly those of the eighteenth century, with an excuse for depicting tenderness with sapphic undertones between two women. In other representations, Diana discovers the pregnancy while bathing and points to Callisto, whom the other nymphs stare at in disapproval (Titian, 1560, Vienna, Kunsthistorisches Museum; Annibale Carracci, c. 1603, Rome, Palazzo Farnese).

Cross-references: Diana. Juno. Jupiter.

Sources: Ovid, *Metamorphoses* II, 401–508; *Festivals* II, 155–92.

Bibliography: *The Loves of the Gods*, ex. cat., Fort Worth, 1992, nos. 24, 49, 57.

CALUMNY OF APELLES *See* Apelles.

CALYDON *See* Meleager.

CALYPSO

Gk. and Ger. Kalypso; Lat. and Fr. Calypso; It. and Sp. Calipso. Nymph.

HISTORY/MYTHOLOGY

Calypso, whose name means "she who hides," was a nymph who lived on the island of Ogygia, near Gibraltar. When Ulysses ran aground at Ogygia during his return voyage from the Trojan War, Calypso detained him there for seven years, promising him immortality in exchange for marriage. Even she, however, could not make Ulysses forget Ithaca or Penelope, and the gods finally compelled her to set him free.

Calypso meets Ulysses' son in the novel by Fénelon, *The Adventures of Telemachus* (1699).

REPRESENTATIONS

Representations of Calypso and Ulysses are rare in both ancient and modern art. A Megarian vase decorated in relief possibly portrays Calypso alongside Ulysses (c. 150 B.C., Volos).

In a painting by Böcklin, the fully illuminated figure of Calypso, in front of her cave and turning toward her lover, is contrasted with the dark silhouette of Ulysses, who looks longingly toward the open sea (1883, Basel, Kunstmuseum). The nymph-seductress whose charms conquered the most courageous of heroes inspired twentieth-century artists such as Max Beckmann, who went so far as to establish an implicit analogy between Calypso and Eve by painting Ulysses being squeezed more tightly by a serpent wrapped around his legs than by the nymph's arms (*Odysseus and Calypso*, 1943, Hamburg, Kunsthalle).

Odysseus [Ulysses] and Calypso.
Max Beckmann, 1943.
Hamburg, Kusthalle.

Fénelon's novel inspired a few eighteenth-century paintings (Natoire, St. Petersburg, Hermitage; J. Raoux, 1722, Paris, Louvre).

Cross-references: Telemachus. Ulysses.

Sources: Homer, *Odyssey* V, 1–281.

CAMBYSES

Gk. and Ger. Kambyses; Lat. Cambyses; It. Cambise; Sp. Cambises; Fr. Cambyse.
Persian king (ruled c. 528–521 B.C.).

HISTORY/MYTHOLOGY

Cambyses succeeded Cyrus II the Great and ruled over Persia in the sixth century B.C. He launched the conquest of Egypt just when the twenty-sixth dynasty's last pharaoh, Psammenitus, acceded to the throne. After driving the pharaoh to suicide, he crowned himself king and founded the twenty-seventh dynasty. He proved to be an extremely cruel monarch, who indulged in atrocities and finally went mad. When, for example, a judge, Sisamnes, was found guilty of maladministration, Cambyses had him skinned alive and then had the magistrate's seat re-upholstered with the skin. Ancient accounts provide other examples of Cambyses' murderous rampages.

REPRESENTATIONS

The horrifying episode with the judge is depicted in two panels by Gérard David entitled *The Justice of Cambyses* (1498, Bruges, Groeningemuseum). The judge is arrested in the first panel and tortured in front of Cambyses and his attendants in the second. In a composition that recalls the clandestine anatomical dissections practiced at the end of the fifteenth century, Sisamnes lies on a table with his face frozen by pain while he is skinned in four different places.

Psammenitus's compulsory suicide is the subject of a painting by André Guignet (1841, Paris, Louvre).

Sources: Herodotus, III, 11–15 (Psammenitus); V, 25 (Sisamnes).

CAMILLUS

Roman general during the Republic (fourth–fifth century B.C.).

HISTORY/MYTHOLOGY

The republican general Marcus Furius Camillus was considered the "second founder of Rome." As leader of the Roman army, he conquered the Etruscan city of Veii after a ten-year siege (396 B.C.) and also drove off the Gauls, who had occupied Rome.

Several of his deeds left legendary traces in Roman history. One of these occurred when he laid siege to Falerii, a town northeast of Rome: he became so outraged when the town's schoolmaster tried to ransom his students—the offspring of Patricians—that he ordered the pupils to strip their teacher and flog him all the way back to Falerii.

Later, the Gauls' chieftain, Brennus, agreed to lift his siege of Rome in exchange for a considerable sum of gold. When a Roman tribune complained that Brennus had added his sword to the scale to make the balance of gold even higher, Brennus retorted with the famous words, "*Vae victis!*"—"Woe to the vanquished!" Camillus responded by declaring void the agreement made with the Gauls and then pounced on the enemy in a line of battle, ultimately crushing them.

REPRESENTATIONS

Camillus often appears as the central figure in representations of triumphs (for example, Francesco Salviati's fresco in the Palazzo Vecchio, Florence, 1543–45).

In addition, the subject of the schoolmaster from Falerii appears in sixteenth- and seventeenth-century painting, where it was intended to emphasize the Roman general's clemency. One noteworthy example is a painting by Poussin (1637, Louvre), in which the judgement of Camillus and his punishment of the guilty party are both shown. The "*Vae victis!*" of Brennus is depicted during the same period, mainly by

Camillus and the Schoolmaster from Falerii (detail).
Nicolas Poussin,
1637.
Paris, Louvre.

Danaë.
Jan Gossaert, called Mabuse, 1527.
Munich, Alte Pinakothek.

Apollo and Daphne.
Giovanni Battista Tiepolo, 1743–4.
Paris, Louvre.

Deianira Abducted by Nessus.
Guido Reni, 1621.
Paris, Louvre.

Democritus.
Antoine Coypel, 1692.
Paris, Louvre.

Italian artists (for example Perino del Vaga, *Brennus Surprised by the Arrival of Camillus*, c. 1530, Genoa, Palazzo Doria).

Attributes: Sword. Whip.

Sources: Plutarch, *Life of Camillus* 10. Livy, *History of Rome* V, 27, 48–9.

CAMPASPE *See* Apelles.

CAP *See* Attis (Phrygian cap). Castor and Pollux (round cap or *pilos*). Charon. Daedalus (artist's cap). Mercury (winged).

CASK *See* Danaïds.

CASSANDRA *See* Ajax (son of Oileus).

CASTOR AND POLLUX (THE DIOSCURI)

Gk. and Ger. Dioscuri; Lat. Tyndaridae; Fr. Dioscures.
Legendary Greek characters.

HISTORY/MYTHOLOGY

Castor and Pollux were the inseparable children of Leda, the wife of King Tyndareus, and Zeus. They are sometimes called the Tyndaridae or the Dioscuri (the sons of Zeus). They were twins with two different natures: Castor was mortal and Pollux divine. Together they joined Jason in the voyage of the Argonauts and took part with Meleager in the Calydonian boar hunt. Castor was killed in a skirmish after the brothers raped their uncle Leucippus's daughters, the Leucippidae, who were betrothed to other cousins. Pollux, however, convinced Zeus to make them both immortal and they became the constellation known as Gemini.

Castor and Pollux.
Silver denarius,
136 B.C.
Paris, Bibliothèque
Nationale de France,
Cabinet des Médailles.

Castor and Pollux are Dorian heroes who were particularly popular in Sparta, whose army they accompanied on campaigns. Although horsemen, they also protected navigators.

REPRESENTATIONS

The Dioscuri often appear alone in ancient art, as divinities; they are identifiable not only by their twin resemblance but by their costume of horsemen and hunters (Attic stela, c. 370 B.C., Bologna, Museo Civico). They may appear in scenes from the Calydonian boar hunt. The rape of the Leucippidae is represented on the south frieze of the Siphnian Treasury at Delphi (c. 525 B.C.) as well as on various Attic vases (hydria by the Meidias Painter, c. 410 B.C., London, British Museum). Archaic iconography preferred the heroic episodes (the hunt, the expedition of the Argonauts, the rape), but this was supplanted in Hellenistic times by imagery linked to the cult of the Dioscuri—

**The Rape
of the Daughters
of Leucippus.**
Peter Paul Rubens,
c. 1616.
Munich,
Alte Pinakothek.

particularly the Theoxony, in which the twins are welcomed to the table of mortals (votive relief, first century B.C., Paris, Louvre).

In *The Rape of the Daughters of Leucippus* by Rubens, Pollux is still on foot while Castor, in armor, is already on horseback (c. 1616, Munich, Alte Pinakothek). The twins are represented up to the beginning of the twentieth century, as demonstrated by Kerr-Xavier Roussel's painting *The Rape of the Daughters of Leucippus*, in which the Dioscuri watch the young girls bathe (1911, Paris, Musée d'Orsay).

Attributes: Horses. Round cap (*pilos*). Star.

Cross-references: Leda. Meleager.

Sources: Ovid, *Festivals* V, 693–720. Theocritus, *Idylls* XXXII, 135–211 (rape of the Leucippides).

Bibliography: S. Alpers, "Manner and Meaning in Some Rubens Mythologies," *Journal of the Warburg and Courtauld Institutes* 30 (1967): 272.

CATO

Lat. and Ger. Cato; It. Catone; Sp. and Fr. Caton.
Historical Roman character (95–46 B.C.).

HISTORY/MYTHOLOGY

Marcus Porcius Cato, called Cato the Younger or Cato of Utica, was the great-grandson of Cato the Censor and lived from 95 to 46 B.C. He sided with Pompey and was therefore Julius Caesar's political adversary. He was a Stoic renowned for his integrity and virtue, and he accordingly preferred suicide over surviving the Republic's defeat: after re-reading Plato's *Phaedrus*, which treats the soul's immortality in the context of the death of Socrates, he drove a sword through his stomach. Although help arrived, he insisted on completing his act and died.

REPRESENTATIONS

The subject of some ancient Roman busts has been identified as Cato (Rome, Musei Vaticani).

Modern artists chose to illustrate the suicide. The chosen moment is either when Cato stabs himself with a sword (Guercino, seventeenth century, Genoa, Galleria Brignole-Sale) or just after he dies (Le Brun, c. 1645, Arras, Musée, the former Abbey of Saint-Vaast). An open book serves as a reminder of the importance that Stoic philosophy places on choosing to die.

The subject of the Prix de Rome competition of 1797 was *The Death of Cato of Utica*, a subject that served as an exemplary model of republican virtue in the Revolution. The candidates were to depict Cato refusing help after mortally wounding himself. Exceptionally, three candidates won prizes: Guérin, Bouillon, and Bouchet. All three interpreted the scene less intimately than their senior colleagues had: Cato's face is twisted with pain as he theatrically pushes away the doctor to the horror of his son and attendants.

Attributes: Book. Sword.

Cross-references: Caesar. Pompey.

Sources: Plutarch, *Life of Cato the Younger.*

CAVE *See* Cacus.

CECROPIDES *See* Aglauros.

CECROPS *See* Aglauros.

CENTAURS

Gk. and Ger. Kentauroi; Lat. and It. Centauri; Sp. Centauros; Fr. Centaures.
Mythical creatures.

HISTORY/MYTHOLOGY

Centaurs were hybrid creatures with the head and chest of a man attached to the hind part of a horse. They were the offspring of Ixion and a cloud, which Jupiter had shaped into Juno. They lived in the mountains of Thessaly, usually on Pelion, in northern Greece. Brutal hunters, violent, and thieves, centaurs were the uncultured and uncivilized inhabitants of a savage world.

At the wedding of Pirithoüs (a Thessalonian hero and the son of Dia and Ixion) and Hippodamia, the daughter of Butes (not to be confused with Hippodamia, daughter of Oenomaüs, Pelops's wife), who was herself the offspring of a centaur, the centaurs became drunk and tried to rape the bride and run off with the female guests. The result was a ferocious battle between centaurs and Lapiths, who were relatives of Pirithoüs and whom Theseus defended.

The centaurs also became violent when Hercules visited Pholus, a hospitable and civilized centaur, in contrast to the rest of his race. Hercules made Pholus open the jar of wine that Bacchus had entrusted to the centaurs. It was hardly opened before the scent attracted and intoxicated the other centaurs, who then attacked Hercules. The hospitable scene degenerated into a battle during which the "good" centaur Pholus was killed.

Battle of the Centaurs.
Arnold Böcklin, 1873.
Basel, Kunstmuseum.

**Centaur Raping
a Woman.**
Honoré Daumier,
drawing,
nineteenth century.
Paris,
Private Collection.

Pholus was not the only civilized centaur. Chiron was another, renowned for both for his wisdom and his medical skill; he educated several heroes, including Achilles, Aesculapius, Jason, and Actaeon.

REPRESENTATIONS

The double nature of the centaurs is indicated in different ways. In Greek art, the "good," civilized centaurs have human feet and may be dressed as men (amphora by Oltos, c. 520 B.C., Paris, Louvre), while savage centaurs have four horselike hooves.

The emotional fury of the centaurs has inspired painters and sculptors since antiquity. The Battle of Lapiths and centaurs is found in the sculptured metopes of several archaic temples. The most celebrated group comes from the pediment of the Temple of Zeus at Olympia and shows Apollo extending his arm in a gesture intended to end the violence (c. 460 B.C.). Other battle scenes pit Hercules against the centaurs as the latter try to reclaim their share of the wine entrusted to Pholus, or against Nessus as he tries to rape Deianira (amphora by the Nessus Painter, c. 620 B.C., Athens, National Museum).

In classical art, the centaurs are often bald, with hairy bodies and bestial faces, similar to those of satyrs. They have no weapons, and instead fight with rocks or uprooted trees. Although there were no female centaurs in the Hellenistic world, Lucian describes a painting which shows one, and this theme is taken up by Renaissance artists (Botticelli, in one of the details of *The Calumny of Apelles*, 1495, Florence, Uffizi). Use of the centaurs as an iconographic motif in mythological subjects lasted into the twentieth century (Picasso, *Combat of Faun and Centaur*, 21 drawings, 1946; *Satyr, Faun, and Centaur*, triptych, 1946, Antibes, Musée Grimaldi).

Attributes: Rocks and trees rather than metal arms. Wild game carried on shoulders (these are hunters).

Cross-references: Achilles. Chiron. Deianira. Hercules.

Sources: Ovid, *Metmorphoses* XII, 210–535 (battle between Lapiths and centaurs); Lucian, *Zeuxis* 4 (family of centaurs).

CEPHALUS AND PROCRIS

Gk. and Ger. Kephalos, Procris; Lat. Cephalus, Procris; It. Cefalo, Procri; Fr. Céphale, Procris.
Athenian hero and his wife.

HISTORY/MYTHOLOGY

Cephalus, the son of Aeolus, was an Athenian hero who rejected the goddess Aurora in favor of his young wife Procris, the daughter of Erechtheus.

Aurora avenged herself by making Cephalus suspicious and jealous. He consequently decided to test his wife's fidelity by trying to seduce her when disguised as someone else. Procris was on the verge of succumbing when she instead fled to Diana. Husband and wife were reconciled, and Procris brought Cephalus two presents from Diana: a very quick dog and a spear that never missed its mark. After a false rumor later made Procris think Cephalus unfaithful, however, she hid herself in the bushes to spy on him while he hunted, and when Cephalus heard noises, he threw his spear and unwittingly killed her.

REPRESENTATIONS

Cephalus often appears in Attic ceramics, dressed as a hunter and holding one or two spears while fleeing from Aurora's advances (amphora by Hermonax, c. 470 B.C., Naples, Museo Nazionale).

In a painting by Poussin, the young hunter is seen resisting Aurora's advances (*Cephalus and Aurora*, 1628, London, National Gallery). The most frequent subject, however, is the death of Procris, which first appears during the Renaissance (Veronese, 1580, Strasburg, Musée des Beaux-Arts). The focus of attention is the young couple, who are often integrated into historical landscapes. Fragonard painted a version that is both erotic and moving (c. 1755, Angers, Musée des Beaux-Arts). Piero di Cosimo's treatment of the subject is unusual in that the dead Procris is accompanied by only a dog and the faun who denounced her to Cephalus (c. 1506, London, National Gallery).

Attributes: Dog. Spear.

Cross-references: Aurora..

Sources: Ovid, *Metamorphoses* VII, 661–866.

Bibliography: S. Kaempf-Dimitriadou, *Die Liebe der Götter in der attischen Kunst des 5. Jahrhundert vor Christus*, Berne, 1979, pp. 16–21, 81–93. I. Lavin, "Cephalus and Procris. Transformations of an Ovidian Myth," *Journal of the Warburg and Courtauld Institutes* (1954): 260–87.

The Death of Procris.
Piero di Cosimo, c. 1506.
London, National Gallery.

**Hercules Bringing
Cerberus
to Eurystheus.**
Caertan hydria,
c. 540 B.C.
Paris, Louvre.

CERBERUS

Gk. and Ger. Kerberos; Lat. Cerberus; It. Cerbero; Sp. Cerbero/Cancerbero; Fr. Cerbère.
Monstrous dog that guarded Hades (the Underworld).

HISTORY/MYTHOLOGY

Cerberus, the son of Typhon and Echidna, was a monstrous dog that guarded the entry to Hades and prevented anyone from leaving. He was most often described as a beast with three heads (or fifty, according to Hesiod), the tail of a serpent, and sometimes the claws of a lion. Only Orpheus's music could make him docile. Hercules' twelfth labor was to fetch Cerberus from Hades for his cousin Eurystheus.

REPRESENTATIONS

Roughly one hundred largely black-figure Attic vases depict Hercules leaving Hades with Cerberus beneath the gaze of Pluto and Persephone or Mercury and Athena (amphora by the Andokides Painter, c. 520 B.C., Paris, Louvre). The monster is as frequently depicted in representations of Hades on Apulian vases (krater by the Darius Painter, c. 340 B.C., Munich, Antikensammlungen).

Hercules' adventure with Cerberus captured the attention of Italian sculptors (Florentine bronze, second quarter of the sixteenth century, Baltimore, Walters Art Gallery) and painters (Schiavone, 1563, Venice, Brass Collection). The subject also appears in a series of paintings by Zurbarán that are dedicated to the Theban hero (c. 1636, Madrid, Prado).

Attributes: Three heads.

Cross-references: Hercules. Orpheus.

Sources: Hesiod, *Theogony*, 310–12.

CERCOPES *See* Hercules.

CERES or DEMETER

Gk. Demeter; Lat. Ceres; Ger. and Sp. Ceres; It. Cerere; Fr. Cérès. Goddess of agriculture.

HISTORY/MYTHOLOGY

Ceres was the daughter of Rhea and Saturn. As the goddess of agriculture and wheat, she was associated with fertility and abundance. After Pluto abducted her daughter, Proserpine, Ceres searched for her on Earth disguised as an old woman. She arrived at Eleusis and there entered the service of King Celeus and Queen Metaneira, whose son Demophoön she tried to make immortal by dipping him into fire. Iambe (others say Baubo) succeeded in making the goddess laugh at her jokes. Out of gratitude, Ceres gave mankind the gift of wheat, which she entrusted to Triptolemus. She also instituted the Eleusinian Mysteries, sacred rituals in honor of Demeter (Ceres), Kora (Proserpine), and Triptolemus.

REPRESENTATIONS

In many statues, the goddess is shown standing and dressed in a simple cloak, which sometimes covers her head (copy of an original from the fourth century B.C., Rome, Villa Doria Pamphili). In a cult statue from Cnidos she is shown enthroned (c. 340 B.C., London, British Museum). Images on offerings left in the goddess's sanctuaries frequently show her holding sheaves of wheat, a piglet, or torches.

As Demeter, she is often grouped with her daughter Kora, especially in Eleusinian reliefs (c. 460 B.C., Eleusis, Archeological Museum). She sometimes holds her daughter on her knee (marble relief from Eleusis, middle of the fourth century B.C.). In Attic ceramics, she is often seen offering wheat to Triptolemus as she anoints him with a libation (skyphos by Makron, c. 480 B.C., London, British Museum). Apart from this subject, however, Demeter is rare in mythological scenes. In her association with the Empire's prosperity and the city's food supply, she appears on Roman coins as Ceres.

In modern painting, Ceres appears in her chariot in triumphal scenes that extol prosperity, as exemplified in the Farnesina ceiling (Rome, 1508–13, Sala delle Nozze d'Alessandro). Pinturicchio incorporated her into a complex grouping of other gods in chariots: Apollo, Mars, and Amphitrite (1513, ceiling for the Palazzo Petrucci, Siena, now in New York, Metropolitan Museum of Art). Rubens and Frans Snyders depicted Ceres surrounded by a profusion of flowers and fruits, and accompanied by either nymphs or Pan (1617, Madrid, Prado). Although the goddess often appears in decorative programs as an allegory of agriculture (Luca Giordano, 1682–83, Florence, Palazzo Medici-Riccardi), she also symbolizes Summer, as seen in a marble sculpture by Houdon (1785, Montpellier, Musée Fabre).

Attributes: Snake. Torches. Wheat (sheaves or crown).

Cross-references: Baubo. Proserpine. Seasons. *Sine Baccho et Cerere.*

Sources: *Homeric Hymn to Demeter*, Hesiod, *Theogony*, 453–506, 969–74.

CHARIOT *See* Achilles. Amphiaraus. Apollo. Aurora. Ceres. Cleobis and Biton. Hector. Medea. Triptolemus.

Ceres.
Silver denarius, 90 B.C.
Paris, Bibliothèque
Nationale de France,
Cabinet des Médailles.

Venus, Juno, and Ceres.
Raphael, fresco, c. 1517.
Rome, Farnesina.

Ceres.
Adam Elsheimer, print,
sixteenth century.
Paris, Bibliothèque
Nationale de France.

Charon's Boat.
Attic lekythos,
c. 440 B.C.
Paris, Louvre.

CHARITY (ROMAN) *See* Cimon and Pero.

CHARON

Gk., Lat., and Ger. Charon; It. Caronte; Sp. Caron; Fr. Charon.
Ferryman of Hades.

HISTORY/MYTHOLOGY

In Greek mythology, Charon ferried the dead by boat across the Styx,
the river that encircled Hades (the Underworld).

REPRESENTATIONS

Charon is represented as an ugly old man with a short beard and conical cap, who maneuvers his boat with a pole. He is frequently seen in a
series of Attic funerary vases from the end of the fifth century B.C.,
where he is accompanied by Hermes (Mercury), who brings him the
dead. In Etruscan iconography, Charon (Charun) is more frightening
and resembles a winged, hook-nosed demon wielding a hammer
(Tarquinia, Tomba dell'Orco).

Charon has hardly been represented in modern times because
competing Christian figures of death received more attention.
Nevertheless, he appears in a painting by Patinir, which shows him
crossing the Styx in an expansive landscape where the Christian
Paradise, with its angels, is contrasted to pagan hell, guarded by
Cerberus (1524, Madrid, Prado). In Subleyras's academic painting,
Charon Transporting the Shadows, the god is nude, and is shown from
behind as he turns toward human forms draped in white cloth
(eighteenth century, Paris, Louvre).

Attributes: Boat. Cap.

Cross-references: Mercury.

CHEST *See* Danaë.

CHILD *See* Aeolus. Andromache. Astyanax. Bacchus. Belisarius.
Camillus. Cupid. Zephyr.

CHIMERA *See* Bellerophon.

CHIRON

Gk., Lat., Fr., and Ger. Chiron; It. Chirone; Sp. Quiron.
Centaur.

HISTORY/MYTHOLOGY

Chiron was the son of Philyra and Cronus. He was a centaur whose hybrid nature resulted from his father having taken on the form of a horse to escape from his wife, Rhea, so he could seduce Philyra. In contrast to the other centaurs who were violent, however, Chiron was a sage: he knew the secrets of plants and the arts of medicine, the hunt, and music. He was entrusted with the education of Achilles, Actaeon, Jason, and Aesculapius.

REPRESENTATIONS

In ancient art, especially in Attic ceramics, Chiron is represented as a complete human body attached to the hind part of a horse (amphora by Oltos, c. 510 B.C., Paris, Louvre). He is often dressed as a man as he welcomes the young Achilles, who is led by his father Peleus (oenochoe, London, British Museum). He is seen teaching Achilles the kithara in a Pompeian fresco (first century A.D., Naples, Museo Nazionale).

During the Renaissance, Chiron was portrayed as Achilles' teacher, as in the frescoes of Rosso, which largely reflect François I's love of fencing, swimming, hunting, and jousting (1535–40, Fontainebleau). Chiron is seen ridden by his young pupil in a cycle by Rubens about the story of Achilles (c. 1631, Madrid, Prado).

Chiron.
Attic oenochoe,
c. 510 B.C.
London,
British Museum.

Attributes: Body of a horse.

Cross-references: Achilles. Actaeon. Aesculapius. Centaurs. Jason. Peleus.

Sources: Statius, *Achilleid* II, 381–452.

CHLOE *See Daphnis.*

CHLORIS *Greek name for Flora.*

CICERO *See Archimedes.*

CIMON AND PERO (ROMAN CHARITY)

HISTORY/MYTHOLOGY

Cimon (sometimes called Micon or Mykon) was condemned to starve to death in prison as an elderly man. His daughter Pero visited each day and nourished him from her breast. This anecdote, related by Valerius Maximus, served as an example of filial piety.

REPRESENTATIONS

Baroque painters often depicted Cimon being breast-fed in prison (Rubens, 1612, St. Petersburg, Hermitage). Caravaggio incorporated the subject into his composition *The Seven Acts of Mercy* (1607, Naples, Church of Pio Monte della Misericorda). Pero often resembles a nursing Madonna.

Sources: Valerius Maximus, V, 4, Ext. 1.

Cimon and Pero.
Anonymous
engraving, 1542.

QVO NON PENETRAT, AVT QVID NON EXCOGITAT PIETAS! QVAE IN CARCERE SERVANDI PATRIS NOVAM RATIONEM INVENIT *c.i.q.*₃   *Ait. 544. rcc.*

Bibliography: A. de Ceuleneer, "La Charité romaine dans la littérature et l'art," *Annales de l'Académie royale de Belgique* (1920). W. Deonna, "La légende de Pero et de Micon et l'allaitement symbolique," *Latomus* XIII (1954): 140–66, 356–75. E. Knauer, "Caritas Romana," *Jahrbuch der Berliner Museen* VI (1964): 9–23.

CINCINNATUS

Character from Roman history (fifth century B.C.).

HISTORY/MYTHOLOGY

Cincinnatus was a native of ancient Rome who became a national hero. He belonged to the patrician class and was twice named dictator during Roman crises, notably in 458 B.C. during the war against the Eques and the Volsques. When not involved in these state activities, he would return to the plow that he himself was driving when the bearers of the insignia of his new position called him to public office. As someone who was simultaneously a peasant, a soldier, and a statesman, and whose principal quality was selflessness, Cincinnatus became a symbol of the original Roman virtues.

REPRESENTATIONS

Renaissance artists often group Cincinnatus with other illustrious ancient Romans in portrait cycles. In such works he is likened to Scipio Africanus (Perugino, c. 1500, Perugia, fresco in the Collegio del Cambio) or to Curius Dentatus, another Roman who led a temperate life.

Cincinnatus.
Detail from Perugino
(Pietro Vanucci),
*Strength and
Temperance with
Six Ancient Heroes*,
c. 1500.
Perugia,
Collegio del Cambio.

The scene most often represented is the Senate's messengers finding Cincinnatus in the middle of tilling the land. Although that scene was depicted from the sixteenth through nineteenth centuries in a few easel paintings (Cabanel, 1823–89, *Cincinnatus Receiving the Senate's Deputies*, Montpellier, Musée Fabre), it was used mainly for large painted decorations, always intended to set an example (Delacroix, cupola of the library of Paris, Palais de Luxembourg, 1840–46).

Attributes: Chariot.

Cross-references: Curius Dentatus. Scipio Africanus.

Sources: Livy, *History of Rome* III, 26.

CIRCE

Gk. and Ger. Kirke; Lat., It., and Sp. Circe; Fr. Circé.
Greek mythical magician.

Circe (detail).
Dosso Dossi, c. 1515.
Rome,
Galleria Borghese.

HISTORY/MYTHOLOGY

Circe, the daughter of Helios (the Sun) and the sister of Pasiphaë, was a sorceress. She was living on the island of Aeaea when Ulysses landed there after losing most of his companions and ships. Ulysses first sent a portion of his surviving crew on a reconnaissance mission to the island, and Circe gave these men a potion that transformed them into swine, although they still retained their human reasoning. The one exception was Eurylochus, who had remained in hiding as an observer and who told Ulysses what had happened. Mercury then gave Ulysses a magical herb, the "moly," that enabled him to escape metamorphosis when he went to rescue his companions, whom Circe later restored to human form. Ulysses stayed with Circe for one year, and the couple had a son named Telegonus. Before he left the island, Circe advised Ulysses on how to avoid danger during the rest of his voyage.

REPRESENTATIONS

A popular episode in ancient art, this adventure was represented from the sixth century B.C. through Roman times on Greek vases and small bronzes, on Etruscan mirrors, and on Roman lamps. Archaic artists were fond of depicting the transformation of Ulysses' men into different animals (horses, lions, bulls, and sheep). On vases and in small bronzes, the men are shown in the middle of their metamorphosis: the upper parts of their bodies are animal, but their hips and legs are still human. Similar representations appear on a black-figure Attic cup (c. 550 B.C., Boston, Museum of Fine Arts) and on a large red-figure Attic krater by the Persephone Painter (c. 450 B.C., New York, Metropolitan Museum of Art).

In modern painting, the sorceress is often surrounded by a variety of animals. The subject appears in the sixteenth, seventeenth, and eighteenth centuries, in Italian as well as French, Flemish, and German painting. One example is Annibale Carracci's fresco in the Palazzo Farnese, Rome (1597–98). A large painting by Wilhelm Schubert von Ehrenberg (1630–76) in the J. Paul Getty Museum, Malibu, depicts Ulysses arriving at Circe's palace, whose approach is overrun by numerous animals. The painter George Romney portrayed Lady Hamilton as Circe (c. 1782, London, Tate Gallery). Sir Edward Burne-Jones showed Circe pouring the poison while Ulysses' ships appear on the horizon (1863–69, England, priv. coll.).

Cross-references: Ulysses.

Sources: Homer, *The Odyssey* X, 133–574.

CLAUDIA QUINTA

Character from Roman history (third century B.C.).

HISTORY/MYTHOLOGY

The Roman vestal virgin Claudia Quinta lived during the second half of the third century B.C. She had a reputation as a flirt, which resulted in aspersions being cast on her purity. Then, in 204 B.C., when Hannibal and his armies threatened Rome, the Cumaean Sibyl was consulted and said that to win against Carthage the Romans most obtain the statue of Cybele owned by Attala, king of Phrygia. The arrival of the ship carrying the sacred image was announced in Rome, but the vessel hit a sandbar near Ostia, and Claudia Quinta, who had meanwhile implored the goddess Cybele to help prove her chastity, succeeded in bringing the ship to land by pulling it with a rope.

The Christian tradition assimilated this character into the group of virgins it reveres.

REPRESENTATIONS

Claudia Quinta was represented on the Temple of Cybele, consecrated in 191 B.C. on the Palatine Hill and destroyed several times. A relief with the figure of the prodigy is in the Musei Capitolini; it bears an inscription referring to Claudia with the epithet "*Navis Salvia*," "Savior of the Ship."

The towing of the boat reappeared as a subject in the early Middle Ages and continued to be represented throughout the Renaissance. Mantegna depicted Claudia Quinta in the middle of a group of Roman women who welcome the statue and surround Scipio Nasica, who was sent to the ceremony by his cousin Scipio Africanus (*The Triumph of Scipio*, 1500, London, National Gallery). In Siena, there is an anonymous portrayal of Elizabeth I of England as Claudia. Claudia Quinta was also grouped with another vestal virgin, Tullia, who carried water in a sieve to prove her virginity.

Claudia Quinta. Detail from Andrea Mantegna, *The Triumph of Scipio*, 1500. London, National Gallery.

Attributes: Rope. Ship. Statue.

Cross-references: Cybele. Scipio Africanus.

Sources: Livy, *History of Rome* XXIX, 14. Ovid, *Festivals* IV, 247–348. Silius Italicus, *Punica* XVII, 1–47.

CLAWS (OF AN EAGLE) *See* Cerberus. Griffin. Harpies.

CLEOBIS AND BITON

Gk. and Ger. Kleobis, Biton; Lat. Cleobis, Biton; Fr. Cléobis, Biton.
Mythical characters.

HISTORY/MYTHOLOGY

The brothers Cleobis and Biton were sons of Hera's priestess,
Cydippe. Once, when leaving for the temple to celebrate the goddess's
feast, Cydippe was delayed for lack of a team. Her sons took the place
of the missing oxen and ran the necessary forty-five stades (five miles)
to bring their mother to Hera's sanctuary. Cydippe then prayed for the
goddess to reward the two youths with the best thing a man could
hope for in life. Hera complied by having them die in the flower of
their youth while asleep in her temple.

REPRESENTATIONS

Two archaic statues discovered at Delphi might represent the Argian
heroes (beginning of the seventh century B.C.). A Roman altar, based
on a fifth-century B.C. model, shows Cleobis and Biton yoked to a cart
that carries their mother (Rome, Museo Nazionale Romano).

In the sixteenth century, Rosso represented the chariot drawn by
the youths (1537–39, Fontainebleau, Galerie François I). Nicolas-
Pierre Loir depicted the chariot's arrival at Hera's temple in a painting
in which numerous people gather to welcome the priestess and her
sons (1624–79, Budapest, Szépmüvészeti Muzeum).

Attributes: Chariot.

Sources: Herodotus, I, 31.

Cleobis and Biton.
Tapestry after
a fresco at
Fontainebleau,
sixteenth century.
Vienna,
Kunsthistorisches
Museum.

93

Cleopatra Bitten by an Asp.
Jean Mignon, c. 1545, Fontainebleau School.

CLEOPATRA

Gk. and Ger. Kleopatra; Lat., It., and Sp. Cleopatra; Fr. Cléopâtre. Queen of Egypt (69–30 B.C.).

HISTORY/MYTHOLOGY

Cleopatra married her brother Ptolemy XIV, who quickly exiled her so that he could rule alone. She was restored to power after becoming Caesar's mistress, however, and tried to reestablish Egypt's leadership in the Mediterranean with Roman support. She met Antony in Cilicia after Caesar died and, according to one story, tried to impress her new lover with a dazzling display of her imagination by preparing a drink with a pearl from one of her earrings dissolved in vinegar. Antony was seduced, sent his wife back to Rome without actually repudiating her, and married Cleopatra. He then proposed that they share the East, with Cleopatra as "queen of queens." Octavius objected to the union, claiming it as a threat to Rome, and conquered Antony and Cleopatra's armies at Actium in 31 B.C. Antony committed suicide, and Cleopatra followed by having an asp bite her. That suicide, however, should not be confused with the one performed by Corneille's Cleopatra, who in the tragedy *Rodogune* is a Syrian queen who takes her own life by drinking poison after uttering curses.

REPRESENTATIONS

With varying degrees of certainty, ancient sculptures of a woman bitten by a snake have occasionally been proposed as representations of Cleopatra committing suicide; one example is the female figure with a snake bracelet in the Belvedere—a work once identified as portraying Cleopatra but which is now known as the *Sleeping Ariadne* (Rome, Vatican).

In modern times, different subjects from Cleopatra's life have captured artists' attention, but most frequently represented are her banquet for Antony and her suicide. In the first, Cleopatra is seated at a table with Antony and a few courtiers (de Lairesse, seventeenth century, Amsterdam, Rijksmuseum; Tiepolo, 1743–44, Melbourne, National Gallery of Victoria). In the second, Cleopatra is dying, surrounded by weeping attendants; soldiers who express shock at the spectacle may also appear. The snake may still be attached to its prey (Guido Cagnacci, c. 1660, Vienna, Kunsthistorisches Museum) or slithering away from it (Lagrenée, eighteenth century, Paris, Louvre; Regnault, 1799, Dusseldorf, Kunstmuseum). Corneille's image of Cleopatra's suicide was depicted by Antoine Coypel (*Cleopatra Drinking the Poison*, 1749, Paris, Louvre).

Cleopatra's love affair with Caesar provided subject matter for the *à l'antique* genre scenes that were so popular among nineteenth-century academic artists (Gérôme, *Cleopatra and Caesar*, painting exhibited at the Salon of 1866). In the context of her love affair with Antony, scenes in which the couple become reunited (Claude Gellée, called Lorrain, *The Disembarkation of Cleopatra at Tarsus*, 1643, Paris, Louvre) or exchange gifts highlight the queen's magnificence and the tributes paid to her.

Attributes: Pearl earrings. Snake.

Cross-references: Caesar.

Sources: Pliny the Elder, *Natural History* IX, LVII, 119–21. Plutarch, *Life of Antony*, 78–86.

CLIO *See* Muses.

___

CLOELIA

Lat. Cloelia; It. Clelia; Fr. Clélie; Ger. Cloelia.
Legendary ancient Roman.

HISTORY/MYTHOLOGY

According to the corpus of legends surrounding ancient Rome, Cloelia
was one of several Roman maidens sent as hostage to Porsena when
the Etruscans laid siege to Rome (end of the sixth century B.C.).
Impressed by the Romans' heroism—particularly that of Mucius
Scaevola—the Etruscans had withdrawn to a certain distance from the
city when the young girl escaped with a few companions from the
enemy camp, crossed the Tiber on horseback to safety, and entered
Rome. To conform with the treaty the Romans had previously signed
with him, Porsena demanded the return of the hostages but was so
filled with admiration for the maiden that he afterward released her
and allowed her to take with her whomever she wished.

Denys of Halicarnassus and Valerius Maximus made Cloelia even
more heroic: they edited the account to have her escape alone.

REPRESENTATIONS

An equestrian statue of Cloelia was erected along the Sacred Way in
Rome, which was rare for a woman; it was still in place during the
Roman Empire, according to ancient authors.

No ancient representation of the heroine survives, but her adventures have often been depicted in modern painting. Cloelia resembles
an Amazon mounted on horseback when she is shown escaping or
appearing before Porsena after returning to the Etruscan camp. She is
sometimes grouped with Mucius Scaevola, Marcus Curtius, Horatius
Cocles, Artemisia, or even Rhodogune in decorative compositions
(Palace of Versailles, the Queen's Antechamber).

**Cloelia Escaping
from Porsena's
Camp.**
Pierre Milan.
Engraving,
c. 1550.

Attributes: Horse. Woman dressed as a horseman.

Cross-references: Artemisia. Horatius Cocles. Marcus Curtius. Mucius Scaevola.

Sources: Livy, *Roman History* II, 13. Plutarch, *Bravery of Women*, 249–50.

CLOTHO *See* Fates.

CLUB *See* Hercules.

CLYTEMNESTRA *See* Agamemnon.

COMMODUS *See* Marcus Aurelius.

CORIOLANUS

Roman general (fifth century B.C.).

HISTORY/MYTHOLOGY

The fifth-century Roman general Gaius Marcius earned the name Coriolanus after he captured the Volscian town of Corioli in about 493 B.C. He sided with the Patricians against the Plebeians, who refused him the consulship. He then avenged himself against the Plebeians by calling into question the sanctity of the magistrature of their tribunes and by making the distribution of wheat to the starving dependent on the suppression of the tribunate. After he was exiled for that, he took refuge among his former enemies, the Volscians, and formed an

Coriolanus.
Nicolas Poussin,
c. 1650–55.
Les Andelys,
Hôtel de Ville.

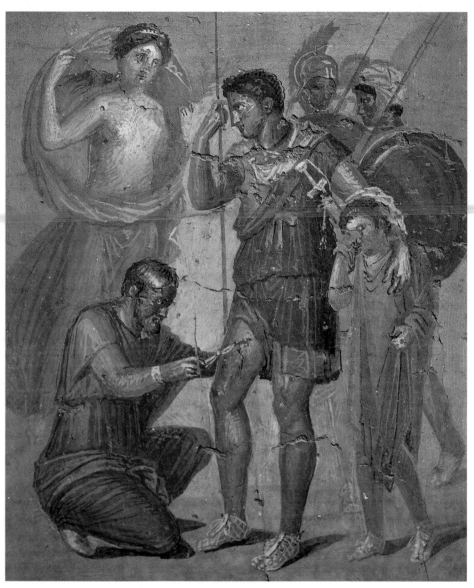

Aeneas Wounded.
Roman painting from Pompeii.
Naples, Museo Archeologico.

Aeneas Carrying Anchises.
Carle van Loo, 1729.
Paris, Louvre.

alliance by means of which he shared command of their army with their leader, Tullius.

When Coriolanus arrived at the gates of Rome, intent on besieging the city, however, he was met by a group of Roman women, led by his mother, Veturia, and his wife, Volumnia, who begged him not to attack their homeland. Coriolanus was overwhelmed by the unexpected embassy, renounced his plans for revenge, and retraced his steps after ordering the Volscian army to retreat. Tullius refused to pardon the about-face and had Coriolanus executed.

REPRESENTATIONS

Coriolanus, swayed by the entreaties of his mother and wife, was frequently illustrated from the fifteenth century onward in compositions depicting opposing emotions. The main characters are the two women, who are posed like supplicants, and the armed general, captured in his vindictive fury. Among the fairly numerous secondary characters are other Roman women, who adopt poses similar to the two heroines, and soldiers, who are grouped behind Coriolanus. The scene is sometimes set in front of the city, conforming to the ancient account, but also occurs inside the city, as in a painting by Januarius Zick in which the presence of two armies increases the intensity (1791, Ulm, Städliches Museum). Roman women brandish their young children, Volumnia and Coriolanus seem about to embrace, and Veturia, dressed in black and kneeling, turns away from her son in prayer.

Occasionally one or two children, either near Volumnia or nestling in her arms, plead with their father and heighten the dramatic atmosphere (Poussin, c. 1650–55, Les Andelys, Hôtel de Ville). Poussin added the figure of Minerva, who observes the scene somewhat aloofly.

Coriolanus bidding his family farewell, a subject proffered as a sequel to the preceding scene, is less common in painting (Tischbein, eighteenth century, Kassel, Schloss Wilhelshöhe). Here, two supporters and two children surround a weeping Volumnia, who almost faints into Coriolanus's arms while Veturia—dressed in mourning like her companions—covers her face and withdraws.

Cross-references: Minerva.

Sources: Plutarch, *Life of Coriolanus*, 34–36. Livy, II, 40.

CORNELIA *See* Gracchi.

CORNUCOPIA *See* Cybele. Fortune. Pluto.

CORONIS *See* Aesculapius. Apollo. Neptune.

COSTUME *See* Achilles (hunter). Amazons (barbarian). Attis (open). Cloelia (horseman). Mercury (voyager). Semiramis (horseman).

COW *See* Daedalus. Io (heifer). Pasiphaë.

**Croesus
on the Funeral Pyre.**
Attic amphora,
c. 480 B.C.
Paris, Louvre.

CRESCENT MOON *See* Diana.

CROESUS

Gk. and Ger. Kroisos; Lat. Croesus; It. and Sp. Creso; Fr. Crésus.
King of Lydia (sixth century B.C.).

HISTORY/MYTHOLOGY

Croesus, who lived between 591 and 546 B.C., reigned over Lydia and
owed his legendary wealth to the gold-bearing sands of the Pactolus.
Since antiquity, his name has been proverbial for a man blessed with
fortune. He once received the Athenian sage Solon at his capital,
Sardes, and asked him if he knew anyone happier than himself. Solon
replied: "Don't call anyone happy before they die." As it happened,
after many victories against the Persians, Croesus was conquered by
Cyrus the Great and condemned to die on the pyre. After he uttered
Solon's name three times during his execution, however, Cyrus not
only spared his life but retained him as an advisor.

REPRESENTATIONS

Croesus seated on the pyre, which a servant is about to light, is found
on an Attic amphora attributed to Myson (c. 480 B.C., Paris, Louvre).
   Two episodes from the life of Croesus have inspired modern
painters: the encounter with Solon and the funeral pyre. They are in
general related, and bear evident moral significance. Frans Francken
the Younger combined them in one painting (*Croesus Showing His
Wealth to Solon*, seventeenth century, Brussels, Musées Royaux des
Beaux-Arts). In the foreground, the Lydian king displays his sparkling
gold to Solon, whose simplicity and expression of wise detachment
strongly contrasts with the magnificent finery of the courtiers. In the
background, Croesus is atop the lighted pyre while Cyrus, surrounded
by his companions-in-arms, watches the torture.
   The subject of Croesus showing his riches to Solon may appear
independently from the pyre scene. Thus in Gerrit van Honthorst's
painting, a soberly dressed Solon addresses Croesus, whose wealth is
ostentatious; although his words seem to disturb the king, a courtier
behind him openly mocks the Athenian sage (*The Legislator Solon
before Croesus, King of Lydia*, 1624, Hamburg, Kunsthalle).

Attributes: Funeral pyre. Gold. Goldsmiths' work (vessels, etc.).

Cross-references: Cyrus.

Sources: Herodotus, I, 86–7.

CROMMYON *See* Theseus.

CRONUS *Greek name for* Saturn.

CROWN *See* Melpomene. Urania (stars). Venus (celestial and victrix).

CUP *See* Apollo (phiale). Artemis. Bacchus (kantharos). Ganymede. Hebe (oenochoe). Sophonisba.

CUPID

Gk. and Ger., Eros; Lat. and Sp., Amor; It., Amore; Fr. Amour.
God of love.

Flying Eros with a Lyre.
Amphora, c. 470 B.C.
Paris, Louvre.

HISTORY/MYTHOLOGY

In Greek cosmogonies, Eros (Cupid), or Love, is the primordial force that permits procreation in Heaven and on Earth. There was another Eros, the son of Aphrodite, who was more directly linked to the passion of love. Traditions regarding that Eros vary, as do the philosophic speculations associated with him. In Plato's *Symposium*, Socrates makes him the son of Artifice and Poverty, and speaks of him as an eternally restless intermediary between mortals and gods. Sacred Love, the son of Aphrodite Ourania (Celestial Venus), was associated with divine contemplation and was sometimes distinguished from Profane Love, the son of Aphrodite Pandemia (Terrestrial Venus), who is associated with sexual gratification.

Specific myths about Eros are uncommon. He is instead the childish prankster—punished, pricked by roses, stung by bees, or cajoled—who accompanies Aphrodite, who occasionally urges him on as he lets his arrows fly at men or even gods, causing Apollo to pursue Daphne and Pluto to abduct Proserpine.

Eros became known as Cupid in Roman mythology. He was also the hero of the romantic tale, *The Story of Cupid and Psyche*, which has come down to us through Apuleius's *The Golden Ass*.

REPRESENTATIONS

In classical and archaic Greek art, Eros is an adolescent who is almost always winged and who incarnates both beauty and desire; he may be accompanied by Himeros or Pothos, other personifications of Desire (Attic vase, London, British Museum; sculptural group by Scopas for the Temple of Aphrodite at Megara). Praxitiles, like Lysippus, portrayed Eros several times in lost works that are known only through Roman copies. Love is not always winged, as evidenced in an example showing him stringing his bow, a work that is now in Rome, Musei Vaticani. Eros becomes somewhat infantile from the late fifth century B.C. onward. In Hellenistic and Roman art, cupids are pudgy little children who fly every which way and playfully mimic human behavior (Pompeian frescoes, Naples, Museo Nazionale). The theme of Cupid kissing Psyche appears on sarcophagi as well as in a marble group, a Roman copy of a Hellenistic original (Rome, Musei Capitolini).

Cupid is an omnipresent mythical subject in painting, sculpture, and the decorative arts. Representations of myths in which the god Cupid played an important role (Cupid and Psyche, the education of Cupid, etc.), however, should be distinguished from the plethora of images in which little cupids abound and function essentially as decorative elements.

Different episodes from the story of Cupid have inspired artists: his birth, education, relations with other Olympian gods, and his loves, to cite only a few. Artists devoted themselves to many variations on the amusing episodes that characterized the god's infancy: he pricks himself on or sharpens an arrow, he is blindfolded, he spills the

The Cupid Seller.
Joseph Marie
Vien, 1763.
Fontainebleau,
Château
de Fontainebleau.

contents of a purse, and so on. Although these anecdotes may carry some symbolic significance, the character of Cupid is also associated with more serious allegories, from Titian's *Sacred and Profane Love*, which links the two types of Venus with the child Cupid (c. 1512, Rome, Galleria Borghese), to the rarer subject of *The Funeral of Cupid*, painted by Antoine Caron in 1556 upon the death of Diane de Poitiers, mistress of Henri IV.

Small cupids become essential ornamental motifs in the visual arts beginning in the fifteenth century, and may often be mistaken for genies or small angels. They are nude children and are called putti, an Italian word that entered all the European languages. Although Donatello is considered the modern inventor of the putto, the artist was directly inspired by Greek and Roman cupids. These laughing children are found in all types of image, from decorative garlands to processions, as musicians or friends of other imaginary creatures, such as fauns and nymphs. In early neoclassicism, Vien reflected a Pompeian motif in *The Cupid Seller* (1763, Fontainebleau) that had been recently taken up again.

Cupids often accompany Olympian gods, especially Venus, and their presence in representations of *The Birth of Venus* is a convention rarely ignored from the Renaissance (Botticelli, 1482, Florence, Uffizi) through the nineteenth century (Cabanel, 1863, Paris, Musée d'Orsay).

Finally, putti unexpectedly appear in *Memento Mori*, an iconographic tradition that invites reflection on the precariousness of existence; examples include Pieter Moninckx's *Cupid Asleep on a Death's Head* (c. 1606–86, Bordeaux, Musée des Beaux-Arts) and Luigi Miradori's *Memento Mori* (active between 1639 and 1657, Cremona, Museo Civico).

Attributes: Bow. Quiver. Torch.

Cross-references: Butades. Hercules. Mars. Nymphs. Psyche. Venus.

Sources: Hesiod, *Theogony*, 120. Ovid, *Metamorphoses* I, 452–80 (Apollo); V, 363–84 (Pluto). Pausanius, I, 43, 6 (sculpture by Scopas at Megara). Plato, *Symposium*.

Bibliography: A. Greifenhagen, *Griechische Eroten*, Berlin, 1957. E. Panofsky, *Studies on Iconology*, New York, 1939. R. Stueveras, *Le Putto dans l'art antique*, Brussels, 1969.

CURIATII *See* Horatii.

CURIUS DENTATUS

Roman consul (third century B.C.).

HISTORY/MYTHOLOGY

Curius Dentatus was a consul and the leader of the Roman army in 290 B.C. He led his troops to victory over the Samnites, a mountain people from the Abruzzi who had long resisted Roman tactics. When the Samnite ambassadors were sent to Curius by the Roman Senate after asking for peace, they found him in his villa seated on a wooden chair and eating plant roots. When the ambassadors tried to appease him by offering him gold and presents, Curius responded by saying that he preferred to command those with gold than to possess it himself. Curius Dentatus went on to win other victories, notably against Pyrrhus (272 B.C.).

REPRESENTATIONS

Curius refusing the Samnite's gifts was abundantly illustrated in painting from the sixteenth through eighteenth centuries. Curius was often grouped with others (such as Cincinnatus and Abdalonymus) who illustrate the integrity and virtuous austerity of the early Romans, particularly in decorative programs for government buildings. He was especially popular among northern European artists, from Holbein the Younger (*Marcus Curius Dentatus and the Samnite Ambassadors*, 1521–22, fresco in Basel, Gross-Ratsaal) to Ferdinand Bol (seventeenth century, Vienna, Albertina).

Cross-references: Alexander. Cincinnatus.

Sources: Plutarch, *Life of Pyrrhus*, 25. Valerius Maximus, IV, 3, 5.

CURTAIN *See* Zeuxis.

CYBELE

Gk. and Ger. Kybele; Lat. Cybele; It. Cibele; Sp. Cibeles; Fr. Cybèle. Phyrgian goddess.

HISTORY/MYTHOLOGY

Cybele was a major Phrygian goddess. She was a protectress of animals, and Attis was her companion. The rites of her cult, which originated in Asia Minor, included ecstatic dances and ritual mutilations. At Pessinus she was worshiped under the name of Agdistis, and her sanctuary housed the black meteorite that the Romans later took to Rome when, on the advice of the Sibyl, they introduced her cult there in 205 B.C. during the Second Punic War.

Attis, Mercury, and Cybele.
Detail from Roman lamp, second century B.C.
Rome,
Museo Communale.

REPRESENTATIONS

Cybele is found mostly on votive reliefs (Piraeus, Archeological Museum) and coins. Lions flank her throne or pull her chariot, and she holds a scepter or cornucopia and, as a symbol of the cities she protects, wears a crown of crenels and towers.

In Andrea Mantegna's depiction of the introduction of Cybele's cult into Rome, Scipio welcomes the goddess's bust, which is carried on a baldachin (*The Triumph of Scipio*, 1504, London, National Gallery). Cybele represents Earth in allegories of the elements and sometimes holds a globe.

Attributes: Globe. Lions. Scepter. Towers.

Cross-references: Attis. Claudia Quinta.

Sources: Lucretius, II, 598 ff. Ovid, *Metamorphoses* X, 686. Pliny, *Natural History* XVIII, 16. Strabo, X, 3, 12, p. 469; XII, 5, 3, p. 567.

Bibliography: *Le Culte de Cybèle, mère des dieux à Rome et dans l'Empire romain*, Paris, 1912. E. Will, "La Grande Mère en Grèce," *Éléments orientaux...*, pp. 95–111.

CYCLOPS

Gk. Kyklops; Lat. Cyclops; It. Ciclopi; Sp. Ciclope; Fr. Cyclopes; Ger. Zyklopen.
Giants.

The Cyclops.
Odilon Redon, 1898–1900.
Otterlo,
Rijksmuseum Kröller-Müller.

HISTORY/MYTHOLOGY

The Cyclops were giants with one eye in the middle of their forehead; Hesiod says that they were the sons of Ouranos and Gaea (Heaven and Earth). Three of them—Brontes (the Thundering One), Sterpes (the Lightning One), and Arges (the Shining One)—forged Jupiter's thunderbolts and helped him battle the Titans. Another of the Cyclops, Polyphemus, captured Ulysses and his men in *The Odyssey*.

REPRESENTATIONS

Polyphemus is the most famous of the Cyclops owing to his love for Galatea and the way he was blinded by Ulysses, and he is the only one frequently represented in both ancient and modern times.

Domenichino painted Apollo killing a Cyclops to avenge the death of his son, Aesculapius, whom Jupiter killed with one of his thunderbolts (*Apollo Slaying the Cyclops*, 1616–18, London, National Gallery). Like satyrs and centaurs, the Cyclops are sometimes grouped with other subjects, and in these instances are usually shown spying on a sleeping nymph (Odilon Redon, *The Cyclops*, 1898–1900, Otterlo, Rijksmuseum Kröller-Müller).

Attributes: One eye.

Cross-references: Aesculapius. Galatea. Polyphemus.

Sources: Hesiod, *Theogony*, 139–46.

CYRUS

Gk. and Ger. Kyros; Lat. and Fr. Cyrus; It. and Sp. Ciro.
King of Persia (558–528 B.C.)

HISTORY/MYTHOLOGY

Cyrus II the Great lived in the sixth century B.C. He conquered Asia and founded the Persian empire. Ancient sources concerning his life do not always agree but the events mentioned below constitute the legendary elements represented in art.

One of these events relates how Astyages, the third king of the Medes and grandfather of Cyrus, had a dream in which a grapevine sprang from his chest and extended its shoots across Asia. The king interpreted this to mean that he would have a grandson who would kill him and seize his crown. He therefore summoned his pregnant daughter to the palace and ordered a courtier, Harpagus, to kill the child as soon as it was born. Harpagus could not bring himself to comply and instead entrusted the child to a shepherd, who raised him. As an adult, Cyrus led the bellicose tribes of Persia and waged war against his grandfather, Astyages, whom he dethroned. After conquering the Medes, he extended his rule into Babylonia and Mesopotamia. The king of Lydia, Croesus, tried to mount a campaign against Cyrus, but was besieged in his own capital, where he was conquered and taken prisoner. Cyrus continued his conquests as far as Egypt but died during an expedition against the Massagetae, a Scythian tribe living north of Iaxartes. After his defeat, Queen Tomyris had him decapitated and plunged his head into a wineskin filled with human blood crying, "See now—I fulfil my threat: you have your fill of blood."

Tomyris with the Head of Cyrus (detail).
Peter Paul Rubens, 1620–25.
Paris, Louvre.

REPRESENTATIONS

Modern artists have represented Astyages condemning the unborn child to die (Perrin, *Cyrus Condemned to Die upon Astyages' Command*, 1802, Paris, Louvre). This subject allowed artists to depict Harpagus's conflicting emotions as he is torn about whether he should disobey his command in order to bring about good, a position which he eventually chose. Cyrus also appears in paintings of Croesus or Tomyris.

Attributes: Funeral pyre. Nursing child. Severed head.

Cross-references: Croesus. Tomyris.

Sources: Herodotus, *The Histories* I. Xenophon, *Cyropaedia*.

CYTHERA

Gk. and Ger. Kythera; Lat. Cythereias; Sp. Citeres; Fr. Cythère.

Pilgrimage to the Island of Cythera (detail).
Antoine Watteau, 1717.
Paris, Louvre.

An island in the south of the Peloponnese where Venus, sometimes called Cythera, was supposed to have landed after she was born from the foam of the sea. Watteau made Cythera famous as a subject in his painting *Pilgrimage to the Island of Cythera*; this implies a voyage to the land of Venus, that is, the promise of love (1717, Paris, Louvre).

Sources: Hesiod, *Theogony*, 192.

DAEDALUS

Gk. Daidolos; Lat. and Ger. Daedalus; It. and Sp. Dedalo; Fr. Dédale. Legendary Athenian hero.

HISTORY/MYTHOLOGY

The Athenian hero Daedalus was first and foremost a clever and skillful artisan, architect, sculptor, and engineer. After being exiled to Crete, he entered the service of King Minos, for whose wife, Pasiphaë, he fabricated a cow, enabling her to couple with the bull she had fallen in love with. He also designed the labyrinth that imprisoned the Minotaur and suggested to Ariadne the strategy of the string, which would enable Theseus to leave the labyrinth alive. Imprisoned in his turn by Minos, Daedalus flew to Sicily with wings he created for himself and his son, Icarus.

Daedalus Making Pasiphaë's Cow.
Hellenistic relief,
second century B.C.
Rome,
Palazzo Spada.

REPRESENTATIONS

Archaic representations of Daedalus are infrequent. He seems to have been popular in Etruria, where he is portrayed as an artisan on gems and engraved bronze mirrors. In Hellenistic reliefs, he is seen making the cow for Pasiphaë, or preparing the wings as Icarus watches (second century A.D., Rome, Villa Albani).

Renaissance artists appropriated the figure of Daedalus, who appears on Giotto's portal for the campanile in Florence (Andrea Pisano, 1337–43). Rubens depicted the labyrinth and Pasiphaë's cow (1636, formerly at La Coruña, Museo de Bellas Artes).

Attributes: Cap (artisan's). Cow. Wings.

Cross-references: Icarus. Minotaur. Pasiphaë.

Sources: Apollodorus, *The Library* III, 5, 8 ff. Diodorus Siculus, *Library of History* IV, 76–9. Ovid, *Metamorphoses* VIII, 152–235.

Bibliography: F. Frontisi-Ducroux, *Dédale, mythologie de l'artisan en Grèce ancienne*, Paris, 1975.

DAGGER *See* Arria and Paetus. Hecate. Lucretia.

DANAË

Gk., Lat., It., Sp., and Ger. Danae; Fr. Danaé.
Mythical Greek princess.

HISTORY/MYTHOLOGY

When Acrisius, king of Argos, learned from an oracle that his grandson would dethrone him, he had his only daughter, Danaë, imprisoned

Danaë with Cupid.
Titian, 1545–46.
Naples, Galleria
di Capodimonte.

in a brass tower, where she was impregnated by Jupiter who changed himself into a shower of gold. Acrisius refused to believe in the role of divine intervention in the subsequent birth of Danaë's son, Perseus, and locked mother and child in a chest, which he cast into the sea.

REPRESENTATIONS

In Greek ceramics, Danaë is clothed and seated on her bed or in a chair while being showered with golden rain. She sometimes reaches to open her dress and welcome the rain to her breast. In Pompeian painting, she is nude and seated while a cupid pours gold from an amphora and Jupiter sits nearby (c. A.D. 70, Pompeii, House of G. Rufus). The ensuing episode, in which Danaë is locked in a chest with her young son Perseus, also appears in Attic ceramics (krater by the Triptolemus Painter, c. 480 B.C., St. Petersburg, Hermitage). Some Imperial Roman mosaics group Danaë with other partners of Jupiter: Leda, Antiope, Europa, and Ganymede (mosaic from Oued Agla, beginning of the fourth century A.D., Algiers).

In medieval art, Danaë is sometimes compared to the Virgin, who also conceived without a husband; a painting by Jan Gossaert, called Mabuse, follows this tradition by depicting Danaë dressed in blue (1527, Munich, Alte Pinakothek). Usually, however, Danaë is regarded as a woman who succumbed to the purchasing power of gold. The loves of Jupiter were a favorite subject in European painting from the Renaissance to the twentieth century, and the episode of the shower of gold was therefore often depicted; this particular subject gave artists an excuse to portray the female nude explicitly in order to introduce the idea of desire in art. Danaë reclines on a bed while Eros-Cupid (in Correggio's painting of 1531, Rome, Galleria Borghese) or small cupids, who help the maiden collect or even test the gold pieces, often witness the scene. Sometimes a maidservant—a pure invention on the part of painters—is present: she watches the scene and lifts the bed curtain (Rembrandt, 1636, St. Petersburg, Hermitage) or her apron to catch the gold (Titian, 1553, Madrid, Prado). The shower of gold is more or less clearly represented, from detailing each coin (Tintoretto, 1577–78, Lyon, Musée des Beaux-Arts) to using a sunbeam as a metaphor. In a cycle dedicated to Perseus, Burne-Jones followed the poetic version of the story by William Morris and has Danaë watching the construction of the brass tower in which her father plans to imprison her (1872, Cambridge, Fogg Art Museum).

Attributes: Gold coins.

Cross-references: Jupiter. Perseus.

Sources: Ovid, *Metamorphoses* IV, 611–13.

DANAÏDS

Gk., Lat., and Sp. Danaides; It. Danaidi; Fr. and Ger. Danaïdes.
Mythical Greek princesses.

HISTORY/MYTHOLOGY

The Danaïds were the fifty daughters of the Libyan king, Danaüs. When Danaüs's twin brother, Aegyptus, tried to force the Danaïds to marry his fifty sons, the maidens fled with their father to Argos, in Greece, where Aegyptus caught up with them. Danaüs made believe he consented to the marriage but secretly advised his daughters to kill their husbands on their wedding night. They all did this, except for Hypermnestra, who spared the respectful Lynceus. The Danaïds later married men of Argos, giving birth to the Danaens. Lynceus ultimately avenged his brothers by massacring the Danaïds and their father, and the Danaïds were thrown into Hades, where their eternal punishment is to fill a bottomless jar.

REPRESENTATIONS

The Danaïds are seen filling their jar on a small number of Greek vases (Attic amphora, c. 510 B.C., Munich, Antikensammlungen; Apulian hydria, Tarentum, Museo Archeologico); water leaks from the bottom of the vessel in a relief in the Vatican. The subject recurs in the context of an odyssean landscape in a fresco of the first century B.C. (Rome, Biblioteca Vaticana).

**The Danaïds
and Sisyphus
in Hades.**
Attic amphora,
c. 510 B.C.
Munich,
Antikensammlungen.

The subject is fairly rare in modern art, but it appears in a drawing by Charles Lebrun (1690, Frankfurt, Städelsches Kunstinstitut), a painting by M.J. Schmidt (1785, Ljubljana, Museum), a sculpture by Rodin (1885, Paris, Musée d'Orsay), and a painting by Waterhouse (1906, Aberdeen, Art Gallery).

Attributes: Cask. Jar for water.

Cross-references: Amymone.

Sources: Ovid, *Metamorphoses* IV, 462–63.

Bibliography: E. Keuls, *The Watercarriers in Hades*, Amsterdam, 1974.

Apollo and Daphne.
Gian Lorenzo
Bernini, 1622–25.
Rome,
Galleria Borghese.

DAPHNE

Gr., Lat., It., Sp., and Ger. Daphne; Fr. Daphné.
Nymph.

HISTORY/MYTHOLOGY

The nymph Daphne was the daughter of the river god Peneus. When Apollo made fun of his fellow archer, Cupid, the latter retaliated by shooting Apollo with a golden arrow to arouse love and Daphne with a lead arrow that made love impossible. Daphne fled from Apollo's amorous advances while begging her father's help, with the result that she was metamorphosed into a laurel tree (*daphne* in Greek) just as Apollo caught up with her; the leaves of that tree served Apollo as a crown for ever after.

REPRESENTATIONS

Artists most often represent Daphne at the moment when Apollo takes hold of her: Daphne is already partially metamorphosed into a tree: the fingers on the hands of her raised arms are growing into branches and her hair is turning to foliage. Medieval illustrators of Ovid sometimes depicted Daphne as a walking tree; Antonio Pollaiuolo replaced her arms with two bushy trees (c. 1460, London, National Gallery). In Poussin's version, a cupid releases an arrow at Apollo, who wraps himself around Daphne as she metamorphoses while trying to rid her of invading leaves; Daphne's father, Peneus, weeps in the foreground (c. 1625, Munich, Alte Pinakothek). An incomplete version by Poussin is more static: Apollo sits and contemplates Daphne, who embraces her father while a cupid aims his bow and while Mercury ironically steals an arrow from Apollo's quiver (1664, Paris, Louvre). Bernini immortalized the very instant of the metamorphosis in sculpture (1622–25, Rome, Galleria Borghese); the same motif is found in a work by Ossip Zadkine (1950, priv. coll.).

Attributes: Laurel.

Cross-references: Apollo. Cupid.

Sources: Ovid, *Metamorphoses* I, 452–567.

Bibliography: Y. Guiraud, *La Fable de Daphné: essai sur un type de métamorphose végétale dans la littérature et les arts jusqu'à la fin du XVIIe siècle*, Geneva, 1968. W. Stechow, *Apollo and Daphne*, 2nd ed., Darmstadt, 1965.

DAPHNIS AND CHLOE

Daphnis and Chloe.
Pierre Bonnard.
Lithograph, 1902.

Gk., Lat., and Ger. Daphnis, Chloe; It. Dafni, Cloe; Sp. Dafne, Chloe; Fr. Daphnis, Chloé.
Mythical characters.

HISTORY/MYTHOLOGY

The shepherd Daphnis was the son of Mercury and a nymph; he invented bucolic poetry, according to Diodorus, and Pan taught him how to play the syrinx.

Another Daphnis is the hero of a Greek novel written by a certain Longus, probably during the Hadrianic period (first–second century A.D.). A short pastoral work situated in Lesbos, the novel tells how Daphnis discovered the innocence and pleasure of love with Chloe, and ends happily by having them, both foundlings, recognized by their parents and married.

REPRESENTATIONS

Some ancient gems show Pan beside a youth who could be Daphnis; the same grouping is found in sculpture (c. 120 B.C., Naples, Museo Nazionale).

Paris Bordone depicted the romantic couple under the gaze of a cupid (1545–50, London, National Gallery). After Amyot translated Longus's novel into French in 1559, some of the scenes inspired School of Fontainebleau artists (Ambroise Dubois, c. 1604, cycle for the Château, known through a drawing). Numerous illustrators repeated the subject, including Prud'hon (with François Gérard, 1800, series of nine drawings), Bonnard (1902, 156 lithographs), Maillol (1938, 45 wood engravings), and Chagall (1961, 42 lithographs). Daphnis and Chloe were sculpted by Carpeaux (1875, Paris, Petit Palais) and Rodin (1866, Paris, Musée Rodin).

Cross-references: Pan.

Sources: Diodorus Siculus, *Library of History* IV, 84. Longus, *Daphnis et Chloe.*

DARIUS *See* Alexander.

DECIUS MUS

Lat. and Ger. Decius; It. Decio; Fr. Decius Mus.
Roman historical character.

HISTORY/MYTHOLOGY

The heroism of the consul Decius Mus during the war against the Latins (340–338 B.C.) was brought about by a dream suggesting that victory would go to whichever leader of the two camps voluntarily sacrificed his life. After pledging himself to the gods, Decius Mus marched alone into the middle of the enemy to secure a Roman victory. He died in battle, whereupon the prophecy was fulfilled.

**Decius Mus Telling
His Dream (detail).**
Peter Paul Rubens,
1618.
Vaduz, Collection
of the Prince of
Liechtenstein.

REPRESENTATIONS

The sacrifice of Decius Mus predominantly inspired Rubens, who illustrated the ancient text with a cycle of eight large paintings that divide the account into episodes entitled *Decius Mus Telling His Dream*, *The Interpretation of the Sacrifice*, *The Consecration of Decius Mus*, *The Sending Away of the Lictors*, *The Death of Decius Mus*, *The Obsequies of Decius Mus*, *Victory and Virtue*, and *The Trophy* (canvases conceived as cartoons for tapestries, c. 1616–18, Vaduz, Collection of the Prince of Liechtenstein).

Sources: Livy, VIII, 6–10.

DEER *See* Apollo. Diana. Iphigenia.

DEIANIRA

Gk. and Ger. Deïaneira; Lat. and It. Deianira; Sp. Deyanira; Fr. Déjanire.
Mythical princess.

HISTORY/MYTHOLOGY

Deianira, the daughter of King Oeneus of Calydon, was Meleager's sister. She married Hercules, who fought the river god Achelous over her, and the couple had a child named Hyllus. The centaur Nessus tried to rape Deianira when she and Hercules tried to cross a river while returning from Calydon. Hercules killed the centaur, but just before Nessus died he made a potion from his blood and gave it to Deianira, claiming it would ensure Hercules' fidelity if ever the need arose. When Hercules later fell in love with Iole at Trachis, Deianira stained his cloak with the ointment, but the "cloak of Nessus" burned the hero so badly that Hercules sacrificed himself on a funeral pyre. Devastated upon discovering her mistake, Deianira committed suicide.

REPRESENTATIONS

Many vases show Deianira's abduction, with Deianira seated on the back of Nessus. In one of the oldest of these works, Hercules seizes the centaur by the hair and prepares to strike him with a sword (Nessos Painter, c. 620 B.C., Athens, National Museum).

In modern times, Deianira's abduction is the most widely represented episode. In a version by Veronese, Hercules is in the foreground and centaurs flee in the distance (c. 1580, Vienna, Kunsthistorisches Museum). Guido Reni painted the opposite composition, underscoring the power and violence of the centaur as he abducts Deianira, while making Hercules barely visible in the background (1621, Paris, Louvre).

Cross-references: Hercules.

Sources: Sophocles, *Trachiniae.*

DEMETER *Greek name for* Ceres.

DEMOCRITUS AND HERACLITUS

Gk. and Ger. Demokritos, Herakleitos; Lat. Democritus, Heraclitus; It. Democrito, Eraclito; Sp. Democrito, Heraclito; Fr. Démocrite, Héraclite.
Ancient Greek philosophers: Democritus (c. 460–370 B.C.), Heraclitus (c. 550–480 B.C.).

Nessus Abducting Deianira.
Detail from a column, thirteenth century. Chartres, Cathedral.

HISTORY/MYTHOLOGY

Popular ancient tradition linked Democritus to Heraclitus, his elder by about one century. The age difference was overlooked in order better to contrast the two philosophers, with Democritus supposedly laughing at everything and Heraclitus crying at everything. That aphorism is a simplistic interpretation of the character traits rooted in each philosopher's theories: the pessimism of Heraclitus, who emphasized the flight of time and the vicissitudes to which all creation is subject, and the optimism of Democritus, who preceded Epicurius in extolling the virtue of calmness as a way to encourage humanity to reap only the good in life. The contrast persisted in medieval philosophy and in some languages exists as a phrase that vividly expressed antagonistic opinions or personalities.

REPRESENTATIONS

The iconography of the two philosophers apparently originates in fifteenth-century Italian painting. Marcello Ficino owned a double portrait of them, a copy of a Roman antique and presumably the first modern representation of the subjects. The philosophers reappear in Raphael's *The School of Athens*, 1509-11. Cornelis Cort's drawings of Democritus and Heraclitus cultivated their image. This type of representation spread to Italy and the Netherlands in the seventeenth

**Democritus and
the Abderians (detail).**
Jean-Baptiste-Camille
Corot, 1841.
Nantes,
Musée des Beaux-Arts.

century, and may have something in common with the genre of "Vanitas" painting: neither crying nor laughing changes anything in human existence. The most widespread type of iconography consists of half-length portrayals showing the philosophers separated by a globe, a symbol of humanity bound to blind destiny, as evidenced in a painting by Jan van Bijlert (1597–1671, Utrecht, Centraal Museum). Both men are often depicted as elderly, although Democritus may be younger, as in Bijlert's painting. Heraclitus always has a serious, occasionally tearful expression, while Democritus smiles and may even be joyful.

Even when separated, the two philosophers retain their individual expressions, as demonstrated in Antoine Coypel's portrait of a mirthful Democritus (1692, Paris, Louvre).

Attributes: Globe. Tears and laughter.

Sources: Seneca, *On Anger* II, 10, 5.

Heraclitus.
Ter Brugghen, 1628.
Amsterdam,
Rijksmuseum.

DEMOSTHENES *See* Phocion.

DEUCALION AND PYRRHA

Gk., Lat., and Ger. Deukalion, Pyrrha; Sp. and Fr. Deucalion, Pyrrha.

Mythical characters.

HISTORY/MYTHOLOGY

Prometheus's son, Deucalion, and his wife, Pyrrha, were the only survivors of the deluge that Jupiter inflicted on humanity. When the flood stopped, an oracle advised the couple to throw their mother's bones over their shoulders; Deucalion understood this to mean the bones of Mother Earth, or stones. The stones thrown by Deucalion were turned into men, those thrown by Pyrrha into women.

REPRESENTATIONS

The subject is rare in ancient art, but a stucco relief found at Ostia shows Deucalion and Pyrrha, under the gaze of Minerva and with their arms bent backward, while men sprout up behind them (c. 120 B.C.).

**Deucalion
and Pyrrha.**
Peter Paul Rubens,
1636.
Madrid, Prado.

The same subject was depicted by Schiavone (1563, Parma, Galleria Nazionale), and was revived in baroque art (Rubens, 1636, Madrid, Prado).

Attributes: Stones.

Cross-references: Prometheus.

Sources: Ovid, *Metamorphoses* I, 348–415.

DIADEM *See* Juno.

Diana of Ephesus.
Naples, Museo
Nazionale.

DIANA

Gk. and Ger. Artemis; Lat., It., and Sp. Diana; Fr. Diane.
Goddess.

HISTORY/MYTHOLOGY

Diana, Apollo's twin and the daughter of Jupiter and Leto, was one of the Olympian deities. Sometimes identified with the Moon (Selene), she was a virgin huntress who lived in forests and the wilds in the company of uncivilized maidens, and would not permit men to approach her. She punished Actaeon cruelly after he unwittingly surprised her while she bathed, and she chased away Callisto, whom Jupiter had seduced. When Niobe insulted Leto by boasting that her children were more beautiful than those of the goddess, Diana joined Apollo in avenging their mother by massacring the Niobids with arrows. Not all events involving Diana's intervention were so violent. When, for example, Agamemnon was about to sacrifice Iphigenia, Diana transformed the girl into a deer. Generally speaking, Diana presided over all that precedes marriage in a young girl's life.

REPRESENTATIONS

The earliest iconography portrays Artemis as the mistress of wild animals; she is shown frontally and holds an animal in each hand. At

Ephesus, in Asia Minor, a very different type existed, which was influenced by oriental models: the immobile goddess is dressed in a tight, richly ornamented garment and is endowed with multiple breasts, which underscore her fertility.

In classical Greek art, Artemis is often represented in the company of Leto and Apollo, with whom she forms the Delian triad. It is sometimes difficult to distinguish mother and daughter, except when Diana is equipped with her bow. Artemis the huntress wears a short tunic and shoulders a quiver in classical sculpture; she also holds a bow and is accompanied by a dog or stag.

Diana is contrasted to Venus, like Chastity to Lust, in medieval allegories. Modern painters often depicted Diana the huntress, sometimes drawing their inspiration from a statue now in the Louvre which has been known since the end of the sixteenth century and often associated with the *Apollo Belvedere* (Roman copy of a fourth century B.C. Greek original).

The School of Fontainebleau freely exploited the relationship between the goddess and Diane de Poitiers, mistress of Henri II (decorative program for the Château d'Anet; idealized portrait in Paris, Louvre).

Diana's chastity isolated her and led her to flee men's company. In addition to depictions of the mythical expression of this chastity (*Diana and Actaeon, Diana and Callisto*, painted by Titian, 1556–59, Edinburgh, National Gallery of Scotland), there are other, occasionally ambiguous representations of this theme, such as *Diana in Her Bath* (Boucher, Amiens, Musée des Beaux-Arts, 1747; Watteau, *Diana Bathing*, 1715, Paris, Louvre), and *Diana Resting with Nymphs, Satyrs, and Booty* (Jordaens, seventeenth century, Paris, Petit Palais).

Diana appears in various nineteenth-century historical landscape paintings (Corot, *The Clearing. Souvenir of the City of Avray*, 1872, Paris, Musée d'Orsay; Böcklin, *The Hunt of Diana*, 1896, Paris, Musée d'Orsay).

Attributes: Bow. Crescent moon. Deer. Stag.

Cross-references: Actaeon. Apollo. Callisto. Iphigenia. Leto. Niobe.

Diana the Huntress.
École
de Fontainebleau,
c. 1550–60.
Paris, Louvre.

Diana in Her Bath.
François Boucher,
eighteenth century.
Amiens,
Musée des Beaux-Arts.

Bibliography: *L'Ecole de Fontainebleau*, ex. cat., Paris, 1972, nos. 54, 234, 455–61.

DICE *See* Achilles. Ajax the Great.

Dido.
Albrecht Altdorfer.
Engraving,
sixteenth century.

DIDO

Gk., Lat., and Ger. Dido; It. Didone; Fr. Didon.
Legendary queen.

HISTORY/MYTHOLOGY

Dido, the daughter of the king of Tyr, fled to Libya after her husband's assassination and there founded Carthage, which she ruled as queen. When storms drove Venus's son, Aeneas, ashore at Carthage after the fall of Troy, it was Dido who welcomed him and his men. Venus feared Juno's vindictiveness, and consequently made Dido fall in love with Aeneas. While Venus and Juno prepared for the wedding, Iarbas, a jealous suitor whom the queen had spurned, appealed to Jupiter, who ordered Aeneas to leave Carthage and abandon Dido. Infuriated, Dido cursed Aeneas and his descendants, climbed a funeral pyre, and stabbed herself with Aeneas's sword. Juno sent Iris to free Dido from her body when she died.

REPRESENTATIONS

The misadventure of Dido and Aeneas is sometimes found in Roman art. The couple hunts together in a mosaic from Halicarnassus (third century A.D., London, British Museum). Represented in succession in another mosaic is the arrival of Aeneas, a hunt, Aeneas and Dido wrapped in each other's arms, and, in the center, Dido flanked by two cupids (beginning of the fourth century A.D., Ham House, England). Miniatures from one of the *Aeneid*'s earliest manuscripts focus on: a sacrifice, the meeting with Aeneas, the departure of Aeneas, Dido's death on the pyre, and Dido mourned at her funeral (beginning of the fifth century A.D., Rome, Vatican).

Modern artists often represented Dido's death. In a painting by Mantegna, the queen stands in melancholy before a tall funeral pyre holding Aeneas's sword in her right hand (a grisaille imitating bronze, c. 1500, Montreal, Musée des Beaux-Arts). The subject is frequent in baroque painting. Rubens created a much more dramatic version, with Dido sitting on a bed atop the pyre and lifting her eyes toward the heavens as she prepares to stab herself (c. 1635–38, Paris, Louvre). Tiepolo depicted a despairing Dido lying on a funeral pyre near an altar; she is supported by mourning attendants, while Aeneas stands watching from the right of the composition (c. 1757, Moscow, Pushkin Museum).

Attributes: Funeral pyre. Sword.

Cross-references: Aeneas.

Sources: Virgil, *Aeneid* I–IV (Aeneas and Dido); IV, 584–705 (death of Dido).

DIOGENES

Gk., Lat., It., Sp., and Ger. Diogenes; Fr. Diogène.
Greek philosopher (fourth century B.C.).

HISTORY/MYTHOLOGY

Diogenes of Sinopia, the most famous of the Cynic philosophers, lived first in Athens and then in Corinth in the fourth century B.C. He broke with the customs, prejudices, and rules of society, and his life was punctuated by a few episodes so celebrated that they are now proverbial. In one episode, the philosopher felt the Athenians had so degenerated that he lit a lantern in broad daylight, claiming he was looking for "a man" and feigning he could find none. On another occasion, he saw a child drinking at a fountain from its mother's cupped hands and subsequently broke his own bowl, deciding it was superfluous. Dressed in brilliant splendor, Alexander once visited Diogenes, who lived in a tub, and offered to grant the philosopher any wish. Diogenes replied with the celebrated phrase, "Remove yourself from my sunlight," which earned Alexander's admiration.

REPRESENTATIONS

Diogenes is very realistically portrayed in second-century B.C. busts (copies after originals); he is generally ugly, unkempt, and has a shaggy beard. Ancient artists retained the motif of the tub, notably in a third-century mosaic in Cologne (Römisch-Germanisches Museum). A dog may accompany Diogenes as an allusion to his fraternity with the Cynics (relief in Rome, Villa Albani).

Diogenes meeting Alexander dominates modern representations. The subject is frequent in seventeenth-century painting and sculpture, as exemplified by a sculptural group by Puget (1693, Paris, Louvre).

Diogenes and Alexander (detail).
Pierre Puget, 1684.
Paris, Louvre.

Diogenes and the lantern is also seen and sometimes bears an undertone of tragic realism, as in a lost painting by Rubens in which the characters seem frightened (c. 1614; copy in Paris, Louvre). The same subject may occur in a contemporary historical setting, as in a painting by the Dutch artist Van Everdingen, in which the philosopher seems to have found true men among the members of an austere Calvinist family (1652, The Hague, Mauritshuis). The episode with the tub adapted well to historical landscape painting, as evidenced in a work by Poussin in which the philosopher's gesture of ultimate detachment occurs in the context of perfect sweetness and serenity. Ultimately, Diogenes became a symbol of privation and misgiving, a symbol that arouses reflection not only in the depicted characters but also in the spectator; one example of this is Jeaurat's painting, *Diogenes Breaking His Bowl* (1747, Paris, Louvre).

Attributes: Bowl. Lantern. Tub.

Cross-references: Alexander.

Sources: Plutarch, *Life of Alexander*, 14, 2–5. Valerius Maximus, IV, 3, Ext. 4.

DIOMEDES

Gk., Lat., Sp., and Ger. Diomedes; It. Diomede; Fr. Diomède.
Mythical character and one of the Greek leaders in the Trojan War.

HISTORY/MYTHOLOGY

Diomedes, the son of Tydeus, led the Argians and the Tirynthians during the Trojan War. With Minerva's help, he succeeded in wounding Venus, who was fighting alongside her son, Aeneas. He often accompanied Ulysses, notably in the expedition against the Thracian king, Rhesus, during which he surprised the Trojan spy, Dolon. He also accompanied Ulysses on his search for Philoctetes, who was wounded at Lemnos and whose presence in the Greek ranks was indispensable in taking Troy.

REPRESENTATIONS

In Attic ceramics, Diomedes accompanies Ulysses in the embassy sent to Achilles (aryballos by the Clinic Painter, c. 470 B.C., Berlin, Staatliche Museen); he also appears with Ulysses in a series of images representing the Dolonie, when the two Greek heroes capture Dolon, who is disguised as a wolf (cup attributed to Onesimos, c. 490 B.C., Paris, Bibliothèque Nationale de France, Cabinet des Médailles). Finally, Diomedes is seen stealing the *Palladium*, the statue of Pallas Athena, during the sack of Troy (amphora, c. 480 B.C., Stockholm, Medelhavmuseet). This last subject also appears on a marble Hellenistic relief (c. 150 B.C., Rome, Palazzo Spada) and on various gems, in which a beardless Diomedes sits holding the *Palladium* and faces a bearded Ulysses (intaglio signed Felix, 40–20 B.C., Oxford, Ashmolean Museum).

The subject is rare in modern painting, when Diomedes' wounding of Venus has most attracted painters' attention. Joseph-Marie Vien chose the moment when Mars helps Venus into her chariot, with Iris at the reins (1755, Columbus Museum of Art). Diomedes appears at left in a painting by Callet in which Apollo intervenes to protect Aeneas and Iris carries away the wounded Venus (1784–85, Paris, Louvre).

**Venus, Wounded
by Diomedes, Returns
to Olympus.**
Jean-Auguste-
Dominique Ingres,
c. 1805.
Basel, Kunstmuseum.

Cross-references: Minerva. Philoctetes. Ulysses. Venus.

Sources: Homer, *The Iliad* V (combat against Aeneas, Venus and
Mars); X (Dolonie).

DIOMEDES, King of Thrace *See* Hercules.

DIONYSUS *Greek name for* Bacchus.

DIOSCURI *See* Castor and Pollux.

DISTAFF *See* Fates. Hercules.

DOG *See* Actaeon. Adonis. Aeneas. Cephalus and Procris.
Cerberus. Diogenes. Hector. Mars. Meleager.

DOLPHIN

The Greek name for dolphin, *delphis*, recalls the place-name Delphi,
and the animal is among those that surround Apollo. Dolphins are
sensitive to music: they rescued the poet Arion when he sang while

pirates threw him into the sea. By contrast, Dionysus turned Tyrrhenian pirates into dolphins when they tried to throw him overboard.

Cross-references: Amphitrite. Apollo. Arethusa. Arion. Bacchus. Galatea. Venus.

DRAGON *See* Cadmus. Hercules. Hesperides. Jason. Medea.

DRAWING *See* Apelles. Butades. Zeuxis.

EAGLE *See* Ganymede. Jupiter. Prometheus.

EARS (OF AN ASS) *See* Midas.

ECHO *See* Narcissus.

ELECTRA *See* Orestes.

ELEUSIS *See* Baubo. Ceres. Proserpine.

ENDYMION

Gk., Lat., Fr., and Ger. Endymion; It. Endimione; Sp. Endimion. Shepherd from mythology.

HISTORY/MYTHOLOGY

Endymion is particularly famous for having aroused love in the goddess Diana, in her guise of Selene (the Moon). After Diana discovered the beautiful shepherd asleep, she asked Jupiter to keep him dozing forever so she might find him every night; according to other versions of the story, it was Endymion himself who chose eternal sleep.

REPRESENTATIONS

The young shepherd is seen sleeping while Selene descends in her chariot, in several Roman works of art, including paintings, reliefs, and especially sarcophagi (three examples in Paris, Louvre, all third century A.D.).

Endymion and Diana. Edmé Bouchardon, 1735. Paris, Louvre, Cabinet des Dessins.

Titian depicted the subject in a landscape (c. 1508, Meryon, Barnes Foundation). Endymion is joined by Diana just as the Sun's chariot, led by Apollo, begins its journey across the sky in a painting by Poussin (c. 1627, Detroit, Institute of Art). Diana descends toward the sleeping shepherd in a painting by van Loo (1731, Paris, Louvre).

Endymion and Selene.
Roman sarcophagus,
second century A.D.
Paris, Louvre.

Sometimes painters endeavored to capture the effect of moonlight (Girodet, 1793, Paris, Louvre). Endymion is grouped with a fantastic representation of an ambiguously shaped moon-woman in a work by the symbolist painter George Frederic Watts (1869–1903, Compton, Surrey, Watts Gallery).

Attributes: Dogs. Shepherd's staff.

Cross-references: Diana.

Sources: Apollodorus, *The Library* I, 75. Hyginus, *Fabulae* 271. Lucian, *Dialogues of the Gods* 19 (11).

Bibliography: F.H. Dowley, "The Iconography of Poussin's Painting Representing Diana and Endymion," *Journal of the Warburg and Courtauld Institutes*, 36 (1973) 305–18. J.H. Rubin, "Endymion's Dream as a Myth of Romantic Inspiration," *Art Quarterly*, spring 1978, no. 1, 47–84.

EOS *Greek name for* Aurora.

EPIMETHEUS *See* Pandora. Prometheus.

ERATO *See* Muses.

ERICHTONIUS

Gk. and Ger. Erichtonios; Lat. Erichtonius; It. Erittonio; Sp. Erictonio; Fr. Érichthonios.
Legendary Athenian king.

HISTORY/MYTHOLOGY

Erichtonius was the result of Hephaestus's (Vulcan's) passion for Athena (Minerva). Hephaestus pursued the goddess in vain and spilled his semen on Athena, who wiped herself clean with a tuft of wool, which she subsequently cast into the sea. Earth then gave birth to Erichtonius, whom Athena gathered up and hid in a basket, which

Cecrops and Gaea Giving Erichtonius to Athena, Hephaestus, and a Cecropide. Cup by the Codrus Painter, c. 440 B.C. Berlin, Staatliche Museen.

she entrusted to Aglauros, the daughter of Cecrops (the Cecropides), after advising her not to open it. Curiosity got the better of Aglauros, who with her sisters looked inside to find an infant guarded by two snakes. Overcome by terror, the Cecropides killed themselves. Erichtonius was then brought up by Athena on the Acropolis; he succeeded Cecrops as king of Athens.

REPRESENTATIONS

The Attic legend occurs on several vases representing the birth of Erichtonius; Earth is seen coming out of the ground and entrusting the child to Athena's care (cup by the Codrus Painter, c. 440 B.C., Berlin, Staatliche Museen).

In modern times, the child's discovery captured the attention of painters (Sebastiano del Piombo, 1511, Rome, Farnesina), especially Flemish baroque painters (Jordaens, 1617, Antwerp, Koninklijk Museum voor Schone Kunsten). A statue derived from the Diana of Ephesus, itself an evocation of fertility, appears in a niche in the background of a painting by Rubens (c. 1615–17, Vaduz, Collection of the Prince of Liechtenstein).

Attributes: Basket. Infant. Snake.

Cross-references: Aglauros. Minerva.

Sources: Ovid, *Metamorphoses* II, 552–61.

Bibliography: C. Bérard, *Anodoi, essai sur l'imagerie de passages chthoniens*, Lucerne and Rome, 1974. W. Stechow, "The Finding of Erichtonius," *Studies in Western Art*, vol. III, Princeton, 1963, pp. 27–35.

ERIGONE

Gk., Lat., It., Sp., and Ger. Erigone; Fr. Érigone.
Mythical character.

HISTORY/MYTHOLOGY

Erigone was an Athenian and the daughter of Icarius. The god Dionysus turned himself into a cluster of grapes to seduce her, and

Erigone.
Detail from
Charles-Joseph Natoire,
Triumph of Bacchus,
1792.
Paris, Louvre.

when he brought the grape to Earth—and wine to mankind—Erigone welcomed him. She later hanged herself when she came across the dead body of her father, who had been murdered by shepherds who believed themselves poisoned when they became drunk after Icarius shared the god's gift of wine with them. Dionysus took revenge by driving the young women of Athens so mad that they in turn hanged themselves. After consulting the Delphic oracle, the Athenians punished the shepherds and honored Erigone by instituting a feast at which small disks decorated with heads (*oscilla*) were customarily suspended from trees.

REPRESENTATIONS

The ancients favored Dionysus meeting Icarius as well as the episode with the drunken shepherds (mosaic from Nea Paphos, Cyprus).

Painters, especially in the eighteenth century, usually depicted Erigone being seduced by a cluster of grapes (Poussin, *Bacchus and Erigone*, c. 1626, Stockholm, National Museum). Carle van Loo shows Erigone plucking a bunch of grapes while gazing defiantly at the viewer (c. 1747, Atlanta, High Museum of Art). Natoire placed Erigone in the foreground of a sweeping composition entitled *Triumph of Bacchus*; visibly predisposed towards pleasure, Erigone fixes her gaze on the cluster of grapes she is about to devour (1797, Paris, Louvre). Boucher added a second female figure (1745, London, Wallace Collection).

Attributes: Cluster of grapes.

Cross-references: Bacchus.

Sources: Apollodorus, *The Library* III, 14, 7. Ovid, *Metamorphoses* VI, 125.

Bibliography: *The Loves of the Gods*, ex. cat., Fort Worth, 1992, no. 40. E. Panofsky, *A Mythological Painting by Poussin*, Stockholm, 1960.

ERINYES *See* Furies.

ERIPHYLE *See* Amphiaraus.

EROS *See* Cupid.

ERYMANTHUS *See* Hercules.

EUCLID *See* Archimedes.

EUDAMIDAS

Character from literature.

HISTORY/MYTHOLOGY

Eudamidas was a poor but noble inhabitant of Corinth. In his last will, which he dictated from his deathbed, he entrusted the care of his elderly mother to one friend, and to another the problem of a dowry and a husband for his daughter. To the great astonishment of the Corinthians, who had scoffed at Eudamidas, both friends respected the testament.

REPRESENTATIONS

The rare subject was made famous by Poussin in *The Testament of Eudamidas* (c. 1653, Copenhagen, Statens Museum for Kunst). The composition includes five characters: three men, stoically determined, and two mourning women, who are separated from the men. In a room which is sparsely decorated to evoke the soldier's virtue, one friend takes down the testament which the dying Eudamidas dictates.

Sources: Lucian, *Toxaris or Friendship*, 22–3.

The Testament of Eudamidas (detail).
Nicolas Poussin, c. 1650. Copenhagen, Statens Museum for Kunst.

EUROPA

Gk., Fr., and Ger. Europe; Lat., It., and Sp. Europa.
Legendary Phoenician princess.

HISTORY/MYTHOLOGY

Europa was the daughter of Agenor, a Phoenician king. Jupiter fell in love with her and, after turning himself into a white bull, went to a shore where she played with companions. She put a crown on the animal, flattered it, and then sat herself on it; no sooner had she done so when the animal carried her off to Crete. Europa had three children with Jupiter: Minos, Sarpedon, and Rhadamanthus. The bull became one of the zodiacal signs.

REPRESENTATIONS

There are many ancient representations of a woman seated on a bull that might be connected to the story of Europa (metope from Selinunte, beginning of the sixth century B.C., Palermo, Museo Nazionale; hydria by the Berlin Painter, c. 500 B.C., Oxford, Ashmolean Museum). The same motif is used to depict a Maenad carried off by the Dionysian bull, but the presence of ivy or grapevines distinguishes one scene from the other.

In the medieval tradition, the bull abducting Europa corresponds to the constellation of the same name; the subject also functions as an allegory for the triumph of love over chastity. In classical iconography, the bull is sometimes on the shore and crowned by Europa's companions (Poussin, preparatory drawing, c. 1649–50, Stockholm, Nationalmuseum; Veronese, 1573, Venice, Palazzo Ducale). Most often, the bull is already in the sea with a frightened Europa holding on to one of its horns (Titian, c. 1560, Boston, Isabella Stewart Gardner Museum).

In the nineteenth century, Gustave Moreau depicted the subject several times. In the first version, he gave the bull the radiant head of Jupiter (1869, Paris, Musée Gustave Moreau). Ingres drew inspiration

The Rape of Europa.
Fresco from Pompeii,
first century B.C.
Naples,
Museo Nazionale.

**The Rape
of Europa (detail).**
Titian, c. 1560.
Boston,
Isabella Stewart
Gardner Museum.

directly from a Greek vase for his rendition of the subject (1863, Cambridge, Fogg Art Museum).

Attributes: Bull.

Cross-references: Jupiter.

Sources: Ovid, *Metamorphoses* II, 836–75.

Bibliography: M. Pastoureau and J.-C. Schmitt, *Europe, mémoire et emblème*, Paris, 1990.

EURYDICE *See* Orpheus.

EURYSTHEUS *See* Hercules.

EURYTUS *See* Hercules.

EUTERPE *See* Muses.

EXOTIC ANIMALS *See* Aristotle.

EYE *See* Argus (eye that never shuts). Cyclopes (sole eye). Graeae (sole eye). Horatius Cocles (blinded in one eye). Oedipus (plucked out). Polyphemus (plucked out). Zaleucus (plucked out).

FACE (DOUBLE) *See* Argus. Janus.

FALERII *See* Camillus.

FANTASTIC ANIMALS *See* Griffin. Phoenix.

FATES

Gk. Moirai (Moires); Lat. Parcae; It. and Sp. Parcas; Fr. Parques; Ger. Parzen.
Divinites of destiny.

HISTORY/MYTHOLOGY

The Fates, daughters of Jupiter and Themis, were Roman divinities of Destiny identified with the Greek Moirai. The three sisters—Atropos, Clotho, and Lachesis—measured the life of every mortal, with the first spinning, the second unwinding, and the third cutting the thread of life. The Fates were also sisters of the Horae (Hours or Seasons).

REPRESENTATIONS

In Rome, the Fates were represented in three statues in the Forum called the *Tria Fata* (Three Fates). They later appeared in painting, busy parceling out and cutting the thread of life. Usually old and not very attractive, they were often grouped with images of death (skeleton, reaper, etc.)

A warrior kneels on bended knee before the Fates in a drawing by Dürer (1515, formerly in Rotterdam, Museum Boymans-van Beunigen), and Atropos cuts the thread of life with a bronze dagger in a painting by Francesco Salviati (1510–63) in the Palazzo Pitti in Florence.

Rubens painted the subject several times, notably in one of twenty-four allegorical compositions narrating the life of Maria de' Medici, who commissioned the series in 1621 to decorate a gallery in the Palais de Luxembourg (now in Paris, Louvre). Camille Claudel named her statuette of a woman with withered breasts and an expressionless face *Clotho*, a work that is in fact an allegory of old age (c. 1893, Paris, Musée d'Orsay). The Fates spin the destiny of a German

The Fates.
Francisco de Goya,
1820–21.
Madrid, Prado.

knight, who holds a figure of Pan, in a watercolor by Mossa (1917, Nice, Musée des Beaux-Arts Jules-Chéret).

Attributes: Basket of spindles. Distaff. Knife. Scissors.

Sources: Hesiod, *Theogony*, 904–6. Plato, *Republic* X, 617 c.

The Barberini Faun.
Engraving
by Robert Auden-
Aert, 1704.

FAUN

Gk. Pan; Lat. and Ger. Faunus; It. and Sp. Fauno; Fr. Faune.
God of fertility, flocks, and fields.

HISTORY/MYTHOLOGY

The Latin name Faunus originally applied to a god who, as the equivalent of the Greek god Pan, protected flocks and shepherds. In the legend of the origin of Rome, Faunus was also a name given to King Evander. In the classical period, fauns degenerated into hybrid, half-goat creatures with hairy thighs and horns on their foreheads. They became known for their lewdness as well as their love of wine and music, and they were particularly fond of the syrinx. Ovid tells the story of Faunus, who entered Omphale's bedroom unaware that she had exchanged clothes with Hercules and mistakenly climbed into bed with the sleeping hero.

REPRESENTATIONS

Fauns are almost indistinguishable from satyrs in ancient iconography. They are particularly plentiful in Hellenistic and Roman sculpture, where the most famous example is the *Barberini Faun*, which represents a drunken sleeping faun (copy of a third-century B.C. original, Munich, Glyptothek), and the *Dancing Faun*, a bronze statue found at Pompeii in 1830 (copy of a Hellenistic original, Naples, Museo Nazionale).

Modern artists have often represented groups or families of fauns; examples include a painting by Lucas Cranach (*A Faun with His Family*, c. 1530, Donaueschingen, Fürstlich Fürstenbergische Collection) and stucco figures by Rosso (1535–40, Fontainebleau, Galerie François I). Piero di Cosimo placed a grieving faun rather than Cephalus beside the dead Procris (1506, London, National Gallery). Fauns are frequently musicians associated with bucolic poetry; they appear in this context in Puget's sculpture *Faun about to Play the Syrinx* (1692–94, Marseille, Musée des Beaux-Arts) and Coysevox's *Faun Playing a German Flute* (1709, Paris, Louvre). Tiepolo mixed *Satyr with Faun*, depicting the satyr as a winged child holding a tambourine (1740, Rome, Galleria Nazionale d'Arte Antica). Picasso united three species of similarly fantastic creatures in his triptych, *Satyr, Faun, and Centaur* (1946, Antibes, Musée Grimani). Tintoretto depicted Faunus climbing into Omphale's bed just as Hercules awakens (*Hercules Driving the Faun from Omphale's Bed*, 1582–84, Budapest, Szépművészeti Múzeum).

Attributes: Hooves of a goat. Horns.

Cross-references: Bacchus. Hercules. Nymphs. Pan. Satyrs.

Sources: Ovid, *Festivals* II, 303–58.

Bibliography: F. Haskell and N. Penny, *Taste and the Antique*, New Haven and London, 1982, pp. 202–15.

The Kiss of the Faun.
Aimé-Jules Dalou,
1890–94.
Paris, Musée d'Orsay.

FAWN *See* Bacchus (fawn skin).

FIRE *See* Marcus Curtius. Prometheus.

FISH *See* Nereids. Ocean.

FLORA

Gk. Chloris; Lat., It., Sp., and Ger. Flora; Fr. Flore.
Goddess of flowers.

HISTORY/MYTHOLOGY

Flora is essentially a Roman goddess whom the Greeks named Chloris. She was pursued by Zephyr, who married her and made her mistress of the flowers. She was the mother of Spring. In Rome, the festival of the Floralia, at which courtesans participated, was celebrated on 1 May.

REPRESENTATIONS

In Roman art, particularly coins, Flora is adorned with garlands of flowers; she holds a bouquet or a crown in sculptures (Roman copy of a fourth-century B.C. original, Naples, Museo Nazionale).

On the right side of Botticelli's famous painting, *Primavera* (1477, Florence, Uffizi), Flora exhales flowers while Zephyr pursues her. She served as an allegory in Titian's portrait of a virtuous woman, entitled *Flora* (1515, Florence, Uffizi). In two large compositions by Poussin, the goddess is grouped with the different heroes whom Ovid tells us were turned into flowers: Narcissus, Hyacinthus, Adonis (anemone), Ajax (carnation), Crocus, Smilax (morning glory), and Clytie (sunflower) (*The Triumph of Flora*, c. 1627, Paris, Louvre and *The Kingdom of Flora*, 1631, Dresden, Gemäldegalerie). A relief by Carpeaux, which was intended for the Tuileries, lent its name to the Pavillon de Flore (1873, Paris, Louvre).

Flora.
Jean-Baptiste Carpeaux,
1870.
Paris, Musée d'Orsay.

Attributes: Flowers.

Cross-references: Adonis. Ajax. Narcissus. Seasons. Zephyr.

Sources: Ovid, *Festivals* V, 193–214.

Bibliography: J.S. Held, "Flora, Goddess and Courtesan," *De artibus opuscula XL, Essays in Honor of E. Panofsky*, Zurich, 1961, pp. 201–18.

FLOWER *See* Adonis. Ajax the Greater (lark's foot). Ceres. Flora. Hyacinthus. Narcissus.

FLUTE *See* Euterpe. Mars. Marsyas. Pan. Satyrs.

Fortune.
Bronze.
Naples,
Museo Nazionale.

FORGE *See* Vulcan.

FORTUNE

Gk. Tyche; Lat., It., Sp., and Ger. Fortuna; Fr. Fortune.
Goddess.

HISTORY/MYTHOLOGY

Fortune was a Roman goddess who distributed her favors according to chance. She corresponds to the Greek goddess Tyche, protectress of cities, and was identified with the Egyptian goddess Isis in the Hellenistic period. She is first and foremost an allegorical figure.

REPRESENTATIONS

Fortune is shown as a draped woman who carries a cornucopia, the source of the favors she distributes, and holds a rudder, symbolic of her association with the uncertainties of sea travel.

In coins from eastern Greece from the time of Alexander onward, Tyche is portrayed as a divine protectress wearing a crown of walls and towers. The most celebrated iconographic model is the Tyche of Antioch, whose prototype derives from a statue by Eutychides, known through a Roman copy (Rome, Vatican).

From the Middle Ages onward, Fortune is often seen with a wheel or a globe to indicate that she is unstable and can make men's fortunes rise as easily as plummet. She is often represented blindfolded because of these qualities (Gentile Bellini, *Allegory of Fortune*, c. 1495, Venice, Accademia). Fortune may appear in nautical subjects, where she is shown nude and standing on a shell, framed by a sail. Although Fortune resembles Venus or Galatea in such cases, the presence of a ball, symbolizing instability, eliminates any ambiguity (engraving after van Gheyn II, end of the sixteenth century). Fortune is nude and balances herself on a globe in two engraved versions of the subject by Dürer. In *The Little Fortune* (c. 1495), however, she holds flowers, a symbol of romantic happiness, whereas in *The Large Fortune* (c. 1501), which actually represents Nemesis (divine justice), she is winged, dominates the world, and holds a vase full of honors and riches as well as a bridle, the latter a symbol of measure and restraint. Rubens revived the formula of a nude Fortune with a sail; in this image, Fortune's foot is posed on a ball that rolls over waves.

Burne-Jones made Fortune's wheel a central motif in a composition that is notable for its emphasis on human suffering (1883, Paris, Musée d'Orsay).

Attributes: Blindfold. Cornucopia. Globe. Rudder. Sail. Wheel.

Bibliography: A. Doren, "Fortuna im Mittelalter und in der Renaissance," *Vorträge der Bibliothek Warburg* (1922–3): 71–144. F. Rodari, ed., *Fortune*, ex. cat., Lucerne, Musée de l'Elysée, 1981.

FROGS *See* Leto.

FRUIT *See* Ceres. Pomona.

The Wheel of Fortune.
Edward Burne-Jones, 1883.
Paris, Musée d'Orsay.

Triumph of Galatea.
Italian majolica, seventeenth century.
Paris, Petit Palais.

FUNERAL PYRE *See* Croesus. Cyrus. Dido. Hercules.

FURIES

Gk. Erinyes/Erinnyes; Lat. Furiae/Erinnyes; It. Furie; Sp. Furias; Fr. Furies; Ger. Rachegöttinnen.
Goddesses of revenge.

HISTORY/MYTHOLOGY

The Furies where demonic goddesses of vengeance who mercilessly pursued their prey, usually murderers, whom they drove mad. The Romans euphemistically called them the Terrible Ones (Dirae). In Greece, the Furies were known as the three Erinyes, who sprang from the blood of Uranus and were individually named Alecto, Megaera, and Tisiphone. Once their thirst for vengeance was satisfied and the murderer purified, the Erinyes could become the Eumenides, or the Benignant Ones. They became known as the Eumenides after they were appeased when Athena and Apollo defended Orestes, who murdered his mother.

REPRESENTATIONS

The Furies have snakes for hair and may be winged. They wield whips or hold torches while they chase their terrified victims. They pursue Orestes or are asleep in Apollo's sanctuary at Delphi in a series of Italiot ceramics (krater, c. 380 B.C., Paris, Louvre), but they are shown walking in peaceful procession in an ex-voto from Argos whose dedication calls them the Eumenides.

    The subject is rare in modern painting, but the Furies appear behind Mars in Rubens' *The Horrors of War* (1638, Florence, Palazzo Pitti). In addition, because they play a role early in the ninth canto of Dante's *Inferno*, they were depicted by the poem's illustrators: Botticelli (c. 1490, Rome, Vatican), Flaxman (c. 1792), and Blake (1824–27, Melbourne, National Gallery).

Attributes: Snakes. Torches. Whip.

Cross-references: Orestes.

The Furies.
Detail
from Peter Paul Rubens,
The Horrors of War, 1638.
Florence, Palazzo Pitti.

Sources: Aeschylus, *Eumenides*. Virgil, *Aeneid* VI, 571; VII, 324; XII, 846.

Bibliography: C. Aellen, *À la recherche de l'ordre cosmique*, Kilchberg, 1994. J. Harrison, *Prolegomena to the Study of Greek Religion*, Cambridge, 1903, pp. 223–56.

GAIUS MARCIUS *See* Coriolanus.

GALATEA

Gk. and Ger. Galateia; Lat., It., and Sp. Galatea; Fr. Galatée.
Nereid.

HISTORY/MYTHOLOGY

Galatea was a Nereid who lived in Sicily and loved the youth Acis, the son of Pan (or Faunus) and a nymph. The Cyclops Polyphemus, however, was also in love with Galatea and sang hopelessly of this until her refusals so infuriated him that he surprised the couple together and crushed Acis with a huge boulder. Galatea then turned Acis into a river.

Pygmalion's statue is also sometimes named Galatea, but the two subjects should not be confused.

REPRESENTATIONS

The subject was frequently incorporated into seascapes and architectural backgrounds in Pompeian painting. Polyphemus sits on a rock or is perched in a high place and plays his syrinx while Galatea rides a

Triumph of Galatea (detail).
Raphael, 1511.
Fresco, Rome,
Farnesina.

dolphin (Pompeii, first century B.C., House of the Colored Capitals, Naples, Museo Nazionale).

Modern artists revived the image of the forlorn giant who plays his syrinx while Galatea wanders away (Carraccio, c. 1597–1600, Rome, Palazzo Farnese); sometimes the Cyclops brandishes a rock over the fleeing couple. Poussin's landscape version downplays the drama of the episode in order to underscore the harmony between man and nature (1649, St. Petersburg, Hermitage). Polyphemus's discovery of the young couple was a continual source of inspiration during the nineteenth and twentieth centuries; artists play on the contrast between the graceful and tender figures of Acis and Galatea and the unsettling force of the Cyclops. Ottin sculpted the subject for the Medici Fountain in the Luxembourg Gardens (1852–57, Paris). In painting, the subject was depicted by Kerr-Xavier Roussel (1867–1944) in a large composition dating from the 1930s and now in Paris, Musée d'Orsay.

In Raphael's *Triumph of Galatea*, the Nereid is in a sea-chariot surrounded by other Nereids and Tritons; cupids fly overhead.

Cross-references: Cyclops. Nereids. Polyphemus. Pygmalion.

Sources: Ovid, *Metamorphoses* XIII, 738–897.

Bibliography: C. Dawson, *Romano-Campanian Mythological Landscape Painting*, New Haven, 1944.

GANYMEDE

Gk., Lat., and Ger. Ganymedes; It. Ganimede; Sp. Ganimedes; Fr. Ganymède.
Mythical character.

HISTORY/MYTHOLOGY

The exceptional beauty of the young Trojan shepherd Ganymede so seduced Jupiter that the god turned himself into an eagle, abducted him, and then had him replace Hebe as his cupbearer.

REPRESENTATIONS

In Attic ceramics, Ganymede is shown serving Zeus. His abduction is found only in Hellenistic or Roman sculpture, where the youth is grouped with an eagle that carries him away or else is served something to drink by him.

The abduction of Ganymede symbolized the soul's ascension towards God in most Renaissance allegorical representations of the subject. Other allegories exploit the homosexual connotations more or less explicitly by varying the eagle's posture (drawing, Michelangelo, c. 1533, Cambridge, Fogg Art Museum). Ganymede's abduction figures in decorative programs devoted to the loves of Jupiter. Correggio made Ganymede carried aloft by the eagle a pendant to Io making love with the cloud (c. 1530–32, Vienna, Kunsthistorisches Museum). Thorwaldsen sculpted Ganymede as a cupbearer several times (1804, Copenhagen, Thorwaldsens Museum).

Attributes: Eagle. Pitcher.

Cross-references: Hebe. Jupiter.

Sources: Ovid, *Metamorphoses* X, 155–61.

Rape of Ganymede.
Antonio da Correggio,
c. 1530–32.
Vienna,
Kunsthistorisches
Museum.

Bibliography: *The Loves of the Gods*, ex. cat., Fort Worth, 1992, no. 36. G. Kempter, *Ganymed: Studien zur Typologie, Ikonographie und Ikonologie*, Cologne and Vienna, 1980. J.M. Saslow, *Ganymedes in the Renaissance: Homosexuality in Art and Society*, New Haven and London, 1986. H. Sichtermann, *Ganymed*, Berlin, 1951.

GERMANICUS

Lat., Fr., and Ger. Germanicus; It. and Sp. Germanico.
Roman general (16 B.C.–A.D. 19).

HISTORY/MYTHOLOGY

Tiberius Drusus Nero, called Germanicus, was born in 16 B.C. He was adopted by his uncle, Tiberius, and married Augustus's granddaughter, Agrippina. As commander of eight legions on the Rhine, he avenged his predecessors' defeats with brilliant victories, but refused the title of emperor offered to him by the German legions out of loyalty to Rome.

His successes aroused the jealousy of Tiberius, and he was consequently sent to Syria, where he came into conflict with the province's hostile governor, Piso. He died suddenly there in A.D. 19, perhaps poisoned by Piso on orders from Tiberius. On his deathbed, Germanicus asked his friends to look after his family and to avenge his death.

REPRESENTATIONS

Germanicus's portrait appears on Caesarian and Cappodocian coins minted during his proconsulate (A.D. 18–19). A statue found at Gabii makes it possible to identify several other busts.

Although he was merely a member of the Caesar family, Germanicus was a highly honored general and was elevated to the status of a god by the emperor. In one representation of this subject, the *Great Cameo* of Saint-Chapelle, he is mounted on a winged horse (Rome, second quarter of the first century A.D., in Paris, Bibliothèque Nationale, Cabinet des Médailles). Germanicus's deification is the subject of another exceptionally fine cameo, sometimes identified as the Emperor Claudius, that shows him carried through space by an eagle with wings spread, like Ganymede (first century A.D., Paris, Bibliothèque Nationale, Cabinet des Médailles).

Several episodes from his life have captured the attention of painters. His German victories inspired *Germanicus Gathering the Bones of the Legions of Varrus*, a work whose political meaning could be a rich source of information about Restoration France (Abel de Pujol, Salon of 1824).

Most representations of Germanicus focus on his death. In general, modern painting reflects the iconography and structure of Poussin's celebrated painting (1627, Minneapolis, Institute of Arts). In that friezelike composition, the dying Germanicus separates two distinct groups of figures: one comprises his grief-stricken wife, her children, and a nurse; the other comprises soldiers and friends who are aroused by thoughts of vengeance.

The remainder of Tacitus's account of the life of Germanicus also inspired painters. Agrippina's grief, for example, was often represented in the eighteenth century. In one noteworthy example, she arrives at Brindisi carrying her husband's ashes in an urn (Benjamin West, Philadelphia Museum of Art and Gavin Hamilton, London, Tate Gallery).

Sources: Tacitus, *Annals* II, 71–72.

Bibliography: L. Curtius, "Germanicus," *Mitteilungen des deutschen archäologischen Instituts* 1 (1948): 69–94. *La Mort de Germanicus de Poussin*, ex. cat., Paris, Louvre, 1973.

GERYON *See* Hercules.

GIANTS

Gk., Lat., Sp., and Ger. Gigantes; It. Giganti; Fr. Géants.
Mythical monsters.

HISTORY/MYTHOLOGY

The Giants were sons of Gaea (Earth), and sprang from the blood of Uranus after Cronus castrated him. Although divine in origin, they were mortal provided they were killed by both a mortal and a god at the same time. They tried to storm Olympus by piling mountain upon mountain (the Pelion on the Oss), but were driven off by the gods with help from Hercules. They were subsequently buried under volcanoes, where they still groan.

REPRESENTATIONS

There are countless representations of the battle between the gods and the Giants (the Gigantomachy), with Attic and Italiot ceramics from the sixth through fourth centuries B.C. providing more than three hundred examples. The subject is found just as often in sculpted programs of temples, where it served as a reminder of the gods' supremacy. The Giants resemble hoplite warriors in the frieze of the Siphnian Treasury at Delphi (c. 525 B.C.) and in metopes from the Parthenon (c. 445 B.C.). The most complex group comes from the Altar of Zeus and Athena at Pergamum (c. 180 B.C., Berlin, Antikensammlungen): some Giants have the bodies of snakes—a characteristic feature in Hellenistic and Roman art—others are winged. Generally in the iconographic repertory, giants are armed like common warriors (hoplites), or with trees and rocks, while battling gods use their

Giants.
Frieze from the Altar of Zeus at Pergamum, c. 180 B.C.
Berlin, Antikensammlungen.

The Sala dei Giganti (detail).
Giulio Romano, 1531–36.
Mantua, Palazzo del Tè.

respective attributes as weapons: Jupiter his thunderbolt, Neptune his trident, Bacchus his grapevine, Vulcan the tools of his forge.

The most impressive example of a Gigantomachy is the Sala dei Giganti at the Palazzo del Tè, Mantua (Giulio Romano and assistants, 1531–36). Here Jupiter uses his thunderbolts to strike down the Giants, who are engulfed by *trompe-l'oeil* architecture. The myth of the thunderstruck Giants easily leant itself to political interpretation as an allegory of Charles V's triumph over the rebel princes. The same type of decoration appears at this time in Perino del Vaga's work at the Palazzo Doria, at Fassolo (Genoa, c. 1530). The Giants are sometimes confused with Titans, who also battled with thunderbolts but who were ultimately chained up rather than buried under volcanoes. Veronese used this subject in an allegory depicting Jupiter striking down the Vices with thunderbolts in the ceiling of the Palazzo dei Doge, Venice (c. 1554, Paris, Louvre).

Attributes: Rocks. Trees.

Cross-references: Jupiter. Thetis.

Sources: Ovid, *Metamorphoses* I, 151–62.

Bibliography: F. Vian, *Répertoire des gigantomachies figurées dans l'art grec et romain*, Paris, 1951.

GIRDLE *See* Amazons. Hercules. Juno.

GLAUCUS AND SCYLLA

Lat. and Fr. Glaucus, Scylla; Gk. and Ger. Glaukos, Scylla;Scylla; It. Glauco, Scilla. Mythical characters.

HISTORY/MYTHOLOGY

Glaucus, a fisherman, was transformed into a sea centaur after eating a magical herb. He fell in love with Scylla, who would have nothing to do with him, and consequently sought help from the sorceress Circe, who herself fell in love with him. When Glaucus rejected Circe's advances, she jealously retaliated by turning Scylla into a monster whose waist was girdled with howling dogs, thinking this would discourage Glaucus from chasing after her. In her monstrous form, Scylla lived near the Straits of Messina.

REPRESENTATIONS

The sea god Glaucus is shown meeting Scylla, still in her maiden form, in a Pompeian fresco. Scylla in her monstrous form was a widespread subject that is found, among other places, in a terracotta relief from Melos (c. 460 B.C., London, British Museum), in a relief from Tarentum (end of the fourth century, London, British Museum), on the coins of several cities (Kyme, Tarsus, Agrigento), and in a fresco from Stabiae (Naples, Museo Nazionale). Different fragmentary sculpted groups link her to Ulysses' adventures.

Ovid's account of this legend inspired Bartholomeus Spranger (*Glaucus and Scylla*, c. 1581, Vienna, Kunsthistorisches Museum) and Rubens (sketch, 1636–38, Bayonne, Musée Bonnat).

Glaucus and Scylla.
Salvatore Rosa.
Engraving, c. 1640.
Paris, Bibliothèque
Nationale de France.

Cross-references: Centaurs. Circe. Ulysses.

Sources: Ovid, *Metamorphoses* XIII, 895–967; XIV, 1–74. Pholostratus, *Imagines* II, 15.

Bibliography: B. Andreae, *Odysseus*, Frankfurt, 1982.

GLOBE *See* Atlas. Cybele. Democritus and Heraclitus. Fortune. Saturn. Urania.

GOAT *See* Bacchus. Satyrs. Venus.

GOLD *See* Croesus. Curius Dentatus. Danaë (gold coins, shower of gold). Midas.

GOLDEN FLEECE *See* Jason.

GOLDSMITHS' WORK *See* Croesus.

GOOSE *See* Philemon and Baucis.

GORDIAN KNOT *See* Alexander the Great.

Medusa (detail).
Michelangelo
da Caravaggio,
1598–99.
Florence, Uffizi.

GORGON

Gk. and Ger. Gorgo; Lat. Gorgon; It. Gorgone; Sp. Gorgona; Fr. Gorgone.
Goddess of revenge.

HISTORY/MYTHOLOGY

Medusa, Stheno, and Euryale, the three Gorgon sisters, were the daughters of the sea divinities Phorcys and Ceto. They were hideous and frightening monsters who lived far in the west, in the confines of the world of the dead. Of the three, only one was mortal: Medusa, who turned into stone all who gazed into her eyes. After Perseus succeeded in outfoxing and decapitating Medusa, her head was affixed to the center of Athena's shield, where it served to avert evil.

REPRESENTATIONS

Medusa was a constant source of inspiration to ancient artists. Representational types range from a simple mask to full-length images, and occur in a variety of media from the seventh century B.C. onward (ivory reliefs from the Heraeum at Samos), from small objects (vases, bronze statuettes, terracottas, ivories, and coins) to monumental ones. First and foremost among these is the Running Gorgon in the center of the pediment from the Temple of Artemis at Corfu (c. 590 B.C., Museum of Corfu).

The Gorgon is found on Athena's shield and on the interior or exterior of many Attic black-figure cups; in the latter, she appears between the evil-averting eyes that are characteristic of the period or, disguised as Iris, in the center of the eyes, as seen on a cup in the Fitzwilliam Museum, Cambridge (c. 520 B.C.).

The iconography of the Gorgon has changed radically over the centuries: her monstrous and hideous image metamorphosed into the beautiful, ambitious, and restless face of a woman. Using a frontal pose—the very essence of the archaic Gorgon—was no longer essential by the Hellenistic period, as demonstrated by the Rondanini Gorgon (Hellenistic or Imperial period), now in the Munich Museum, which deeply inspired Goethe. In the Tazza Farnese (Naples, Museo Nazionale), a sumptuous example of Alexandrian glyptics from the Hellenistic period (second century B.C.) composed of two layers of sardonyx, the Gorgon Medusa is represented as a mask whose swollen face is lost in a spreading mass of hair. Two entwined serpents on the Gorgon's neck end in a crown of reptiles that coil around her; on the inside of the tazza an engraved cameo represents the fertility of the Nile.

Medusa has enjoyed enormous popularity in modern times, but the two most fascinating works are probably still Benvenuto Cellini's bronze *Perseus and Medusa* of 1533 (Loggia dei Lanzi, Florence)—an example of the "beautiful Gorgon" type—and Caravaggio's frightful *Medusa*, with gaping mouth, eyes that bulge from their sockets and a tangle of snakes for hair (1598–99, Florence, Uffizi). Painted on a tournament shield, the second serves to avert evil and must have petrified all enemies of Prince Cosimo II de Medici, who received the symbolic object as a wedding gift in 1608.

The ambiguity of the Perseus and Medusa myth is made manifest in Paul Klee's print, *The Triumph of Wit over Misfortune* (1904), in which the adversaries seem to exchange character traits: an unsettling and oppressive Perseus, soaked in evil after his battle with Medusa, is shown frontally and occupies most of the space, while an anemic Medusa, shown in profile, is relegated to a corner.

Attributes: Enormous, hanging tongue. Snakes. Wings.

Cross-references: Minerva. Pegasus. Perseus.

Sources: Aeschylus, *Prometheus Bound*. Homer, *The Iliad* XI, 36–7. Hesiod, *Theogony*, 275 and 55. Ovid, *Metamorphoses* IV, 772–804.

Bibliography: J. Clair, *Méduse*, Paris, 1989. *Images de la Gorgone*, ex. cat., Cabinet des médailles, Paris, 1985. J.-P. Vernant, *La Mort dans les yeux*, Paris, 1985.

GRACCHI

Lat. and It. Gracchi; Sp. Graco; Fr. Gracques; Ger. Graachen.
Tribunes from the Roman Republic (second century B.C.).

HISTORY/MYTHOLOGY

Tiberius and Gaius Gracchus were born in 162 and 154 B.C. respectively and were raised by their mother, Cornelia, who was widowed early and was determined to instill her sons with republican virtues. Although opposites in temperament (Tiberius, calm, serious and moderate; Gaius, more spirited and impassioned), the Gracchi are inseparable because of the role they played in Roman history.

Cornelia, Mother of the Gracchi.
Pierre-Jules Cavelier, 1861.
Paris, Musée d'Orsay.

Tiberius became a tribune of the Plebeians in 133 B.C. and tried to bring in agrarian reform by proposing the *Lex Sempronia*, a law that called for redistribution to the poor of some of the public land that had been accorded to a few wealthy Patricians. The law was adopted, but Tiberius was killed during a riot the same year.

Gaius took up his brother's program and allied himself with the *equites* (cavalry) as well as with the federated Italian cities. To encourage those who lived in war-ravaged areas, he had wheat sold at reduced prices and planned to have Roman citizenship granted to all Italians. Some Romans found his program threatening and assassinated Gaius and many of his supporters in 121 B.C. during a battle against the consul Opimius's troops.

REPRESENTATIONS

There are no known ancient representations of the brothers, who appear infrequently even in modern painting. Fuseli sketched and painted Gaius's death near the Temple of the Furies, a pure invention since the tribune is recorded, without mention of a temple, as dying near the Bridge of Sublicus in a forest consecrated to the Furies (1778, New York, Pierpont Morgan Library). The Gracchi were represented more often as a result of neoclassicism, beginning with the French Revolution and the successful staging of a play by André Chénie in 1792. Because Tiberius and Gaius served as models of republican virtue, Topino-Lebrun exhibited the *Death of Gaius* in homage to the revolutionary Babeuf at the Salon of 1798.

Sculptures tend to make historical and stylistic allusions to antiquity and show the Gracchi as children with Cornelia (Cavelier, 1861, Paris, Musée d'Orsay) or portray them on a cenotaph with the scroll for the *Lex Sempronia* in hand (Guillaume, 1847–49, Paris, Musée d'Orsay).

Sources: Plutarch, *Life of the Gracchi*.

The Three Graces.
Fresco from Pompeii,
first century B.C.
Naples,
Museo Nazionale.

The Three Graces.
Detail from Sandro
Botticelli, *Primavera*,
1477–78.
Florence, Uffizi.

GRACES

Gk. Charites; Lat. Gratiae; It. Grazie; Sp. Gracias; Fr. Grâces; Ger. Grazien.
Goddesses of beauty.

HISTORY/MYTHOLOGY

The Graces (or Charites) were goddesses of beauty who lived on Olympus in the company of either Apollo and the Muses, or Venus. They are generally considered daughters of Jupiter, and although their number varied, the classical period counted three: Aglaia (Splendor), Euphrosyne (Serenity), and Thalia (Prosperity).

REPRESENTATIONS

The Graces walk in procession with gods on their way to celebrate the marriage of Thetis and Peleus (François Vase, c. 570 B.C., Florence, Museo Archeologico). They are shown clothed, advancing in procession, and being welcomed by Hermes in an archaic relief from Thasos (c. 480 B.C., Paris, Louvre). In the fourth century B.C., they began to be shown as nudes with arms placed on one another's shoulders; this became the model for them. The standard grouping in which the central figure is seen from the back and the two others from the front is known in sculpture through innumerable copies, the most famous of which is in the Cathedral at Siena; it is also known through a Pompeian fresco (Naples, Museo Nazionale). According to Seneca, the Graces' pose reflects the triple aspect of the gift: giving, accepting, and returning.

Renaissance humanists revived the subject and at the same time elaborated on it by adding the triple dimension of Love (beauty, desire, and satisfaction) or by creating a triple personification (Chastity, Beauty, and Love). The three Graces are clothed and dance to the left of Venus in Botticelli's *Primavera* (1477–78, Florence, Uffizi). Raphael (c. 1505, Chantilly, Musée Condé) and Correggio (1519, Parma, Camera di San Paolo) echoed the ancient disposition of three nude Graces viewed alternatively from front and back. Some versions of the Judgement of Paris are clearly analogous to representations of the three Graces (Lucas Cranach, *The Judgement of Paris*, 1527, Copenhagen, Statens Museum). The Graces became a successful subject because they made it possible for the female anatomy to be shown from multiple perspectives. Rubens supplied four versions and Boucher five. Among the sculptors clearly inspired by the subject are Germain Pillon (1561, Paris, Louvre), Antonio Canova, who reversed the position of the three Graces by representing the central figure frontally (1813, St. Petersburg, Hermitage), and Bertel Thorwaldsen, who added a small cupid (1817–19, Copenhagen, Thorwaldsens Museum).

Attributes: Apples. Myrtle. Roses.

Cross-references: Paris.

Sources: Hesiod, *Theogony*, 905. Seneca, *On Benefits* I, III, 2.

Bibliography: H. Damisch, *Le Jugement de Pâris*, Paris, 1992. E. Wind, *Pagan Mysteries of the Renaissance*, New York, 1968.

GRAEAE

Lat. Grae; Fr. Grées; Gk. Graiai.
Minor divinities.

Perseus and the Graiae (detail).
Edward Burne-Jones, 1884–88.
New York,
Huntington Gallery.

HISTORY/MYTHOLOGY

The Graeae (or Graiae) were minor Greek divinities from the generation of gods who preceded the Olympians. They were the three elderly sisters of the Gorgons, and between them had but one eye and one tooth, which they took it in turns to use. Despite their handicap, the Graeae were constantly vigilant and blocked the way to the Gorgons, but Perseus succeeded in getting past them by stealing their eye.

REPRESENTATIONS

The subject is rare in both ancient and modern art. However, on an Attic pyxis, Perseus intercepts the Graeae's eye as it is passed from one sister to the other (c. 425 B.C., Athens, National Museum).

The subject also appears in a cycle by Burne-Jones devoted to the story of Perseus (begun in 1875, Stuttgart, Staatsgalerie and New York, Huntington Gallery).

Attributes: Eye (sole). Tooth (sole).

Cross-references: Gorgons. Perseus.

Sources: Hesiod, *Theogony*, 270–94. Ovid, *Metamorphoses* IV, 614–20, 770–803.

GRAPES *See* Bacchantes. Bacchus. Erigone. Zeuxis.

GRIFFIN

Gk. Gruph; Lat. Grypos; It. Griffone; Sp. Grifo; Fr. Griffon; Ger. Greif.
Fantastic monster.

HISTORY/MYTHOLOGY

Griffins were mythical monsters with the head, wings, and claws of an eagle, and the body of a lion. They originated in Near Eastern artistic models and reputedly lived north of Greece, in the lands of the

Apollo Riding a Griffin.
Attic cup, c. 380 B.C.
Vienna,
Kunsthistorisches
Museum.

Scythians, the Arismapsi, and the Hyperboreans, where, according to myth, Apollo spent the winters.

REPRESENTATIONS

Griffins appear as ornamental motifs as early as the sixth century B.C. in so-called orientalizing ceramics. The front parts of their bodies often decorate archaic caldrons from Olympia. From the fourth century B.C. onward, they appear in Attic ceramics, fighting the Arismapsi as often as they are mounted by them (pelike, Paris, Bibliothèque Nationale de France, Cabinet des Médailles).

In modern heraldry, the griffin symbolizes the perspicacity of an eagle and the courage of a lion, and, in the Christian tradition, Christ's dual nature.

Attributes: Body of a lion. Wings.

Cross-references: Apollo.

Sources: Herodotus, *Histories* III, 102, 116.

Bibliography: H. Metzger, *Les Représentations dans la céramique attique du IVe siècle*, Paris, 1951, pp. 327–32.

GYGES

Ger., Gk., and Lat. Gyges; Fr. Gygès.
Legendary character.

HISTORY/MYTHOLOGY

The legendary Gyges was a simple shepherd who became king of Lydia (between 708 and 670 B.C.). Several versions of his story exist, but the one that most influenced painters tells how he found a mysterious ring that made its wearer invisible. As a favorite of King Candaules, he was then invited to gaze upon the beautiful queen while she slept nude. The queen was so outraged that she promised Gyges both her hand in marriage and the throne in exchange for killing her husband.

REPRESENTATIONS

The voyeuristic scene in which the king conducts Gyges to the queen's bedroom greatly inspired seventeenth-century Dutch painters. Gyges and the king watch the queen undress as she prepares to get in to her bed nude, in a work by Jordaens (Stockholm, Nationalmuseum). The subject endured through the nineteenth century (Gérôme, *King Candaules*, 1844, Puerto Rico, Ponce Museum, Museo de Arte). The death of Candaules was depicted in 1720 by Pittoni as a contrasting pendant for Dido founding Carthage.

Attributes: Ring.

Sources: Cicero, *On Duties* III, 9; Herodotus, I, 8–14 (both without the voyeurism episode). Plato, *Republic* II, 359d–360b.

HADES *Greek name for* Pluto. *For Hades as the Underworld, also see* Cerberus. Charon. Hercules. Ixion. Orpheus. Proserpine. Psyche. Sisyphus. Tantalus. Tityus.

HANNIBAL

Gk. Annibas; Lat., Fr., and Ger. Hannibal.
Carthaginian general and statesman (247–183 B.C.).

HISTORY/MYTHOLOGY

The Carthaginian general and statesman Hannibal (247–183 B.C.) learned to hate Rome as a child. He accompanied his father, Hamilcar, on expeditions in Spain, and distinguished himself with courage under the command of his brother-in-law, Hasdrubal, after whose assassination he was appointed commander-in-chief. Determined to take revenge on Rome, he triggered the Second Punic War, and crossed the Alps with hopes of winning over cities already allied with Rome. He scored brilliant victories but, rather than dare attack Rome itself, took up winter quarters in nearby Capua. The war of attrition led by Fabius Maximus Cunctator, battles won by Claudius Marcellus, and reversals suffered by the Carthaginian armies (under the command of his brothers Hasdrubal Barca and Magon) justified Hannibal's great strategic intelligence. The Carthaginian government took fright after Rome attacked Africa and recalled Hannibal. Defeated by Scipio Africanus at Zama in 202 B.C., Hannibal nevertheless continued to foster a fierce hostility toward Rome until the end of his life.

REPRESENTATIONS

There are no representations of the Carthaginian general in antiquity. In contrast, there are many in modern times, particularly in decorative programs, such as the one by Jacopo Ripanda (late fifteenth–early sixteenth century) in the Palazzo dei Conservatori, Rome, and in sculpted reliefs devoted to the Second Punic War. At Caserta, the eighteenth-century sculptor Persico made a parallel between Roman history and the donation of Naples by the Bourbons. Such cycles often parallel Hannibal's deeds with those of the Roman general Scipio.

As a child, Hannibal reputedly took an oath of eternal hatred against Rome, a subject illustrated by painters: in a setting that exudes solemnity, the youth is surrounded by important figures, most of them portrayed as magistrates of Carthage. In a painting by Schönfeld, the scene takes place in an enormous temple, and the oath is sworn before the statue of a warrior, which is placed on a high altar (seventeenth century, Nuremberg, Germanisches Nationalmuseum).

Hannibal's desire for revenge against the Romans is also depicted by Tiepolo in one of nine panels that originally formed part of a decorative program devoted to Roman history in the Palazzo Dolfini, Venice; Hannibal is shown gazing at the head of Hasdrubal, which has just been brought back to camp (1725–30, Vienna, Kunsthistorisches Museum). Other allusions to the Carthaginian general are frequent in painting; these include David's equestrian portrait of Napoleon, in which Hannibal's name is inscribed on a stone. The subject of Hannibal crossing the alps provided the setting for Turner's representation of the violence of nature (1812, London, Tate Gallery).

Cross-references: Scipio Africanus.

Sources: Livy, *History of Rome* XXI, 1 (the oath).

HARMONIA *See* Cadmus.

HARPIES

Gk. Harpuai; Lat. Haryia; It. Arpiee; Sp. Arpias; Fr. Harpies; Ger. Harpyien.
Monstrous divinities.

HISTORY/MYTHOLOGY

The Harpies were the daughters of Thaumus, son of Pontus, and an Oceanid. Two, sometimes three, in number, they were monstrous pre-Olympian divinities with the heads of women and the bodies of sharp-clawed birds, and they were originally linked to the sea and to storms. Their Greek name means "the snatchers": they abducted children and the souls of the dead, and Virgil later accordingly placed them at the entrance to Hades. The Harpies are famous for having tormented King Phineus by fouling his food. They were hunted down by Boreas's sons, Calaïs and Zetes, who destroyed them during one of the Argonauts' expeditions.

REPRESENTATIONS

The Harpies are represented as winged female bodies on a proto-Attic vase, which identifies them with an inscription (c. 620 B.C., Berlin, Antikensammlungen). That iconographic type recurs in a series of Attic vases devoted to the Boreads chasing away the Harpies from Phineus's table. In a Lycian funerary monument, which is traditionally called the "Monument of the Harpies," the Harpies are represented as birds with women's faces, and they hold the dead in their arms; the typology of those figures, however, suggests that they are more probably Sirens (beginning of the fifth century B.C., London, British Museum).

The Harpies are found in medieval allegories of Virtues and Vices, where they represent Greed. They are again depicted as birds with monsters' claws in a sketch by Rubens, *The Harpies Driven away by Zetes and Calaïs* (executed by Quellyn, c. 1636–38, Madrid, Prado).

Attributes: Claws (of an eagle). Wings.

Cross-references: Argonauts. Phineus. Silenus.

Sources: Virgil, *Aeneid* III, 209–18.

Bibliography: M. Vojatzi, *Frühe Argonautenbilder*, Würzburg, 1982, pp. 51–71.

HEAD *See* Caesar (severed). Cerberus (triple). Cyrus (severed). Gorgon. Perseus. Tomyris (severed).

HEBE

Gk., Lat., Sp., and Ger. Hebe; It. Ebe; Fr. Hébé.
Goddess of youth.

HISTORY/MYTHOLOGY

Hebe, the daughter of Jupiter and Juno, was the Greek goddess of youth. She married Hercules when the hero became immortal and entered Olympus, and she was the gods' cupbearer until Jupiter abducted Ganymede, who took over this role from her.

REPRESENTATIONS

Hebe is represented as a young woman who pours drink for the gods; she holds a pitcher (oenochoe) or a cup. She is nevertheless not always easily identifiable in Attic ceramics without an inscription (cup by Oltos, c. 520 B.C., Tarquinia). She also appears on Argian coins.

The young goddess is seen advancing toward Jupiter at an assembly of gods in the clouds in Veronese's *Coronation of Hebe* (c. 1586, Boston, Isabella Stewart Gardner Museum). It was popular in seventeenth-century England to portray women as Hebe as a way of honoring the model's youth (Reynolds, 1772, Ascot, Rothschild Collection). In a sculpture by François Rude, *Hebe and the Eagle*, the goddess lifts her cup high, and a spread-winged eagle on the ground eyes the cup with eager anticipation (marble, 1857, Dijon, Musée des Beaux-Arts).

A sculpted group by Carrier-Belleuse, composed of a monumental eagle enveloping the sleeping Hebe in its wings, has been interpreted as an allegory of the imperial eagle protecting France.

Attributes: Cup. Pitcher.

Cross-references: Ganymede. Hercules.

Sources: Hesiod, *Theogony*, 950–55.

Hebe and the Eagle of Jupiter.
Albert-Ernest Carrier-Belleuse, 1869.
Paris, Musée d'Orsay.

HECATE

Gk. and Ger. Hekate; Lat. and Sp. Hecate; It. Ecate; Fr. Hécate.
Greek divinity.

HISTORY/MYTHOLOGY

Hecate was a Greek divinity descended from the Titans but faithful to Jupiter, who gave her privileges over earth, sea, and sky. She distributed material prosperity. She was associated with the new moon and related to Diana. Often evoked by sorcerers and witches, whom she protected, Hecate was linked to the world of the Shadows. Herself a sorceress, she was generally associated with crossroads.

REPRESENTATIONS

Hecate is mainly the object of cult representations, and is often portrayed as a three-bodied figure backed against a column; she wears a type of basket (*calathos*) as a headdress, holds torches, and is accompanied by a dog. On the frieze of the Great Altar of Pergamum, she has two heads and four arms (Berlin, Antikensmuseum). In a more recent iconographic type, known through gems, she has six arms and holds torches, keys, a whip, a dagger, a sword, and snakes.

Although Hecate is rarely represented in modern painting, she appears in the Renaissance mythological tradition as a figure whose three heads are those of a horse, a dog, and a boar (Cartari, *Le imagini de i dei*, 1571).

Attributes: Dogs. Snakes. Torches. Triple head.

Cross-references: Diana.

Sources: Hesiod, *Theogony*, 411–52.

Hecate.
First century A.D.
Paris, Bibliothèque Nationale de France, Cabinet des Médailles.

Hector's Farewell to Andromache. Pompeo Batoni, study, eighteenth century. Besançon, Musée des Beaux-Arts.

HECTOR

It. Ettore; Fr. Hector.
Trojan prince.

HISTORY/MYTHOLOGY

Hector was a Trojan prince who played a leading role in *The Iliad*. His parents were Priam and Hecuba, and he was the husband of Andromache and the father of Astyanax. He was the true leader and defender of Troy. He avoided confronting Achilles during the first years of the Trojan War, but decimated the Greek ranks in Achilles' absence. His role was particularly brilliant and decisive during the attack by sea, when only the intervention of the gods saved Nestor and Diomedes. After Achilles' inseparable friend, Patroclus, took up arms and was killed by Hector, Achilles retaliated by killing Hector's brother, Polydorus. Hector then challenged Achilles to one-on-one combat, but proved no match for Achilles and was slain. In fact, Zeus had previously weighed the destiny of each adventurer, and the balance tipped against Hector. Despite the dying Hector's entreaties, Achilles refused to surrender his body to Priam, and instead attached it by its ankles to his chariot and dragged it around the city's walls. After Aphrodite and Apollo took pity on him, his body was restored to Priam in exchange for a hefty ransom, and the funeral rite was celebrated with dignity.

REPRESENTATIONS

A large number of themes connected with Hector's story were represented in antiquity. Notable are: Hector's arming, his farewells to his family, his departure, his individual combats (especially the duel with Achilles), and the sea battle. Predominantly, vase painters treated these subjects, particularly in the fifth century B.C. The dragging of Hector's body around the walls of Troy and the ransom episode were more popular among black-figure painters of the sixth and very early fifth centuries B.C. and, later, among Italiot painters. Other media such as mural painting (at Pompeii), Roman sarcophagi, and metal vases, evoke several episodes of the hero's life, notably in a single artifact. In

Hercules and the Lernaean Hydra.
Guido Reni, 1620.
Paris, Louvre.

Apollo and Marsyas.
Perugino (Pietro Vanucci), 1495.
Paris, Louvre.

Triumph of Neptune and Amphitrite.
Roman mosaic from Constantine, third century.
Paris, Louvre.

Oedipus Solves the Riddle of the Sphinx.
Jean-Auguste-Dominique Ingres, 1808–25.
Paris, Louvre.

Hector Dragged Before the Walls of Troy.
Attic lekythos,
c. 510 B.C.
Paris, Louvre.

a first-century B.C. Pompeian painting from the so-called Casa del Sacello Iliaco e del Criptoportico, Hector leaves the city, confronts Achilles, is killed by Achilles, and is dragged behind the chariot.

In a pair of vases (oenochoes) from the end of the first century A.D. that form part of the silver treasury from the Temple of Mercury at Berthouville (Paris, Bibliothèque Nationale de France, Cabinet des Médailles), Hector is dragged behind Achilles' chariot, his body weighed, and his ransom paid.

Since antiquity, Hector has appeared as a warrior who is valorous but nevertheless conquered or at least ready to be conquered. He was generally portrayed as a mature man with a glittering, high-crested helmet; he is bearded until the fifth century B.C. and usually beardless afterward.

Hector has served as the Jack of Diamonds in playing cards in the West since the fifteenth century.

Artists occasionally depicted the dead hero being dragged around the walls of Troy (for example, Donato Creti's painting in the Palazzo Communale in Bologna, c. 1740), but they mostly portrayed him bidding farewell to Andromache and Astyanax, a subject that conforms more with seventeenth- and eighteenth-century sensibilities: drawings by Tiepolo, paintings by Antoine Coypel (Tours, Musée des Beaux-Arts), and a cartoon by Joseph-Marie Vien for a tapestry (1787, Paris, Louvre).

Cross-references: Achilles. Andromache. Astyanax. Nestor. Patroclus. Priam. Troy.

Sources: Homer, *The Iliad* VI, VII, XII, XIV.

HELEN

Gk. and Ger. Helene; Lat. and Sp. Helena; It. Elena; Fr. Hélène.
One of *The Iliad*'s principal heroines.

HISTORY/MYTHOLOGY

According to Homeric tradition, Helen was the daughter of Jupiter and Leda. She was the sister of the Dioscuri, Castor and Pollux, and of Clytemnestra. Her beauty was famous throughout the ancient world. When it was time for her to marry, the enormous number of suitors overwhelmed her mortal father, Tyndareus (Leda's husband). He followed Ulysses' advice on how not to offend any of the suitors by asking them all to accept whatever choice Helen herself made and to pledge their support to her future husband. Helen chose Menelaus. She had, however, already been promised by Venus to Paris, the son of the Trojan king, Priam, in recompense for his having judged Venus winner in a competition with Minerva and Juno. Paris therefore abducted Helen and, because the Greek chiefs had sworn to rally around Menelaus if it were ever necessary, triggered the Trojan War.

Helen of Troy.
Dante Gabriel Rossetti,
1863.
Hamburg, Kunsthalle.

145

**The Abduction
of Helen.**
Guido Reni, 1631.
Paris, Louvre.

The result of the ten-year combat was that Helen was found by
Menelaus and taken back to Sparta.

Helen's beauty was proverbial. Pliny reports that Zeuxis painted a
portrait of her for the Temple of Hera at Croton, reputedly selecting
the most perfect features from five models.

REPRESENTATIONS

The iconography involves two principal events: Helen's abduction by
Paris, and Helen meeting Menelaus at the end of the Trojan War, prior
to the couple's return to Sparta. The wedding of Menelaus and Helen
also appears on ancient vase paintings. A lekythos attributed to the
Brygos Painter gives special emphasis to King Menelaus, who wears a
helmet and a cloak, and looks back toward his young fiancée who
timidly follows (beginning of the fifth century B.C., Berlin, Staatliche
Museen). Helen appears with Paris in a great many Attic and Apulian
ceramics, with a cupid either fluttering above her or crouched beside
her (pelike, middle of the fourth century B.C., Cassel, Staatliche
Kunstsammlung; Apulian krater, c. 370 B.C., Rome, Vatican). In other
vases and in mural paintings, Helen appears with Venus, who tries to
influence her. In a Pompeian painting, for example, Venus sits beside
and embraces the apparently troubled figure of Helen, whose head is
covered with a himation and whose hands are on her knees; a small
cupid gestures to Helen with one hand and rests the other on Paris
(Pompeii, House of Sacerdos Amandus, A.D. 35–45).

The abduction of Helen was a very popular subject throughout
antiquity. Depending on the specific date, it occurs with or without a
chariot. In archaic art, a warrior on foot and with drawn sword turns
toward a woman who follows (Attic amphora by the Amasis Painter
(c. 550 B.C., Munich, Antikensammlungen). Paris's ship is occasionally
seen in Roman art (painting from Pompeii, House of the Tragic Poet,
A.D. 70–79, Naples, Museo Nazionale).

**Helen at the Scaean
Gate.**
Gustave Moreau,
c. 1880–85.
Paris,
Musée Gustave Moreau.

Helen's return is found on an enormous number of ceramics, especially in fifth-century B.C. Athens. While Troy falls, Menelaus draws his sword and threatens Helen, who flees (skyphos by Makron, c. 480 B.C., Boston, Museum of Fine Arts). In the second half of the fifth century B.C. one theme dominates: Menelaus moved by Helen's beauty when he sees her again and lets his sword fall.

In modern times, Helen's abduction has captured most attention. The subject was already popular in fifteenth- and sixteenth-century Italy. Noteworthy representations include works by Giulio Romano (Mantua, Palazzo Ducale) and Guido Reni (1631, Paris, Louvre). Giovanni Francesco Romanelli (1610–62) painted the subject on the ceiling of the Galerie Mazarine (Paris, Bibliothèque Nationale de France). Helen's abduction also inspired sculptors; one noteworthy example is Johann C.W. Beyer's group in Schönbrunn Park in Vienna (c. 1775).

Helen is also represented in amorous adventures with Paris (David, 1789, Paris, Louvre) or alone (Rossetti, 1863, Hamburg, Kunsthalle). Her beauty, which engendered so much misfortune, is celebrated in these works.

Cross-references: Leda. Menelaus. Paris. Troy. Venus. Zeuxis.

Sources: Pliny the Elder, 35, 64 (Zeuxis).

Bibliography: L. Ghali-Kahil, *Les Enlèvements et les retours d'Hélène*, Paris, 1955.

HELIOS *See* Apollo.

HELLE *See* Phrixus.

HELMET *See* Belisarius. Hector. Mars. Mercury (winged helmet).

HEPHAESTUS *Greek name for* Vulcan.

HERA *Greek name for* Juno.

HERACLITUS *See* Democritus.

HERAKLES *Greek name for* Hercules.

Hercules Strangling the Snakes.
First century A.D.
Pompeii, House of the Vettii.

HERCULES

Gk. Herakles; Lat. and Ger. Hercules; It. Ercole; Fr. Hercule.
Greek hero.

HISTORY/MYTHOLOGY

Hercules, the most famous Greek hero, was the son of Jupiter and Alcmena, a Theban princess. To seduce Alcmena, who was renowned for her fidelity, Jupiter had to disguise himself as her husband, Amphitryon, a transformation that added a note of legitimacy to an otherwise illegitimate union. Hercules was the butt of Juno's jealousy from the day he was born. Even while he was still in the cradle, the goddess sent snakes to bite and kill him, but Hercules strangled them. By contrast, another story claims that Juno was tricked into nursing him and that the milk that gushed from her breast became the Milky Way. Hercules received some form of musical education but could not tolerate criticism from his teacher, Linus, whom he killed in a violent attack. He was sent to live among the shepherds of Mount Cithaeron to atone for that murder, and he afterward returned to Thebes, where he helped his mortal father, Amphitryon, fight the city of Orchomenus. When Amphitryon died, his successor, Creon, married his daughter Megara to Hercules. In another attempt to avenge herself, however, Juno drove the hero mad and he massacred his own children. When he came to his senses, he sought purification at Delphi, where the Pythia had him go to his cousin Eurystheus, king of Tiryns, and do whatever he bid.

Juno's hatred pursued Hercules wherever he went and manifested itself in the form of all sorts of monsters and trials that the hero had to overcome. These episodes are often grouped into a cycle comprising twelve labors, although the list varies and also contains other adventures.

The Twelve Labors of Hercules

The Nemean Lion
The first labor was to strangle the invulnerable Nemean Lion, whose skin Hercules afterward wore as a talisman.

The Lernaean Hydra
The Hydra was a creature whose many heads regrew whenever one was cut off. With help from his companion, Iolaus, Hercules progressively cauterized each wound with a torch to prevent the heads from reforming.

**Hercules and
Omphale with
the Labors
of Hercules.**
First century A.D.
Naples,
Museo Nazionale.

The Stag with the Golden Horns (The Ceryneian Hind)
On Mount Ceryneus lived a golden-horned and brass-footed stag
sacred to Diana. Hercules hunted the animal for a year before he captured it and brought it back to Tiryns alive.

The Erymanthian Boar
Near the Erymanthus, a tributary of the Alpheus, was an enormous
boar, which Hercules took back to Eurystheus alive. The hero met
Pholus on the way and with him opened the jug of wine that Dionysus
had entrusted to the centaurs, who then became so intoxicated by the
odor that they attacked Hercules and precipitated a pitched battle
during which Pholus died.

The Augean Stables
Next, Hercules diverted the course of the Alpheus to clean the stables
of Augeas, king of Elis.

The Stymphalian Birds
With a sling or arrows, Hercules succeeded in killing the man-eating
birds that clouded the skies near Lake Stymphalus.

The Cretan Bull
In Crete, Hercules captured the bull that Neptune gave to Minos and
brought it to Tiryns. The animal subsequently devastated the area

before retracing its steps as far as Marathon, where Theseus next captured it.

The Horses of Diomedes
The ravenous mares of Diomedes, king of Thrace and son of Ares, devoured the bodies of shipwrecked sailors until Hercules tamed them.

The Girdle of Hippolyta
Hercules was next ordered to find the girdle of Hippolyta, queen of the Amazons, for Eurystheus's daughter. The queen died during the battle between Hercules and the Amazons. While returning from this expedition, Hercules rescued Laomedon's daughter, a Trojan princess named Hesione, from a ferocious sea monster sent by Neptune. He then killed Laomedon for refusing to pay the promised reward.

The Cattle of Geryon
Geryon, son of Chrysaor (the Gorgon Medusa's son) and Callirhoe, was a three-bodied monster whose cattle Hercules had to bring back to Tiryns. The Sun loaned Hercules a golden bowl as a vessel in which to cross the ocean and catch up with Geryon, who lived far away in the west beyond the pillars that bore the hero's name. After killing Geryon and his shepherd, Eurytion, Hercules traveled through the Iberian peninsula and Gaul and then returned to Rome, where he slew the monster Cacus.

Hercules Slaying the Lernaean Hydra.
Antonio del Pollaiuolo, c. 1460.
Florence, Uffizi.

The Golden Apples of the Hesperides
Hercules' next labor was to retrieve the Golden Apples of the Hesperides, a task that took him on another long expedition. He turned to Nereus, the old man of the sea, for directions, which he extracted only after blocking Nereus's cycle of metamorphoses with locked arms. Passing through Libya, Hercules fought the Giant Antaeus, son of Gaea (Earth), and succeeded in strangling him by preventing him from touching the ground to replenish his strength. Hercules was soon afterward assaulted in his sleep by pygmies. He arrived in Egypt only to be captured by the pharaoh Busiris's men, who would have sacrificed him had he not broken free of his chains and sent them running. Continuing on his way, he freed Prometheus, who had been chained to the Caucasus, and who then pointed out the way to the Hesperides. Some say that Hercules made his own way into the garden where the Golden Apples were guarded by a serpent; others say that he temporarily shouldered the sky for the Giant Atlas, father of the Hesperides, who then gathered the apples for him.

Cerberus
For his last labor, Hercules brought Cerberus, the three-headed dog guarding the entry to Hades, to Eurystheus, whom the animal then terrorized.

Other Adventures
Other exploits took Hercules to different parts of Greece and the ancient world, although the sequence of events is not always logical. The following are noteworthy examples from the numerous and sometimes contradictory accounts.

The Labors of Hercules.
After the metopes from the Temple of Zeus at Olympia, c. 456 B.C.

Eurytus, king of Oechalia, challenged his daughter's suitors to an archery contest. Hercules won the competition but destroyed Oechalia when Eurytus refused to give up his daughter. After killing Eurytus's son, Iphitus, he went to Delphi to consult the oracle and purify himself of the crime. There he got into a fight with Apollo over the god's

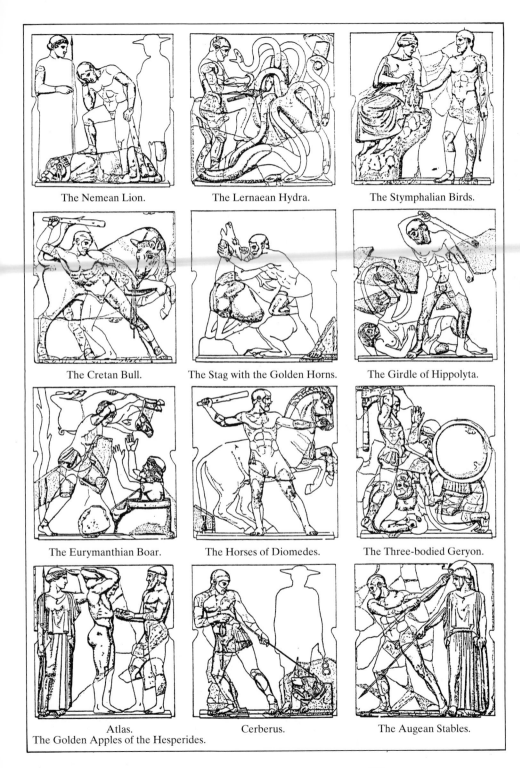

The Nemean Lion.

The Lernaean Hydra.

The Stymphalian Birds.

The Cretan Bull.

The Stag with the Golden Horns.

The Girdle of Hippolyta.

The Eurymanthian Boar.

The Horses of Diomedes.

The Three-bodied Geryon.

Atlas.
The Golden Apples of the Hesperides.

Cerberus.

The Augean Stables.

151

Hercules.
Pierre Courteys.
Enamel, 1559.
Château d'Ecouen,
Musée National
de la Renaissance.

sacred tripod, which Hercules had stolen because the Pythia refused to answer him. As a result, Hercules was sold as a slave to the Lydian queen, Omphale, for whom he spun wool and with whom he exchanged clothes. He also had to till the land for Syleus, a winegrower who habitually pressed passersby into his service, but he finally rebelled and devastated the vineyard.

Hercules fought a number of other giants and fantastic creatures. He captured the Cercopes, the pair of mocking dwarfs who tried to steal his weapons. He battled Geras, the misshapen personification of old age. He subdued Alcyoneus, the Giant who stole the Sun's oxen and whose strength was replenished whenever he touched the earth, by attacking him in his sleep. Hercules also took part in the Gigantomachy, the battle between gods and Giants, which the gods could not have won without a mortal's presence. He fought Achelous, who tried to gain Deianira's hand by threatening her father, and married Deianira himself after killing the river god. The episode involving Nessus took place later, when the couple was crossing a river near the centaur's home. After making believe he wanted to help Deianira, Nessus tried to rape her, and Hercules killed him with an arrow. Before dying, however, Nessus secretly gave Deianira some advice that would one day prove fatal to Hercules: he told her to make a potion from his blood and to soak the hero's tunic in it if she ever needed to ensure his fidelity. Finally, Hercules battled Cycnus, who robbed pilgrims on their way to Delphi and gave the spoils to his father, Mars.

Hercules' death is connected to the episode with Nessus. Deianira eventually became jealous and followed the centaur's advice, but the potion caused such painful burning that life became unbearable for Hercules, who built a funeral pyre on Oeta, climbed on to it, and had Philoctetes light it after giving him his bow. When Hercules' bones were about to be gathered, it was discovered that they had disappeared, indicating that the hero had become a god. Hercules was considered both hero and god after this, and many cities established cults in his honor.

Hercules was a very changeable personality in the ancient tradition. To authors of comedies, he was a big eater or a divine glutton, but a heroic symbol of endurance and a model of virtue to philosophers. A parable by the philosopher Prodicus, reported by Xenophon, tells how Hercules came upon a crossroads as an adolescent and was forced to choose between the easy road of pleasure and the rougher, more difficult road of virtue; the hero ultimately followed the difficult road.

REPRESENTATIONS

Ancient representations of Hercules almost always show him wearing a lionskin whose jaws cover his head; he has a short beard and sometimes carries a skyphos, or small drinking cup. His weapons vary according to his adversaries: they are most often a club and a bow, but may be a sword (to fight centaurs or Amazons), a sickle (to cut off the Hydra's heads), or even a sling (to shoot down the Stymphalian birds).

Several of Hercules' adventures were grouped together as early as the sixth century B.C. Examples include the metopes from the Heraeum at Sele, near Paestum (Deianira and Nessus, the quarrel over the tripod, the Cercopes, Pholus, and perhaps Antaeus), and an amphora by the Kleophrades Painter (c. 500 B.C., Malibu, Getty Museum: the Lernaean Hydra, Amazons, the Hesperides, and Atlas). The Twelve Labors of Hercules, however, first appear as a cycle on metopes from the Temple of Zeus at Olympia (completed c. 456 B.C., Museum of Olympia and Paris, Louvre). The series can vary according to the ensemble, as exemplified in the Temple of Hephaestus at Athens (c. 450 B.C.), where they are paralleled with Theseus's labors.

Cycles are more frequent in Roman art, particularly in mosaics (for example, a mosaic from Saint-Paul-lès-Romans, c. A.D. 150–200, Valence, Musée) and sarcophagi, where the hero's adventures are tightly juxtaposed, with as many as eight in a single panel (c. A.D. 170, Mantua, Palazzo Ducale; c. A.D. 200, Florence, Uffizi). Hercules and Omphale are shown surrounded by representations of the Twelve Labors on a small votive relief (middle of the second century A.D., Naples, Museo Nazionale).

The adventure with the Nemean Lion is by far the most frequent among individual representations of Hercules' labors, especially in Attic ceramics. It also appears on coins from Heraclea, a city in Lucania (fourth century B.C.). By contrast, other isolated labors, such as the Stymphalian Birds and the Horses of Diomedes, are extremely rare.

Hercules on His Funeral Pyre. Guillaume Coustou. Marble, 1704. Paris, Louvre.

In some sculptures, Hercules is shown resting. The most well known is the Farnese Hercules, a colossal statue probably derived from a Greek model and signed by Glycon of Athens (third century A.D., Naples, Museo Nazionale); here the hero leans on his club with one hand behind his back. Alexander the Great used Hercules in his court iconography and often had himself represented on coins with a lionskin over his head; the Emperor Comodus (A.D. 180–192) also likened himself to Hercules (statue, Rome, Vatican; bust, Rome, Musei Capitolini).

Modern artists have represented the Labors of Hercules in cycles that may be more or less developed. In Florence, Vasari created the decorative program for a Hercules room (1558, Palazzo Vecchio). Giambologna executed a series of small bronze sculptures of the Labors (end of the sixteenth century). Hercules is the subject of Annibale Carracci's decorations for the Camerino in the Palazzo Farnese (1595–97, Rome); *Hercules at the Crossroads*, in the center, is flanked by *Hercules Bearing the Globe* and *Hercules Resting*, and various other episodes are depicted in grisailles (the snakes, the lion, the Hydra, Achelous, Nessus, and the funeral pyre). Guido Reni magnified the hero's muscular power in a series of four paintings (1617 and 1620, Paris: the Hydra, Achelous, Nessus, and the funeral pyre). Zubarán painted one of the most complete ensembles (ten canvases, 1637, Madrid, Prado), and Rubens planned four subjects for the Torre de la Prada (1636–38: *Hercules and the Hydra*, London, Courtauld Institute; *Hercules and Cerberus*, Madrid, Prado; *The Apotheosis of Hercules*, Brussels, Musées Royaux des Beaux-Arts; and an extremely rare subject, Hercules' dog discovering *The Tyrian Purple*, (Bayonne, Musée Bonnat).

Hercules Killing the Stymphalian Birds. Detail from Émile-Antoine Bourdelle, *Herakles the Archer*, 1909. Paris, Musée d'Orsay.

There are very many representations of isolated themes. Noteworthy among the principal themes are: the infant Hercules strangling Juno's two snakes (Annibale Carracci, c. 1600, Paris, Louvre), the battle with Achelous, Hercules bringing Alcestis up from Hades to the palace of Admetus, the fight between Hercules and Antaeus, Hercules shouldering the vault of the sky, Hercules recovering the cattle that Cacus stole from him, and Hercules fetching Cerberus from Hades. Geryon's murder and the theft of his cattle were relatively infrequently represented by modern artists, but they were illustrated by Langetti (1625–76, Vienna, Kunsthistorisches Museum); Hercules freed Hesione from the rock to which she was chained and succeeded in gathering the Golden Apples of the Hesperides. This subject is relatively infrequent but endures into the twentieth century (Desvaillières, Paris, Musée d'Orsay). Hercules' victory over the Hydra is much more frequently represented, especially in Italian painting and in sculpture

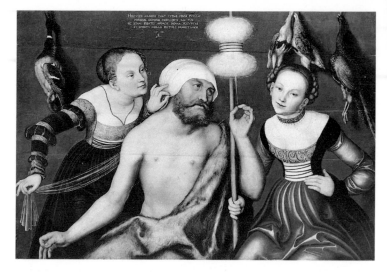

**Hercules
and Omphale.**
Lucas Cranach,
1532.
Formerly
Göttingen,
destroyed 1945.

(Puget, c. 1670, Rouen, Musée des Beaux-Arts). The adventure with the Nemean Lion is found in both painting and sculpture (Giulio Romano, after a model from antiquity, c. 1530, Mantua, Palazzo del Tè). The two most popular subjects since the sixteenth century are, however, Hercules and Omphale, an example of the world turned topsy-turvy or of sexual ambiguity and transvestism (Lucas Cranach, 1537, Brunswick, Herzog Anton-Ulrich Museum; Luca Giordano, 1670, Dresden, Gemäldegalerie; François Le Moyne, 1724, Paris, Louvre), and the parable of Prodicus, which is treated as a moral allegory (Veronese, *Allegory of Virtue and Vice*, c. 1580, New York, Frick Collection, and Annibale Carracci, *Hercules at the Crossroads*, c. 1596, Naples, Galleria di Capodimonte).

Along the same lines as a moral allegory is Rubens' *Heroic Virtue (Hercules) Overcoming Discord*, which served as a pendant to *Prudence (Minerva) Conquering Sedition* (1630–34, London, ceiling of Banqueting House, Whitehall).

Hercules was a symbol of not only physical strength but also earthly glory. He marches in front of the chariot of Fame in a majolica from Castel Durante (c. 1490, London, Victoria and Albert Museum). He has served as a model for some modern rulers (especially French king Henri IV) who had themselves represented with a club and lionskin (cameo, end of the sixteenth century, Paris, Bibliothèque Nationale de France, Cabinet des Médailles; polychrome enamel, Écouen, Musée National de la Renaissance).

Attributes: Bow. Club. Lionskin.

Cross-references: Achelous. Alcestis. Amazons. Antaeus. Atlas. Busiris. Cacus. Centaurs. Cerberus. Deianira. Hylas. Juno. Milky Way. Philoctetes. Prometheus. Triton.

Sources: Diodorus Siculus, IV, 11-27. Apollodorus, *The Library* II, 4, 8–7, 8. Xenophon, *Memorabilia* II, 1, 21 (Prodicus's parable).

Bibliography: F. Brommer, *Herakles* I, II, Darmstadt, 1979, 1983. R. Volkommer, *Herakles in the Art of Classical Greece*, Oxford, 1988. J.-P. Uhlenbrock, *Herakles, Passage of the Hero through 100 Years of Classical Art*, ex. cat. Bard College, 1986. *The Loves of the Gods*, ex. cat., Fort Worth, 1992, nos. 23, 33, 42, 54. E. Panofsky, "Hercules am

Scheidewege," *Studien der Bibliothek Warburg,* Leipzig, 1930. Tietze-Conrat, "Notes on Hercules at the Crossroads," *Journal of the Warburg and Courtauld Institutes* 14 (1951): 304–7.

HERMAPHRODITUS

Gk. and Ger. Hermaphroditos; Lat. Hermaphroditus; It. Ermafrodito; Sp. Hermafrodita; Fr. Hermaphrodite.
Mythical character with a double nature (both masculine and feminine).

HISTORY/MYTHOLOGY

Hermaphroditus's name was created from those of his parents, Hermes and Aphrodite (Mercury and Venus). He was originally a male youth of exceptional beauty living in Asia Minor. One of Diana's nymphs, Salmacis, fell in love with him when he went bathing in her lake, however, and when Hermaphroditus spurned her embraces, Salmacis begged the gods to unite their two bodies. Her wish was granted and the two became one: a being both male and female.

By extension, the term hermaphrodite designates all bisexual beings, and is sometimes applicable to Priapus and Cupid (Eros).

REPRESENTATIONS

Hermaphroditus appears in the procession of Bacchus in Hellenistic reliefs and Pompeian frescoes (House of O. Rufus). He often stands alone, either nude or lifting up his garment to expose his genitals. He is aggressed by a satyr, who mistakes him for a woman, in several representations. Sculptures of Hermaphroditus portray him lying face down on a bed; the most famous version of this model, which dates to the second century B.C. and is now in the Louvre, formerly formed part of the Borghese collection and was restored by Bernini.

Two scenes occur in baroque painting, both painted by Francesco Albani: Salmacis falling in love with Hermaphroditus (c. 1660, Rome, Galleria Borghese) and Salmacis kissing Hermaphroditus in the water (1660, Turin, Pinacoteca); the second has been known since the Renaissance (Jan Gossaert, beginning of the sixteenth century, Rotterdam, Museum Boymans van Beuningen; Bartholomeus Spranger, c. 1581, Vienna, Kunsthistorisches Museum).

Attributes: Bisexuality.

Sleeping Hermaphrodite.
Second century B.C.
Paris, Louvre.

Cross-references: Priapus.

Sources: Ovid, *Metmorphoses* IV, 285–388.

Bibliography: F. Haskell and N. Penny, *Taste and the Antique*, New Haven and London, 1982, pp. 234–5.

HERMES *Greek name for* Mercury.

HERO AND LEANDER

Gk. Hero, Leandros; Lat. and Ger. Hero, Leander; Sp. Hero, Leandro; Fr. Héro, Léandre; It. Èno, Leàndro.
Legendary characters.

HISTORY/MYTHOLOGY

The youth Leander lived in Abydos on the southern banks of the Black Sea and fell in love with Hero, a priestess of Venus. Hero lived on the opposite shore, at Sestos, and each night Leander would swim out to join her, guided by the lantern she lit. One evening, however, a storm put out the lantern and Leander drowned; Hero was overcome by grief and threw herself into the sea.

REPRESENTATIONS

The legend's two heroes appear on Imperial Roman coins from Abydos and Sestos; Hero is at the top of a tower, and Leander is below, swimming.

  The subject was enormously popular in the seventeenh century, especially in Italian painting; there are versions by Annibale Carracci

Hero and Leander. Théodore Chassériau, sketch, c. 1840–41. Paris, Louvre.

(1597–1600, Rome, Palazzo Farnese), Luca Giordano (priv. coll.), and Carpioni (seven examples with one in Dijon, Musée des Beaux-Arts). Rembrandt owned a version, now lost, painted by Rubens. Artists generally portrayed Leander swimming out to Hero in her tower; sometimes Nereids carry the drowned Leander while Hero throws herself into the sea (Domenico Fetti, seventeenth century, Vienna, Kunsthistorisches Museum).

Sources: Musaeus, *Hero and Leander*. Ovid, *Heroides* 18, 19.

HERSE *See* Aglauros. Mercury.

HESPERIDES *See* Hercules.

HESTIA *Greek name for* Vesta.

HIPPODAMIA *See* Pelops.

HIPPOLYTA *See* Amazons. Hercules.

HIPPOLYTUS *See* Phaedra.

HOMER

Gk. and Sp. Homero; Lat. Homerus; It. Omero; Fr. Homère; Ger. Homeros.
Greek epic poet (ninth century B.C.).

Homer.
Rembrandt van Rijn, 1663.
The Hague, Mauritshuis.

HISTORY/MYTHOLOGY

The two epic monuments in Greek literature, *The Iliad* and *The Odyssey*, are each attributed to the mythic poet Homer, who is believed to have been born in the ninth century B.C. and to have died on the island of Ios, after traveling throughout the Mediterranean world. Homer is traditionally portrayed as a highly venerated, elderly, blind man who recites his epic poems before an audience drawn from all parts of Greece. His name derives from his impairment: Homer means "blind" in the Cymean dialect.

REPRESENTATIONS

Homer is shown as blind in all the many ancient busts and sculpted figures traditionally identified as him. He wears the traditional philosopher's band around his head in herm figures in the Louvre, Paris, and in the Musei Capitolini, Rome. He is shown as a blind man walking with the aid of a staff in a marble statue discovered at Herculaneum and now in Naples.

The Apotheosis of Homer.
Jean-Auguste-Dominique Ingres, 1827.
Paris, Louvre.

Homer has been a popular subject in modern times. Painters depict him singing verse to the accompaniment of a lyre or sometimes a violin, or they illustrate events from the legendary poet's life. A maiden supports the elderly Homer and serves as his guide after fishermen abandon him in *Homer on the Island of Chio* (Gérard, nineteenth century, known through an engraving by Massard); in representations of Homer being bitten by dogs, the poet may be accompanied by a young man, a shepherd named Claucaus, who pulls him away from his flock's dogs (sculptural group by Clodion in terracotta, 1810, Paris, Louvre). The subject of an elderly person being accompanied by another in each of the above works is related to Belisarius and Oedipus, who were each guided by a young man or a maiden. This motif was particularly popular in the years 1790–1820.

The iconography of Homer is more symbolic than anecdotal in large-scale compositions. This is true of Ingres' *Apotheosis of Homer* (1827, Paris, Louvre), a work that retraces the history of human genius by surrounding the Greek poet with portraits of his spiritual progeny from the arts and literature. An influential work, Ingres' painting inspired other academic artists, who used precise archaeological reconstructions in their attempts to situate the poet in his original context (Leloir, *Homer*, Salon of 1841, Paris, Louvre).

Cross-references: Troy.

Sources: Herodotus (attributed to), *Life of Homer*. Mme Dacier, *Essai dur la vie, les écrits et le savoir d'Homère*, 1779.

HOOVES *See* Centaurs (horse). Faun (goat). Satyrs.

HORATII

Lat. and Ger. Horatii; It. Orazi; Fr. Horaces.
Legendary Romans (seventh century B.C.).

HISTORY/MYTHOLOGY

The war between Rome and Alba marked the reign of Tullus Hostilius (672–640 B.C.). As a way out of the conflict, each city chose three champions: the Horatii for Rome and the Curiatii for the Alba. After two of the Horatii brothers were killed in the combat, the third pretended to flee but then killed each of the Curiatii in turn. As it happened, the Horatii's sister, Camilla, was betrothed to one of the Curiatii, and when her brother returned triumphantly to Rome with the spoils of his victory, she recognized an object that had belonged to her betrothed. Horatius spotted her overcome by tears and drove his sword through her crying, "Behold how any Roman who mourns the enemy should die." Horatius was tried for murder but acquitted by the people.

The ancient account inspired Corneille's celebrated tragedy, *Horace*, and was later embellished; the oath that the Horatii swear before their father—to win or die—for example, appeared in Rollin's *Roman History*, a much-consulted work in the eighteenth century.

The Horatii.
Detail from
Jacques-Louis David,
The Oath of the Horatii,
study, 1784.
Bayonne,
Musée Bonnat.

REPRESENTATIONS

Three elements of the Horatii legend inspired modern painters: the oath sworn by the brothers in their father's presence, the battle, and the murder of Camilla.

The first subject is rare, but was selected by David for the most celebrated example of French neoclassicism, *The Oath of the Horatii* (1784, Paris, Louvre), which expresses the triumph of public interest over self-interest by establishing a contrast between the male figures, held taut by their unified gesture, and the women, limp with grief.

The battle scene itself was fairly often represented in the sixteenth and seventeenth centuries, notably by Italian artists (for example, Paris Bordone, 1500–71, Vienna, Kunsthistorisches Museum). Horatius killing his sister, however, appears to have predominated representations from the seventeenth through the first half of the nineteenth centuries. Inspired directly by Corneille's tragedy (act 4, scene 5), the subject aroused the spectator's emotions by having the

Horatius Killing His Sister.
Jean-Louis-François Lagrenée,
1753.
Rouen,
Musée des Beaux-Arts.

two characters evoke the limit of their separate passions; this was translated successfully into painting by Lagrenée, whose Horatius points an accusing finger (1753, Rouen, Musée des Beaux-Arts), and by Girodet, whose Horatius flashes the fratricidal sword (1787, Montargis, Musée Girodet).

Attributes: Battle. Swords (broadswords).

Sources: Livy, *History of Rome* I, 24–6.

HORATIUS COCLES

Lat. and Ger. Horatius Cocles; Fr. Horatius Coclès.
Legendary Roman hero.

HISTORY/MYTHOLOGY

During the war between the Romans and Etruscans in 507 B.C., Horatius Cocles was the sole defender of the Sublician Bridge, which Porsena's soldiers threatened to cross. He successfully held the Etruscans at bay until the Romans could demolish the bridge. He then dived into the Tiber, complete with armor, and swam to safety on the opposite bank. Horatius lost an eye in the battle and for this earned the name Cocles, or "one-eyed."

REPRESENTATIONS

Horatius Cocles became a model of self-sacrificing patriotism, and a medal with his image was struck in the Antonine period to encourage soldiers to resist the enemy.

He was a very popular subject in the Renaissance, when he was often grouped with Marcus Curtius and Mucius Scaevola, as demonstrated in mid-sixteenth-century Florentine chests in the Rijksmuseum, Amsterdam, and by Pinturiccio's decorative program (c. 1500, Rome, Palazzo della Rovere Colona). In addition, in a number of Roman interiors, Horatius is represented with weapons in hand

Horatius Cocles.
Charles Le Brun, 1642.
London, Dulwich Picture Gallery.

Orion.
Detail from Nicholas Poussin, *Blind Orion Searching for the Rising Sun*, 1658.
New York, Metropolitan Museum of Art.

The Death of Orpheus.
Emile Lévy, 1866.
Paris, Musée d'Orsay.

or swimming across the Tiber. Such depictions were often inspired by fifteenth- and sixteenth-century illuminated manuscripts of Livy. Marcus Curtius and Horatius Cocles also appear in the painted decorations of Nuremberg Town Hall (1622); the iconography of these heroes continued into the seventeenth century (Charles Le Brun, 1642, London, Dulwich Picture Gallery).

Attributes: Bridge. River.

Cross-references: Marcus Curtius. Mucius Scaevola.

Sources: Livy, *History of Rome* II, 10.

HORNS *See* Achelous. Actaeon (stag). Faun. Io. Muses (Melpomene: animal horn as musical instrument). Ocean. Satyrs.

HORSE *See* Bellerophon (winged). Castor and Pollux. Centaurs (body of horse). Chiron (body of horse). Cloelia. Hecate. Hercules. Marcus Curtius (rearing). Pegasus (winged).

HOURS *See* Seasons.

HUNT

A large number of myths center around the theme of the hunt, and one might say that most Greek heroes at one time or another were heroes of the hunt. The hunt educated heroes on how to master the savage world and confront the most ferocious animals; it also initiated the hero into the arts of cunning and war. Diana, along with her companions, the nymphs, was the supreme huntress.

Hunting was also a perilous activity: accidents could precipitate a hunter's death (Adonis), the hunter could be mistaken for the hunted (Cephalus), or a quarrel could break out between two hunters (Meleager). The metaphor of the hunt as the pursuit of love sometimes entailed tragic reversals, as in the deaths of Procris and Actaeon.

Cross-references: Actaeon. Adonis. Atalanta. Centaurs. Cephalus. Chiron. Diana. Meleager.

HYACINTHUS

Gk. and Ger. Hyakinthos; Lat. Hyacinthus; It. Giacinto; Sp. Hiacinto; Fr. Hyacinthos.
Legendary Spartan prince.

HISTORY/MYTHOLOGY

Hyacinthus was the son of Oebalus, king of Sparta. The youth's beauty seduced Apollo, who would have made him his lover had it not been for a fatal accident: the god was in training one day when the discus he threw struck the young man in the head and killed him. Apollo mourned

Hyacinthus and caused the flower that bears the young prince's name, the hyacinth, to spring from the blood that spilled onto the grass.

REPRESENTATIONS

In Greek art, Hyacinthus is shown astride Apollo's swan (cup, around 500 B.C., Paris, Louvre).

In a painting by Rubens (1636, Madrid, Prado), he lies spread out on the grass with his head near the fatal discus, while Apollo tries to revive him.

Cross-references: Apollo.

Sources: Ovid, *Metamorphoses* X, 162–219; Philostratus, *Imagines* I, 24.

HYLAS

Gk., Lat., Fr. and Ger. Hylas; Sp. Hilas.
Mythical character.

HISTORY/MYTHOLOGY

Hylas was a young man who accompanied Hercules on the voyage of the Argonauts. He was sent ashore to search for water and came upon a spring, where his beauty so charmed the nymphs that they engulfed him. Hercules heard him cry out and searched for him in vain while the Argonauts continued on their way.

REPRESENTATIONS

The subject appears in both Hellenistic and Roman art, particularly in Pompeian painting (House of the Epheboi): the youth is near a spring and tries to break free from the nymphs, who have grabbed hold of him.

A preparatory sketch suggests that the subject interested Giulio Romano for a painting that is now lost (c. 1530, Vienna, Albertina). Bertel Thorwaldsen sculpted the subject (1831, Copenhagen, Thorwaldsens Museum), and John William Waterhouse painted it (1896–97, Manchester, City Art Gallery).

Attributes: Pitcher.

Cross-references: Argonauts. Hercules.

Sources: Ovid, *Metamorphoses* VII, 1 ff. Theocritus, *Idyll* XIII. Virgil, *Eclogues* VI, 44 ff.

Bibliography: R. Ling, "Hylas in Pompeian Art," *Mélanges de l'École française de Rome. Antiquité* 91 (1979): 773-816.

HYPNOS

Gk., Fr., and Ger. Hypnos; Lat. Somnus/Sopor; Sp. Hypnos/Hipnos; It. Somno.
God of sleep.

HISTORY/MYTHOLOGY

Hypnos (Sleep) and his brother, Thanatos (Death), were sons of Night and lived in Hades near Lethe, the river of Forgetfulness. Hypnos's son was Morpheus, the god of dreams.

REPRESENTATIONS

Hypnos was a young man endowed with wings. He may appear in Attic ceramics as a miniature figure crouching down beside another who is asleep or as a figure accompanied by an old and bearded Thanatos. Hypnos and Thanatos together removed dead warriors from the battlefield, most notably Sarpedon after he was stripped of his armor (krater by Euphronius, c. 510 B.C., New York, Metropolitan Museum of Art). In Hellenistic and Roman sculpture, Hypnos has small wings on his head and holds a poppy.

The kingdom of Hypnos was a subject in Renaissance (Primaticcio, c. 1544, Château de Fontainebleau) and baroque painting. Giulio Carpioni portrayed Iris paying a visit to Hypnos (mid-seventeenth century, Budapest, Szépmüvészeti Múzeum). In a painting by Toussaint Dubreuil, Cybele awakens Hypnos while Night takes flight. Hypnos is surrounded by Night's attributes of an owl and masks (c. 1600, Château de Fontainebleau); in the background are the god's children: Morpheus, Phobetor (Nightmare), and Phantasus (god of dreams).

Attributes: Mask. Owl. Poppy. Wings.

Cross-references: Iris. Sarpedon.

Sources: Ovid, *Metamorphoses* XI, 592–615, 633–75 (Morpheus).

Bibliography: *De Nicolo dell'Abate à Nicolas Poussin*, ex. cat., Meaux, 1988, no. 5, pp. 59–61.

Hypnos and Thanatos.
Lekythos, c. 430 B.C.
London,
British Museum.

ICARUS

Gk. and Ger. Ikaros; Lat. Icarus; It. and Sp. Icaro; Fr. Icare.
Legendary character.

HISTORY/MYTHOLOGY

Icarus, the son of Daedalus, was imprisoned with his father in the labyrinth that Daedalus had designed to contain the Minotaur. To

The Fall of Icarus.
Carlo Saraceni,
seventeenth century.
Naples,
Galleria di Capodimonte.

make their escape, Daedalus fabricated wings of feathers held together by wax. He advised his son to follow him, and to fly neither too high nor too low. However, Icarus became overconfident and flew too near the sun, which melted the wax, and he fell to earth.

REPRESENTATIONS

The fall of Icarus appears frequently in Roman art: in sweeping seascapes, on reliefs, and on gems, which show Icarus alone in flight.

Sebastiano del Piombo took up the theme of Daedalus and Icarus at the Farnesina (1511, Sala di Galatea), as did Giulio Romano at Mantua (1546, lost). A painting by Pieter Bruegel the Elder reduces the fall of Icarus to a detail within a large panorama that depicts a peasant at work (1558, Brussels, Musées Royaux d'Art et d'Histoire).

The subject underscored the virtues of moderation, but in some allegories it also represented the difficulties of spiritual ascent. Icarus is grouped with Phaëthon, Ixion, and Tantalus in a series of fallen figures (engravings by Golzius, 1588, after Corneliz van Haarlem).

Attributes: Wings.

Cross-references: Daedalus. Ixion. Phaethon. Tantalus.

Sources: Ovid, *Metamorphoses* VII, 183–235.

Bibliography: P. von Blanckenhagen, "Daedalus and Icarus on Pompeian Walls," *Römische Mitteilungen* 70 (1968): 106–43.

INO *See* Bacchus. Cadmus. Juno. Phrixus.

IO

Lat., Gk., Fr., and Ger. Io.
Young girl metamorphosed into a heifer.

HISTORY/MYTHOLOGY

The striking beauty of Io, the daughter of the river god Inachus, so seduced Jupiter that he turned himself into a cloud so he could escape Juno's jealous watch and make love to the girl, whom he then turned into a heifer. Juno, however, asked her husband to give her the heifer as a gift and then set the hundred-eyed Argus to watch over it. Jupiter in turn sent Mercury to liberate Io, which the messenger-god did by putting Argus to sleep and then killing him. Juno retaliated by sending a gadfly, which chased the crazed heifer all the way to Egypt, where Io reverted to human form and was worshiped by a cult similar to the one devoted to Isis.

REPRESENTATIONS

In archaic art, Io is shown as a heifer guided by Argus, until the fifth century B.C., when she becomes a horned woman. She appears as a woman seated on a rock between Argus and Mercury in a fresco from the House of Livy (first century, Rome).

In Correggio's series, *The Loves of Jupiter*, Io makes love with the cloud (1531, Vienna, Kunsthistorisches Museum). Andrea Schiavone painted *Jupiter and Io Spied upon by Juno* (sixteenth century, St. Petersburg, Hermitage).

Io and Jupiter.
Antonio da Correggio, 1531.
Vienna, Kunsthistorisches Museum.

Attributes: Heifer. Horns.

Cross-references: Argus. Juno. Jupiter. Mercury.

Sources: Ovid, *Metamorphoses* I, 583–663, 724–50.

IOLAUS *See* Hercules.

IOLE *See* Hercules.

IPHIGENIA

Gk. and Ger. Iphigeneia; Lat. Iphigenia; It. and Sp. Ifigenia; Fr. Iphigénie.
Legendary princess.

HISTORY/MYTHOLOGY

Iphigenia was the daughter of Clytemnestra and Agamemnon, king of Mycenae. She was a young girl when, upon the advice of the prophet Calchas, her father agreed to sacrifice her on Diana's altar to appease the angry goddess, who kept the Achaean fleet from leaving Aulis for Troy. She was summoned to Aulis on the pretence that she was to marry Achilles, but Diana substituted her there with a deer at the crucial moment. Having been spared, she became a priestess of Artemis at Tauris, in the Crimea, where she was assigned the task of sacrificing all strangers stranded on the surrounding coast. One day she recognized among the strangers her brother Orestes and his friend Pylades, who were sent to steal the cult statue; she gave them the effigy and then fled with them to Greece.

The Sacrifice of Iphigenia.
Giovanni Battista Tiepolo, Fresco, 1757.
Vicenza, Villa Valmarana.

REPRESENTATIONS

Iphigenia was not enormously popular in the iconography of ancient Greece, and was better represented in southern Italy and later in Rome. Among the heroine's adventures, those that took place in Tauris were most often highlighted by artists.

Iphigenia (identified by inscription) is shown being led to the sacrificial altar in a white-ground lekythos attributed to Douris (c. 470 B.C., Museo di Palermo). The most important representation of this subject is lost: a mid-fourth-century B.C. work that Pliny described as the masterpiece of Timanthus, a Greek painter from Kythnos. Often cited as a model for the expression of grief, the painting appears to have been influential throughout Roman times. A mosaic from Ampurias and a painting from the House of the Tragic Poet at Pompeii (first century A.D.) are thought to have been influenced by this lost work. They show Iphigenia, half-naked and with arms raised, being led to the altar by Ulysses and Diomedes; Calchas stands on the right while Agamemnon, at left and veiled, turns away from the scene. Iphigenia is carried off by a deer toward the sky, where Diana awaits her. A very similar scene is represented in a mosaic from Ampurias (Spain, first century A.D. or end of the Imperial period). The fact that the sacrifice itself has never been represented is noteworthy. An Apulian krater shows Iphigenia, whose shadow doubles for that of a deer, advancing towards the altar while Agamemnon raises a large knife in preparation for the sacrifice (370–355 B.C., London, British Museum).

Iphigenia's adventure in Tauris, a subject not treated in Greek art, also inspired Apulian painters. The arrival of the prisoners Orestes and Pylades, their meeting with Iphigenia, the message from the Delphic oracle enjoining them to steal the statue of Diana, and the flight of the protagonists, were all subjects in ceramics. The characters are shown in a temple, which occupies the center of the image. The heroine is usually richly dressed, covered with jewels, and wearing a long veil; she often holds a large key or the message she must relay to Pylades.

In Roman art, it is largely mural paintings from Herculaneum and Pompeii (first century A.D.) and sarcophagi (second century A.D.) that narrate the different events taking place at Tauris: the arrival of Orestes and Pylades, who are led in chains before Iphigenia, the recognition of Orestes, and the three heroes' escape by boat.

In modern times, the sacrifice has unquestionably most captured the attention of artists. Diana is often shown in a cloud making the deer appear. The subject was frequently treated in eighteenth-century Italian and French art. Notable are a painting by Sebastiano Ricci (Venice, Academia) and a painted ceiling by Domenico Carvi for the Palazzo Borghese in Rome. Tiepolo treated the theme as a cycle several times, most importantly in the Sala d'Ifigenia of the Villa Valmarana (1757), near Vicenza, where the ceiling portrays Diana and Aeolus and where *The Sacrifice of Iphigenia* and the *Greek Fleet at Aulis* decorate the walls. In France, Charles Le Brun, Charles-Antoine Coypel, and Carle van Loo illustrated the myth. Iphigenia's recognition of Orestes and Pylades appears in some rare Flemish and German works (Pieter Lastman, seventeenth century, Amsterdam, Rijksmuseum).

Attributes: Key. Message. Veil.

Cross-references: Agamemnon. Orestes.

Sources: Euripides, *Iphigenia in Aulis*, *Iphigenia in Tauris*. Ovid, *Metamorphoses* XII, 24–38. Pliny the Elder, XXXV, 73 (painting by Timanthes).

IRIS

It. Iride; Lat., Gk., Ger., and Fr. Iris
Personification of the rainbow.

HISTORY/MYTHOLOGY

Iris was the Harpies' sister and therefore a descendant of Ocean. She personified the rainbow, the link between Heaven and Earth, and accordingly served as messenger to the gods, especially Juno, who sent her and others to end Dido's torment. Iris intervenes in *The Iliad* by rescuing Venus from battle after Diomedes wounds the goddess of love.

REPRESENTATIONS

Iris appears alone or at divine assemblies in Attic ceramics; she is winged and holds a caduceus, an object that distinguishes her from Victory (skyphos by the Kleophrades Painter, c. 500 B.C., Florence, Museo Archeologico); she sometimes holds a pitcher for pouring libations.
    She is identifiable in modern representations through her wings and rainbowlike nimbus. She awakens Sleep in a painting by Carpioni (*Iris, Messenger in the Realm of Hypnos*, 1555–60, Budapest, Szépmüvészeti Múzeum). She rescues the wounded Venus in a painting by Vien (1775, Ohio, Columbus Museum), a work inspired by a description by Caylus, the celebrated eighteenth-century art and archeology critic who suggested the composition and coloring according to Homer's text. Rodin sculpted several heads of Iris, as well as a headless *Iris, Messenger of the Gods* (c. 1890, Paris, Musée Rodin).

Attributes: Caduceus. Pitcher. Rainbow. Wings.

Cross-references: Dido. Harpies. Hypnos. Juno.

Sources: Ovid, *Metamorphoses* XI, 585–91. Virgil, *Aeneid* IV, 694–705.

Bibliography: *The Loves of the Gods*, ex. cat., Fort Worth, 1992, no. 62, pp. 496–9.

IVY *See* Bacchantes. Bacchus. Silenus (crown).

IXION

It. Issione; Lat., Ger., and Fr. Ixion.
Legendary king.

HISTORY/MYTHOLOGY

**Ixion Condemned
to the Wheel for Eternity.**
First century B.C.
Pompeii, House
of the Vettii.

Ixion was a particularly cruel and violent Thessalonian king. He slew his father-in-law rather than give him the dowry he had promised. Faithless and sacrilegious, no one but Jupiter would consent to purify him. The god freed Ixion from his madness and gave him the gods' ambrosia to drink, but Ixion relapsed and tried to seduce Juno. Jupiter retaliated by shaping a cloud to resemble the goddess, and Ixion made love to it; the centaurs' father, Centaurus, resulted from this union. Jupiter punished the sacrilege by attaching Ixion to a wheel that turns eternally in either the sky or Tartarus.

Ixion, King
of the Lapiths,
Tricked by Juno.
Peter Paul Rubens,
c. 1615.
Paris, Louvre.

REPRESENTATIONS

Ixion is shown attached to a wheel (Attic cup, c. 500 B.C., Geneva, Musée d'Art et d'Histoire), sometimes surrounded by the Furies (Campanian amphora, c. 320 B.C., Berlin, Staatliche Museen). He appears between Sisyphus and Tantalus on the shorter side of a Roman sarcophagus (c. A.D. 170, Rome, Vatican).

Modern artists have followed Ovid and grouped Ixion with the other great sinners: Tantalus, Tityus, and Sisyphus (Ribera, 1632, Madrid, Prado). Rubens represented the mock coupling of Ixion and Juno (c. 1615, Paris, Louvre).

Attributes: Wheel.

Cross-references: Centaurs. Furies. Sisyphus. Tantalus. Tityus.

Sources: Ovid, *Metamorphoses* IV, 461. Pindar, *Pythian Odes* II, 22–44.

Janus.
Silver denarius,
119 B.C.
Paris, Bibliothèque
Nationale de France,
Cabinet
des Médailles.

JANUS

Lat. and Fr. Janus; It. Giano; Sp. Jano; Ger. Ianus.
Roman divinity.

HISTORY/MYTHOLOGY

Janus was an archaic Roman divinity. His name is linked to *janua*, or gate, and he was the guardian of passages and boundaries, as well as the protector of beginnings. He lent his name to the first month of the year, *Januarius*. An enclosure in the Roman Forum, consisting of a vaulted passage closed only during times of peace, was consecrated to him.

REPRESENTATIONS

Janus's double nature—temporal and spatial—translated into a double face (*bifrons*) that looked forward and backward, and it is in this form that he appears on Roman coins.

Full-length representations, which are sometimes endowed with a quadruple face, first appear in the Hadrianic period. Janus's head is sometimes a crowning element on quadrangular pillars (herms).

Renaissance painters used the double face as a symbol to express the past and the future, a function that it also serves on a pillar in Poussin's *Dance of Human Life* (c. 1638, London, Wallace Collection).

A few paintings depict the emperor Augustus closing the doors of the Temple of Janus and offering a sacrifice to the god in celebration of the reestablishment of peace (Louis Boullogne, 1681; Carle van Loo, c. 1750, both in Amiens, Musée des Beaux-Arts).

Attributes: Double face.

Cross-references : Augustus: Double face.

Sources: Suetonius, *Life of Augustus* XXII. Virgil, *Aeneid* VII, 180.

JAR *See* Danaeds (earthenware jar).

Jason.
Gustave Moreau, 1865.
Paris, Musée d'Orsay.

JASON

Gk., Lat., and Ger. Iason; It. Giasone; Sp. and Fr. Jason.
Greek hero.

HISTORY/MYTHOLOGY

Jason is one of the most famous Greek heroes. His father, Aeson, was king of Iolcus in Thessaly until his half-brother, Pelias, dethroned him, and Jason was entrusted to the care of the centaur Chiron, who took charge of his education. Jason returned to Iolcus as an adult to claim his father's heritage and his rightful kingdom. Pelias agreed to restore the kingdom to him in exchange for the Golden Fleece, the skin of the magical ram that had saved Phrixus and which was now in the possession of King Aeëtes of Colchis (on the Black Sea). He organized a sea voyage on the *Argo* and, leading the Argonauts, arrived at Colchis. With the help of Medea, whom he later married, he overcame various obstacles and took the Golden Fleece. He returned to Ioclus, where Medea avenged him by inducing Pelias's daughters to kill their father, and then fled with Medea to Corinth, where he fell in love with Creusa, King Creon's daughter. He was about to repudiate his wife in order to marry Creusa when Medea went mad with jealousy, gave a poisoned robe to Creusa, and killed her and Jason's children.

REPRESENTATIONS

An Attic cup by Douris (c. 480 B.C., Rome, Musei Vaticani) depicts an otherwise unknown episode in the adventures of Jason: the hero is regurgitated by the dragon that protects the Golden Fleece while his protectress, Athena, looks on. Other images conform more to tradition: the hero approaches the Fleece (Attic krater, c. 470 B.C., New York, Metropolitan Museum of Art) or meets King Pelias (Pompeian fresco, House of the Golden Cupids).

The story of Jason occasionally appears on Renaissance *cassoni* (Bartolomeo di Giovanni, end of the fifteenth century, England, priv. coll.). Jason was the subject of a series of twenty-six engravings by René Boyvin, after drawings by Léonard Thiry, which were published in Paris in 1563. Jean-François de Troy created a series of cartoons on the same subject for the Manufacture des Gobelins (first half of the eighteenth century).

Jason with the Golden Fleece.
Bertel Thorwaldsen, 1803–28.
Copenhagen, Thorwaldsens Museum.

Minerva, Jason, and the Dragon.
Cup by Douris, c. 480 B.C.
Rome, Musei Vaticani.

Juno.
From an Attic cup, c. 470 B.C.
Munich, Antikensammlungen.

Cross-references: Argonauts. Chiron. Hylas. Phrixus.

Sources: Apollonius of Rhodes, *Argonautica*. Ovid, *Metamorphoses* VII, 1–400. Pindar, *Pythian Odes* IV.

JUNO

Gk. and Ger. Hera; Lat. and Sp. Juno; It. Giunone; Fr. Junon.
Goddess and wife of Jupiter.

HISTORY/MYTHOLOGY

The daughter of Cronos (Saturn) and Rhea, Juno was both sister and wife to Jupiter, with whom she reigned on Olympus. She was protectress of wives and childbirth, and herself had four children: Vulcan, Mars, Ilithyia, and Hebe. She was above all else, however, the victim of Jupiter's infidelity, and often turned jealous and vindictive. Among those she tormented were her husband's lovers—Io, Semele, and Ino. She hindered Leto in childbirth and also took against Jupiter's children, Bacchus and Hercules. As punishment for her vindictiveness against his children, Jupiter suspended her from the sky; she ultimately acknowledged the existence of Hercules, whose name in Greek means "glory of Hera." Hephaestus (Vulcan) so resented his mother after he was thrown out of Olympus that he gave her a trick chair, which she could not get out of until Bacchus succeeded in bringing Hephaestus back to Olympus.

Juno was, nevertheless, more than just a maligned wife. She could be the object of sacrilegious desire, as when Ixion tried to rape her. To seduce and hold on to Jupiter, she sought help from Venus, who gave her a magical girdle. She was the rival of Venus and Minerva in the Judgement of Paris, and sided with the Greeks during the Trojan War because the shepherd chose Venus; she then tormented Venus's son, Aeneas, when he fled the fallen city.

REPRESENTATIONS

In Greece, Hera (Juno) was particularly venerated at Argos and Samos, as well as at Olympus, where her temple was near that of Zeus and where a head from her cult statue is preserved. As a sovereign goddess, she is often enthroned, which sometimes makes it difficult to distinguish her from Demeter (Ceres). She has a conical hairstyle (*polos*) or wears a crown, and her head is often covered by her cloak. Zeus and Hera are frequently seen as a couple in scenes about sacred marriage (*hiérogamie*), most notably in a small wooden group found at Samos (beginning of the sixth century B.C., Museum of Samos) and in a metope from the Temple of Hera at Selinunte (c. 470 B.C., Palermo, Museo Archeologico). The episode with Hephaestus's trick chair occurs on several vases (krater by the Kleophrades Painter, c. 500 B.C., Paris, Louvre). Hera is distinguishable in the Judgement of Paris through her scepter and the lion that sometimes accompanies her.

Juno was a Roman state divinity and reigned on the Capitoline with Jupiter and Minerva. Thus she appears on Imperial coins that evoke the temple and this triad.

In modern times, Juno appears with Minerva and Venus in representations of the Judgement of Paris. She is sometimes shown watching Jupiter's loves from afar, especially in baroque painting. Her chariot is drawn by peacocks whose tails are decorated with Argus's eyes. She symbolizes Air in allegories of the elements. She symbolizes

Prosperity just as often, and is found in allegories by Veronese (*Juno Pouring Gifts over Venice*, 1553, Venice, Palazzo Ducale) and Tintoretto (*Juno Conferring Power and Nobility on Venice*, 1577, Venice, Palazzo Ducale). Correggio depicted her punishment exactly as *The Iliad* described it: she is suspended by her arms from the sky and her feet are weighted down with anvils (c. 1520, Parma, Camera di San Paolo).

Attributes: Belt. Diadem. Peacock. *Polos*. Pomegranate. Scepter.

Cross-references: Argus. Bacchus. Hercules. Io. Ixion. Jupiter. Leto. Milky Way. Semele. Vulcan.

Sources: Hesiod, *Theogony* 453–506. Homer, *The Iliad* XIV, 153–351 (seduction by Jupiter); XV, 18–21 (punishment). *Homeric Hymn to Hera*. Ovid, *Metamorphoses* I, 722–3 (peacock).

Juno.
Fulgentius Metaforalis, fifteenth century. Rome, Musei Vaticani.

JUPITER

Gk. and Ger. Zeus; It. Giove; Fr. and Lat. Jupiter.
Ruler of Olympus and the greatest god of the Greek and Roman Pantheon.

HISTORY/MYTHOLOGY

Jupiter was the son of Cybele (Rhea) and Saturn (Cronos). Saturn customarily devoured his children as soon as they were born for fear that they would dethrone him, but Rhea saved Jupiter by wrapping a stone in swaddling clothes and having her husband swallow this rather than the child. The nymphs of Mount Ida raised the infant in Crete and nourished him with milk from a goat named Amalthea. Once grown, he allied himself with Metis, and together they forced Cronos to regurgitate all the children he had swallowed, overthrew Cronos and the Titans and formed the generation of Olympian gods, with Jupiter as king. He also fought the monstrous Typhon and the Giants.

As a celestial power, Jupiter mastered lightning, rain, and storms. He was the reigning source of order and justice on Mount Olympus and Earth.

Jupiter's love affairs were lively and complicated. He was the husband of Juno, with whom he conceived Hebe, Ilithyia, and Mars, but had numerous other children through both mortal and divine unions. After swallowing Metis, who would otherwise have supplanted him, he gave birth himself to Minerva. Through Themis, or Order, he brought forth the Seasons and the Fates; through Ocean's daughter Eurynome, the Graces; through Mnemosyne (Memory), the Muses. He fathered Apollo and Diana through Leto, a Titan, and had a daughter, Proserpine, with his sister Ceres.

Jupiter seduced many mortals and often had to resort to metamorphosis to escape Juno's jealousy at his infidelity, becoming a shower of rain (for Danaë), a cloud (for Io), a bull (for Europa), a swan (for Leda), or an eagle (for Ganymede). He sometimes had to take on someone else's identity: a satyr (for Antiope), Diana (for Callisto), or Amphitryon (for Alcmena). When he regretfully revealed his true form to Bacchus's mother, Semele, the lightning emanating from his divine countenance struck her dead.

REPRESENTATIONS

In many images from Olympus and Dodona, Jupiter brandishes his thunderbolt as a weapon against adversaries (fifth century B.C.,

Jupiter Giving Birth to Minerva.
Attic pyxis,
c. 560 B.C.
Paris, Louvre.

Athens, National Museum). He is seen wrestling, especially with Typhon (Chalcidian hydria, c. 550 B.C., Munich, Antikensammlungen) or the Giants (deinos by Lydos, c. 570 B.C., Athens, National Museum). In addition to representations of Jupiter fighting are those that show him enthroned among the gods (cup by Oltos, c. 510, Tarquinia, Museo Archeologico) or reclining at a feast (cup by the Codrus Painter, c. 440 B.C., London, British Museum). He is also seated when he gives birth to Athena (Minerva), who pops out of his head fully armed; standing beside him are the goddesses of childbirth, the Ilithyias, and Hephaestus (Vulcan), who opened Zeus's head with his ax (Attic pyxis by the C Painter, c. 570 B.C., Paris, Louvre). On a cup by Phrynos (c. 570 B.C., London, British Museum), the ruler of Olympus appears twice, giving birth to Athena on one side and receiving Hercules, accompanied by Athena, on another.

The loves of Jupiter were also frequently represented. Zeus (Jupiter) meets Hera (Juno) in a metope from Selinunte (Temple E, c. 470 B.C., Palermo, Museo Archeologico). However, it was Jupiter's extramarital affairs that most often captured artists' attention (see the various entries on Jupiter's partners). From among the nymphs Jupiter pursued, attention should be drawn to Aeginia, daughter of the river Asopus, who is often represented in Attic ceramics (stamnos by the Copenhagen Painter, c. 470 B.C., Rouen, Musée Départemental d'Archéologie). Jupiter abducting Ganymede is the subject of an important terracotta group at Olympus (c. 480 B.C., Olympus Museum).

The gold and ivory statue of Jupiter enthroned, created by Phidias around 450 B.C. for the Temple of Olympus, was one of the seven wonders of the world. Although known only through the ancient descriptions it inspired, this majestic work served as model for the statue of Jupiter Capitolino in Rome, where the god is flanked by Juno and Minerva; it is also found on Imperial Roman coins.

In modern painting, Jupiter nursed by the goat Amalthea was frequently represented from the sixteenth through eighteenth centuries. Among known versions are those by Schiavone (1542–44, Vienna, Kunsthistorisches Museum), Jordaens (1630–35, Paris, Louvre), and Poussin (c. 1635, London, Dulwich Picture Gallery; c. 1639, Berlin, Staatliche Museen, Dahlem Gemäldegalerie), as well as a sculpture by Bernini (c. 1615, Rome, Galleria Borghese). Most representations,

**The Infant Jupiter
Entrusted to Nymphs.**
Courtin,
eighteenth century.
Arras,
Musée des Beaux-Arts.

however, focus on Jupiter's loves (see the entries for the different partners), and these are sometimes treated in cycles: Correggio, for Federico Gonzaga at Mantua (1527–31, now in Vienna, Kunsthistorisches Museum and Rome, Galleria Borghese); Natoire, for the château of the Godefroy Chapel (c. 1730, Troyes, Musée des Beaux-Arts); and Girodet (series of lithographs published in 1825). Giulio Romano devoted a series of paintings to Jupiter's childhood, loves, and rejections (c. 1533; originally twelve paintings of which six survive, at Hampton Court and London, National Gallery). There also exist scenes of sacrifices being made to Jupiter (Giulio Romano, c. 1527–30, frescoes, Mantua, Palazzo del Tè; Noël Coypel, Palace of Versailles, Salle des Gardes de la Reine, end of the seventeenth century). Finally, Jupiter also appears in various allegories, such as those by Dosso Dossi (*Jupiter, Mercury, and Virtue*, c. 1525, Vienna, Kunsthistorisches Museum) and Veronese (*Jupiter Expelling the Vices*, 1553, Paris, Louvre).

Attributes: Beard. Eagle. Scepter. Thunderbolt.

Cross-references: Antiope. Bacchus. Callisto. Danaë. Europa. Ganymede. Hebe. Io. Juno. Leda. Leto. Minerva. Muses. Semele.

Sources: Homer, *The Iliad* XIV, 312–28. Ovid, *Festivals* V, 121–4 (childhood); *Metamorphoses* VI, 103–15 (loves of Jupiter).

Bibliography: *The Loves of the Gods*, ex. cat., Fort Worth, 1992. A.B. Cook, *Zeus*, Cambridge, 3 vols., 1914–40. S. Kaempf-Dimitriadou, *Die Liebe der Götter*. E. Verheyen, "Corregio's Amori de Giove," *Journal of the Warburg and Courtauld Institutes* 29 (1966): 160–92.

KAINEUS *See* Caeneus.

KEYS *See* Hecate. Iphigenia.

KITHARA *See* Apollo.

KNIFE *See* Agamemnon. Fates.

KORA *See* Proserpine.

LABYRINTH *See* Daedalus.

LACHESIS *See* Fates.

LANDSCAPE

Two contrasting traditions in landscape painting have existed since the Renaissance: the rustic landscape, in which humans are absent or are shown in contemporary dress (usually peasants), and what is known as the heroic, historical, or mythological landscape, in which characters are selected from history, Greco-Roman legend, or the Bible. The subject of a landscape is of such minor importance to the representation of nature that it is sometimes hardly identifiable. However, the fact that landscape painting has a subject at all raises it one notch in the hierarchy established by the academic tradition, where it normally holds a next-to-last position, just above still-life painting. As a result, a Prix de Rome for historical landscape painting was established in 1816.

The titles of historical landscape paintings most often allude to the episodes depicted in them.

LANTERN *See* Diogenes. Hero and Leander.

LAOCOÖN

Gk. and Ger. Laokoon; Lat. and Fr. Laocoon; It. Laocoonte; Sp. Laoconte. Priest of Apollo in the legend of Troy.

HISTORY/MYTHOLOGY

Laocoön was a Trojan priest of Apollo who committed sacrilege by making love to a woman in the god's temple. After the Greeks made believe they lifted their siege of Troy by withdrawing their fleet and leaving a wooden horse ashore, Laocoön was about to sacrifice a bull when two huge snakes arose from the waves to strangle his two sons and, when he rushed to their aid, himself also. The Trojans interpreted this as Minerva punishing Laocoön for having opposed the delivery to

Troy of the horse that many believed was an offering to her. With Laocoön dead, the Trojans no longer hesitated and welcomed the Trojan horse, and consequently their demise, into the city.

REPRESENTATIONS

Laocoön's iconography is both celebrated and exceedingly rare. There are two known representations on southern Italian vases (one c. 430 B.C. and the other, fragmentary, c. 300 B.C.; formerly in Ruvo, now lost). The snakes wrap themselves around the father and one son, while the other son lies dead and torn to pieces. Two Pompeian paintings from the first century A.D. depict the story in a dramatic context; one is still *in situ* in the House of Menander. In the center, a snake imprisons Laocoön and menaces his head with its tongue; at the foot of an overturned table, one son still struggles while the other is already dismembered; the sacrificial bull appears in the background. The same scene appears in a manuscript illumination for Virgil's *Aeneid* (fifth century A.D., Rome, Vatican). The work that is universally accepted as the emblematic representation of Apollo's priest, however, is still the marble group discovered in 1506 near Santa Maria Maggiore in Rome. That work was immediately purchased by Pope Julius II and installed in the Belvedere (Rome, Musei Vaticani); it was brought to Paris during the Napoleonic Wars (1797), but restored to the Vatican in 1815. The repercussions of the statue's discovery were enormous, for the work was acknowledged as a masterpiece comparable to the largest Pergamene creations and definitely the group described by Pliny as decorating the Palace of Titus and sculpted in the second century B.C. by Hagesandros, Polydoros, and Athenodoros. This enthusiasm inspired many copies in all sizes and materials, including marble, bronze, terracotta, and carved *pietra dura* (Giovanni Pinchler, 1734–91).

A few rare works predate the Vatican group's discovery. Among them is a drawing by Filippino Lippi (c. 1457–1504) in the Museum of Haarlem. By contrast, many copies or interpretations incorporating the statue appeared after the 1506 excavation. Titian drew inspiration from the group for the pose of a satyr in *Bacchus and Ariadne* (1522–23, London, National Gallery); he also caricatured it by substituting monkeys for the priest and his sons. El Greco reinterpreted the sculpture in a painting that isolates each figure against a background representing Toledo (1610–14, Washington, National Gallery).

Attributes: Snakes.

Cross-references: Troy.

Sources: Pliny the Elder, XXXVI, 37 (statue). Virgil, *Aeneid* II, 199–228.

Bibliography: B. Andreae, *Laocoon und die Gründung Roms*, Mayence, 1989. M. Bieber, *Laocoon: The Influence of the Group since Its Discovery*, Detroit, 1942. F. Haskell and N. Penny, *Taste and the Antique*, New Haven and London, 1982, pp. 243–7. G.E. Lessing, *Laokoon, oder über die Grenzen der Malerei und Poesie*, Berlin, 1766.

Laocoön.
Marble,
first century A.D.
Rome,
Musei Vaticani.

LAOMEDON *See* Hercules.

LAPITHS *See* Centaurs.

LAUREL

The laurel tree is sacred to Apollo. To escape from the god, Daphne was transformed into a laurel tree (*daphne*, in Greek).

Cross-references: Apollo. Augustus. Calliope (crown). Clio (crown). Daphne.

Leda.
After Leonardo
da Vinci,
sixteenth century.
Rome,
Galleria Borghese.

LEDA

Legendary queen.

HISTORY/MYTHOLOGY

Leda, the wife of the Spartan king Tyndareus, was loved by Jupiter, who visited her in the form of a swan. She consequently laid an egg (or two), giving birth to two boys, Castor and Pollux (the Dioscurides), and two girls, Helen and Clytemnestra.

REPRESENTATIONS

In Attic ceramics, Leda's egg is seen on an altar. There are two distinct types of sculpture for Leda: in one, she stands and opens her dress while a swan snuggles up against her (Rome, Musei Capitolini); in the other, she is nude and couples with an enormous swan.

There are many versions of Leda and the swan in Italian Renaissance painting and baroque art. Leonardo da Vinci depicted Leda standing and holding the swan's neck (lost, but known through copies); Michelangelo shows her reclining and welcoming a far more insidious swan (lost, copy by Rosso, 1530, London, National Gallery). The swan's long supple neck was painted in many ways (Correggio, 1531, Berlin, Staatliche Museen); some have erotic connotations and show the swan's head approaching the young woman's genitals (Clément La Belle, *Leda*, 1778, Paris, Louvre). This licentious

Leda and the Swan
Théodore Géricault.
Drawing,
nineteenth century.
Paris, Louvre.

ambiance endured into the nineteenth century, particularly in statuettes, such as *Leda* by Hughes (Paris, Musée d'Orsay). The subject also inspired sculptors, including Bourdelle (1904, relief, Paris, Musée Bourdelle) and Brancusi (1920, Chicago, Art Institute).

Attributes: Swan.

Cross-references: Castor and Pollux. Clytemnestra. Helen. Jupiter.

Sources: Hyginus, *Fabulae*, 77.

Bibliography: *The Loves of the Gods*, ex. cat., Fort Worth, 1992, no. 46.

LEONIDAS

Lat. Leonidas; Fr. Léonidas; It. Leonida; Gk. and Ger. Leonidas.
King of Sparta.

HISTORY/MYTHOLOGY

Leonidas was king of Sparta from 491 to 480 B.C. During the Persian invasion under Xerxes, he defended the pass of Thermopylae, a strategic passageway between Thessaly and Greece. A traitor informed the Persians about how to outflank the defile, but Leonidas nevertheless opted to engage them in battle in hopes of breaking through Xerxes' camp. With three hundred loyal soldiers prepared to die, Leonidas attacked six thousand Persians. He perished along with all his soldiers, and his remains were transported to Sparta, where a tomb was erected in his honor.

REPRESENTATIONS

As with other great deeds from ancient history, Leonidas's heroism has occasionally been represented from the sixteenth through eighteenth centuries. David's depiction is, however, the most celebrated one (completed in 1814, Paris, Louvre). The artist captured the moment prior to the assault led by the handful of fearless Lacedaemonians; the attitudes of the young soldiers manifest a courage and equanimity that corresponds to the ancient ideal of *virtus* as understood by neoclassical

Leonidas.
Detail from
Jacques-Louis David,
*Leonidas
at Thermopylae*,
1813.
Paris, Louvre.

painters. The French Revolution revived an interest in portrayals of Lacedaemonians, who were renowned for their strict and unflinching patriotism.

Sources: Herodotus, VII, 220–24.

Leto and Artemis, with Hermes, beneath the Palm Tree of Delos.
Attic amphora, c. 510 B.C.
Paris, Louvre.

LERNA *See* Hercules.

LETO

Gk., Sp., and Ger. Leto; Lat. and It. Latona; Fr. Léto.
Mythical character.

HISTORY/MYTHOLOGY

Leto became the mother of the twins Apollo and Diana through Jupiter. Juno became jealous and kept her from giving birth for such a long time that she was finally forced to seek refuge on the floating island of Delos, which Jupiter anchored down for the occasion. Leto later incited her children to avenge her against Niobe, who insulted her by boasting that her own progeny was more beautiful than Leto's: with their mother looking on, Apollo and Diana massacred the Niobids. Another story tells how Leto transformed the peasants of Lycia into frogs for having stopped her from drinking water from their lake.

REPRESENTATIONS

Leto, who is sometimes identifiable by her cylindrical hairstyle (*polos*), often serves with Diana to frame Apollo in representations of the Delian triad (many Attic black-figure vases). She sometimes carries her young offspring in her arms (lost originals by Praxiteles and Euphranor, Roman copy, Rome, Museo Torlonia; Hadrianic coins from Ephesus). She also appears behind Apollo and Artemis in the Gigantomachy on the frieze of the Great Altar from Pergamum (second century B.C., Berlin, Antikensammlungen).

The subject of the Lycian peasants transformed into frogs appeared frequently in Italian and Flemish painting from the sixteenth and seventeenth centuries (Tintoretto, c. 1544, Modena, Galleria Estense; Albani, 1660, Dôle, Musée). The same subject inspired a fountain by René Frémin and Jean Thierry for La Granja of the Escorial (1721–38).

Cross-references: Apollo. Diana. Niobe.

Sources: Ovid, *Metamorphoses* VI, 317–81.

LEUCIPPIDAE *See* Castor and Pollux.

LION

The lion accompanies Cybele, who turned Atalanta and Hippomenes into lions after they profaned her temple. Hercules used the Nemean Lion's skin as a garment after he strangled it to death.

Cross-references: Alcestis. Atalanta. Bacchantes. Cybeles. Hercules. Hippomenes. Milon of Croton. Pyramus and Thisbe.

LOOM *See* Arachne. Penelope.

LUCRETIA

Lat. and Ger. Lucretia; It. Lucrezia; Sp. Lucrecia; Fr. Lucrèce.
Historical Roman character (sixth century B.C.).

HISTORY/MYTHOLOGY

Lucretia.
Lucas Cranach, c. 1530.
Munich,
Alte Pinakothek.

According to Livy, the tragic death of Lucretia in 510 B.C. had far-reaching political consequences, for it involved the advent of the Roman Republic. When the Romans besieged Ardea under the command of King Tarquinius Superbus, the king's son, Sextus Tarquinius, proposed to his debauched companions, who included Lucretia's husband, Collatinus, that they return to Rome at night in order to catch their wives by surprise in the middle of their trysts. Only one wife, Lucretia, was found to be beyond reproach. Lucretia's striking beauty and virtue so impressed Sextus Tarquinius, however, that he later returned, forced himself on her hospitality and broke into her bedroom. He then made her succumb by threatening her with blackmail: if she resisted, he would stab her and tell others that, having found her faithless, he only avenged the honor of Collatinus. Lucretia gave in to his demands, but the next day exposed the outrage she endured and killed herself in front of her husband, Valerius, and Brutus.

REPRESENTATIONS

Lucretia has been a frequent source of inspiration to modern artists, who have focused mainly on two episodes from Livy's account: her rape and suicide. Both those subjects usually result in representations of despairing women of stoic virtue: whether Lucretia is facing her aggressor or holding the dagger, her look is one of tragic resignation to her destiny.

The violence of the confrontation in the rape scene varies: Lucretia, seated on the edge of her bed, pushes away her aggressor or more forcefully—but still hopelessly—attempts to break free from his grasp (Tintoretto, *The Violence of Tarquinius*, fifteenth century, Madrid, Prado). Representations of the events leading up to the rape are rare. Gustave Moreau, however, depicted Lucretia nude and inscrutable in the face of her aggressor (1850–55, Paris, Musée Gustave Moreau). When shown at the moment of her suicide, Lucretia is often portrayed half-length and in contemporary dress (Veronese, 1580, Vienna, Kunsthistorisches Museum; Rembrandt, 1664, Washington, National Gallery) or, more rarely, as a full-length nude (Titian, 1523, Hampton Court). She is always armed with a dagger, which she points toward her breast.

Lucretia.
Detail from
Sandro Botticelli,
The Story of Lucretia,
1500.
Boston, Isabella
Stewart Gardner
Museum.

Attributes: Dagger.

Cross-references: Brutus.

Sources: Livy, I, 57–9.

LYRE

In mythology, the lyre is the stringed instrument which Hermes (Mercury) invented as a child and offered to his brother, Apollo, in recompense for having stolen his herd of cattle. It became Apollo's favorite instrument, one that was superior to the flute, which cannot be played while singing and which distorts the face. Several exceptional musicians also played the lyre: Amphion, Arion, and Orpheus.

Cross-references: Amphion. Apollo. Arion. Marsyas. Mercury. Muses. Orpheus. Terpsichore.

MAENADS *See* Bacchantes. Pentheus.

MAIA *See* Mercury.

MANLIUS TORQUATUS

It. Manlio Torquato; Sp. Manlio Torcuato; Fr. and Ger. Manlius Torquatus.
Roman consul and dictator (fourth century B.C.).

HISTORY/MYTHOLOGY

The Roman tribune Titus Manlius earned his surname Torquatus (from *torques,* or collar) when he distinguished himself in the war against the Celts: he overcame a giantlike warrior before whom everyone else retreated, and then stole his golden collar. A stern and principled man, he had his own son executed on the simple excuse that he had killed an enemy without waiting for orders. For this reason, Titus Manlius was denied the customary honors when he returned to Rome.

REPRESENTATIONS

In Germany and the Netherlands, Manlius is portrayed in public buildings as a symbol of rigor and civic duty, as exemplified in the façade of the Ulm Town Hall (sixteenth century). In the decorative program for the Nuremberg Town Hall, Manlius condemning his son is grouped with the Judgement of Solomon and the Last Judgement. Manlius Torquatus also appears in Italian painted decoration, as in the former chapel of the Palazzo Publico in Siena (fifteenth century), near a personification of Fortitude, accompanied by Cato of Utica (Berthélemy, *Manlius Torquatus Condemning His Son to Death*, 1785, Tours, Musée des Beaux-Arts). Easel paintings also depict his son's condemnation, and these works served as a warning to the viewer: Woe to he who acts without orders. In a spectacular fresco in the Loggia del Capitaniato in Vicenza, a captivating low-angle perspective emphasizes the marching soldiers who accompany Manlius, the son's corpse, and the sword the father still holds (Giovanni Antonio Fasolo, 1572).

Cross-references: Cato of Utica.

Sources: Aulus Gellius, IX, 13. Livy, VII, 10; VIII, 7.

MARCUS AURELIUS

Lat. and Ger. Marcus Aurelius; It. and Sp. Marco Aurelio; Fr. Marc Aurèle.
Roman emperor (A.D. 121–180).

HISTORY/MYTHOLOGY

Marcus Aurelius is the prototype of the emperor-philosopher. He impressed Hadrian at a very young age, was adopted by Antoninus Pius, and acceded to the throne in A.D. 161. Ancient documents praising his virtue and magnanimity suggest that he was renowned in his own lifetime for his dedication to Stoic principles. He led military campaigns aimed at pacification at the same time as he wrote several texts, of which only the *Meditations* have come down to us. He died during an expedition in Germany, but biographers are undecided about the cause. Among the possibilities cited are: plague, self-inflicted malnutrition in the name of Stoic convictions, and poisoning, incited by his son, Commodus, who was eager to accede to the throne.

Equestrian Statue of Marcus Aurelius.
Bronze,
end of second century A.D.
Rome, Capitoline.

REPRESENTATIONS

There are ancient portrait-busts in the Vatican, the Uffizi, the Louvre, and other museums. The most famous equestrian statue is that erected on the Capitoline on a pedestal made by Michelangelo, who deeply admired the emperor: Marcus Aurelius, mounted on a horse of colossal proportions, extends his right hand in a gesture that is typical of Roman orators. Three ancient reliefs have long been regarded as portrayals of Marcus Aurelius (c. A.D. 76, Rome, Musei Capitolini).

Several moralizing episodes from the emperor's life have captured the attention of modern artists; they celebrate Marcus Aurelius's generosity toward his people (Vien, *Marcus Aurelius Having Bread and Medicine Distributed to the People*, 1765, Amiens, Musée) as well as his clemency toward enemies. The most frequent subject is the emperor's death: Marcus Aurelius, faithful to the Stoic tradition, speaks his last words before an audience of followers. In a painting by Delacroix, the emperor's benevolent and serene expression is contrasted with the weak and scornful one of his son, Commodus, who is beside him (*The Last Words of Marcus Aurelius*, 1845, Lyon, Musée des Beaux-Arts).

Cross-references: Hadrian.

Sources: Dio Cassius, *Roman History*, 71. Marcus Aurelius, *Mediations*.

Bibliography: Collective, *La Colonna di Marco Aurelio*, Rome, 1955.

Marcus Curtius Flinging Himself into the Gulf.
Marble,
first century A.D.
Rome,
Villa Borghese.

MARCUS CURTIUS

It. Marco Curzio; Sp. Marco Curtio; Fr., Ger., and Lat. Marcus Curtius.
Roman hero.

HISTORY/MYTHOLOGY

According to ancient legend, a chasm opened up on the site of the Roman Forum in the fourth century B.C. Augurs declared that the greatest Roman would need to sacrifice himself to fill the chasm. Marcus Curtius, a young Patrician, took this to mean that someone with fighting spirit was needed and, after consecrating himself to the gods, plunged into the pit armed and on horseback, which immediately closed over him. A small lake along the Sacred Way and between the Curia and the Rostra bears the hero's name and has been connected with this event.

In the twelfth century, an extra element was added to the original story in a collection of memorable deeds called the *Gesta Romanorum*: Curtius knew a year in advance that he would perform a heroic deed. This premonition related his sacrifice to that of Christ.

REPRESENTATIONS

Marcus Curtius is one of the rare Republican heroes to appear in Roman art. In 9 B.C., the emperor Augustus had a relief of the hero placed on the site of the mythical event. The subject is also found on some Imperial Roman gems and lamps.

There are a number of Renaissance murals showing Marcus Curtius. The subject of a rearing horse on the verge of plunging offered spectacular artistic possibilities; sometimes fire is added to the pit, as if it were a volcano. A ceiling by Veronese places the spectator beneath the leaping horse, creating a captivating visual scene (c. 1556, Vienna, Kunsthistorisches Museum). The hero's adventure was abundantly illustrated in other media, including sculpture (Bernini's 1665 equestrian statue of Louis XIV so displeased the king that he ordered Girardon to transform it into a statue of Marcus Curtius, Louvre, Cour Napoléon), engraving (a series of Roman heroes by Goltzius), and ceramics (sixteenth-century southern German enameled stove tiles).

Marcus Curtius is sometimes grouped with other Roman heroes, including Horatius Cocles, Manlius Torquatus, and Scipio Africanus.

Attributes: Fire. Horse (rearing).

Cross-references: Horatius Cocles. Manlius Torquatus. Scipio Africanus.

Sources: Livy, VII, 6, 1–6. Valerius Maximus, V, 6, 2.

Bibliography: S. Hoog, *Le Bernin, Louis XIV, une statue déplacée: une œuvre déplacée*, Paris, 1989.

MARS

Gk. and Ger. Ares; Lat. Mars; It. and Sp. Marto; Fr. Mars.
God of war.

HISTORY/MYTHOLOGY

Mars, the son of Jupiter and Juno, formed part of the second generation of Olympian gods (with Apollo and Mercury). Accompanied by Fear and Panic (Phobus and Deimos), he is the aggressive and cruel epitome of war. He sided with the Trojans during the Trojan War, and clashed with Minerva, who wounded him after taking the appearance of Diomedes. In contrast to Minerva, who defended the arts and represented the positive side of war, Mars was above all violent. He tried in vain to defend his son, Cycnus, a bandit who robbed pilgrims on their way to Delphi, against Hercules, who was aided by Minerva; but once again the goddess wounded the god.

Mars never laid down his arms unless he was in love. His most famous affair was with Venus, whose husband, Vulcan, caught them embracing, trapped them in a huge net, and then exposed them to the ridicule of the other Olympians.

To Romans, Mars was the father of their founding heroes, Romulus and Remus. The god was also associated with spring, the season when war began.

REPRESENTATIONS

Ares (Mars) is infrequently represented in Greek art. He stands beside Aphrodite (Venus) in the procession of gods on their way to

The Triumph of Mars.
Antoine Caron, c. 1570.
New Haven, Yale
University Art Gallery.

Venus, Mars, and Cupid.
Piero di Cosimo,
c. 1505.
Berlin, Staatliche
Museen.

the wedding of Thetis and Peleuson in a krater by Sophilos (c. 580 B.C., London, British Museum). He also appears with the other Olympians in depictions of the Gigantomachy (frieze on the Siphnian Treasury, c. 525 B.C., Delphi). In the struggle between Hercules and Cycnus, he lends a strong hand to his son while Minerva sides with Hercules (Attic oenochoe, c. 560 B.C., Berlin, Staatliche Museen).

In Pompeian painting, Venus and Mars appear together, surrounded by cupids (House of Venus and Mars, first century A.D., Naples, Museo Nazionale). Mars is usually nude in Roman statuary, except for his helmet, shield, and sword (Borghese Ares type, Hadrianic copy, Paris, Louvre). The god is at rest and seated beside his weapons in the Ludovisi Ares (copy from the Antonine period after an original by Scopas, fourth century B.C., Rome, Museo delle Terme).

The love affair between Venus and Mars inspired a number of paintings from the Renaissance onward; works include those by Botticelli (1483, London, National Gallery) and Piero di Cosimo (c. 1505, Berlin, Staatliche Museen). The two lovers meet (Veronese, *Venus and Mars United by Love*, 1580, New York, Metropolitan Museum of Art) or are surprised by Vulcan, who throws a net over them (Tintoretto, *Mars and Venus Surprised by Vulcan*, c. 1555, Munich, Alte Pinakothek). Cupids disarm the god, and the scene functions as an allegory of Peace. Daumier created a delightful caricature of Vulcan's humiliation of the two lovers.

Mars and Venus being caught by surprise was also romantically depicted by such baroque painters as Luca Giordano (seventeenth century, Vienna, Kunsthistorisches Museum) and Boucher (c. 1750, London, Wallace Collection).

In Rubens' *The Horrors of War*, Venus hopelessly tries to restrain Mars while Fury pulls him onward (1637–38, Florence, Palazzo Pitti). David represented Minerva's victory over Mars when the god defended Cycnus (1771, Paris, Louvre).

Attributes: Arms. Dog.

Cross-references: Dimedes. Minerva. Venus. Vulcan.

Sources: Homer, *The Iliad* V, 825 (Diomedes); *The Odyssey* VIII, 266–366. Ovid, *Metamorphoses* IV, 171–89 (Venus and Mars).

MARSYAS

It. Marsia; Sp. Marsias; Fr., Ger., Gk., and Lat. Marsyas.
Satyr and flautist.

HISTORY/MYTHOLOGY

Marsyas, the son of Olympus, was a satyr who lived in Phrygia. It was
he who took hold of the double flute which Minerva invented after she
tossed it away because it made her cheeks puff out when she played.
Marsyas then got so carried away with his own musical talent that he
challenged Apollo to a competition, with the god playing his lyre and
the satyr his flute. King Midas judged the contest and leaned in favor
of the satyr, but the god finally won, for he could play his instrument
backward and Marsyas could not. Marsyas was punished for his arro-
gance by being skinned alive.

REPRESENTATIONS

A sculpted group by Myron reputedly represented Marsyas with
Athena, at the moment when the goddess throws away the flute. The
competition between the satyr and Apollo is found on Attic vases of the
fifth century B.C., but it is not until fourth-century B.C.. Italiot ceramics
that the punishment of Marsyas appears. A Hellenistic sculpture has
him hanging by his arms from a tree (Florence, Uffizi; numerous other
copies). This statue is associated with the *Blade Grinder*, which represents
a Scythian slave sharpening the torturer's knife (Hellenistic original,
Florence, Uffizi).

Renaissance painters revived the motif of a musical competition between wind instruments and string instruments; for them, it symbolized
the contest between sensual and intellectual forms of music. Raphael,
like Titian (c. 1570, Czechoslovakia, Kremsier, Archiepiscopal
Palace), depicted the torture of Marsyas. Titian accentuated the
violence of the subject, however, by showing Marsyas hanging by his
feet and being skinned by Apollo himself. It is this version, faithful to
Ovid's text, that baroque painters favored (Ribera, 1637, Naples, San
Martino; Luca Giordano, c. 1660, Florence, Museo Bardini).

Attributes: Flute.

Cross-references: Apollo. Midas.

Sources: Ovid, *Festivals* VI, 703–8 (invention of the flute);
Metamorphoses VI, 382–400 (torture). Pausanias (statue by Myron).

Bibliography: J.P. Small, *Cacus and Marsyas in Etrusco-Roman
Legend*, Princeton, 1982.

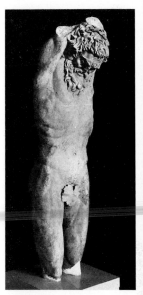

**Marsyas Suspended
from a Tree Trunk.**
Hellenistic sculpture,
c. A.D. 150.
Istanbul, Museum.

Apollo and Marsyas.
Raphael, 1502.
Rome, Vatican.

MASK *See* Bacchus. Hypnos. Muses (Melpomene, Thalia).

MAUSOLUS *See* Artemisia.

MEDEA

Gk. and Ger. Medeia; Lat., It., and Sp. Medea; Fr. Médée.
Legendary sorceress.

Medea about to Kill Her Children.
Eugène Delacroix, 1838.
Lille, Musée des Beaux-Arts.

Medea.
Campanian amphora, c. 370 B.C.
Paris, Bibliothèque Nationale de France.

HISTORY/MYTHOLOGY

Medea, the daughter of King Aeëtes of Colchis, was endowed with magical powers. She helped her husband, Jason, triumph over many obstacles so that he could secure the Golden Fleece. She also enabled the Argonauts to escape from King Aeëtes: after killing her young brother, Apsyrtus, she scattered the pieces of his body and escaped with Jason when her father stopped to gather them up.

The couple arrived in Iolchus, where Medea plotted Jason's revenge against Pelias, who had usurped the throne from his father, Aeson. She began by rejuvenating Aeson by boiling him with magical herbs in a cauldron. She then convinced Pelias's daughters, the Peliades, that the same magic would work its powers on their father, but this time substituted powerless herbs, whereupon Pelias died.

Medea then fled with Jason to Corinth, where her husband grew weary of her and decided to repudiate her in order to marry the king of Corinth's daughter, Creusa. Beside herself with anger and jealousy, Medea pretended to accept the situation but killed the bride by giving her a poisoned robe as a present. She then slew her own children so that Jason would have no descendants.

REPRESENTATIONS

In Greek art, Medea sometimes resembles an oriental princess (Apulian krater, c. 350 B.C., Munich Antikensammlungen). She may appear before a cauldron—rejuvenating Aeson—or setting her trap for the Peliades. She is also seen preparing to leave Corinth in a chariot drawn by dragons after assassinating her children. In a Pompeian fresco, she contemplates the murder of her children, with sword in hand. Several Roman sarcophagi represent various episodes from the story of Medea, especially the death of Creusa, the deaths of Jason's children, and Medea's departure (c. A.D. 150, Rome, Museo delle Terme).

Modern artists were more faithful to Ovid than to Euripides and accentuated Medea's skills as a magician. Medea may be shown rejuvenating Aeson (Vassallo, 1637, Florence, Uffizi) or deceiving Pelias's daughters (Pietro de Mariscalchi, c. 1584, Verona, Museo Civico di Castelvecchio). She holds an important place in a series of twenty-six engravings executed by René Boyvin after Léonard Thiry's drawings for *The Conquest of the Golden Fleece*, which was published in Paris in 1563.

The tragic scene of the children's murder was treated in two drawings by Poussin (c. 1648–50, Windsor) and again by Delacroix (1838, Lille, Musée des Beaux-Arts; 1862, Paris, Louvre).

Cross-references: Jason.

Sources: Euripides, *Medea*. Ovid, *Metamorphoses* VII, 1–452.

Bibliography: M. Meyer, *Medeia und die Peliaden*, Rome, 1980. M. Schmidt, *Der Basler Medeiasarcophag*, Basle, 1969.

MEDUSA *See* Gorgons.

MELEAGER

Gk. Meleagros; Lat. and Ger. Meleager; It. and Sp. Meleagro; Fr. Méléagre.
Greek hero.

HISTORY/MYTHOLOGY

Meleager was the son of Althea and Oeneus, king of Calydon, in Aetolia. It was he who organized a group of youths for the Calydonian boar hunt when Diana sent an enormous bull to ravage the country after Oeneus neglected to make a sacrifice to her. Atalanta was the first to wound the animal, but Meleager finished the kill and was awarded the skin, which he turned over to Atalanta, with whom he was in love. Jealous, Meleager's uncles tried to recuperate the coveted prize but were killed by their nephew in the ensuing skirmish. As it happened, the Fates had announced upon Meleager's birth that he would live as long as a certain log were never consumed by fire; when Althea, who had long ago saved the log from burning and stored it away, learned how her brothers died, she killed her son by throwing the log into the flames.

REPRESENTATIONS

The central episode in the story of Meleager is the Calydonian boar hunt, which appears on the neck of the François Vase (570 B.C., Florence, Museo Archeologico) as well as on archaic Greek vases: the boar is assailed by dogs and surrounded by hunters, some of whom are identified by inscriptions (Melanion, Peleus, Castor and Pollux, Atalanta, etc.). The subject was developed in a series of Roman sarcophagi that juxtapose several episodes from the story: the meeting of Meleager and Atalanta, the hunt, and the death of Meleager (second century A.D., Paris, Louvre). The statue of a young man, which a copyist turned into a representation of Meleager by adding a boar's head, was for a long time as famous as the *Apollo Belvedere* (second century A.D. copy of a fourth-century B.C. Greek original, Rome, Vatican).

The Hunt of Meleager and Atalanta. Charles Le Brun, c. 1658. Paris, Louvre.

The most frequently represented subject in modern painting is Meleager returning the animal skin to Atalanta, a subject that mixes bravery and romance. It was depicted several times by Rubens (*Meleager and Atalanta*, c. 1635, Munich, Alte Pinakothek and Madrid, Prado) and Jordaens (1628, Madrid, Prado). The entire story of Meleager was illustrated by Le Brun for a series of tapestries (c. 1658, Paris, Louvre).

Attributes: Boar. Hunting dog. Spear.

Cross-references: Atalanta.

Sources: Homer, *The Iliad* IX, 430–605. Ovid, *Metamorphoses* VIII, 270–547.

Bibliography: F. Haskell and N. Penny, *Taste and the Antique*, New Haven and London, 1982, pp. 263–4. A. Schnapp, *Revue archéologique* (1979): 195–218.

MELPOMENE *See* Muses.

MEMNON

It. Memnone; Fr., Ger., Gk., and Lat. Memnon.
Legendary Ethiopian king.

Memnon.
Cup by Douris,
c. 480 B.C.
Paris, Louvre.

HISTORY/MYTHOLOGY

The Ethiopian king, Memnon, was the son of the goddess Aurora (Eos) and Priam's nephew Tithonus. He was the hero of a number of adventures in the Trojan War, including an equally matched battle with Ajax and a battle in which he had the advantage over Antilochus, who had come to save his aged father, Nestor. Achilles challenged Memnon to a duel to avenge his friend's death after the second struggle. Aurora and Thetis, the combatants' divine mothers, sought help from Jupiter, each asking that her own son be saved. The psychostasia, or the weighing of destinies, ensued: Jupiter placed the souls of each hero on a balance, which tipped against Memnon. Nevertheless, Aurora obtained immortality for her son, whose corpse she gathered up and transported to Ethiopia. It is said that the tears that the goddess of the dawn sheds in mourning over her son are drops of dew.

REPRESENTATIONS

There are only a few representations of Memnon, almost all from Greek vases. The main themes are Memnon accompanied by Ethiopian soldiers, the psychostasia, the one-on-one combat between Achilles and Memnon in the presence of their mothers (or simply Minerva for Achilles), and Aurora lifting up her son's body.

Memnon is always shown with Caucasian (Greek) features, even when accompanied by Ethiopian soldiers, who are black (amphora by Exekias, c. 540 B.C., London, British Museum). The weighing of the souls is well illustrated in a fragmentary krater attributed to the Kleophrades Painter (c. 490 B.C., Paris, Bibliothèque Nationale, Cabinet des Médailles): Mercury holds the balance over a platter on which stands a small, armed hoplite; Jupiter has his lightning bolt in hand. Memnon and Achilles are shown fighting one-on-one over the prostrate body of Antilochus in a famous relief from the Siphnian Treasury at Delphi (525 B.C.) in which inscriptions identify the three characters. The same three figures battle each other on a red-figure Attic cup from the beginning of the fifth century B.C., a work signed by the potter Gorgos (Athens, Agora Museum); in this depiction, Memnon's lance becomes useless after it gets stuck in his adversary's shield, and a frantic Aurora bares her chest. The sequel to this story appears on a cup in the Louvre, signed by Douris (c. 480 B.C.): Aurora sadly lifts the broken corpse of her son. By tradition, a monumental statue of pharaoh Amenhotep III (the so-called "Colossus of Memnon"), visible on the site of Thebes in Egypt (eighteenth dynasty, 1403–1364 B.C.) has been identified as Memnon. Pausanias writes that each morning at sunrise the statue emitted melodious sounds, as if in honor of Memnon's mother, Aurora.

Memnon has rarely been represented in modern painting. In Henry Fuseli's lost *Psychostasia*, Achilles stands before the body of Memnon beneath the gaze of Jupiter, who is accompanied by Tithonus and Aurora (1803, known through drawings).

Cross-references: Achilles. Aurora. Thetis. Troy.

Sources: Ovid, *Metamorphoses* XIII, 576–622. Pausanias, I, 42,3 (colossus of Memnon).

MENELAUS *See* Helen.

MENTOR *See* Telemachus.

MERCURY

Gk. and Ger. Hermes; Lat. Mercurius; It. and Sp. Mercurio; Fr. Mercure.
Messenger-god.

HISTORY/MYTHOLOGY

Mercury, the son of Jupiter and Maia, was born in Arcadia at Cyllene and was one of the twelve Olympian gods. He most often acted as messenger to the other gods and can be characterized as the god of trade and commerce. He accompanied the dead to the Underworld, distributed wealth, and protected tradesmen and thieves. He was known for his skill, inventiveness, and wiles. Hardly had he seen the light of day when he stole Apollo's heifers; to be forgiven, he gave Apollo the lyre, which he had just invented from a tortoise shell.

As the gods' messenger and as ferryman, Mercury plays only a secondary role in many accounts: he leads the goddesses to the Judgement of Paris; he receives the child Bacchus from Jupiter and hands him over to the nymphs; he is assigned by Jupiter the task of killing Argus. He often accompanied Jupiter, for example during the visit to Philemon and Baucis, or when the father of the Olympians disguised himself as Amphitryon to seduce the faithful Alcmena, for which Mercury disguised himself as Sosia, the Theban king's servant. Finally, Jupiter also sent Mercury to kill Argus, whom Juno had assigned the task of keeping watch over Io.

REPRESENTATIONS

In archaic and classical art, Mercury is portrayed as bearded and dressed in a traveler's cloak; he wears a wide-brimmed hat (*petasus*) and winged sandals, and he holds a caduceus. He often appears on funerary urns, accompanying the deceased to the Underworld; he is also seen with Orpheus and Eurydice on a relief whose original dates from the end of the fifth century B.C. (Naples, Museo Nazionale). At the end of the classical period, he sometimes appears as a youth, as in the famous *Hermes* by Praxiteles in which he plays with the child Dionysus (fourth century B.C., Olympia), or as in the seated Mercury from Herculaneum (bronze copy of a fourth-century B.C. original, Naples, Museo Nazionale). In his role of protector of flocks, he sometimes carries a ram (bronze, sixth century B.C., Athens, National Museum). The theft of Apollo's herds appears on a hydria from Caere (c. 530 B.C., Paris, Louvre) as well as on two cups by the Brygos Painter (c. 480 B.C., Rome, Musei Vaticani and Princeton, Art Museum).

In antiquity, there is a special type of statue known as a herm: a quadrangular pillar topped by the god's bust and endowed with genitals. Such figures were placed like stakes along roads or at crossroads to indicate boundaries or to demarcate space, in a reflection of Hermes' role. This type of image, however, does not represent only Hermes: some are sculpted with busts of Dionysus, Athena, or even historical characters (for example, the double herm showing Herodotus and Thucydides in the museum at Naples). Such figures appear in sculpture through the nineteenth century (Moulin, 1879, Paris, Musée d'Orsay).

In Renaissance emblems, Mercury personifies Eloquence and Reason. He and Venus are sometimes seen teaching Cupid (Carle van Loo, 1765, Aix-en-Provence, Musée Granet). Mercury appears in

Hermes of Alcamenes.
From Pergamum,
150–200 B.C.
Istanbul, Museum.

Mercury.
Hydria from Caere,
c. 530 B.C.
Paris, Louvre.

Mercury and Paris.
Annibale Carracci,
1597–1600.
Rome,
Galleria Farnese.

many scenes, most notably in the Judgement of Paris. He is one of the main characters in the story of Io and is shown putting Argus to sleep with his music (Velázquez, 1659, Madrid, Prado; Fragonard, c. 1761, Paris, Louvre) as often as he is shown preparing to kill the latter (Rubens, c. 1638, Madrid, Prado). He may appear in the sky, falling in love with Herse, the daughter of the Athenian king, Cecrops, as he spots her on her way to visit Athena's temple (Boeckhorst, middle of the seventeenth century, Vienna, Kunsthistorisches Museum); he is also found punishing Aglauros, Herse's jealous sister (Veronese, c. 1580, Cambridge, Fitzwilliam Museum; Lagrenée, 1767, Stockholm, National Museum). Mercury inventing the caduceus is a subject treated by Chapu (1860, Paris, Musée d'Orsay).

Attributes: Caduceus. Winged hat and shoes.

Cross-references: Aglauros. Apollo. Argus. Bacchus. Io. Orpheus. Paris. Philemon and Baucis. Sarpedon.

Sources: *Homeric Hymn to Hermes.* Ovid, *Metamorphoses* I, 668–721 (Argus); II, 708–832 (Herse).

Bibliography: P. Zanker, *Wandel der Hermesgestalt in der attischen Vasenmalerei*, Berlin, 1965.

METAMORPHOSIS

Metamorphoses are frequent in ancient mythology, and accounts of them were gathered together several times by scholars and poets such as Ovid and Antoninus Liberalis.

Most often, a metamorphosis is an irreversible transformation inflicted by the gods; it entails passing from human into animal, vegetable, or mineral form. A glance from the Gorgon, for example, resulted in permanent petrification. There also existed metamorphoses that involved only a sex change (Caeneus, Tiresias). The gods themselves metamorphosed, but only temporarily. Certain marine divinities, including Thetis, sometimes transformed themselves in order to escape a pursuer. Jupiter often used metamorphosis to satisfy his amorous desires, making himself become mineral (gold for Danaë), animal (bull, swan, and eagle), or human (Amphitryon for seducing Alcmena, satyr for Antiope, and Diana for Callisto).

Cross-references: Actaeon. Adonis. Ajax the Greater. Arachne. Arethusa. Atalanta. Caeneus. Callisto. Circe. Danaë. Daphne. Flora.

Metamorphosis of Men into Dolphins.
Detail from an
Etruscan hydria,
c. 530 B.C.
Toledo, Museum
of Art.

Ganymede. Hyacinthus. Io. Jupiter. Leda. Leto. Narcissus. Niobe. Tereus. Thetis. Tiresias.

Sources: Antoninus Liberalis, *The Metamorphoses*. Ovid, *Metamorphoses*.

MIDAS

It. Mida; Fr., Ger., Gk., and Lat. Midas.
Legendary Phrygian king.

HISTORY/MYTHOLOGY

The Phrygian king, Midas, earned Bacchus's gratitude by being kind to elderly Silenus, the god's follower, when Silenus was found drunk by peasants. Offered a reward, Midas asked that whatever he touched be turned to gold. The gift became a curse, for he could no longer eat or drink, and he asked Bacchus to free him of the power, whereupon he was told to purify himself in the river Pactolus, which has run with gold ever since.

Midas judged the musical contest between Apollo and Pan (or sometimes Marsyas). He leaned in favor of Apollo, and that poor judgement made the angry god turn his ears into those of an ass.

REPRESENTATIONS

In fifth-century B.C. ceramics, Silenus is shown as a prisoner being led before Midas, who is identifiable by his long ears.

The episode with Midas, Silenus, and the gold of the Pactolus inspired Poussin several times (c. 1626–30, New York, Metropolitan Museum of Art). The judgement scene is more frequent in the Renaissance. It appears in a fresco by Giulio Romano (1527–28, Mantua, Palazzo del Tè) and in a sketch by Rubens (1636–38, Madrid, Prado).

Midas
Detail from a drawing
by Antoine Caron,
sixteenth century.
Paris,
École des Beaux-Arts.

Attributes: Ears of an ass.

Cross-references: Apollo. Marsyas. Pan.

Sources: Ovid, *Metamorphoses* XI, 84–145 (gold); 146–79 (music contest).

MILKY WAY

HISTORY/MYTHOLOGY

As a child, Hercules was the butt of Juno's jealousy. Minerva, however, arranged for their chance meeting, and Juno not only took pity on the child but let Minerva talk her into nursing him. Hercules pressed her breast so hard that the milk gushed out into the sky and became the Milky Way.

REPRESENTATIONS

The subject does not appear prior to baroque and mannerist painting. In a work by Tintoretto, it is Mercury, commanded by Jupiter, who brings the child to the sleeping Juno (1582, London, National Gallery).

Attributes: Gushing milk.

Cross-references: Hercules. Juno. Jupiter.

Sources: Diodorus Siculus, *Library of History* IV, 9.

Milon of Croton.
Pierre Puget, 1683.
Paris, Louvre.

MILON OF CROTON

It. Milone; Fr. Milon de Crotone; Lat. Milon; Ger. Milon von Kroton.
Greek athlete, born in Croton (probably between 540 and 516 B.C.).

HISTORY/MYTHOLOGY

The celebrated athlete Milon of Croton lived in Magna Graecia during the sixth century B.C. According to Diodorus Siculus, he was six times victor at the Olympic Games and seven times victor at the Pithian Games. A man with prodigious strength and an appetite no less remarkable, he made an effort at training his mind by studying Pythagoras. Nevertheless, Milon's death would appear to symbolize his *hybris*, the sort of pride that Greek philosophy liked to discourage in the wise. He overestimated his strength one day by attempting to split a partially cracked tree trunk with his bare hands and became trapped in the cleft; wild beasts caught him by surprise and devoured the now defenseless athlete.

REPRESENTATIONS

Modern representations focus on Milon's death. Two highly celebrated and often copied sculptural groups represent this subject; one is by Puget (1683, Paris, Louvre), the other by Falconet (1755, Paris, Louvre). The first leaves the spectator with the impression that Milon would subdue the animal were not his hand trapped: his upright body is taut with effort as well as pain (the lion is already biting him), and he lifts his head imploringly toward the heavens. By contrast, Falconet's Milon is already on the ground after being tackled by the ferocious lion.

Attributes: Lion. Tree trunk.

Sources: Diodorus Siculus, *Library of History* XII, 9. Pausanias, VI, 2–3. Strabo, VI, 263.

Athena Parthenos.
Sculpture after
Phidias,
second century A.D.
Athens,
National Museum.

MINERVA

Gk. Athena, Pallas; Lat., It., Sp., and Ger. Minerva; Fr. Minerve.
Goddess.

HISTORY/MYTHOLOGY

Minerva, one of the Olympian gods, was the daughter of Metis, whom Jupiter swallowed up pregnant for fear that his children would dethrone him. She was therefore born without a mother, popping out of Jupiter's head a fully developed adult. She was a virgin goddess (*parthenos*) and refused to marry. Only Hephaestus (Vulcan) dared approach her, and Erichtonius, who sprang from the earth, was the offspring of this rejected passion. Minerva was also a warrior-goddess and participated in the gods' battle against the Giants. She is often associated with Victory (Nike). Almost always helmeted, she wears the aegis, a sort of tunic made from the scaled skin of a dragon and decorated with Medusa's head, which Perseus gave her after he slew the monster.

Athena protected many Greek cities, especially Athens, which bears her name. She became Athens's principal goddess after her victory over Neptune in the quarrel over who would possess Attica:

Perseus and Andromeda.
Paolo Veronese, 1583.
Rennes, Musée des Beaux-Arts.

Phaëthon.
Gustave Moreau, 1878.
Paris, Louvre.

the god of the sea made saltwater spring forth and Minerva made an olive tree spring up. The goddess's sanctuary was in the Parthenon, which was consecrated to her, on the Acropolis.

Minerva was one of the three goddesses who competed in the Judgement of Paris. After she was not chosen by the Trojan prince, she sided with the Greeks during the Trojan War, as did Juno; she often intervened in favor of Ulysses, during his years of combat as well as during his odyssey, or his return to Ithaca. Minerva protected other heroes as well: Jason, Theseus, and especially Hercules, whom she introduced to Olympus when he was elevated to the status of a god.

Minerva was prudence and wisdom incarnate, and the owl that accompanies her may symbolize her perspicacity. Since the Alexandrian period, she has been associated with the Muses because of these qualities. Nevertheless, the goddess could hardly have called herself a musician: after Medusa was beheaded, Minerva invented the flute (*aulos*), which imitates the plaintive cries of the other Gorgons, but threw away the instrument when she found that it puffed out her cheeks unattractively (the satyr Marsyas then grabbed hold of it). An expert weaver, she was also the protectress of artisans. It was she who punished the proud Arachne by turning her into a spider after the maiden boasted that she surpassed the goddess at weaving.

REPRESENTATIONS

Athena was frequently represented, especially at Athens; she appeared helmeted on the city's coins, and was also depicted on ceramics. She is seen being born from Jupiter's head (pyxis by the C Painter, c. 560 B.C., Paris, Louvre), fighting the Giants (cup by the Brygos Painter, c. 490 B.C., Berlin, Antikensammlungen), assisting at the birth of Erichtonius (hydria by the Oonanthè Painter, c. 470 B.C., London, British Museum), and participating at the Judgement of Paris (pyxis, c. 440 B.C., Copenhagen, Archeological Museum). Athena's birth is represented on the east pediment of the Parthenon, and her dispute with Poseidon on the west pediment (c. 438–432 B.C., now destroyed). In sculpture, one of the most famous statues was the *Athena Parthenos* by Phidias (c. 440 B.C.), a colossal work in gold and ivory known only through a small, mediocre copy of the Roman period (second–third centuries A.D., Athens, National Museum). Here the goddess stands upright with her shield on the ground; on her right hand is a small figure of Victory. In statues, Athena brandishes a lance in fighting position (*Athena Promachos*, votive bronze from the Acropolis, c. 470 B.C.), or she is immobile and leans on the lance (*Athena Meditating*, stela, c. 460 B.C., Athens, Acropolis Museum). The Promachos type was regularly reproduced on panathenaic amphorae, which contained the oil given as a prize to victorious athletes at the Panathenae, the festivals held in the goddess's honor.

Athena Meditating.
Stela, c. 460 B.C.
Athens,
Acropolis Museum.

Minerva.
Detail
from Andrea Mantegna,
*Pallas Expelling
the Vices*, 1504.
Paris, Louvre.

Roman art reflects the same iconography but also integrates Minerva into the Capitoline triad, alongside Jupiter and Juno.

Minerva functions as a symbol of Wisdom in modern painting. She plays this role in Mantegna's *Triumph of Virtue*, where she chases the Vices from the garden of Virtue (c. 1504, Paris, Louvre) and in the foreground of Bartholomeus Spranger's *The Triumph of Wisdom* (1591, Vienna, Kunsthistorisches Museum). In eighteenth-century portraiture, women were sometimes represented in the guise of Minerva, as in Tassard's marble bust of Catherine II of Russia (1774, St. Petersburg, Hermitage).

The dispute over the possession of Attica is occasionally represented, either statically, as in a painting by Garofalo (1512, Dresden, Gemäldegalerie), or more turbulently, as in a work by Hallé (1748, Paris, Louvre).

Attributes: Aegis. Gorgon's head. Helmet and weapons. Owl.

Cross-references: Aglauros. Arachne. Erichtonius. Giants, Hercules. Jupiter. Marsyas. Neptune. Paris. Perseus.

Sources: Hesiod, *Theogony*, 886–900. Pausanias, I, 24.

Bibliography: R. Wittkower, "Transformations of Minerva in Renaissance Imagery," *Journal of the Warburg and Courtauld Institutes* 2 (1938–9): 194–205.

Maria de' Medici as Minerva, Patroness of the Fine Arts.
Engraving after Peter Paul Rubens, c. 1625.

MINOS *See* Ariadne. Daedalus. Europa.

MINOTAUR

Gk. and Ger. Minotauros; Lat. Minotaurus; It. and Sp. Minotauro; Fr. Minotaure.
Monster that was half-man, half-bull.

HISTORY/MYTHOLOGY

The Minotaur was a monster with a human body and the head of a bull; he was born after Pasiphaë, the wife of the Cretan king, Minos, coupled with a bull sent by Neptune. Minos had promised to sacrifice the bull to the god, but changed his mind because it was so beautiful. Neptune aroused a monstrous passion in Pasiphaë, and Daedalus enabled her to mate with the bull. Minos locked the offspring of this union, the Minotaur, in a labyrinth constructed by Daedalus. After the Athenians were conquered by Minos, they had to deliver seven young men and seven maidens every year to Crete, where they were locked up with the Minotaur. With the help of Minos's daughter, Ariadne, Theseus succeeded in killing the monster and escaping from the labyrinth.

Theseus and the Minotaur.
Antoin Louis Barye, bronze, nineteenth century. Reims, Musée des Beaux-Arts.

REPRESENTATIONS

The Minotaur appears on its own on coins from Knossos. A number of important Attic vases represent the local hero, Theseus, slaughtering the monster; a column may mark the entry to the labyrinth (cup by the Aison Painter, c. 410 B.C., Madrid, Museo Arqueologico). The same scene appears in the "Thesion" of Athens and in Pompeian painting.

The death of the Minotaur is rarely represented in modern painting. Carle van Loo painted an imposing version of the subject (1746, Nice, Musée des Beaux-Arts Jules-Chéret) and Canova sculpted several groups (*Theseus and the Minotaur*, 1804–19, Vienna, Kunsthistorisches Museum). From 1928 onward, Picasso created a number of works in which the Minotaur appears as either a voyeur contemplating a sleeping maiden (etching, 1933) or a monster dying at the sight of his own reflection (drawing, 1937).

Cross-references: Daedalus. Pasiphaë. Theseus.

Sources: Ovid, *Metamorphoses* VIII, 169–73. Plutarch, *Life of Theseus* I, 19.

MIRROR *See* Venus.

MNEMOSYNE *See* Muses.

MOIRAI *See* Fates.

MONSTER

Mythology abounds with monstrous characters. They are often creatures composed of several different parts of animals (the Chimera, griffins, Pegasus) or of human and animal parts (Achelous, fauns, satyrs, Silenus, centaurs, the Minotaur). Some monsters are deformed (the Cyclopes, Polyphemus, Giants, Antaeus, Alcyone, Geryon, Cecrops) or terrifying humans (the Gorgons, Harpies); others are strange animals (Cerberus, the Hydra). Many monsters were the opponents of Hercules, Bellerophon, Theseus, and other Greek heroes.

Cross-references: Achelous. Antaeus. Bellerophon. Cacus. Centaurs. Cerberus. Cyclopes. Faun. Giants. Glaucus and Scylla. Gorgons. Griffins. Harpies. Hercules. Minotaur. Pegasus. Polyphemus. Satyrs. Silenus. Theseus. Triton.

MOON *See* Diana (crescent moon). Hecate (new moon).

MORPHEUS *See* Hypnos.

MUCIUS SCAEVOLA

It. Muzio Scevola; Fr. and Ger. Mucius Scaevola.
Legendary Roman.

HISTORY/MYTHOLOGY

Mucius Scaevola's legendary adventure took place at the end of the sixth century B.C., during the war waged by the budding Roman

Mucius Scaevola.
Engraving after
Giovanni Battista
Tiepolo, 1753.

Republic against the Etruscans. The enemy had besieged Rome, and the young man penetrated the invaders' camp with the goal of assassinating the Etruscan king, Porsena. He instead mistakenly killed a guard and was brought before his intended victim. At that point, Mucius punished his right hand for having failed by letting it burn on a lighted sacrificial brazier. The act earned him the name *scaevola*, or left-handed. The young hero's courage so impressed Porsena that he was set free.

REPRESENTATIONS

Mucius Scaevola became the *exemplum virtutis* (model of courage) par excellence, and his story, which glorifies both determination and physical courage, has been illustrated from the Renaissance through neoclassical times, especially during the French Revolution and the Consulate, to which it was particularly suited. The two main characters are Mucius and Porsena: Mucius stands and resolutely extends his right hand over the brazier while Porsena, seated, contemplates the scene. That grouping is the essential element in other versions which are faithful in varying degrees to the ancient account. Sometimes the guard whom Mucius mistakenly killed is shown lying at the foot of the brazier with the sword protruding from his body (Rubens, 1616–18, Budapest, Szépmüvészeti Muzeum); sometimes the guard is already shrouded and carried away (Le Brun, c. 1642, Mâcon, Musée des Ursulines). Spectators of varying number are added, including attending soldiers who are impressed by the hero's exceptional courage (Tiepolo, 1753, Würzburg, Martin von Wagner Museum).

Attributes: Bloody sword. Brazier.

Sources: Livy, II, 12. Plutarch, *Life of Publicola*, 17. Valerius Maximus, III, 3, 1.

Terpsichore.
Eustache Le Sueur,
c. 1647–50.
Paris, Louvre.

MUSES

Gk. Mousai; Lat. Musae; Ger. Musai; It. Muse.
Goddesses of the arts and sciences.

The nine Muses presided over all intellectual creativity. They are sometimes said to be the daughters of Uranus and Gaea (the Sky and the Earth), but they were most often acknowledged as the fruit of nine consecutive nights of love between Jupiter and Mnemosyne. They were classified into several groups until classical times; the two main groups were the Muses of Thrace, who were neighbors of Olympus and linked to the cult of Dionysus and the myth of Orpheus, and the Muses of Mount Helicon, whom Apollo led. It was only in Hellenistic times that the number, names, and realms of activity of the Muses became definitively fixed. As a result, identifying the Muses is often difficult: their attributes vary and, apart from a few amorous adventures, their appearance in art is not linked to specific episodes in their lives, which is often the case with secondary divinities. The Muses customarily participated at the gods' feasts and at important ceremonies (the wedding of Thetis and Peleus, for example).

The problem of identification continued into modern times, when the Muses sometimes bear no attribute, although artists generally follow the iconography established by Cesare Ripa, whose *Iconologia*, published in 1593, presented an alphabetical repertory of the signs and symbols of Western civilization, including Greek and Roman mythology.

Melpomene, Erato, and Polyhymnia.
Eustache Le Sueur,
c. 1647–50.
Paris, Louvre.

The Muses and Their Possible Attributes:
Calliope (epic poetry, eloquence): trumpet, tablet and stylus, books, a laurel crown held in hand.
Clio (history): book, scroll, tablet and stylus, swan, trumpet, a laurel crown held in hand.
Polyhymnia (mime): small organ or other musical instrument.
Euterpe (music): simple or double flute, trumpet, or other musical instrument.
Terpsichore (dance and lyric poetry): viol, lyre, or stringed instrument.
Erato (hymns, love poetry): tambourine, lyre, viol, sometimes a swan.
Melpomene (tragedy): tragic masks, horn, sword, scepter at her feet, a crown held in hand.
Thalia (comedy): scroll, comic masks, viol or other musical instrument.
Urania (astronomy): globe and compass, a crown of stars.
The Muses sometimes appear with cupids playing at their feet, and they wear crowns of flowers and long tunics.

REPRESENTATIONS

Although the Muses have no specific legendary cycle, they were often represented in classical and Hellenistic Greece. They may appear alone in vase painting (white-figure lekythos by the Achilles Painter, c. 450 B.C., Munich, Antikensammlungen), but they are most often accompanied by Apollo (red-figure stamnos, middle of the fifth century B.C., Rome, Villa Giulia).

Urania.
Eustache Le Sueur,
c. 1647–50.
Paris, Louvre.

There are many other examples on vases from southern Italy. More impressive, however, are the Hellenistic and Roman sculpted groups and reliefs that have come down to us. In one of these, by Archelaos of Pierna, Muses appear in the context of the *Apotheosis of Homer* (c. 125 B.C., London, British Museum). An even more important example is the great marble sarcophagus in the Louvre known as the *Sarcophagus of the Muses* (which inspired an ode by Paul Claudel). This imposing Roman work of more than six feet in length dates from the middle of the second century A.D. and was found very near Rome at the beginning of the eighth century. The nine Muses are depicted one beside the other, each draped in a tunic and bearing an attribute.

Clio, Euterpe, and Thalia.
Eustache Le Sueur,
c. 1647–50.
Paris, Louvre.

Calliope.
Eustache Le Sueur,
c. 1647–50.
Paris, Louvre.

The Muses are also represented individually in large statues (*Thalia*, London, British Museum), as well as in small terracotta figurines from Tangara and Myrina.

The subject has been an enormous source of inspiration to modern artists. Frequently represented in Italy, France, and the Netherlands in the sixteenth century, the Muses continued to be popular among artists in subsequent centuries. The subject was highly suited for ceiling and mural decorations of châteaux and townhouses.

Primaticcio adapted the subject to pendentives for the Salle de Bal at the Château de Fontainebleau (sketch for *Apollo and the Muses on Parnassus*, 1552–56, London, British Museum); in 1655–57, Giovanni Francesco Romanelli decorated the ceiling of the Salle des Saisons in the summer apartment of Anne d'Autriche in the Louvre with a painting of *Apollo and the Muses*. Another example is the *Cabinet des Muses*, painted around 1647–50 by Eustache Le Sueur in the Hôtel Lambert, which was constructed by Le Veau on the Île Saint-Louis in Paris for Thorigny, president of the Chambre des Comptes; in five panels that are now in the Louvre, separate groups of Muses with delicate faces and vibrant colors are harmonized by a pastoral setting. The Muses continued to inspire artists into the nineteenth century (Denis, *The Muses*, 1893, Paris, Musée d'Orsay).

Cross-references: Apollo. Peleus. Thetis.

Sources: Hesiod, *Theogony*, 35 ff. Pausanias, 1, 2, 5; IX, 29, 2 ff.

Bibliography: P. Boyance, *Le Culte des muses*, Paris, 1936.

MUSICAL INSTRUMENT *See* Apollo (stringed instruments). Euterpe. Minerva (flute). Pan (flute, syrinx). Polyhymnia. Satyrs (flute, syrinx). Terpsichore (stringed instruments). Thalia.

MYRRH *See* Adonis.

MYRTLE *See* Graces.

NAIADS

Gk., Lat., and It. Naiades; Fr. Naïades; Ger. Najade.
Water divinites.

HISTORY/MYTHOLOGY

The Naiads were water nymphs who were mainly associated with springs, rivers, and lakes. They were often said to be the daughters of river gods or, according to Homer, the daughters of Zeus.

REPRESENTATIONS

The Naiads are rarely distinguishable from Nereids, or sea nymphs, in ancient iconography.

Some of the modern female figures in fountains are actually expansions on the Naiad theme, as exemplified in Jean Goujon's reliefs for the Fontaine des Innocents (1550, Paris). Antonio Canova sculpted a *Naiad and Cupid* in marble (1815–17, London, Buckingham Palace). A reflection of the fountain motif is found in Ingres' *The Source*, in which a Naiad carries an urn (1856, Paris, Louvre).

Cross-references: Arethusa. Hylas. Nereids. Nymphs.

Sources: Callimachus, *Hymns* III, 13.

NARCISSUS

Gk. Narkissos; Lat. and Ger. Narcissus; It. and Sp. Narciso; Fr. Narcisse.
Greek hero.

HISTORY/MYTHOLOGY

Narcissus was the son of the river god Cephissus and the nymph Liriope. His story is linked to that of the nymph Echo, who kept Juno distracted with long conversations while Jupiter courted the nymphs. When Juno caught on to the ruse, she punished Echo by making her unable to say anything but the last words spoken to her.

Echo was enraptured with Narcissus's beauty, but the youth spurned her. Venus subsequently doomed Narcissus to love only his own image. Seated on a bank and leaning over his own reflection in the water, he died in despair over never being able to possess his beloved. The gods then transformed him into the flower that bears his name; Echo also disappeared, becoming only a voice.

REPRESENTATIONS

The subject appears frequently in Pompeian painting (Naples, Museo Nazionale). Narcissus is dressed as a hunter on the shore, leaning over his reflection in the water; a cupid often accompanies him.

The story of Narcissus has been of great interest to modern artists, who found that the story provided an excellent image. Narcissus may be shown leaning over a well, as is often the case in *mille fleurs* tapestries (fifteenth century, Paris, Musée Cluny). There are, however, an

Narcissus.
Detail from
Mille fleurs tapestry,
fifteenth century.
Boston,
Museum of Fine Arts.

Echo and Narcissus.
Nicolas Poussin,
c. 1629.
Paris, Louvre.

enormous number of examples focusing on the play between the reflected image and the reaction it provokes in the youth, who is both surprised and melancholic. Narcissus is shown prostrate and dying while Echo and a cupid look on in Poussin's version of the subject (c. 1644, Paris, Louvre). Claude Lorraine incorporated Narcissus into a landscape (1644, London, National Gallery). In contrast, a painting attributed to Caravaggio focuses solely on the figure of Narcissus in order to emphasize the illusion of a composition reflected in a mirror.

Attributes: Spring.

Sources: Ovid, *Metamorphoses* III, 339–510. Philostratus, *Imagines* I, 23.

Bibliography: D. Panofsky, "Narcissus and Echo," *Art Bulletin* XXXI (June 1949): 112–20.

NAUSICAÄ

Fr., Ger., Gk., It., and Lat. Nausicaa.
Legendary princess.

HISTORY/MYTHOLOGY

Nausicaä was the daughter of Alcinoüs, king of the Phaeacians. After leaving Calypso, Ulysses washed ashore naked and exhausted near the mouth of a river. He fell asleep only to be awakened by the sound of voices. Coming out from the bushes, he encountered the Princess Nausicaä and her servants on their way to wash clothes in the river. Nausicaä came to his aid and took him to her father's palace, where Alcinoüs and his queen, Arete, offered Ulysses their hospitality and held a banquet in his honor.

REPRESENTATIONS

The encounter between Ulysses and Nausicaä is rare in ancient art, but Pausanias described a painting by Polygnotus of this subject. An

Nausicaä.
Friedrich Preller,
1864.
Poznan,
Nationalmuseum.

Attic red-figure amphora may reflect its composition: Ulysses and Nausicaä meet under the benevolent eye of Minerva while the princess's frightened companions run away (c. 440 B.C., Munich, Antikensammlungen).

In modern times, the subject is found largely in Flemish painting; it provided an occasion for representing a vast, rocky landscape bordering the sea, as demonstrated in a work by Rubens, *Landscape with Ulysses on the Island of the Phaeacians* (1630–35, Florence, Palazzo Pitti) and another by Peter Lastman, who depicted Nausicaä standing before Ulysses, who kneels nude at a river bank. The subject recurs in a similar setting in a painting by Preller (1864, Poznan, Nationalmuseum).

Cross-references: Ulysses.

Sources: Homer, *The Odyssey*, ch. 6. Pausanias, I, 22, 6.

Bibliography: O. Touchefeu-Meynier, *Thèmes odysséens dans l'art antique*, Paris, 1968.

NEMESIS *See* Fortune.

NEOPTOLEMUS *See* Polxena.

NEPTUNE

Gk. Poseidon; Lat. Neptunus; It. Nettuno; Sp. Neptuno; Fr. Neptune; Ger. Neptun.
God of the sea.

HISTORY/MYTHOLOGY

Neptune, one of the great Olympian gods, was the son of Saturn and the brother of Jupiter and Pluto. His share of the world centered on water: he could command waves, trigger storms, and create springs.

Neptune and Amphitrite.
Mosaic
from Nea Paphos,
third century A.D.

Although Neptune was first and foremost master of saltwater bodies, he also caused earthquakes and was thought to possess special powers over horses, which he could tame; bulls were sacrificed to him.

With his wife, Amphitrite, Neptune had a son, Triton. He also fathered Polyphemus, with the sea goddess Thoosa; Chrysaor and Pegasus, with the Gorgon Medusa; Nauplius, with the Danaïd Amymone, whom he seduced after saving her from a satyr. Neptune also loved Caeneus (Kaineus), who convinced him to change her into an invulnerable man. Princess Coronis, daughter of Coroneus, escaped from Neptune's assaults by fleeing and crying out for help from Minerva, who transformed her into a crow.

Neptune and Apollo together put themselves in the service of King Laomedon to construct Troy's ramparts, but when the king later refused to pay the agreed price, Neptune had the city ravaged by a sea monster, which Hercules killed.

Neptune and Minerva competed for possession of Attica, he by striking the ground and causing a saltwater spring to appear on the Acropolis, she by making an olive tree grow there. Minerva was declared the winner and became the patron goddess of the city that borrowed her Greek name—Athena.

Neptune is portrayed as a long-haired, bearded man; he often holds a trident and is surrounded by Tritons, dolphins, and fish; seahorses (hippocampi) draw his chariot.

REPRESENTATIONS

Neptune is clothed, holds a trident, and faces Athena in an amphora by the Amasis Painter (c. 540 B.C., Paris, Bibliothèque Nationale, Cabinet des Médailles). Without his trident, he is sometimes difficult to distinguish from Zeus (Jupiter). For this reason, the large bronze statue discovered at Artemisium, which shows Neptune with his arm positioned as if wielding a trident, is sometimes regarded as a representation of Zeus hurling one of his thunderbolts (c. 460 B.C., Athens, National Museum). Neptune appears in a similar pose in coins from Poseidonia (Paestum). In representations of the Gigantomachy he not only fights with his trident but also uses the island of Nisyros as a projectile (Attic cup, c. 480 B.C., Berlin, Antikensmuseum).

Neptune appears alongside Amphitrite in divine assemblies (dinos by Sophilos, c. 580 B.C., London, British Museum) and in sea processions (mosaic from Utica, third century A.D., Tunis, Bardo

**Triumphal
Procession
of Neptune
and Amphitrite.**
Edmé Bouchardon,
eighteenth century.
Paris, Louvre.

Museum). The subject is frequent in Roman mosaics, particularly those decorating baths (Thermae, Ostia, A.D. 140). The quarrel between Neptune and Minerva over the possession of Attica was represented on the west pediment of the Parthenon (c. 438–432 B.C., now destroyed); it is also found on a hydria in the style of Kertsch (end of the fourth century B.C., St. Petersburg, Hermitage). Neptune and Amymone are found in ceramics and various mosaics.

In modern times, Neptune often forms a central element in fountains, such as the one by Giambologna (1566, Bologna, Piazza del Nettuno), or in basins, as at Versailles (Lemoyne, seventeenth century, Basin of Neptune). He was popular in baroque painting, especially in triumphal scenes (Poussin, c. 1634, St. Petersburg, Hermitage; Le Brun, end of the seventeenth century, Louvre, Galerie d'Apollon); more rarely, he calms the storm that troubled Aeneas (Rubens, *Quos Ego*, 1634–35, Dresden, Staatliche Kunstmuseum). The quarrel between Neptune and Minerva is illustrated in a painting by Nallé (1784, Paris, Louvre).

Neptune symbolizes maritime power in political allegories, such as *Mars and Neptune (Protectors of Venice)* by Veronese (1575–78, Venice, Palazzo Ducale, Sala del Collegio).

Among Neptune's love affairs, the one with Amymone is most represented (Boucher, 1764, Versailles, Grand Trianon); also noteworthy is a drawing by Spranger, engraved in 1580 by J. Sadeler, of Neptune raping Caeneus, and a painting by Carpioni, *Neptune Pursuing Coronis* (1665–70, Florence, Uffizi).

The link between the sea and horses is underscored in a symbolist composition by Walter Crane, *Neptune's Steeds* (1892, Munich, Neue Galerie), in which the foam from the sea blends with the horses' galloping legs.

**Neptune
and Amphitrite.**
Jan Gossaert (called
Mabuse), beginning
of the sixteenth century.
Berlin, Staatliche
Museen.

Attributes: Fish. Trident.

Cross-references: Amphitrite. Amymone. Caeneus. Hercules. Nereids. Polyphemus. *Quos Ego*. Triton.

Sources: Ovid, *Metamorphoses* II, 569–94 (Coronis); 12, 189–207 (Caeneus).

Nereid.
Jean-Baptiste
Clésinger,
nineteenth century.
Paris, Musée d'Orsay.

NEREIDS

It. Nereidi; Sp. Nereidas; Fr. Néréides; Ger. Nereïden; Lat. Nereids.
Sea nymphs.

HISTORY/MYTHOLOGY

The Nereids, daughters of the sea god Nereus and his wife Doris, were
sea divinities who personified the waves. There were at least fifty of
them. They were imagined as striking, long-haired beauties who lived
in their father's palace at the bottom of the sea, spending their time
spinning, weaving, and singing. They were most often present at
events without necessarily being personally involved, but some of
them made exceptions: Achilles' mother Thetis, Neptune's wife
Amphitrite, and Acis' beloved Galatea.

REPRESENTATIONS

Equally esteemed by Greeks, Romans, and Etruscans, the Nereids are
present in all categories of ancient monument, from the smallest to the
largest. They are shown alone or with Nereus, and they sometimes
appear in narrative contexts (the legends of Achilles, Amphitrite,
Thetis, etc.). Most often, they walk, run, hang on to a fish, or straddle
a sea monster. They are usually dressed in short chitons or long tunics
with himations; a saccos (a type of string) binds their hair and they are
adorned with different jewels.

The Nereids lent their name to a celebrated monument known as
The Nereid Monument (c. 410 B.C., London, British Museum) from
Xanthos in Lycia (Asia Minor). That work, which has no mythological
basis, comprises a marble funerary monument composed of a high
podium surmounted by a small temple; Nereids, their transparent drapery animated by the wind, occupy the spaces between the columns
that surround the temple.

Nereids appear in many murals and mosaics. The back view of a
Nereid astride a bull appears in a mosaic from the Baths of Cronion at
Olympia (late first century B.C.–early second century A.D., Olympia
Museum). Other examples are found at Ostia in the Thermae of the
Trinacria, the Forum of the Corporations, and the House of the
Monnus Dog (between the first and third centuries A.D.). Nereids also

appear in Pompeian painting (House of Meleager, *in situ*) and in paintings from Stabie (Villa of Ariadne, first century A.D., Naples, Museo Archeologico).

Nereids are used as decorative elements in the minor arts: in jewelry, on gems (notably an amethyst signed by Delio and dating from the second half of the first century B.C., The Hague, Royal Cabinet), and in goldsmiths' work. Artisans from Alexandria engraved bone ornamental plaquettes with Nereids (third century A.D.). The subject's versatility, coupled with the fact that its forms were easily simplified, made it especially suitable for use on decorative friezes adorning such aquatic settings as baths, thermae, and fountains.

The Nereids often decorated Renaissance and seventeenth-century fountains and gardens (Grotto of Thetis and Neptune Basin, Versailles). A Nereid carried off by a horn-blowing Triton (half-man, half-sea serpent) is the subject of a sketch by Rubens (1636–38, Rotterdam, Museum Boymans van Beuningen). This same motif inspired a painting by Böcklin (1873–74, Munich, Bayerische Staatsgemäldesammlungen) and a sculpture by Rodin (c. 1886, terracotta, New York, Metropolitan Museum of Art).

Attributes: Sea animals.

Cross-references: Achilles. Amphitrite. Galatea. Neptune. Thetis.

Sources: Homer, *The Iliad* XVIII, 38–49. Hesiod, *Theogony*, 240–64.

NERO

Lat. and Ger. Nero; It. Nerone; Sp. Neron; Fr. Néron.
Roman emperor (A.D. 37–68).

HISTORY/MYTHOLOGY

Lucius Domitius Claudius Nero was born at Antium (Latium) in A.D. 37 and was emperor of Rome from A.D. 54 until his death in 68.

He came to the throne largely through the intrigues of his mother, Agrippina, who adopted him when she became the second wife of the emperor Claudius. The first five years of the young emperor's reign were calm. In her desire to govern through her son, however, Agrippina assigned him as advisors the prefect Burrus and the philosopher Seneca. Both subsequently urged Nero to break free from his mother's grip and from the calamitous influence of a new courtesan, Petronia, who was turning him into a debauched aesthete. Worried by this, Agrippina turned to Claudius's son, Britannicus, whom Nero quickly had assassinated. The emperor then killed his mother: he first arranged a shipwreck and, when that failed, had one of his henchman execute her in A.D. 59. This new murder is reputed to have been suggested by Nero's mistress, Poppaea Sabina, whose hold afterward grew stronger. Poppaea also urged Nero to divorce, exile, and finally assassinate his wife, Octavia. With Burrus dead in A.D. 62 and Seneca preferring exile, Nero became a cruel and extravagant despot. Public rumor accused him of having started the fire that ravaged Rome in July 64, but Nero himself blamed the Christians, whom he violently suppressed. He physically attacked Poppaea in a fit of anger, kicking her ruthlessly, and the empress died giving birth to the child she was bearing.

In spite of Nero's demagogic initiatives, which consisted of spectacles and lavish extravaganzas, opposition grew and the Senate finally declared him a public enemy. The emperor fled but was assassinated by his secretary at the moment when he was taken prisoner.

Nero.
Bust,
first century A.D.
Paris, Louvre.

Nero reputedly died while uttering the famous words: "*Qualis artifex pereo!*" ("What an artist dies in me!").

REPRESENTATIONS

The emperor is shown with somewhat soft, even weak, traits in the many busts, statues, and coins that portray him (Louvre, Vatican, Uffizi, etc.), although he is portrayed as *Apollo citharede* in a statue in the Musei Vaticani. His excesses, however, were such that representations of him were forbidden for a time after his reign.

Modern painters have drawn on numerous episodes from the life of Nero solely to evoke the crimes of "the bad emperor." The incident with the largest iconographic repertoire is the death of Agrippina, in which Nero commits matricide. The arranged shipwreck from which Agrippina finally escaped, for example, was painted by Carlotto (Munich, Bayerische Staatsgemäldesammlungen); Nero contemplating the lifeless body of his mother has also been illustrated, as demonstrated by a painting attributed to Antonio Zanchi (seventeenth century, Kassel, Gemäldegalerie).

From the Renaissance through the nineteenth century, artists also represented Octavia's repudiation in favor of Poppaea Sabina (Pietro da Cortona, seventeenth century, Lyon, Musée des Beaux-Arts), as well as the murderous kick inflicted on the latter (Antonio Molinari, 1665–1727, Verona, Museo Civico). Finally, Nero watching Rome burn is a theme that provided spectacular subject matter (attributed to Giulio Romano, c. 1546, Hampton Court).

Cross-references: Seneca.

Sources: Tacitus, *Annals* XIV, XV, XVI. Suetonius, *Lives of the Twelve Caesars*.

NESSUS *See* Centaurs. Deianira. Hercules.

NESTOR

It. Nestore.
Legendary king of Pylos.

HISTORY/MYTHOLOGY

Nestor, king of Pylos, lived a very long time; some say three generations. He comes across as an elderly, grey-haired man, who is renowned for his wisdom and whose advice is often sought. Despite his age, he was active in the field and also participated in the battle between centaurs and Lapiths, as well as in the Calydonian boar hunt. He served as Menelaus's advisor after Helen's abduction, and in this capacity helped group the Greek armies; he himself supplied ninety boats and set sail for Troy with two sons, Antilochus and Thrasymedes. During the Trojan War itself, he played the role of mediator, doing whatever was necessary to settle arguments among the Greeks. Nestor is particularly noteworthy for being one of the select few who returned to their kingdoms without mishap after the fall of Troy.

Nestor.
Attic amphora,
c. 470 B.C.
Paris, Louvre.

REPRESENTATIONS

Nestor rarely appears as a solitary figure. Exceptions to this include an Attic skyphos from the middle of the fifth century B.C. (Boston,

Museum of Fine Arts), which shows Nestor putting on his armor, and an amphora from the same period, which shows his son, Antilochus, on the other side (Paris, Louvre). Nestor is present in certain scenes from the Trojan War, appearing, for example, on a large silver plate that illustrates a complex episode interpreted as Briseïs either returning to or leaving Achilles' tent (*Shield of Scipio*, fifth century A.D., Paris, Bibliothèque Nationale, Cabinet des Médailles). Nestor is among the ten figures on the plate, bearded and leaning on a staff; but only the context of the scene enables him to be identified.

In modern painting, Nestor appears only as a secondary character in representations of scenes from *The Iliad*. Indeed, the only episode from the Trojan War in which Nestor's role was important is the one in which Telemachus arrives at Nestor's home in Pylos in search of his father. Nestor appears in that context in Bourdelle's relief, *Telemachus Welcomed to Pylos by Nestor* (1884, Montauban, Musée Ingres).

Cross-references: Telemachus. Troy.

Sources: Homer, *The Iliad, passim*; *The Odyssey* III.

NIKE *See* Victory.

NIOBE

Lat., Gk., and Fr. Niobé; Ger. and It. Niobe.
Queen of Thebes.

HISTORY/MYTHOLOGY

Niobe, the daughter of Tantalus, married Amphion, king of Thebes, and with him had a large number of sons and daughters, the Niobids. She was so proud of her progeny that she claimed to be worthy of the worship normally accorded Leto, who had only two children, Apollo and Diana. This offended Leto, who asked her children to avenge her: Apollo's arrows killed Niobe's sons and Diana's arrows killed her daughters. Sobbing with grief, Niobe was turned into a rock that drips water.

REPRESENTATIONS

Apollo avenging Leto is found on vases from the fifth century B.C. (krater by the Niobid Painter, c. 460 B.C., Paris, Louvre); Niobe's metamorphosis into a stone statue appeared in the fourth century B.C. The death of the Niobids is particularly famous because of a sculpted group whose original dates from the fourth century B.C.; discovered in Rome in the sixteenth century, the group formed part of the Medici collections and is now in Florence (Uffizi).

In classical and baroque painting, the massacre of the Niobids is depicted in a sculpted group in the gardens of the Villa Medici. The scene unfolds in the woods: the children run to escape the shower of arrows released from the sky by Apollo and Diana, while Niobe begs for the gods' mercy. Luca Giordano treated the subject several times, distinctly contrasting the flight of Niobe's children with Apollo's fury (c. 1658–60, Memphis, Brooks Memorial Art Gallery). Rodin sculpted a *Niobid* (c. 1900, Toledo Museum of Art).

Cross-references: Apollo.

Sources: Ovid, *Metamorphoses* VI, 146–313.

Niobe.
Copy after
a fourth-century B.C.
original.
Florence, Uffizi.

Nymph (detail).
Jean Goujon,
c. 1550.
Paris, Fontaine
des Innocents.

NYMPHS

Gk. and Ger. Nymphai; Lat., Nymphae; It. Ninfe; Sp. Ninfas; Fr. Nymphes.
Divinities of nature.

HISTORY/MYTHOLOGY

Nymphs were divinities of nature, and were sometimes considered Jupiter's daughters. They lived in grottoes, in the countryside or the woods, singing and spinning wool. As young maidens, they personified fertility, grace, and the spirits of nature. Nevertheless, it was best to be on their good side since they were easily offended and could become dangerous.

As secondary divinities, nymphs most often accompanied first-rank gods and goddesses (Apollo, Diana, and so on), or served higher-ranking nymphs, such as Calypso, Circe, Nysa, and Oenone. Their habitual companions were the male divinities of nature: Pan, Priapus, and the satyrs. Their love affairs were spirited, however, and they were not above abducting young boys (Hylas). The gods, for their part, were not immune to their beauty (Jupiter, Apollo, Mercury, Bacchus); on the other hand, the nymphs were assigned the task of caring for Jupiter and Bacchus in their infancy. Some nymphs were grouped into specific classes: Dryads were tree nymphs, Oreades were mountain nymphs, Naiads were freshwater nymphs, Nereids were saltwater nymphs. Their sanctuaries, or Nymphaea, were often linked to grottoes and springs.

REPRESENTATIONS

In a marble relief from the end of the fifth century B.C. the nymphs are represented as draped figures who follow one another in procession as they leave a grotto, where the river god Achelous is visible (Berlin, Staatliche Museen). The difficulties involved in identifying nymphs outside a precise context are demonstrated in a work with a figure seated in the pose of someone playing at knucklebones, a work known as the *Nymph on a Shell* but also called *Thetis* or *Venus* (second century B.C., Paris, Louvre). In another sculpture, a nymph is shown trying to break free from a young satyr's grip (Roman copy after a second-century B.C. Alexandrian group, Rome, Palazzo dei Conservatori).

As in antiquity, modern painting has rarely treated nymphs as independent subjects. However, nymphs have a positive presence in representations of the birth of Adonis and the punishment of Eros, and they surround Apollo and Marsyas, or Diana and Actaeon. They are most often accompanied by satyrs.

A nymph serves as the main subject, however, in the *Nymph of Fontainebleau*, for which Cellini, inspired by one of Rosso's compositions, provided the model (1542–43, bronze relief, Paris, Louvre). The composition, rendered in high relief, comprises a nymph wearing a crown of fruit and reclining beside a stream of water, which flows from her urn; forest animals and dogs surround her while she caresses the fully three-dimensional head of a stag, which springs out from the center of the sculpture. Cellini arrived in France in 1540 to work for François I, and his *Nymph* decorated the portal of the Château de Fontainebleau until Henri II gave it to his mistress, Diane de Poitiers, for her residence at Anet. Luca Giordano grouped a nymph with a centaur in his *Centaur and Nymph* (1682–85, Naples, Galleria di Capodimonte), a motif that endured into the nineteenth century (group by Rodin, Paris, Musée d'Orsay).

Prometheus.
Titian, 1549.
Madrid, Prado.

Romulus and Remus Discovered by Faustulus.
Pietro da Cortona, 1643.
Paris, Louvre.

Nymph.
Lucas Cranach
the Elder, after 1537.
Washington,
National Gallery.

The French sculptor Clodion (1738–1814) often treated the subject of nymphs, whose freshness and charm stems from the fact that they are modeled as young, almost pre-adolescent girls (*The Nymph and the Satyr*, eighteenth cenury, New York, Metropolitan Museum of Art; *The Nymph with a Child Frightened by a Serpent*, terracotta, 1799, Washington, National Gallery; *Two Nymphs Carrying a Bowl of Fruit*, plaster, Paris, Musée des Arts Décoratifs). Nymphs were often represented in sweeping landscapes in the seventeenth century; they were frequently grouped with small cupids by eighteenth-century artists, especially Boucher (1746, Stockholm, National Museum). Corot revived these two compositional types in *Morning: The Dance of the Nymphs* (c. 1850, Paris, Musée d'Orsay) and *Nymphs Playing with a Cupid* (1857, Paris, Musée d'Orsay).

Cross-references: Actaeon. Callisto. Calypso. Circe. Diana. Hylas. Paris.

Sources: Homer, *The Odyssey* X, 348–59 (servants of Circe).

Nymphs.
François Boucher.
Drawing, 1749.
San Francisco,
Fine Arts Museum.

Ocean.
François Le Moyne,
eighteenth century.
Versailles,
Neptune Basin.

OCEAN

Gk. and Ger. Okeanos; Lat. Oceanus; It. Oceano; Sp. Océano; Fr. Océan
Sea god.

HISTORY/MYTHOLOGY

Ocean, the father of the river gods, belonged to the generation of
Titans and was the son of Uranus (Sky) and Gaea (Earth).

REPRESENTATIONS

Ocean is represented as a bearded god with abundantly flowing hair. In
a krater by Sophilos, he has horns, a human bust, and the body of a fish;
he holds a snake and a fish (c. 580 B.C., London, British Museum). In
Roman art, he has the traits of a river god (Rome, Musei Vaticani).

Modern representations of Ocean are rare; however, he forms the
central element of a marble fountain created by Jean Boulanger for
the Boboli Gardens (1570–75, Florence, now in the Bargello) and later
appears in Flaxman's illustrations for Hesiod's *Theogony* (1807–14). In
a painting by Magritte that otherwise follows Roman iconography, the
god's genitals are replaced by a standing female nude taken from
images of Venus rising from sea foam (1943, priv. coll.).

Attributes: Fish.

Sources: Hesiod, *Theogony*, 133.

OCTAVIA *See* Cleopatra.

OEDIPUS

Gk. and Ger. Oidipus; Lat. Oedipus; It. and Sp. Edipo; Fr. Œdipe.
Hero from Theban legend.

HISTORY/MYTHOLOGY

The legend of Oedipus is one of the most famous in antiquity, and is
known to us through the Greek tragedies.

Oedipus was the son of Jocasta and Laius, king of Thebes. An oracle told his father that he would one day have a son who would kill him and bring misfortune to his family; to prevent the oracle from coming true, Laius abandoned Oedipus at birth. The infant was found, however, and raised by Polybus, king of Corinth. He remained ignorant of his origins until, in the middle of an argument, he learned that he was adopted. He was troubled by this and went to question the oracle at Delphi, where the Pythia revealed that he would kill his father and marry his mother, and that his descendants would continue the tragedy.

Oedipus was returning to Corinth when he unknowingly killed Laius during an altercation with other travelers in a narrow road on the outskirts of Thebes. While deep in gloom and on his way to Thebes, he encountered the Sphinx, who devoured any wayfarer unable to solve her riddle. Oedipus was the only one to provide the solution, and the monster threw herself from a cliff.

Oedipus and the Sphinx.
Attic cup, c. 480 B.C.
Rome, Vatican,
Museo Etrusco.

Creon, who had administered Thebes since Laius's death, had meanwhile promised Jocasta's hand to whoever rid the country of the Sphinx. Oedipus accordingly married Jocasta (his mother) and became king of Thebes. The couple had two sons : Eteocles and Polyneices, and two daughters, Antigone and Ismene. The years passed and then a plague broke out in the city. Creon was sent to Delphi to consult the Pythia and returned to report that the plague would continue until Laius's murderer was found and punished. Consequently Oedipus consulted the seer Tiresias and little by little learned the tragic truth. Jocasta killed herself in despair, and Oedipus plucked out his eyes, left the city, and began the life of a wanderer, accompanied by his daughter Antigone. After long and difficult travels, he arrived at Colonus, in Attica, where Theseus took him in and where he remained until his death.

REPRESENTATIONS

In antiquity, the episode involving the Sphinx was illustrated by Greek and southern Italian vase painters. Oedipus, dressed as a voyager, stands or is seated while facing the Sphinx, who gazes at him from the top of a column or a rock. The most beautiful of these representations is undoubtedly the one found on the interior of a red-figure Attic cup in Rome, Musei Vaticani (470–460 B.C.). A single vase bears the touching image of the young Oedipus nestled in the arms of the shepherd who found him (amphora by the Achilles Painter, c. 460 B.C., Paris, Bibliothèque Nationale, Cabinet des Médailles).

A Roman painting now in the museum at Palermo might represent Oedipus and the messenger who informed him of his adoptive father's death (first century A.D.). The blind Oedipus supports himself on two children, who guide him, while his two daughters follow, in an ivory relief from late antiquity (beginning of the sixth century A.D., St. Petersburg, Hermitage).

Representations of Oedipus are equally rare in modern art. The two themes illustrated are the shepherd finding the infant attached to a tree by the leash that was passed through his pierced ankles (Félix Lecomte, marble, 1771, Paris, Louvre) and *Oedipus Solves the Riddle of the Sphinx*, painted by Ingres in 1808 (Louvre) and again by Moreau (1864, New York, Metropolitan Museum of Art).

Oedipus Exiling Himself from Thebes.
Henri Lévy,
nineteenth century.
Paris, Musée d'Orsay.

Sources: Homer, *The Odyssey* XI, 271–80. Sophocles, *Oedipus Rex*; *Oedipus at Colonus*.

Bibliography: J.-M. Moret, *Œdipe, la sphinx et les Thébians. Essai de mythologie iconographique*, Institut suisse de Rome, 1984.

**Jupiter
in the Middle
of the Olympians.**
Pierre Milan.
Engraving, c. 1550.

OENONE *See* Paris.

OLYMPUS

Mount Olympus, in northern Greece, was considered the habitual abode of the gods, who dwelt there in assembly under Jupiter's authority while nourishing themselves with nectar and ambrosia. The traditional number of Olympian gods is twelve, but the list was not fixed until later times.

Cross-references: Bacchus (Dionysus). Ceres (Demeter). Diana (Artemis). Juno (Hera). Jupiter (Zeus). Mars (Ares). Mercury (Hermes). Minerva (Athena). Neptune (Poseidon). Pluto (Hades). Venus (Aphrodite). Vulcan (Hephaestus).

OMPHALE *See* Hercules.

ORESTES

Gk., Lat., and Ger. Orestes; Fr., It., and Sp. Oreste.
Greek hero.

HISTORY/MYTHOLOGY

Orestes, the son of Agamemnon and Clytemnestra, was the brother of Iphigenia and Electra. An early episode from his story takes place at the beginning of the Trojan War, during the Greek attack on the kingdom of Telephus in Mysia. After the king was wounded in the thigh by Achilles, an oracle informed him that only the weapon that caused the wound could cure him, while another oracle told the Greeks that they could not take Troy without the help of Telephus. The latter therefore threatened to kill the infant Orestes unless Achilles healed him. Achilles agreed, and Orestes was released.

Upon returning from the Trojan War, Agamemnon was assassinated by Clytemnestra and her lover, Aegisthus. Orestes was saved by his sister, Electra, and then secretly raised by his uncle, Strophius, with his own young son, Pylades, who became Orestes' inseparable companion. Orestes returned to Mycenae as an adult and, urged on by Electra, took revenge on his mother and her lover for his father's murder. He was then hounded and driven mad by angry Erinyes (The Furies), goddesses of vengeance. He sought refuge in Apollo's sanctuary at Delphi, where the sun god purified him of the murder, but it was only at Athens that the Erinyes finally stopped tormenting him: the tribunal of the Aeropagus, instituted by Athena, was divided until the goddess's vote tilted the balance in favor of Orestes, who was finally acquitted. According to another version of the story, Orestes had to bring the statue of Artemis from Tauris to Athens in order to be rid of the Erinyes; he was accompanied by Pylades and aided by Iphigenia, who had become a priestess in the sanctuary of Artemis.

REPRESENTATIONS

Several vases depict Telephus seated as a supplicant on an altar and holding the infant Orestes, whom he threatens with his sword (Attic krater, c. 410 B.C., Berlin, Antikensmuseum). The murder of

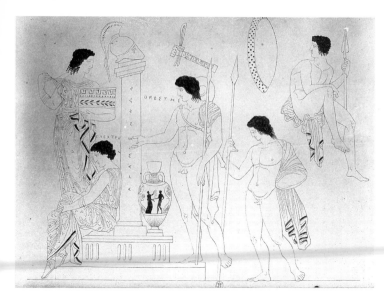

Orestes and Electra.
Lucanian amphora,
c. 380 B.C.
Naples,
Museo Archeologico.

Aegisthus is equally frequently depicted. An Attic krater, attributed to the Dokimasia Painter, groups the death of Agamemnon, on one side, with that of Aegisthus, on the opposite side; Orestes is helmeted and armed with a sword (c. 480 B.C., Boston, Museum of Fine Arts). Most images involving Orestes at Delphi show him seeking sanctuary on the altar of Apollo, or near the omphalus (Apulian krater, c. 380 B.C., Naples, Museo Nazionale). He is also seen fleeing the Erinyes, who brandish snakes. He is purified by piglet's blood (krater by the Eumenides Painter, c. 390 B.C., Paris, Louvre). The meeting between Orestes and Iphigenia at Tauris is also found in ceramics (krater by the Iphigenia Painter, c. 400 B.C., Ferrara, Museo Nazionale).

The main episodes from Orestes' story appear on Roman sarcophagi, in particular a sarcophagus from the Vatican (mid-second century A.D.) where several scenes in succession are shown: the visit to Agamemnon's tomb, the murders of Aegisthus and Clytemnestra, and Orestes pursued by the Erinyes at Delphi; on the cover are Iphigenia in Tauris and the theft of the statue of Artemis.

In modern painting, attention focuses largely on Orestes' madness. The subject of a drawing by Fuseli is *Orestes Pursued by the Furies* (1762–64, Dresden, Staatliche Kunstsammlungen); *The Remorse of Orestes* was painted by Hennequin (1800, Paris, Louvre). Flaxman created a series of thirteen drawings as illustrations to the *Oresteia* (1793–94).

Attributes: Traveler's clothes.

Cross-references: Agamemnon. Furies. Iphigenia.

Sources: Aeschylus, *Oresteia*. Sophocles, *Electra*. Euripedes, *Electra*, *Orestes*, *Iphigenia in Tauris*.

Bibliography: A.J.N.W. Prag, *The Oresteia. Iconographic and Narrative Tradition*, Warminster, 1985.

ORION

It. Orione; Fr., Ger., Gk., and Lat. Orion.
Giant and legendary hunter.

HISTORY/MYTHOLOGY

Orion was a gigantesque Boeotian hunter whose story has several variations. He supposedly tried to rape Perope, the daughter of his host, Oenopion; the latter blinded him in retaliation. He then went to Hephaestus and, guided by a child perched on his shoulders, walked toward the rising sun and regained his sight. His death is told in different ways. According to most authors, Diana sent a scorpion to kill him after he tried to rape her; both the scorpion and Orion were then transformed into constellations, with the first continuously chasing the second. According to Vincenzo Cartari's adaptation (*Le imagini de i dei*, 1556), on the other hand, Diana was in love with Orion.

REPRESENTATIONS

The subject is rare in antiquity, but Lucian briefly described a painting of Orion regaining his sight. It is also possible that Orion is the hunter who appears with other figures condemned to Hades in a fresco from Esquili (50 B.C., Rome, Musei Vaticani).

Poussin, following Cartari, provided the most famous depiction of Orion: the giant walks toward the sun while an enamored Diana stands and watches from a cloud (1658, New York, Metropolitan Museum of Art). Orion stung to death by a scorpion is the subject of a fresco by Raffaelino da Reggio in the Palazzo Farnese at Caprarola (1574, Sala del Mappamondo).

Sources: Lucian, *La Salle* LX, 28–9.

Bibliography: E. Gombrich, *Symbolic Images*, London, 1993, pp. 119–22.

ORITHYIA *See* Boreas.

Orpheus and Eurydice. Majolica dish from Urbino, c. 1550. Venice, Museo Correr.

ORPHEUS

Gk., Lat., and Ger. Orpheus; It. and Sp. Orfeo; Fr. Orphée.
Hero and musician.

HISTORY/MYTHOLOGY

A native of an area near Olympus, this Thracian hero was the son of the river god Oeagrus and the Muse Calliope. He was first and foremost a musician who enchanted wild beasts and savages with his song. He took part in the expedition of the Argonauts, during which he set the rhythm for the oarsmen and calmed the waves. His song charmed infernal monsters and got Pluto and Proserpine to free his wife, Eurydice, the daughter of a nymph, who was killed by a snake when the king of the Lapiths, Aristaeus, tried to abduct her. The gods agreed to allow Eurydice to leave Hades provided Orpheus did not look back before reaching the light of day. He could not resist, however, and lost Eurydice forever. His death was violent: jealous of his power over men, the Thracian women tore him to pieces. His head was carried away by the sea and floated ashore on the island of Lesbos, according to some, or on the coast of Asia Minor, according to others. The sound of his lyre continued to be heard after his death, and from his mouth came oracles.

**Orpheus and
the Thracian Men.**
Attic krater, c. 460 B.C.
Berlin, Staatliche
Museum.

REPRESENTATIONS

In Attic ceramics, Orpheus is dressed in Greek costume and plays his lyre before a captive audience of Thracian warriors (krater by the Orpheus Painter, c. 440 B.C., Berlin, Antikensmuseum). Several vases also show him being killed by Thracian women, who are sometimes tattooed and who assault him with spindles, sickles, and sticks while he tries to defend himself with his lyre (Attic stamnos, c. 460 B.C., Paris, Louvre). A cup shows the head of Orpheus on the ground in front of a young man, who records the oracles on a tablet (c. 420 B.C., Cambridge, Fitzwilliam Museum). The most popular subject from the myth in Roman mosaics was Orpheus charming the animals (Arles, third century A.D.). Orpheus appears in Hades, wearing oriental costume, in some Italiot vases (krater by the Hades Painter, c. 320 B.C., Munich, Antikensammlungen). His meeting with Eurydice is rarer, but appears in a funerary painting from Ostia (first century A.D.). In paleochristian iconography, Orpheus the musician is sometimes assimilated with King David or the Good Shepherd (Rome, Catacomb of Domitilla, fifth century A.D.).

Mantegna depicted the three main episodes of the Orpheus myth in grisaille reliefs for the Camera degli Sposi: two women and a lion listen to him play his music; Orpheus in Hades before Cerberus and one of the Erinyes; and Orpheus killed by women (1468–74, Mantua, Palazzo Ducale). Orpheus is seated in a forest glade surrounded by animals, nymphs, and a faun in a painting attributed to Bellini (1513, Washington, National Gallery). Orpheus charming the animals seems to have been one of the favorite subjects of the Flemish painter Roelandt Savery, whose virtuosity as an animal painter is shown differently in a dozen known versions (1600–28, Paris, Louvre).

Orpheus.
Alabaster
from Sabbartha.
Tripoli, Museum.

Modern painters have most often focused on the subject of Eurydice. Rubens depicted the *Death of Eurydice* (1636–38, Madrid, Prado); Poussin created a *Landscape with Orpheus and Eurydice* (1648–50, Paris, Louvre). Tiepolo incorporated *Orpheus Leading Eurydice from Hades Past Cerberus* into a fresco dedicated to the *Power of Eloquence* (c. 1725, Venice, Palazzo Sandi). Orpheus's grief was dramatized by Moreau (1890, Paris, Musée Gustave Moreau) and Rodin (*Orpheus Imploring the Gods*, bronze, 1892, Paris, Musée Rodin).

The death of Orpheus is a rarer subject. The Thracian women are portrayed as Bacchantes, as exemplified in a painting by Luca Giordano (c. 1700, Madrid, Prado). Moreau, in a fully original work,

Orpheus.
Gustave Moreau,
1865.
Paris,
Musée d'Orsay.

represented a young girl gathering up the lyre and head of Orpheus, which she gravely contemplates (1865, Paris, Musée d'Orsay); the subject was repeated by Redon (c. 1904, Paris, Musée d'Orsay).

For many artists, Orpheus was the figure *par excellence* of the poet and musician. Delacroix portrayed him as a civilizing hero in mural paintings for the library of the Palais Bourbon (*Orpheus Bringing Civilization*, 1838–47, Paris, Chambre des Députés). Orpheus served as a model for other artists, including Dufy, who illustrated Apollinaire's *Bestiary of Orpheus* (1911, wood engravings), and Cocteau, who devoted a cycle of frescoes to him and others (1957–58, Menton, Hôtel de Ville).

Attributes: Lyre.

Cross-references: Argonauts.

Sources: Ovid, *Metamorphoses* X, 1–105.

Bibliography: *Orphée*, ex. cat., Tourcoing, France, 1994.

OWL *See* Hypnos. Minerva.

PAINTING *See* Apelles. Zeuxis.

PALLAS *See* Minerva.

PALM TREE *See* Apollo.

PAN

Gk. Pan; Lat. and Ger. Faunus; It. and Sp. Fauno; Fr. Faune.
Greek god.

HISTORY/MYTHOLOGY

Pan, the son of Hermes and a nymph, was a snub-nosed and horned Greek god with the ears and hooves of a goat. He was particularly venerated in Arcadia by shepherds as a protector of flocks, but he was also associated with woods and mountains. The Romans identified him with Faunus. He was renowned for his lewdness, like the satyrs he often accompanied. He once pursued the nymph Syrinx, who fled to the river Ladon for protection and was turned into reeds as a way of escaping Pan's assaults, whereupon Pan picked a handful of the reeds and with them created the musical instrument that bears the nymph's name—the syrinx or panpipe.

The cult of Pan was introduced in Athens after the Battle of Marathon (490 B.C.) in gratitude for the god's intervention during the war: his appearance triggered a "panic" among the Persian enemy.

Pan.
Bronze from Lousoi,
fifth century B.C.
Berlin,
Antikensammlungen.

**Pan Chasing
after a Shepherd.**
Attic krater,
c. 470 B.C.
Boston, Museum
of Fine Arts.

REPRESENTATIONS

In a series of Attic reliefs (fourth century B.C., Athens, National
Museum), Pan is seen grouped with nymphs in a grotto where believers
have gathered to worship him. He is also seen pursuing a shepherd on a
krater attributed to the Pan Painter (c. 470 B.C., Boston, Museum of Fine
Arts). From the end of the fifth century B.C., Pan's image is multiplied and
Pans collectively surround Bacchus like satyrs. A chorus of Pans
accompanied by a flutist is seen on a krater attributed to the Niobid
Painter (c. 460 B.C., London, British Museum). Pan also appears in
representations of Venus and cupids. He appears frequently in

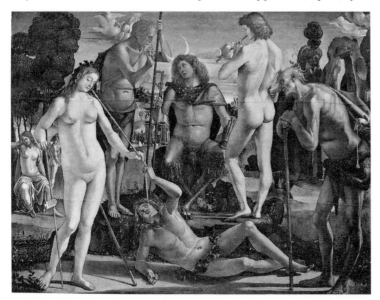

The School of Pan.
Luca Signorelli, 1488.
Destroyed, formerly
Berlin, Kaiser
Friedrich Museum.

Pan and Syrinx.
Jacob Jordaens,
c. 1620.
Brussels,
Musées Royaux
des Beaux-Arts.

Hellenistic sculpture: Venus repels his assaults with her sandal in a group discovered at Delos (100 B.C., Athens, National Museum) and he teaches music to Daphnis in a group for which there are several known Roman copies (Imperial period, Rome, Museo dei Termi).

In Luca Signorelli's *The School of Pan*, the god sits enthroned in the center (c. 1490, Berlin, destroyed). He is grouped with Ceres in *Ceres and Pan* by Rubens and a work by Frans Snyders in which Ceres holds a cornucopia and Pan holds fruit (c. 1617, Madrid, Prado). Jordaens depicted Pan playing the flute (1630–35, Amsterdam, Rijksmuseum), and Poussin painted the *Triumph of Pan* in the context of a series of Bacchanals for the château of Richelieu (c. 1635, London, National Gallery). In the nineteenth century, the subject of Pan inspired Böcklin several times, most notably for *Pan Among the Reeds* (1859, Munich, Neue Pinakothek) and *Pan Frightening a Shepherd* (c. 1858, Basel, Kunstmuseum).

Attributes: Syrinx.

Cross-references: Bacchus. Daphnis. Faun. Venus.

Sources: Herodotus, VI, 105. Ovid, *Metamorphoses* I, 689–712.

Bibliography: P. Borgeaud, *Recherches sur le dieu Pan*, Geneva, 1979.

PANDORA

Gk., Lat., It., and Ger. Pandora; Fr. Pandore.
The first woman.

HISTORY/MYTHOLOGY

In Greek legend, Pandora was the first woman. She was modeled by Hephaestus, and all the gods immediately gave her different qualities as gifts, as indicated by her name, *pan dora*, which means she who has "all gifts" or she who is the "gift of all." Zeus married her to Prometheus's brother, Epimetheus, as mankind's misfortune. She had charge of a jar full of banes and disasters that she was never to open under any circumstances but, overcome by curiosity, she opened it and released all the misfortunes until there remained only hope at the bottom of the jar.

Pandora.
Detail
from Jean Cousin,
Eva Prima Pandora,
1549.
Paris, Louvre.

REPRESENTATIONS

In antiquity, Pandora's creation attracted special artistic interest. She is called Anesidora and appears between Hephaestus and Athena, who adjusts her clothing, in an Attic white-ground cup (c. 460 B.C., London, British Museum). She is seen standing in the middle of an assembly of gods in a krater attributed to the Niobid Painter (c. 460 B.C., London, British Museum). Pausanias says that her birth was also represented on the base of the *Athena Parthenos* by Phidias in the Parthenon (c. 440 B.C.).

In the Renaissance, the iconography of Pandora changed under the influence of Erasmus and following the fusing of her story with that of Psyche. She holds the box from which misfortunes escape, and is seen opening it in a drawing by Rosso (c. 1530–40, Paris, École des Beaux-Arts). She is sometimes likened to Eve, the first woman in the biblical tradition, as indicated by the inscription on Jean Cousin's painting of a reclining female nude, *Eva Prima Pandora* (1549, Paris, Louvre). Although scarcely represented from the baroque through rococo periods, Pandora again became popular in neoclassical art, particularly in England. In a large canvas by James Barry (1791, Manchester, City Art Gallery), Pandora is shown dressed and ready to carry out her destiny in an assembly of gods. A painted ceiling by Howard, who was influenced by Flaxman's drawings for illustrations to Hesiod (engraved by William Blake and published in 1817), reflects the three main episodes of the account: in the center is *Pandora Receiving Gifts from the Gods* and in two framing lunettes are *Pandora Brought to Epimetheus by Mercury* and *Epimetheus Opening Pandora's Vase* (1834, London, Sir John Soane's Museum). Rossetti revived the misogynic theme of Pandora's box (1871, unknown location), and Paul Klee endowed *Still Life with Pandora's Box* with obvious sexual connotations (1920, priv. coll.).

Pandora Born from the Ground. Attic krater, c. 450 B.C. Oxford, Ashmolean Museum.

Attributes: Box. Jar.

Cross-references: Prometheus. Psyche. Vulcan.

Sources: Hesiod, *Works and Days*, 57–101; *Theogony*, 570–90. Pausanias, I, 24, 7.

Bibliography: D. and E. Panofsky, *Pandora's Box*, Princeton, 1991.

PANTHER *See* Bacchantes. Bacchus.

PARCAE *See* Fates.

PARIS

Gk. Alexandros; It. Paride; Sp. Paris; Fr. Pâris; Ger. and Lat. Paris. Trojan prince.

HISTORY/MYTHOLOGY

Paris, the son of Priam and Hecuba, was a Trojan prince. He was abandoned at birth on Mount Ida after a prophet announced that he would be the ruin of Troy, but shepherds found him, named him Alexander, and brought him up as one of them. Although the nymph Oenone was in love with him, he preferred Helen, whom Venus awarded him for the

The Judgement of Paris (detail). Lucas Cranach the Elder, 1528. Basel, Öffentliche Kunstsammlung.

judgement he passed in her favor. The story of the famous Judgement of Paris actually begins at the wedding feast of Thetis and Peleus, to which all the gods were invited except Discord (Eris), who tossed an apple among the guests saying that it was "for the most beautiful." With three goddesses—Juno, Minerva, and Venus—believing themselves thus designated, Jupiter refused to take sides and instead decided that the first mortal to arrive would act as judge. This mortal happened to be Paris. Each of the goddesses then promised him a present. Juno promised power; Minerva, wisdom. Venus promised him the most beautiful woman in the world, Helen of Troy, the wife of Menelaus. Paris chose Venus and consequently abducted Helen, triggering the Trojan War. During the war, Juno and Minerva sided with the Greeks, and Venus with the Trojans. Although Paris was not a major hero in the war and instead fought from a distance with his bow, it was one of his arrows that killed Achilles by wounding the hero in the heel, his only weak spot. Paris himself died by the bow in a duel with Philoctetes.

REPRESENTATIONS

Paris is found most often in representations of the judgement, in which the three goddesses are led by Hermes (Mercury). In Attic ceramics, he is sometimes dressed as shepherd (cup by Makron, c. 480 B.C., Berlin, Antikensmuseum); later, especially in Italiot ceramics, he wears a Phrygian cap and oriental costume. The abduction of Helen, which also appears in ancient art, is probably the subject of a geometric Attic krater from 730 B.C. (London, British Museum), and it appears in

220

**The Judgement
of Paris.**
Michele Corneille,
c. 1685.
Lyon,
Musée des Beaux-Arts.

relief on a Laconian ivory (c. 600 B.C. Athens, National Museum) and on a skyphos by Makron (c. 480 B.C., Boston, Museum of Fine Arts). The bow-and-arrow duel with Philoctetes, during which Paris dies, is depicted on a series of Etruscan urns (second century B.C., Volterra, Museo Guarnacci).

In modern painting, the Judgement of Paris is one of the most common mythological subjects. An important composition by Matthias Gerung, *The Destruction of Troy and the Judgement of Paris* (1540, Paris, Louvre), combines various scenes from the life of the Trojan hero. The judgement alone was very often treated by Lucas Cranach the Elder (thirteen known versions) and Luca Giordano (eight versions, one from c. 1670, Vienna, Kunsthistorisches Museum). The subject is also encountered in a work by Raphael (lost painting, known through an engraving by Marcantonio Raimondi), Tintoretto (1543–44, Padua, Museo Civico), and Rubens (1601, London, National Gallery, and 1607, Madrid, Prado). Fra Angelico depicted Helen's abduction (c. 1450, London, National Gallery). The same scene appears in a landscape by Martin van Heemskerck (1535–36, Baltimore, Walters Art Gallery), and it is represented as a naval battle by Tintoretto (1580–85, Madrid, Prado). David created a more original version by representing Paris and Helen seated on a bed (1788, Paris, Louvre).

Representations have also been made of Paris and Oenone; Paris may hold the nymph under a tree whose bark is inscribed with the couple's names (Jacob van Loo, Dresden).

Attributes: Apple. Bow. Costume of a Phrygian shepherd.

Cross-references: Achilles. Helen. Juno. Minerva. Troy. Venus.

Bibliography: C. Clairmont, *Das Parisurteil in der antiken Kunst*, Zurich, 1951. H. Damisch, *Le Jugement de Pâris*, Paris, 1992.

PARNASSUS

Lat. Parnassus; Ger. andGk. Parnassos; Fr. Parnasse; It. Parnasso. Mountain in Greece.

HISTORY/MYTHOLOGY

Parnassus, a mountain north of Delphi, was traditionally frequented by Apollo and the Muses, and it therefore became the setting *par*

Parnassus.
Raphael,
1510–11.
Rome, Vatican,
Stanza della
Segnatura.

excellence for poetry and music. In classical art, Parnassus often served as a backdrop for allegories of the arts.

REPRESENTATIONS

Parnassus itself was not the main subject of representations in antiquity, but it has commonly been so since the Renaissance. Mantegna provided a version with Mars and Venus for the *studiolo* of Isabella d'Este at Mantua (1497, Paris, Louvre). Raphael peopled his Parnassus with gods, goddesses, and poets united around Homer (1510–11, Rome, Vatican, Stanza della Segnatura). Poussin provided the classic portrayal of Apollo and the Muses (c. 1630, Paris, Louvre), and Claude Lorraine painted a *Landscape with the Parnassus* (1652, Edinburgh, National Gallery of Scotland). Mengs took up the subject of *Apollo with the Nine Muses and Mnemosyne* (fresco, 1760–61, Rome, Villa Albani), a subject also explored by Bourdelle for the façade of the Théâtre des Champs-Élysées (1912, Paris). Parnassus is reduced to the pure form of a pyramid in a work by Paul Klee, *Ad Parnassum* (1932, Bern, Kunstmuseum).

Cross-references: Apollo. Muses.

Bibliography: M. Fumaroli, *L'École du silence*, Paris, 1994, pp. 53–147.

Pasiphaë.
First century B.C.
Pompeii,
House of the Vettii.

PASIPHAË

Gk., Lat., It., and Ger. Pasiphae; Fr. Pasiphaé.
Cretan heroine.

HISTORY/MYTHOLOGY

Pasiphaë, the daughter of Helios (the Sun), was the wife of Minos, king of Crete. After her husband neglected to honor his promise to sacrifice a bull to Poseidon, the angry god had Pasiphaë fall passionately in love with the animal. She consequently asked Daedalus to fabricate a hollow cow for her to slip into so that she could couple with the bull, and the offspring of this unnatural passion was the Minotaur.

REPRESENTATIONS

Pasiphaë watching Daedalus make the cow is a subject that appears in Pompeian painting, in an Imperial Roman relief (Rome, Palazzo Spada), and on a Roman sarcophagus (c. A.D. 140, Paris, Louvre).

Giulio Romano relied on Philostratus's description for his portrayal of Daedalus fabricating the cow (1528, Mantua, Palazzo del Tè). Although infrequently represented, the subject also inspired Poussin's friend John Lemaire, who used it in his architectural landscapes (seventeenth century, Paris, Louvre).

Attributes: Cow.

Cross-references: Daedalus. Minotaur.

Sources: Philostratus, *Imagines* I, 16.

Bibliography: A. Blunt, "Poussin Studies IX. Additions to the Work of Jean Lemaire," *Burlington Magazine* 101 (1959): 438–43.

Pasiphaë and the Bull.
Gustave Moreau,
c. 1897. Paris,
Musée Gustave Moreau.

PATROCLUS

Gk. and Ger. Patroclos; Lat. Patroclus; It. and Sp. Patroclo; Fr. Patrocle.
Greek hero and friend of Achilles.

HISTORY/MYTHOLOGY

Patroclus was the son of Menoetius, king of Locris. He was raised with Achilles and became his inseparable friend. In *The Iliad*, he fought with Achilles' weapons after the hero himself refused to take part in the combat because Agamemnon had offended him. Patroclus was momentarily able to contain the attacking Trojans, but he soon died at the hands of Hector. Achilles then rejoined the battle to avenge his friend's death, killed Hector, and organized a solemn funeral ceremony for Patroclus.

REPRESENTATIONS

Patroclus is most often represented with Achilles. On a cup attributed to the Sosias Painter, Achilles is seen attending to Patroclus, who is wounded in the arm by an arrow (c. 510 B.C., Berlin, Antikensmuseum). The funeral games held in honor of Patroclus appear on the fragment of a

The Obsequies of Patroclus.
Jacques-Louis David,
1779.
Dublin, National Gallery of Ireland.

**Patroclus
and Achilles.**
Attic cup,
c. 500 B.C.
Berlin,
Antikensamm-
lungen.

krater signed by Sophilos (c. 580 B.C., Athens, National Museum). Patroclus appears with Achilles and Briseïs in a Pompeian painting (first century B.C., House of the Golden Cupids). A group known since the Renaissance as the *Pasquino* in fact portrays Menelaus lifting the corpse of Patroclus (original, c. 240 B.C.; Roman copies in Rome, Palazzo del Pasquino, and Florence, Loggia dei Lanzi).

In modern painting, Patroclus is rarely the main character except in scenes that take place after his death. Giulio Romano, for example, represented the *The Battle around the Body of Patroclus* in the Sala de Troia (1538–39, Mantua, Palazzo Ducale) and David painted *The Obsequies of Patroclus* (1778, Dublin, National Gallery of Ireland). In a visionary painting, Fuseli showed how *Achilles Grasps at the Shade of Patroclus* (1803, Zurich, Nusthaus).

Cross-references: Achilles.

Sources: Homer, *The Iliad* XVI, XXIII.

PEACOCK *See* Argus. Juno.

PEARLS *See* Cleopatra.

PEGASUS

Fr. Pégase; Lat. Pegasus; Ger. and Gk. Pegasos; It. Pegaso.
Fabled winged horse.

HISTORY/MYTHOLOGY

Pegasus.
Attic lekythos,
c. 480 B.C.
Oxford,
Ashmolean Museum.

The winged horse, Pegasus, was born with the Giant Chrysaor from the wound of the beheaded Gorgon, Medusa, who was pregnant by Neptune, and immediately sped off to Olympus to bring the thunderbolt to Jupiter. He then served as a mount for Perseus when the hero freed Andromeda, and he is equally important for the legend of Bellerophon, who bridled him while he drank from the Pirene Spring in Corinth. Another tradition claims that Pegasus was a gift to Bellerophon from Athena or Poseidon to help in his fight against the Chimera. Bellerophon indeed fought the Chimera as well as the Amazons, and then arrogantly attempted to climb with Pegasus to Olympus, whereupon Jupiter took offense and dashed Bellerophon to earth.

Pegasus also played a role in the legend of the Pierides. When the daughters of Pierus attempted to rival the nine Muses in a song contest, Mount Helicon became so swelled with pleasure that Neptune sent Pegasus to assuage it. The animal struck the mountain with its hoof, and a spring—the Hippocrene Spring—gushed forth. Pegasus was ultimately transformed into a constellation; he sometimes represents the incarnation of poetic inspiration.

REPRESENTATIONS

This very attractive and ever-popular subject appears as early as the seventh century B.C. In Corinthian, Thasian, and Melian ceramics, Pegasus serves as Bellerophon's mount while the hero battles the Chimera alone or surrounded by gods. The themes and media diversify in the sixth century B.C. The winged horse appears on Corinthian coins until the end of the Roman period. A magnificent bronze helmet from Axos is decorated on two sides with a standing Pegasus in high relief (first quarter of the sixth century B.C., Crete, Herakleion Museum). In this period, bronze workers used the forepart of the winged horse (*protome*) as a decorative motif and even as handles for bronze vessels, as is demonstrated on a dish from Dodona, now in Berlin (c. 540 B.C.).

The theme of filiation or birth emerges in this period. Noteworthy is a scene with Medusa squeezing Pegasus to her breast while Perseus decapitates her (metope from Temple C at Selinunte, c. 530 B.C., Palermo, Museo Archeologico). Chrysaor is shown peacefully leaving the scene with a basket containing Medusa's head attached to the end of a rod, in a Cypriot sarcophagus from Golgoï (early fifth century B.C., New York, Metropolitan Museum of Art). Pegasus is seen rushing out from Medusa's bloody wound while Perseus runs away and lets the beheaded Gorgon fall to earth, in an Attic white-ground lekythos (c. 480 B.C., New York, Metropolitan Museum of Art).

Pegasus.
Odilon Redon,
drawing.
Paris, Louvre.

Another theme treated by artists is that of the horse climbing to the starlit sky (Attic hydria, c. 440 B.C., Paris, Bibliothèque Nationale).

All these images endured into Roman and Hellenistic times. They were also represented in Etruscan art; Bellerophon stands holding a majestic Pegasus by the halter, for example, on a large Etruscan chest of engraved bronze (c. 300 B.C., London, British Museum).

The surface of the celestial globe held by the marble Atlas Farnese, which was discovered in the sixteenth century, is sculpted in relief with personifications of the constellations that astronomers had identified since the fourth century B.C.; among those personifications is the *protome* of Pegasus (Roman copy after a Greek original, A.D. 117–138, Naples, Museo Nazionale).

Pegasus as a constellation is present throughout the Middle Ages and the modern period in treatises on astronomy and in manuscripts whose text is relevant to astronomy. One example is al-Sufi's *Book on the Constellations of the Fixed Stars*—the Arab translation of Ptolemy's *Almagest*, translated in the ninth century (end of the twelfth century for Latin translations).

Many medieval miniatures illustrate the various legends that surround the winged horse. The singing contest between the Muses and the Pierides, for example, is illustrated in a manuscript for the *Moralized Ovid*, a work attributed to Chrétien Legouais; here, the Pierides are turned into magpies while Pegasus, with his hoof, creates the spring where nine Muses bathe and while Apollo, dressed like a medieval ruler, plays his lyre (c. 1380, Paris, Bibliothèque Nationale, ms. fr. 871, f. 116 v). The singing contest also appears in Mantegna's *Parnassus* (1497, Paris, Louvre).

The subject persists into the nineteenth century, notably in symbolist art (for exemple Moreau, *The Traveling Poet*, 1891, Paris, Musée Gustave Moreau).

Cross-references: Bellerophon. Perseus.

Sources: Hesiod, *Theogony*, 276–86, Ovid, *Metamorphoses* V, 256–9.

Bibliography: N. Yalouris, *Pegasus, the Art of the Legend*, 1975.

PELEUS

It. and Sp. Peleo; Fr. Pélée; Ger., Gk., and Lat. Peleus.
Legendary Thessalian king.

HISTORY/MYTHOLOGY

Peleus, a Thessalian king, was the father of Achilles. He was driven out of Aegina by his own father when he and his brother, Telamon, became so jealous of their half-brother, Phocus—particularly with respect to his athletic prowess—that they decided to murder him by throwing a discus at his head. He subsequently fled to the court of Eurytion at Phthia, in Thessaly, where Eurytion purified him of the murder and betrothed his daughter to him. Peleus accidentally killed his father-in-law, however, during the Calydonian boar hunt and was again forced into exile. He then went to the court of Acastus at Iolcos, where the king's wife, Astydamia, tried to have him killed by falsely accusing him of rape. Acastus consequently invited him to a hunt on Mount Pelion with the intention of killing him there. The gods, however, rushed to the aid of Peleus, who, with additional help from Jason and the Dioscuri, beseiged the city and killed the royal couple.

Jupiter and Neptune then promised him a beautiful Nereid, Thetis, whom they themselves had stopped fighting over as soon as a prophecy predicted that her son would be more powerful than his father. Thetis at first refused to accept the arranged marriage and tried to get out of it by using her powers of metamorphosis to change herself into each of the elements and then into a tree, a bird, a tiger, a snake, etc. Peleus finally won when, upon advice from the centaur Chiron, he held Thetis fast until she turned back into a goddess and a woman.

The wedding feast of Thetis and Peleus was celebrated on Mount Pelion in the gods' presence and while Muses sang. Each guest offered a present, notably Neptune, who gave the couple the two immortal horses, Balius and Xanthus, that would later be harnessed to Achilles' chariot. During the banquet, Eris (Discord) threw a golden apple among the guests, saying it was for the most beautiful of three goddesses: Minerva, Juno, or Venus. No one wanted to decide the question, and the dispute that consequently erupted was settled only when Jupiter asked Paris to act as judge. That event, known as the Judgement of Paris, formed the prelude to the Trojan War. Peleus died at an elderly age after the war. According to one tradition, this occurred on the island of Cos, where he had met his grandson, Neoptolemus, after being chased out of Phthia by Acastus's sons. According to another tradition, although Acastus's sons imprisoned Peleus, he died in his own lands after being rescued by Neoptolemus, who restored him to his kingdom.

Peleus Hiding in a Tree.
Attic white-ground oenochoe, 510 B.C. New York, Metropolitan Museum of Art.

REPRESENTATIONS

The struggle between Peleus and Thetis was painted on Corinthian and Attic ceramics from 575 B.C. By the middle of the sixth century B.C., these images evoke Thetis's transformations: a small lion appears on either one of the protagonists' backs or shoulders, the couple is surrounded by snakes, or flames emerge from Thetis (black-figure neck amphora, c. 540 B.C., London, British Museum; superb cup, signed Peithinos, c. 510 B.C., Berlin; cup by Douris, c. 475 B.C., Paris, Bibliothèque Nationale, Cabinet des Médailles).

The marriage has also appeared as a subject in art since the sixth century B.C., particularly on vases made for wedding celebrations. Such works focus on the marriage procession: the newlyweds are escorted by the gods, who may be in chariots or on foot, or Peleus welcomes the gods from in front of his house, with Thetis modestly standing beside him. The most famous examples of this scene are doubtless those found on the François Vase (a large volute krater signed by the painter Kleitias and the potter Ergotimos, c. 570 B.C., Florence, Museo Archeologico) and on a dinos signed by Sophilos (c. 580 B.C., London, British Museum).

Modern artists have depicted the wedding of Thetis and Peleus as well as the apple of discord episode. There have been many examples since the sixteenth century, especially from the Netherlands and Germany (Abraham Bloemaert, 1638, The Hague, Mauritshuis; Rubens, 1636, Madrid, Prado and Chicago, Art Institute).

Cross-references: Achilles. Chiron. Thetis. Troy.

Sources: Homer, *The Iliad* XVIII, 85 ff., 432 ff.

Bibliography: R. K. Davis, *Peleus and Thetis*, Oxford, 1924.

PELIAS *See* Jason.

PELOPS

Fr. Pélops; Ger., Gk., and Lat. Pelops; It. Pelope.
Greek hero.

HISTORY/MYTHOLOGY

Pelops was the son of Tantalus, the father of Atreus and Thyestes. He was killed by his father, who served him as a meal to the gods to try their patience. The gods discovered the murder and restored Pelops to life, but not before Demeter had eaten his shoulder, which then had to be replaced by an ivory one. Pelops later won the hand of Hippodamia by outfoxing her father, Oenomaüs, who challenged his daughter's suitors to a chariot race and killed the losers. He bribed Oenomaüs's charioteer, Myrtilus, into sabotaging his master's chariot, whereupon Oenomaüs was killed and Pelops won the race, married Hippodamia, and reigned over Elis in the region that now bears his name: the Peloponnese.

Pelops.
Attic red-figure
amphora, c. 410 B.C.
Arezzo,
Museo Archeologico.

REPRESENTATIONS

Preparations for the race between Pelops and Oenomaüs are represented on the east pediment of the Temple of Zeus at Olympia (c. 470 B.C.). Several Italiot vases repeat the chariot race motif or sometimes group Pelops with Tantalus's daughter, Niobe (Apulian loutrophoros, c. 350 B.C., Malibu, J. Paul Getty Museum). Sculptors of Roman sarcophagi highlighted the race and the accident that caused Oenomaüs's death: horses rear and Oenomaüs lies on the ground (vat of sarcophagus, c. A.D. 230–240, Paris, Louvre).

Pelops appears not to have been represented by modern artists.

Attributes: Chariot.

Cross-references: Tantalus.

Sources: Apollodorus, II, 4, 5.

PENELOPE

Gk., Lat., Ger., and It. Penelope; Fr. Pénélope.
Wife of Ulysses.

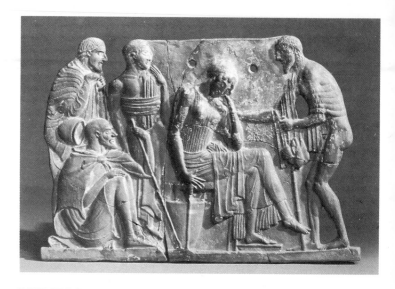

Penelope.
Terracotta
from Melos,
fifth century B.C.
New York,
Metropolitan
Museum of Art.

HISTORY/MYTHOLOGY

Penelope was the exceptionally faithful wife of Ulysses, with whom she had a son, Telemachus. Ulysses was presumed dead when a ten-year voyage in the Mediterranean after the fall of Troy kept him far from Ithaca. Penelope had many suitors as a result, and each one pressed her to choose a new spouse (and therefore a king) while taking up residence in her husband's palace. Forever faithful to Ulysses, whose return she alone awaited, she put off the suitors day after day by pretending she first had to finish weaving a tapestry and then untiringly waking up each night to undo secretly the previous day's work.

Penelope finally organized a contest and promised her hand to whoever was best with Ulysses' bow, which none of the suitors could even string. As it happened, Ulysses had just returned incognito and demanded that he try. His first arrow hit the target of circularly placed ax-heads—a pre-arranged signal to begin the massacre of his wife's suitors. It was only afterward that Ulysses revealed his true identity to Penelope.

REPRESENTATIONS

In ancient art, Penelope appears either near her tapestry or seated in front of it with a distant, melancholic look while resting her head on her hand (skyphos by Penelope Painter, c. 450 B.C., Chiusi). The suitors are often shown trying to string Ulysses' bow during a banquet. These subjects were familiar throughout Greece and were depicted with considerable uniformity. They are found in both Attic and Boeotian ceramics, in carved gems, in goldsmiths' work, and on reliefs from eastern Greece.

Renaissance artists illustrated the same themes. Notable among these artists is Pinturicchio, who depicted Penelope at her loom, surrounded by suitors (c. 1509, London, National Gallery). Rossetti revived this motif in a drawing (1869, priv. coll.), as did Waterhouse (1912, Aberdeen Art Gallery).

Attributes: Loom.

Cross-references: Telemachus. Ulysses.

Sources: Homer, *The Odyssey* XIII–XXIV.

Bibliography: O. Touchefeu, *Thèmes odysséens dans l'art antique*, Paris, 1968.

PENTHESILEA

Fr. Penthésilée; Ger. and Gk. Penthesileia; Lat. Penthesilea.
Queen of the Amazons.

HISTORY/MYTHOLOGY

Penthesilea, the daughter of Ares (Mars), was queen of the Amazons. She came to the aid of the Trojans and fought Achilles in a duel. Achilles won but fell in love with her at the very moment of killing her.

Penthesilea.
Attic cup, c. 460 B.C.
Munich,
Antikensammlungen.

REPRESENTATIONS

The duel between Penthesilea and Achilles appears on an amphora by Exekias (c. 540 B.C., London, British Museum); a cup attributed to the Penthesilea Painter dramatically depicts the exchange of glances between her and Achilles as the hero stabs her (c. 460 B.C., Munich, Antikensammlungen). In a Roman sarcophagus, Achilles is seen lifting the Amazon's dead body (c. A.D. 225–250, Rome, Musei Vaticani).

The subject is rare in modern painting. It has been treated in sculpture by Canova (terracotta model, 1798–99, Possagno, Gipsoteca Canoviana) and Thorwaldsen (marble relief, 1837, Copenhagen, Thorwaldsens Museum). In 1969, Kokoschka illustrated Kleist's tragedy, *Penthesilea* (1808), with a series of ten engravings.

Cross-references: Achilles. Amazons.

Sources: Quintus Smyrnaeus, *Posthomerica* I, 538–629. Virgil, *Aeneid* I, 490–93.

PENTHEUS

Gk., Lat., and Ger. Pentheus; It. and Sp. Penteo; Fr. Penthée.
Legendary Theban king.

HISTORY/MYTHOLOGY

Pentheus, the son of Agave, was a descendant of Cadmus and ruled over Thebes, where Bacchus's mother, Semele, was born. When Bacchus returned from Asia, he arrived incognito in Thebes to establish his cult there. He also intended to avenge his mother, who was a victim of Theban contempt, and he accordingly drove the Theban women mad. Pentheus consequently imprisoned the stranger (Bacchus), who immediately freed himself and persuaded the king to see for himself what the women of his city were up to. Pentheus consequently disguised himself as a woman and went to Mount Cithaeron, where all the women had fled in their madness and where now—led by Pentheus's own mother, Agave—they mistook Pentheus for a lion and tore him to pieces. As a result of this legend, Pentheus came to exemplify an arrogantly impious person who encounters Bacchus's inexorable anger.

Pentheus Dismembered by Maenads. Attic hydria, c. 500 B.C. Berlin, Antikensammlungen.

REPRESENTATIONS

Antique images focus on the most violent moment of this tale, when the king's body is dismembered by frenzied Maenads, who each hold a piece of it (psykter of Euphronius, c. 510 B.C., Boston, Museum of Fine Arts).

This episode is rare in modern painting. It appears in a fresco by Daniele da Volterra (1548–50, Rome, Palazzo Farnese). Laurent de La Hyre devoted two paintings to the *Story of Pentheus* (c. 1634, Montluçon, Museum and Chicago, Art Institute).

Cross-references: Bacchantes. Bacchus. Semele.

Sources: Euripides, *Bacchae.* Ovid, *Metamorphoses* III, 511–63.

Bibliography: H. Philippart, *Iconographie des Bacchantes d'Euridipe*, Brussels, 1930.

PERO *See* Cimon.

PERSEPHONE *See* Proserpine.

PERSEUS

Gk., Lat., and Ger. Perseus; It. and Sp. Perseo; Fr. Persée. Greek hero.

HISTORY/MYTHOLOGY

Perseus, an Argian hero, was the son of Jupiter and Danaë, the mortal daughter of Acrisius. After an oracle predicted to Acrisius that he would have a grandson who would kill him, he had an underground room built and imprisoned his daughter there out of fear that the prediction might come true. Danaë, however, conceived a child after Jupiter visited her in the form of a shower of gold. When Acrisius discovered the child, he locked Perseus and Danaë in a chest, which he threw into the sea. Mother and son then drifted to the island of Seriphos, where they were both welcomed.

The island's tyrant, Polydectes, however, coveted Danaë, and Perseus conceived the mad idea of bringing the Gorgon Medusa's head to Polydectes in order to save his mother. Assisted by Minerva and Mercury, he outfoxed and decapitated Medusa by using her reflection in his polished shield—held by Minerva herself—to guide his *harpe* (a knife with a curved blade). Because Medusa's head retained its power to turn others to stone even after it was severed, Perseus then hid it in a wallet. Although the two other Gorgons, who were immortal, pursued him, Perseus escaped with the help of Mercury's winged sandals and a helmet from Pluto that made him invisible. The winged horse, Pegasus, and the Giant Chrysaor sprang from Medusa's wound. In his next adventure, Perseus mounted the former and, while brandishing Medusa's head, liberated Andromeda, who had been attached to a rock and was about to be devoured by a sea monster. He then fell in love with the beautiful Andromeda, married her, and went back to the island of Seriphos, where he avenged himself on the tyrant Polydectes. As a conclusion to this particular adventure, Perseus offered the Gorgon's head to Minerva, who placed it in the center of her breastplate as a figure to avert evil, and he returned Pluto's helmet, the sandals, and the wallet to Mercury, who restored them to the nymphs.

Perseus later re-entered Argos with Andromeda. While there, he competed in games organized by the king of Lorissa, and during a discus-throw involuntarily but mortally wounded his grandfather, Acrisius, thus fulfilling the oracle's prediction.

Perseus.
Benvenuto Cellini,
1554.
Florence,
Loggia dei Lanzi.

REPRESENTATIONS

Ancient representations of the myth of Perseus are innumerable and very old (seventh century B.C.). They appear in a wide variety of media: architecture, frescoes, ceramics, bronze, coins, cameos, ivory, and so on. The iconography is most often mixed with that of Medusa and Andromeda. In an ivory relief from Samos, Perseus and Medusa appear frontally to avoid exchanging glances while the Gorgon's head falls (c. 630–620 B.C., Athens, National Museum). A parallel scene is found in two sixth-century B.C. works from architectural settings: the

Perseus Freeing Andromeda.
Charles-Antoine Coypel,
1727.
Paris, Louvre.

Gorgon pediment from the Temple of Artemis at Corfu (beginning of the sixth century B.C., Museum of Corfu) and a metope from Temple C at Selinunte (c. 540 B.C., Palermo, Museo Nazionale).

The entire story of the beheading is told on the body of an Attic black-figure lekythos (c. 530 B.C., Paris, Bibliothèque Nationale, Cabinet des Médailles); included is a scene from Perseus's escape that shows the hero hiding Medusa's head in his wallet, dripping blood; also represented are Minerva and Mercury, who help Perseus escape the immortal sisters, Stheno and Euryale. In a Pompeian painting, Perseus hides Medusa's head behind his back and grabs Andromeda's delicate arm (first century B.C., from the House of the Dioscuri and now in Naples, Museo Nazionale).

The different episodes of the myth have been treated frequently in modern art: Perseus and Medusa, Perseus rescuing Andromeda, and Perseus and Phineus (who was betrothed to Andromeda and plotted against Perseus). This last episode is notably illustrated in a drawing by Polidoro da Caravaggio that shows Perseus violently brandishing Medusa's head, which he holds by the hair (sixteenth century, Paris, Louvre, Cabinet des Dessins).

The most important work, however, is probably still Benvenuto Cellini's bronze statue, *Perseus*, which represents a synthesis of the myth: Danaë with the child Perseus appears as one of the four bronze statuettes in the pedestal's niches and, in a bronze relief beneath the pedestal, Perseus comes to the aid of Andromeda (1554, Florence, Loggia dei Lanzi).

Attributes: Head (of Medusa). Shield. Sword. Wallet. Winged sandals.

Cross-references: Danaë. Gorgon. Minerva.

Sources: Ovid, *Metamorphoses* IV, 604–803; V, 1–249.

Bibliography: J.-C. Boyer, *L'Andromède de Pierre Mignard*, Paris, Louvre, 1990. John Pope-Hennessy, *Benvenuto Cellini*, Paris, 1985.

PHAEDRA

Gk. and Ger. Phaidra; Lat. Phaedra; It. Fedra; Fr. Phèdre.
Cretan heroine.

HISTORY/MYTHOLOGY

Phaedra, the daughter of Minos and Pasiphaë, married Theseus and became the stepmother of Hippolytus, Theseus's son by his first wife, the Amazonian queen Antiope. As it happened, Hippolytus, a young, chaste, and surly hunter, worshiped Diana but neglected Venus. This made the goddess of love so jealous that she caused Phaedra to fall in love with him. Then, because Hippolytus rejected her advances, Phaedra wrote a letter accusing him of trying to rape her, whereupon Theseus chased his son away and begged Neptune to punish him. Consequently, while Hippolytus was fleeing in his chariot along the shore, a sea monster rose out of the water and terrified the horses, causing the chariot to overturn and kill Hippolytus. Phaedra hanged herself in despair.

REPRESENTATIONS

The subject of Phaedra and Hippolytus is found particularly on Roman sarcophagi, where several episodes from the story are juxtaposed. On an example in the Louvre (c. A.D. 290), a lovesick Phaedra sits

Phaedra.
Alexandre Cabanel,
1880.
Montpellier,
Musée Fabre.

surrounded by servants and small cupids; in the center is Hippolytus, dressed in hunting clothes, reading Phaedra's letter; finally, Theseus is seen listening to the account of his son's death. Only two scenes appear on another, older sarcophagus: on the left, Phaedra sits while a servant speaks to Hippolytus on her behalf; on the right, Hippolytus hunts a boar (c. A.D. 200, Paris, Louvre).

Modern artists have highlighted the dramatic moment of Hippolytus's death. In a work by Rubens, for example, the monster rises from the sea to frighten the team and cause the chariot to overturn (1611–12, Cambridge, Fitzwilliam Museum). The same subject is reflected in sculpture by Lemoyne (1715, Paris, Louvre). In a painting by Guérin, Hippolytus stands before Phaedra and Theseus, who sit side-by-side (1802, Paris, Louvre).

Cross-references: Theseus.

Sources: Euripides, *Hyppolytus*. Seneca, *Phaedra*. Ovid, *Metamorphoses* XV, 497–546 (death of Hippolytus).

PHAËTHON

Gk., Lat., and Ger. Phaethon; It. Fetone; Sp. Faeton; Fr. Phaéton.
Greek hero.

HISTORY/MYTHOLOGY

Phaëthon was the son of the Titan Helios (the Sun) and the nymph Clymene. His mother withheld his true identity from him until he became an adult, whereupon he sought out his father and asked him, as a sign of recognition, for the right to drive the Sun's chariot for a day. Helios agreed, and Phaëthon was entrusted with the chariot. Despite considerable instruction from his father, however, Phaëthon drove dangerously close to the Earth, which caused him to be struck down by Jupiter's thunderbolts and fall into the Eridanus (now the Po River). Phaëthon's sisters, the Heliades, wept over him and were changed into poplars.

The Fall of Phaëthon.
Jean Mignon.
Engraving, c. 1545.

REPRESENTATIONS

The fall of Phaëthon, along with the metamorphosis of the Heliades, appears in relief on an Arretine bowl (first century A.D., Boston, Museum of Fine of Arts). Phaëthon's story is also told on a series of Roman sarcophagi: on the left, he stands before the Sun, accompanied by the Hours; in the center, the chariot overturns and he falls backward head first; on the right, the Heliades cry over him near the river god Eridanus (sarcophagus third century A.D., Copenhagen, Ny Carlsberg Glyptothek).

The *Fall of Phaëthon* by Sebastiano del Piombo is in the Villa Farnesina (c. 1511, Rome). Giulio Romano used that same subject for a ceiling in the Palazzo del Tè at Mantua (1527–28). Michelangelo drew three versions of Phaëthon (one in London, British Museum, 1533). Poussin painted an *Apollo with the Chariot of Phaëthon* (c. 1630, Berlin–Dahlem, Gemäldegalerie).

Sources: Ovid, *Metamorphosis* I, 750–II, 366.

PHILEMON AND BAUCIS

Gk. and Ger. Philemon, Baukis; Lat. Philemo, Baucis; It. Filemone, Bauci; Sp. Filemon, Baucis; Fr. Philémon, Baucis.
Legendary characters

HISTORY/MYTHOLOGY

Jupiter and Mercury once sought shelter in Phrygia disguised as mortals. Nobody offered hospitality except an elderly couple named Philemon and Baucis, who lived in a simple hut and invited the visitors to their modest table. The couple owned but one goose, which they were about to kill when the fowl fled for protection to the guests, who then unmasked themselves and safely led the couple to high ground before flooding the region. All that remained after the inundation was the couple's hut, which was transformed into the temple where

Jupiter and Mercury in the House of Philemon and Baucis.
Adam Elsheimer,
c. 1600.
Dresden,
Gemäldegalerie.

Philemon and Baucis would serve as guardians for the rest of their days before dying and becoming trees.

REPRESENTATIONS

There are no ancient representations of this subject.

In baroque painting, the story is represented in the form of a meal among peasants, during which the goose flees toward Mercury's legs; Jordaens painted several versions of the subject (1642–51, Helsinki, Atheneum). Rubens represented Philemon and Baucis in a vast stormy landscape, just before the flood (c. 1625, Vienna, Kunst-historisches Museum).

Cross-references: Jupiter. Mercury.

Sources: Ovid, *Metamorphoses* VIII, 621–720.

Bibliography: W. Stechow, "The Myth of Philemon and Baucis in Art," *Journal of the Warburg and Courtauld Institutes* 4 (1940–41): 103–13.

PHILOCTETES

Gk., Lat., and Ger. Philoctetes; It. Fiolotte; Sp. Filoctetes; Fr. Philoctète.
Greek hero.

HISTORY/MYTHOLOGY

According to Homeric tradition, Philoctetes, the son of Demonassa and Poeas, king of Maliaus in Thessaly, received Hercules' bow and arrows after he lit the hero's funeral pyre. Philoctetes was nevertheless later severely punished for revealing the pyre's secret location: he was bitten in the foot by a snake on his way to Troy during a sacrifice on the island of Tenedos or Chryse, and the wound's repugnant odor convinced Ulysses to suggest abandoning him on Lemnos.

Philoctetes Bitten by a Snake.
Attic krater,
c. 470 B.C.
Paris, Louvre.

After Agamemnon gave the order to move on without him, Philoctetes lived alone for ten years on the island and survived on animals he hunted with Hercules' weapons. The Greeks were meanwhile still laying siege to Troy when Helenus, who had the same gift of prophecy as his twin sister, Cassandra, predicted that only Hercules' arrows could conquer the city.

Ulysses accordingly left for Lemnos with Neoptolemus and Diomedes to ask Philoctetes to rejoin the Greeks at Troy. Philoctetes was less than willing, but was ultimately convinced by either Ulysses' wiles or his persuasiveness and, once healed, he took part in the combat and then returned to his native city after the fall of Troy. According to a post-Homeric legend, he settled in the south of Italy.

REPRESENTATIONS

Pliny writes that in 400 B.C. the Greek painter Parrhasius created a work whose subject was Philoctetes on Lemnos (*Natural History* XXXV, 67). Although the painting is lost, the goldsmith Cheirisophos transposed its composition on to a silver one-handled canthara, which was found at Hoby in Denmark (first century B.C., Copenhagen, Nationalmuseet). The vase shows Philoctetes, whose face is diverted and whose bandaged foot is clearly represented, seated on a boulder and leaning on a stick while facing Ulysses, who wears a *pilos* and clearly tries to persuade him to return.

Aside from this superb example, however, only a few objects represent the legend: two Attic vases from the middle of the fifth century B.C., both in the Louvre, and a fragment of Arretine ceramic found at Saint-Bertrand de Commiges (first century A.D.). A noteworthy modern work is by James Barry, dating from 1770 (Bologna, Pinacoteca Nazionale).

Cross-references: Hercules. Troy. Ulysses.

Sources: Homer, *The Iliad* II, 716 ff.; *The Odyssey* III, 190, VIII, 219 ff. Ovid, *Metamorphoses* IX, 229; XIII, 45 ff., 313 ff. Sophocles, *Philoctetes*.

PHINEUS *See* Perseus.

PHOCION

Gk. and Ger. Phokion; It. Focione; Sp. Foco; Fr. and Lat. Phocion. Athenian general (c. 400–317 B.C.).

HISTORY/MYTHOLOGY

The Athenian general and orator Phocion was a paradoxical figure. Serious, austere, and morally irreproachable, he nevertheless advocated making concessions with Philip of Macedon and then with Alexander in order to establish peace. Thus, he opposed Demosthenes, whose harangues urged the Athenians to resist and fight. After the Athenian defeat at Chaeronea, in 338 B.C., Alexander reputedly renounced the idea of destroying Athens out of respect for Phocion, who nevertheless refused all his presents. However, because he gave the Macedonians permission to take possession of some Athenian strongholds, Phocion was condemned as a traitor and forced to drink hemlock. He accepted the sentence and expressed astonishment only at having to pay for the poison (even dying in Athens was not free). As was customary for this kind of condemnation, it was forbidden to bury Phocion, but a man and a woman did so.

REPRESENTATIONS

Phocion is not represented in antiquity and only relatively infrequently in modern times. Nevertheless, artists have illustrated three episodes: Phocion's refusal to be swayed by the Macedonians' presents, Phocion's death (the subject of the Prix de Rome in 1804), and the transfer and burial of Phocion's remains (Poussin, *Landscape with the Funeral of Phocion*, 1648, Oakley Park, Count of Plymouth).

Cross-references: Alexander.

Sources: Plutarch, *Life of Phocion*. Cornelius Nepos, *Phocion* XIX.

PHOEBUS *See* Apollo.

PHOENIX

Gk. and Ger. Phoinix; Lat. Phoenix; It. Fenice; Sp. Fénix; Fr. Phénix.
Fantastic bird.

HISTORY/MYTHOLOGY

The phoenix was a fabled bird that fed on incense, lived for five centuries,
and was then reborn from its own ashes. According to Herodotus, the
bird was sacred to Egyptians and once appeared at Heliopolis.

REPRESENTATIONS

In ancient representations, particularly on Imperial Roman coins, the
phoenix resembles a wader with its head either surrounded by a nim-
bus of rays or set off by a sort of halo (coins of Antoninus Pius at
Alexandria).

The phoenix became more developed as a subject in the context
of Christian iconography. In the Renaissance, it became a symbol for
the Resurrection and eternal life, and it appears in a sixteenth-century
French tapestry with the legend *Figura Resurrectionis* (*Allegory of
Sacred Love*, Paris, Musée des Arts Décoratifs).

Sources: Herodotus, *The Histories* II, 73. Ovid, *Metamorphoses* XV,
391–407.

Bibliography: R. Van den Broek, *The Myth of the Phœnix*, Leiden,
1972.

Phoenix.
Mosaic,
fifth century A.D.
Paris, Louvre.

PHOLUS *See* Centaurs.

PHRIXUS AND HELLE

Lat. Phrixus, Helle; It. Frisso, Elle; Sp. Frixo, Helle; Fr. Phrixos, Hellé.
Ger. Phrixos, Helle; Gk. Phrixos, Hellē.
Boeotian prince and princess.

HISTORY/MYTHOLOGY

Phrixus and Helle were respectively the son and daughter of Athamas
and Nephele. They were about to be sacrificed to Jupiter by their
father, who acted on advice from his second wife, Ino, when the god
sent a ram with a golden fleece to carry them into the sky and off
toward the Orient. Helle fell into the sea on the way, thereby lending
her name to the Hellespont. Phrixus continued until he arrived at the
palace of King Aeëtes of Colchis, where he sacrificed the ram to
Jupiter. The ram's fleece, on the other hand, was consecrated by the
king to Ares and was later the object of Jason's quest.

Phrixus and Helle.
Amphora,
c. 440 B.C.
Naples,
Museo Archeologico.

REPRESENTATIONS

Phrixus is represented in ancient art at the moment when the ram carries
him away: the youth hangs on to the ram's flank while the animal
hovers above the waves (plate from Melos and Pompeian painting).

The same motif appears in a panel from the workshop of
Pinturicchio (c. 1509, ceiling from the Palazzo Pondolfo Petrucci, now
in New York, Metropolitan Museum of Art).

Attributes: Ram.

Cross-references: Argonauts. Jason.

Sources: Apollonius of Rhodes, II, 1140–56.

PHRYNE

Gk., Lat., and Ger. Phryne; It. Frine; Fr. Phryné.
Famous courtisan at Athens (fourth century B.C.).

HISTORY/MYTHOLOGY

Born at Thespiae, in Boeotia, in the fourth century B.C., Phryne
became a famous courtesan. She reputedly served as Praxiteles' model
for his statues of Aphrodite. Accused of impiety, she was defended by
the orator Hyperides, who succeeded in convincing the members of
the jury that she was not responsible for the passions she aroused
and—by unveiling her body in front of them—that she was innocent.

REPRESENTATIONS

Phryne's trial was depicted by Baudon in a work that Diderot harshly
criticized (Salon of 1763): the attorney unveils only a breast and a
shoulder of the young woman who has a shy, even modest expression.
By contrast, Phryne is entirely nude in a painting by Gérôme, in which
the judges are portrayed as elderly men who become filled with surprise and admiration before such a flawless body (1861, Hamburg,
Kunsthalle). Sculptors also celebrated the courtesan's beauty (Pradier,
1845; Clésinger, 1878; Falguière, 1884).

Sources: Athenaeus, XIII, 590–91. Pliny the Elder, XXXIV, 70.

Phryne.
Detail from
Jean-Léon Gérôme,
*Phryne Before
the Areopagus*, 1861.
Hamburg, Kunsthalle.

PIG *See* Ceres. Circe.

PIRITHOÜS *See* Centaurs.

PITCHER *See* Amymone (hydria). Ganymede. Hebe. Hylas. Iris.

PLEIADES

Gk. and Lat. Pleiades; It. Pleiadi; Sp. Pleyades; Fr. Pléiades; Ger. Pleiaden.
Constellation.

HISTORY/MYTHOLOGY

The Pleiades were the seven daughters of Atlas and Pleione: Taygete,
Electra, Alcyone, Sterope, Celaeno, Maia, and Merope. Jupiter transformed them into stars—the constellation that bears their name—so
that they could escape the hunter Orion, who pursued them relentlessly. According to another tradition, their metamorphosis was
prompted by the grief they suffered when Jupiter condemned Atlas to
shoulder the heavens. Their sisters, the Hyades, were also transformed
into stars. In antiquity, the rising of the Pleiades announced the season
for tilling and sowing.

REPRESENTATIONS

The Pleiades are mentioned by Homer in his description of Achilles'
shield, and by Euripides in a description of an embroidered tapestry.
Both allusions are to a constellation similar to one that appears on a
zodiacal gem with Taurus and the Pleiades (St. Petersburg, Hermitage).
The Pleiades are also represented on an Etruscan mirror from
Praeneste (Messter of Ravenstein Collection; end of fourth century
B.C.). A miniature from a manuscript for Germanicus's *Aratea* represents
them as seven female heads: six in a circle and a seventh, veiled and in the
center, for Merope, the lost Pleiade who disappeared as the sisters escaped Orion (ninth century A.D., Leiden, University Library).

The Pleiades have rarely been represented in modern times, but
Flaxman portrayed them in an illustration to Hesiod (drawing engraved
by Blake, published in 1817). There also exists a painting of the *Lost
Pleiade* by Bouguereau (1884, United States, priv. coll.).

Cross-references: Atlas.

Sources: Euripides, *Electra*, 468. Hesiod, *Works and Days*, 383.
Homer, *The Iliad* XVIII, 485. Ovid, *Festivals* IV, 172; V, 83 ff.

PLOW *See* Cincinnatus.

PLUTO

Gk. Hades/Ploutos; Lat. Pluto; It. Plutone; Sp. and Fr. Pluton; Ger. Ploutos.
God of the Underworld.

HISTORY/MYTHOLOGY

Pluto, son of Saturn and Cybele and brother of Jupiter, guarded the
Underworld, which he ruled. He married Ceres' daughter, Proserpine,
after he abducted her.

**Pluto and
Persephone.**
Detail
from Apulian krater,
c. 330 B.C.
Munich, Bayerische
Staatgemäldesamm-
lungen.

The Greeks, for whom the Underworld was very much a world
without light, called him Hades, meaning "invisible." His realm was
circled by various rivers, including Acheron, across which Charon
transported the dead, and its entrance was guarded by Cerberus, a
monstrous three-headed dog with a snakelike tail.

Covetous of his wards, Pluto allowed no one to leave Hades. There
were only rare exceptions to that rule: Eurydice, who almost returned to
the world of the living with Orpheus, and Alcestis, who had taken
Admeta's place but was liberated by Hercules, who also unchained
Cerberus and brought him to King Eurystheus as one of his labors.

REPRESENTATIONS

The Greek word *ploutos* means wealth, and serves as an antiphrastic
nickname for the god, who therefore holds a horn of abundance. Pluto
himself is bearded and holds a scepter in scenes situated in Hades, but
it is particularly Cerberus's presence that identifies him. Attic painters
hardly ever represented him except in the episode in which Hercules
unchains Cerberus. On the other hand, the abduction of Proserpine is
frequent on Roman sarcophagi, in which one rarely encounters a subject
so clearly linked to the Underworld.

In modern times Pluto is rarely portrayed for himself, other than in
series of ancient gods. Proserpine's abduction, however, was often
depicted in the Renaissance: Leonardo da Vinci (lost painting),
Sebastiano del Piombo at the Farnesina (1511), Giulio Romano in
Mantua (1527–28, Palazzo del Tè), and Primaticcio at Fontainebleau.
Rembrandt's version is one the most dramatic and shows Pluto's chariot
being swallowed up by Hell (1628–39, Berlin, Antikensammlungen).

Attributes: Cornucopia. Scepter.

Cross-references: Ceres. Proserpine.

POLLUX *See* Castor and Pollux.

POLYDECTES *See* Danaë. Perseus.

POLYHYMNIA *See* Muses.

POLYPHEMUS

Gk., Lat., and Ger. Poliphemus; It. and Sp. Polifemo; Fr. Polyphème.
One of the Cyclops.

HISTORY/MYTHOLOGY

The giant Polyphemus lived in a cave on the island of the Cyclopes. He
sang in vain for love of the nymph Galatea, who preferred the beautiful
Acis, until he caught the couple together by surprise and crushed Acis
under a rock.

Polyphemus later captured Ulysses and twelve of his companions,
and was about to devour them one by one when Ulysses intoxicated
him and blinded him by sinking a red-hot stake into his sole eye after

The Sabine Women.
Detail from Jacques-Louis David, *The Sabine Women*, 1799.
Paris, Louvre.

Saturn Devouring One of His Children.
Francisco de Goya, 1821–3.
Madrid, Prado.

Landscape with
Polyphemus (detail).
Nicolas Poussin,
c. 1649.
St. Petersburg,
Hermitage.

he had fallen sound asleep. The survivors then escaped by hanging upside down from the thick belly-fleece of rams as the animals left the cave to graze.

REPRESENTATIONS

In ancient art, the two most popular subjects from this legend are the blinding of Polyphemus and the escape under the rams, which are found from the seventh century B.C. in proto-Attic ceramics and from the sixth through early fifth centuries B.C. in Attic black-figure ceramics. Engraved stones, bronzes, and terracottas also show these episodes from the voyage of Ulysses.

The classical period seems, by contrast, to have favored the lone figure of the Cyclops, who, although he has an enormous eye on his forehead or at the base of his nose, preserves traces of the two other eyes in the normal position (Hellenistic and Roman terracotta or marble figurines). In Imperial Roman times, the preferred subject was Ulysses offering wine to Polyphemus; in second place was the blinding of Polyphemus. Both subjects also occur in decorated interiors of that period, as demonstrated by a group of sculptures discovered at Sperlonga in 1957, but which may have come from one of the emperor Tiberius's villas. Other representations are found in the "Ninfeo Bergantino" of the emperor Domitian's villa at Castel Gandolfo, in emperor Claudius's decoration at Baiae, and in Hadrian's villa at Tivoli.

Jordaens illustrated Polyphemus's encounter with Ulysses in a series of cartoons dedicated to the story of the hero (1630–35, Moscow, Pushkin Museum). Polyphemus is shown throwing a boulder at Ulysses' ship in a painting by Rubens (1636–38, Madrid, Prado). He appears in Poussin's *Landscape with Polyphemus* (1660–65, St. Petersburg, Hermitage), a subject that Turner later depicted (1829, London, National Gallery).

Attributes: Eye (sole).

Cross-references: Cyclops. Galatea. Ulysses.

241

Sources: Homer, *The Odyssey* IX, 105–566. Euripides, *The Cyclops*.

Bibliography: O. Touchefeu-Meynier, *Thèmes odysséens dans l'art antique*, Paris, 1968.

Polyxena Carried to Sacrifice.
Pio Fedi,
nineteenth century.
Florence,
Loggia dei Lanzi.

POLYXENA

Gk., Lat., and Ger. Polyxena; It. Polissena; Fr. Polyxène.
Trojan princess.

HISTORY/MYTHOLOGY

Polyxena was the daughter of Priam, king of Troy, and Hecuba. After the fall of Troy, the ghost of Achilles demanded that she be sacrificed on his tomb; Achilles' son, Neoptolemus (sometimes called Pyrrhus), led the sacrifice.

REPRESENTATIONS

Polyxena appears in Attic ceramics of Achilles ambushing Troilus: as Achilles leaps from his hiding place, she lets her hydria fall and flees with her brother, who has come to a fountain to water his horses. The subject is frequent in black-figure ceramics (hydria, c. 520 B.C., Berlin, Antikensmuseum) and early red-figure ceramics (pelike, c. 470 B.C. Paris, Louvre). Also represented is the sacrifice of Polyxena: the Trojan princess is seen either being led by the hand before the tumulus (hydria, c. 520 B.C., Berlin, Antikensmuseum) or, more rarely, slain on the sacrificial altar by Neoptolemus (amphora, c. 550 B.C., London, British Museum).

The most popular subject from this legend in modern times is Polyxena's sacrifice, which was depicted in Primaticcio's *Polyxena Immolated by Pyrrhus* (1541–47, Fontainebleau, Galerie d'Ulysse), works by Pietro da Cortona (c. 1625, Rome, Musei Capitolini), and several times by Pittoni (1730–35, Paris, Louvre).

Attributes: Hydria.

Cross-references: Achilles.

Sources: Ovid, *Metamorphoses* XIII, 439–81.

POMEGRANATE *See* Juno. Proserpine.

POMONA

Lat., It., Sp., and Ger. Pomona; Fr. Pomone.
Goddess of fruit.

HISTORY/MYTHOLOGY

Pomona was an exceptionally beautiful nymph who kept watch over gardens and fruit. Vertumnus, god of orchards and wine, kept watch over the changing of the seasons. To seduce Pomona, Vertumnus assumed different forms one after another, becoming a plowman, a wine grower, and a harvester until finally, in the guise of an old woman, he showed her a vine shoot rolled around a branch of elm, whereupon they engaged in a discourse on love to which Pomona listened unsuspectingly.

REPRESENTATIONS

Pomona is represented as a sturdy young woman, dressed in a long robe whose folds may be filled with fruit; she sometimes holds fruit, or has a fruit basket nearby. This iconography is found into the twentieth century, as demonstrated in a sculpture by Maillol (*Draped Pomona*, 1921, Paris, Musée d'Orsay).

In depictions of Vertumnus meeting Pomona, the god is generally in his last metamorphosis. Two female figures are shown side-by-side in a natural setting; the eldest either approaches the youngest or speaks into her ear. Three paintings in the Louvre represent the scene: by Boucher, Frans II Francken, and Jan van den Hoecke. The theme has also provided a motif for the decorative arts.

Sources: Ovid, *Metamorphoses* XIV, 622–771.

Vertumnus and Pomona.
François Boucher, engraving after Antoine Watteau.

POMPEY *See* Caesar.

POPPY *See* Hypnos. Venus (celestial).

PORTIA

Fr. Porcia.
Roman historical character (first century B.C.).

HISTORY/MYTHOLOGY

Portia, the daughter of Cato of Utica, became a model of Republican virtue and morality. She married one of Caesar's future assassins, Marcus Junius Brutus, in 45 B.C., and followed him to suicide after defeat in the Battle of Philippi in 42 B.C. confirmed Octavius and Antony as victors over Republican party leaders. Concerned about Portia's suicidal intentions, those close to her hid all weapons from sight, but she took her life by swallowing burning coals.

REPRESENTATIONS

This impressive chapter in conjugal fidelity and determination in the face of death has inspired artists since the end of the fifteenth century; a woman may be represented in the act of committing suicide, which arouses as much admiration as it does fear. In a relief by Francesco Mosca, for example, the emphasis is less on Portia's physical pain than on her determination (sixteenth century, Venice, Museo Archeologico).

Cross-references: Cato.

Sources: Plutarch, *Life of Brutus*, 53. Valerius Maximus, IV, 6.

POSEIDON *Greek name for* Neptune.

PRIAM

Gk. and Ger. Priamos; Lat. Priamus; Fr. Priam; It. Priamo.
Legendary Trojan king.

HISTORY/MYTHOLOGY

The Trojan War unfolded during Priam's reign as king of Troy. He
was already very old by that time, however, and did not participate in
combat leaving all important decisions to his son, Hector.

Tradition attributes some fifty sons to Priam through concubines
and two wives, but he had his most famous children with his second
wife, Hecuba: Hector, Paris, Cassandra, and Troilus. All his children
perished during the long war, and Priam had to beg Achilles to accept
an enormous ransom in exchange for Hector's corpse.

After Troy was captured, Priam sought sanctuary with Hecuba
beside an altar in his palace and begged the gods' protection, but
Neoptolemus dragged him from the sacred altar, slew him, and left his
corpse unburied (post-Homeric tradition).

REPRESENTATIONS

Two subjects from the story of Priam were depicted in Greek and
Italiot ceramics: the ransom being paid to Achilles and, from the
middle of the sixth century B.C., Priam's death.

On the outside of a red-figure cup by the Brygos Painter in the
Louvre (480 B.C.), a white-haired Priam sits on the altar and extends
his arms toward Neoptolemus in a plea for mercy. In another work,
the old king, who is portrayed frontally and with a diadem around his
white hair, raises his left hand to his eye in a dignified gesture of sadness
while Hector prepares for battle nearby (red-figure amphora with
twisted handles, c. 440 B.C., Rome, Musei Vaticani).

The violence of Priam's death is also the focus of attention in a
marble relief: Neoptolemus tears the king from the altar and ignores
Hecuba's horrified cries as he prepares to drive a sword through her husband (Hellenistic period, reused in the Roman period, as demonstrated
by the Latin inscription; Boston, Museum of Fine Arts). The payment
of the ransom appears on silver vases of the Augustan period.

Modern representations of Priam are as rare as ancient ones,
although Priam begging for mercy was the subject of a few lost
seventeenth- and eighteenth-century paintings (by Tiepolo, Lebrun,

Priam.
Cup, c. 510 B.C.
Munich,
Antiken-
sammlungen.

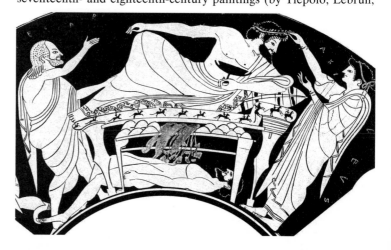

Priam Paying Hector's Ransom.
Jean Mignon.
Engraving, c. 1545.

and Coypel for the Grande Galerie of the Palais Royal, Paris). The neoclassical Danish sculptor Bertel Thorwaldsen revived the subject in a marble relief from a series with ancient subjects; the artist intended to create an abstract effect, which he achieved through the archaistic stylization of the figures (1815, Copenhagen, Thorwaldsens Museum).

Cross-references: Hector. Hecuba. Paris. Troy.

Sources: Homer, *The Iliad* XXIV.

PRIAPUS

Gk. and Ger. Priapos; Lat. Priapus; It. Priapo; Fr. Priape.
Phrygian god.

HISTORY/MYTHOLOGY

Priapus, the son of Venus and Bacchus, is a god who originated in Asia Minor, at Lampsacus, and was endowed with a grotesquely enlarged penis. His effigy was believed to ward off the evil eye, and the god therefore became guardian of orchards and gardens. Priapus was also associated with flocks of goats and sheep. Because of his obscenity, he is close at hand wherever there are satyrs or Bacchic processions. The ass that sometimes accompanies him is an allusion to an ill-fated attempt to seduce the nymph Lotis in her sleep: Priapus was just about to surprise her when Silenus's ass began to bray and awoke the nymph. According to another version of the story, Vesta rather than Lotis was warned by the animal's noise.

REPRESENTATIONS

In Roman and Hellenistic art, Priapus is bearded and lifts his garment to expose his perpetually erect penis; he appears in this pose on coins from

Priapus.
Roman bronze,
second–third centuries A.D.
Augsburg,
Römisches Museum.

Priapus in a Small Temple.
Roman gem,
c. first century A.D.
Berlin,
Staatliche Museum.

Lampsacus (second century A.D.). The folds of his lifted robe may be filled with fruit (marble statue, second century A.D., Rome, Musei Vaticani).

Priapus is seen approaching Vesta in Bellini's *Feast of the Gods* (1514, Washington, National Gallery). The birth of Priapus is the subject of a drawing by Poussin (1620–23). Picasso created a highly energetic bronze sculpture of the god (1952, Geneva, Grantz Collection).

Attributes: Fruits. Phallus.

Cross-references: Bacchus. Vesta.

Sources: Ovid, *Festivals* I, 391–440 (Lotis); VI, 319–48 (Vesta).

Bibliography: E. Wind, *Bellini's Feast of the Gods*, 1948.

PROCRIS *See* Cephalus.

PROCRUSTES *See* Theseus.

PROMETHEUS

Gk., Lat., and Ger. Prometheus; It. and Sp. Prometeo; Fr. Prométhée.
Mythical character.

HISTORY/MYTHOLOGY

Prometheus, the son of Iapetus and Clymene, was Jupiter's cousin and a Titan. His name, which means "forethinker," alludes to both his intelligence and his wiliness. He was sometimes thought of as the creator of the first man, and he was generally regarded as a benefactor for mortals, whom he defended against the gods' hostility. He once divided into two lots a sacrificed animal that was to be shared by gods and mortals, and covered one, consisting of flesh and entrails, with hide and the other, consisting of only bones, with fat. Jupiter was invited to choose the former, but grew suspicious and instead chose the fat, thinking that the meat lay there. Furious at having been deceived this way, he retaliated by withholding the gift of fire from Prometheus's man. Prometheus then stole fire from either the Sun's chariot or, according to others, Vulcan's forge, and gave it to man, whereupon Jupiter created the first woman, Pandora, as a punishment for man and sent her to Prometheus's brother Epimetheus ("the one who plans too late"). He also chained Prometheus to the Caucasus and sent an eagle to pick at his liver continuously. Prometheus was finally unbound by Hercules, who killed the eagle, and he later became reconciled with Jupiter by revealing to him what an oracle had said about Thetis.

Depending on the period, Prometheus may represent the incarnation of sacrilegious pride, as he did for Hesiod, or, on the contrary, creative intelligence and even the spirit of revolution and freedom, as he did for the romantics.

REPRESENTATIONS

The earliest subject from this legend to appear in art is Prometheus unbound. Hercules shoots arrows at the eagle as it flies toward the Titan, who is seated on the ground and attached to a stake (Tyrrhenian amphora, c. 550 B.C., Florence, Museo Archeologico). The subject of the creation appears only later, in the fourth century B.C. In a carved-stone example of that subject, Prometheus is shown assembling man's skeleton (late third century B.C., London, British Museum). The creation theme reappears in more elaborate form in Roman art, particularly on sarcophagi. Three episodes are juxtaposed in one example in the Louvre (c. 220 B.C.): the creation (Prometheus is seated while he models the figure with the help of Minerva), man's death (Mercury and the Fates watch as the soul escapes from the body), and the theft of fire (Prometheus leaves Vulcan's forge, torch in hand). Another sarcophagus shows Prometheus modeling man and bringing him to life (beginning of the fourth century A.D., Rome, Musei Capitolini). Represented on two different sides of the same work are Hercules unbinding Prometheus and Prometheus stealing fire from Vulcan's forge. In what is one of the earliest examples of Greco-Roman iconography being combined with the biblical version of creation, Adam and Eve appear in relief on the border of the same sarcophagus.

Prometheus.
Cornelis Cort.
Engraving, 1566.

Two Renaissance panel paintings by Piero di Cosimo are devoted to the story of Prometheus (c. 1510). Seen in one panel are: the dispute between Prometheus and Epimetheus, the statue of the new man, and Prometheus escorted to the heavens by Minerva (Munich, Alte Pinakothek). On the other panel, Prometheus steals fire from the Sun's chariot, brings man to life, and is bound to a tree by Mercury (Strasbourg, Musée des Beaux-Arts). The punishment of Prometheus was the preferred subject in baroque painting among such artists as Rubens (1612–18, Philadelphia, Museum of Art) and Salvatore Rosa (1665, Rome, Galleria Nazionale). The same subject was also sculpted by Nicolas-Sébastien Adam (1762, Paris, Louvre). In representations of the punishment of Prometheus, a torch distinguishes the scene from a similar one with Tityus, who was devoured by a vulture. The subjects of two frescoes by Domenichino are *Prometheus and Minerva* and *Prometheus Freed by Hercules* (1602, Rome, Palazzo Farnese). The creation appears in Luca Giordano's *Allegory of Life* (c. 1680, Florence, Palazzo Medici-Riccardi).

In the nineteenth century, Prometheus was seen as the "great sacrifice dying for humanity," as Gustave Moreau described him. In Moreau's own depiction of the subject, *Prometheus Struck by Lightning*, Prometheus resembles a pagan Christ (c. 1869, Paris, Musée Gustave Moreau). In a work by Böcklin, which is painted from a vantage point below the horizon, the Titan is stretched out on a mountain and his profile merges with the surrounding rock and clouds (1882, Florence, priv. coll.).

Attributes: Eagle. Torch.

Cross-references: Pandora. Titans. Tityus.

Sources: Hesiod, *Theogony*, 507–616; *Works and Days*, 41–105. Aeschylus, *Prometheus Bound*.

Bibliography: O. Raggio, "The Myth of Prometheus: Its Survival and Metamorphosis up to the Eighteenth Century," *Journal of the Warburg and Courtauld Institutes* 21 (1958): 44–62.

PROSERPINE

Gk. and Ger. Persephone/Kora; Lat., It., and Sp. Proserpina; Fr. Proserpine.
Goddess of the Underworld.

**The Abduction
of Proserpine.**
Niccolò dell'Abbate,
sixteenth century.
Paris, Louvre.

**Proserpine and
Pluto.**
Tablet from Locri,
470–460 B.C.
Naples,
Museo Nazionale.

**The Rape
of Proserpine.**
François Girardon,
end of seventeenth
century.
Palace of Versailles.

HISTORY/MYTHOLOGY

Proserpine was the daughter of Ceres and Jupiter. Pluto, the god of
the Underworld fell in love with her and abducted her while she was
picking flowers with her friends in the plain of Enna, in Sicily. While
in Hades, Proserpine broke the fast imposed on her by eating a
pomegranate and as a result was definitively bound to the
Underworld. Her mother, Ceres, searched the earth for her and then
convinced Jupiter to agree that Proserpine could spend at least part
of the year with her; the alternation of Proserpine's stays below and
above the earth correspond to the rhythm of the seasons and the renewal
of vegetation.

REPRESENTATIONS

Proserpine has all the allure of a young woman, and her Greek name,
Kora, denotes the ideal maiden. In Eleusinian works of art, she is
accompanied by Demeter and Triptolemus. In depictions on some
Attic vases, Hermes or astonished satyrs watch as she rises up from
the earth. Her abduction by Pluto is represented on a number of
Roman sarcophagi.

In modern times, Proserpine is shown either innocently dancing with
her companions while Pluto stands at a distance, or being swallowed up
by the earth along with Pluto and his chariot while he abducts her. In a
statue by Bernini, Proserpine struggles to break free from Pluto, who
lifts her off the ground (1622, Rome, Villa Borghese; the statue formed
a pair with Bernini's more famous *Apollo and Daphne*).

Attributes: Pomegranate.

Cross-references: Ceres. Pluto. Triptolemus.

Sources: *Homeric Hymn to Demeter.*

Bibliography: C. Bérard, *Andoi, essai sur l'imagerie des passages
chthoniens*, Lausanne, 1974.

PSYCHE

Gk., Lat., Ger. Psyche; Fr. Psyché; It. Psiche.
Greek heroine.

HISTORY/MYTHOLOGY

Psyche, whose name means "soul" in Greek, was the youngest and most beautiful of three daughters of a king who had lost all hope of seeing her marry. Indeed, her beauty was so striking that it intimidated all suitors and aroused jealousy even in Venus, who tolerated rivalry poorly from any mortal.

Consequently, the king sought advice from an oracle, who told him to leave his daughter exposed on a mountain, where a frightening monster would come to claim her as his wife. The king had no other choice but to listen to the oracle. Alone on the mountain's summit, however, Psyche felt herself lifted into the air and carried off by the winds to an unfamiliar place, where she fell asleep exhausted.

She awoke to find herself in a magnificent palace. Although she seemed alone, she felt a mysterious presence beside her each evening. This was the spouse spoken of by the oracle. He warned her that she would lose him forever should she try to learn what he looked like. Undaunted, Psyche awaited her mysterious spouse's arrival each evening, and by day lived happily among the invisible voices that served her.

Little by little, however, Psyche longed to see her family, and her pleas were so moving that the wind brought her back to where it had

Cupid and Psyche.
Jean-Honoré
Fragonard.
Engraving.

Cupid and Psyche.
Anthony van Dyck,
c. 1640.
London,
Buckingham Palace.

found her. Psyche then rushed to her family laden with presents and so full of stories about her happiness that her sisters became jealous and badgered her into agreeing to find out what her lover looked like. Upon returning to her palace, Psyche waited until nightfall and then lit a lamp only to find Cupid himself asleep beside her. Taken aback by the god's startling beauty, however, she spilled a drop of oil from her lantern, whereupon Cupid awoke and fled.

Psyche desperately searched the world for her beloved, but incurred the wrath of Venus, who assigned her such tedious tasks as sorting seeds, gathering wool from wild sheep, and, finally, descending into Hades to fetch her a bottle of rejuvenating waters from Persephone.

Although forbidden by Venus to open the bottle, she disobeyed and fell into a profound sleep. Cupid, who had meanwhile remained deeply in love, finally awakened Psyche by stinging her with his arrows. He then ascended to Olympus to ask Jupiter for permission to marry the mortal; the ruler of the gods agreed, and Venus and Psyche became reconciled.

The pagan legend was readily endowed with Christian connotations during the first century A.D., when Psyche's adventures became symbolic of the wanderings of the soul, and when the love she quested after became the love of God. The semantic ambiguity in Psyche's name made it easy to move from legend into Christian myth.

The ancient legend, whose most complete account is found in Apuleius's *Metamorphoses*, has been an exceptionally fertile source of inspiration in the figurative arts; in addition, a number of works from literature echoed the story and consequently contributed to the development of the modern iconography of Psyche. Among those texts is La Fontaine's 1669 prose and verse version, *The Loves of Cupid and Psyche*, which added some half-precious, half-ironic episodes to Apuleius's account.

REPRESENTATIONS

In Attic ceramics, dead warriors are occasionally accompanied by a miniature armed figure, sometimes winged, which represents the soul of the deceased. This figure is named Psyche in an inscription on a hydria in Munster (c. 510 B.C.); white-ground lekythoi are similarly decorated with small, winged silhouettes that hover around stelae or Charon's boat (Attic lekythos, c. 440 B.C., Athens, National Museum). When her amorous adventures with Cupid are the subject, Psyche is a pretty maiden, who is sometimes endowed with butterfly wings. Pompeian painting includes several examples in which the small maiden plays with cupids who, like herself, are winged. These representations suggest an allegorical meaning to the extent that in Roman belief the soul was represented by a butterfly that escapes from a dying body with the victim's last sigh; this probably explains Psyche's presence on Roman sarcophagi. In an ancient marble group—famous since its discovery in the middle of the eighteenth century and sometimes interpreted as the invention of the kiss—Cupid and Psyche are portrayed as two entwined adolescents who join their lips (Rome, Musei Capitolini); the figures are winged in other versions of the same work. Psyche and Cupid were very often represented in other ancient works.

Psyche's iconography was sustained in the first centuries of the Christian era through catacomb paintings and sarcophagi; it was more amply developed in the Renaissance and persisted into the twentieth century. One of its most characteristic guises is found in great decorative programs, such as the one in the Villa Farnesina in Rome, where Raphael devoted ten pendentives and the hall's ceiling to the tale of

Cupid and Psyche.
Antonio Canova,
1787–93.
Paris, Louvre.

Psyche. Here the legend is separated into individual episodes that include: *Venus Points out Psyche to Cupid*; *Cupid Presents Psyche to the Graces*; *Venus withdraws from Juno and Ceres Who Intercede in Favor of Psyche*; *Venus Climbs to Olympus to Implore Jupiter to Punish Psyche*; *Venus Implores Jupiter*; *Mercury Descends from the Sky to Publicly Announce Jupiter's Commands*; *Psyche Brings the Bottle of Rejuvenating Water from Hades*; *Psyche Presents the Bottle to Venus*; *Jupiter Agrees the Marriage of Cupid and Psyche*; *Psyche Carried to Olympus by Mercury*. Between 1543 and 1548, another decorative cycle with the same theme but organized slightly differently was created by Perino del Vaga for a room in the Castel Sant'Angelo: *Psyche Contemplating Cupid*; *Venus Reprimanding Cupid*; *Venus Demands that Psyche Descend into Hades*; *Psyche Tormented by Venus's Servants*; *The Nuptial Procession of Psyche*; *The Wedding Feast of Psyche*. A shortened version of the legend is found in the cartouches of a stained-glass cycle created in the sixteenth century by a French artist for the Château d'Écouen and which is now in the Musée Condé at Chantilly.

Such decorative programs involving Psyche are frequent even into the twentieth century, when Maurice Denis created one for the townhouse of the Russian enthusiast Morosov, a program whose original sketches are now in the Musée d'Orsay.

Psyche also inspired many easel paintings. In the seventeenth and eighteenth centuries, La Fontaine's revival of the legend resulted in lively, sometimes mundane, and even erotic representations. With the advent of neoclassicism, the legend was once again endowed with spiritualist symbolism: the soul reintegrates this myth about the soul. In a painting by Gérard, Cupid is about to place a chaste kiss on Psyche's forehead (1798, Paris, Louvre). Canova sculpted six different versions of the two adolescents, each time rendering the figures as chaste and slender bodies formed into graceful arabesques. Pushing that Neoplatonic and purely metaphysical notion of the myth to its limits comes Chaudet, who sculpted the solitary figure of Cupid who kneels to seize a butterfly by its wings. By contrast, David revived the sensual interpretation in a late work that shows Cupid leaving

Psyche at daybreak without awakening her; here Cupid is a rebellious adolescent who—with sleeping Psyche's arm still resting on his thigh—flashes a smile in the direction of the viewer (1817, Paris, Louvre).

Attributes: Butterfly. Butterfly wings.

Cross-references: Cupid. Venus.

Sources: Apuleius, *Metamorphoses* IV, 28–VI, 24.

Bibliography: E. Pfeifer, *Eidola und andere mit dem Sterben verbunden Flügelwesen in der attischen Vasenmalerei*, Frankfurt, 1989.

Psyche Carried away by Zephyr. Stained glass, sixteenth century. Chantilly, Musée Condé.

PYGMALION

Gk., Lat., Ger., and Fr. Pygmalion; It. Pigmalione.
King of Cyprus.

HISTORY/MYTHOLOGY

Pygmalion, a legendary king of Cyprus, modeled a statue of absolute beauty in ivory and then fell so in love with it that he begged Venus to send him a woman of equal beauty, whereupon the goddess brought the statue to life and he married her. Pygmalion's creation is sometimes called Galatea but otherwise bears no relation to the nymph with that name. They had a child together named Paphos.

REPRESENTATIONS

Although the subject inspired no ancient ceramists or sculptors, it proved particularly attractive to eighteenth-century artists, who saw in it an exaltation of the love of art and beauty, and their representations focused on the moment when the statue comes to life.

In a painting by Carle van Loo (1705–65) in the National Museum of Warsaw, Pygmalion is seen sculpting his statue on bended knee while Venus reclines on a cloud and touches her hand to the figure's hair. In a painting by Deshayes, *Pygmalion and Galatea*, Pygmalion is shown standing alone in the foreground while he sculpts a figure placed high on a pedestal, bathed in a halo of light and surrounded by the putti and nymphs who accompany Venus (eighteenth century, Tours, Musée des Beaux-Arts). A similar setting appears in a work by François Boucher, but the artist, who gazes in stupefaction at the scene, is relegated to the painting's lower right corner (*Pygmalion in Love with His Statue*, 1742, St. Petersburg, Hermitage).

In a marble group of 1763 by Maurice Falconet, the female figure is shown leaning slightly toward Pygmalion, who kneels before her and clasps his hands together in astonishment (*Pygmalion and Galatea*, better known as *Pygmalion at the Feet of His Statue*, Baltimore, Walters Art Gallery). Burne-Jones painted a number of works that highlight different episodes from the myth (*Pygmalion and the Image*, 1869–79, Birmingham, City Museum).

Pygmalion. Master L.D. Engraving, sixteenth century.

Sources: Ovid, *Metamorphoses* X, 243–97. H. Coignet and J.-J. Rousseau, *Pygmalion*, 1770 (a lyric staging; Rousseau is the author of the music and libretto of two pieces).

Bibliography: J. L. Carr, "Pygmalion and the Philosophers," *Journal of the Warburg and Courtauld Institutes* XXIII (1960): 239–55.

Pyramus and Thisbe.
Lucas van Leyden.
Engraving, 1514.
Amsterdam,
Rijksmuseum.

PYRAMUS AND THISBE

It. Piramo, Tisbe; Fr. Pyrame, Thisbé; Gr. Pyramos, Thisbe; Lat.
Pyramus, Thisbe; Ger. Pyramos, Thisbe.
Legendary young Babylonian couple.

HISTORY/MYTHOLOGY

Pyramus and Thisbe were two young lovers whose parents refused
them permission to marry. They spoke to each other in secret through
a hole in the wall that separated their houses, until one night they
agreed to meet beyond the city's walls, near a spring. Thisbe arrived
first but was frightened off by a lioness that had come to the fountain
to quench its thirst after a bloody meal. In her haste to escape, she lost
her veil, which the animal then chewed and shredded. When Pyramus
found the bloody veil on the deserted site, he thought his beloved had
been devoured and immediately killed himself with his sword in despair.
When Thisbe later returned and found her lover dead, she pulled the
sword from his body and killed herself.

REPRESENTATIONS

Although scarcely represented in antiquity, the story became popular
in the Renaissance. It was a favorite subject on marriage chests made
from small carved-bone plaques in the Venetian workshop of the
Embriacchi (active between 1396 and 1433).

Painters favored the scene of the lovers' death, and frequently
depicted either Thisbe returning to the site of the tryst to find her
lover dead or the death of Thisbe herself (Poussin, *Landscape with
Pyramus and Thisbe*, 1650–51, Frankfurt, Städelsches Kunstinstitut);
the lioness sometimes appears in the background (Tintoretto, c. 1541,
Modena, Galleria Estense). Known versions also include works by
Albrecht Altdorfer (c. 1513, wood engraving) and Rembrandt
(1652–53, drawing, Berlin, Kupferstichkabinett).

Sources: Ovid, *Metamorphoses* IV, 55–166. Shakespeare, *A
Midsummer Night's Dream.*

Bibliography: O. Bätschmann, *Nicolas Poussin, Landschaft mit
Pyramus und Thisbe*, Frankfurt, 1987.

PYRRAH *See* Deucalion.

PYTHON *See* Apollo.

QUIVER *See* Cupid.

QUOS EGO

A citation from Virgil's *Aeneid* (I, 35): Juno released the Winds in an effort to prevent the Trojans, who were led by Aeneas, from reaching land, and this enraged Neptune, who threatened the Winds without specifying what he would do by saying, "I [who could] do unto you...." The phrase became a celebrated expression of reserve and was sometimes used as the title of various paintings of Neptune calming a storm (Rubens, 1634–35, Dresden, Staatliche Kunstmuseum).

Cross-references: Neptune.

Quos Ego (detail).
Peter Paul Rubens,
1634–35.
Dresden, Staatliche
Kunstmuseum.

RAINBOW *See* Iris.

RAM *See* Phrixus and Helle.

RAPE

Amorous relations between mortals and gods often ended in rape. It was dangerous for a mortal to enter into a sexual relationship with a divinity; this explains why the mortal is often gripped by fear as well as why violence often ensues. Examples of rape include those between Pluto and Proserpine, Boreas and Orythia, and Jupiter and Ganymede. Goddesses sometimes followed the male gods' example, for example Aurora, who raped Cephalus. Conversely, the mortal Peleus took the divine Thetis by force after the other gods had promised her to him.

Cross-references: Aurora. Boreas. Cephalus. Ganymede. Jupiter. Peleus. Pluto. Proserpine. Thetis.

Bibliography: S. Kaempf-Dimitriadou, *Die Liebe der Götter in der attischen Kunst des 5. Jahrhunderts vor Christus*, Berne, 1979.

REMUS *See* Romulus.

RHEA *Greek name for* Cybele.

RING *See* Gyges.

RIVER

The rivers were represented as bearded figures who often recline with an elbow resting on an urn that pours out water. Some rivers adopt human form, as Alpheus did in pursuit of the nymph Arethusa; others, such as Achelous, have the bodies of bulls and human heads.

Cross-references: Achelous. Arethusa. Cloelia. Horatius Cocles.

ROCK *See* Atlas. Centaurs. Galatea. Giants. Niobe. Polyphemus. Sappho. Sisyphus.

ROMULUS AND REMUS

Lat. Romulus, Remus; It. Romolo, Remo; Sp. Romulo, Remo; Fr. Romulus, Rémus; Ger. Romulus, Remus.
Heroic founders of Rome.

HISTORY/MYTHOLOGY

The founding of Rome is linked to the legend of Troy through a mythical genealogy that makes Romulus, Rome's founder and first king, the descendent of Aeneas.

After the destruction of Troy, Aeneas inadvertently landed in Italy with his son, Ascanius, who there founded Latium's capital, Alba Longa, after his father died. Ten generations later, a struggle erupted

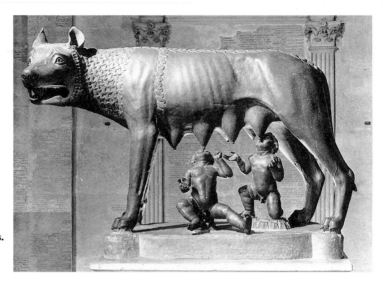

Romulus and Remus.
Bronze, c. 500 B.C.
Rome,
Musei Capitolini.

between two brothers: Numitor, the elder, and Amulius, the younger. As the victor, Amulius assassinated Numitor's son and forced his daughter, Rhea Silvia, to become a Vestal Virgin.

Rhea Silvia, however, received a visit from Mars and consequently gave birth to Romulus and Remus. Amulius abandoned the twins in the Tiber, but the river deposited them safely beneath a fig tree at the foot of the Palatine. A she-wolf then came down from the mountains and nursed the newborns with her milk. Faustulus, who guarded the king's flocks, witnessed that portentous event and gave the twins to his wife to raise as their own, whereupon the wolf withdrew to the Grotto of the Lupercal.

At the age of eighteen, the twins learned the truth about their origins. They then placed themselves in the service of Numitor, whom they restored to the throne of Alba, and decided to found their own city on the Palatine, where the Tiber's currents had long ago left them. They agreed to let the gods decide which of them would be the new city's king, and the prophesies of an augur, based on an interpretation of the flight of birds, favored Romulus. In a sacred ritual that served to establish the foundations of the eternal city of Rome (c. 753 B.C.), Romulus then took up his plow and with it mapped out the *pomoerium*, the furrow that would surround the city walls. Remus meanwhile became filled with resentment and, in defiance of the gods, crossed the boundary, whereupon he was killed by his outraged brother.

REPRESENTATIONS

Romulus and Remus appear frequently in many different media in Roman art. They are seen nursed by the legendary she-wolf on coins, engraved stones, and in sculpted reliefs. The most famous representation of this kind is doubtless the Musei Capitolini bronze group in which the two babies suck at the wolf's nipples. In reality, although the animal is of ancient, probably Etruscan, origin (c. 500 B.C.), the two children are modern additions (before the sixteenth century), and the group's fame is explained by the fact that historians mistakenly identified it with a work of similar composition that Livy and Cicero mentioned as having been installed on the Capitoline. Numerous scenes from the life of

Ulysses and His Companions Blinding the Cyclops.
Detail from Laconian cup, 560 B.C.
Paris, Bibliothèque Nationale de France, Cabinet des Médailles.

Venus, Satyr, and Cupid.
Correggio, 1528.
Paris, Louvre.

Romulus were sculpted on the frieze of the Basilica Aemilia, of which some fragments survive.

In a juxtaposition that at first seems strange but which can be justified as a symbolic representation of the tie between Rome and the church, the twins and she-wolf appear at the base of a medieval ivory crucifix in the Musei Vaticani.

A few episodes from the legendary life of Romulus have inspired modern artists; most important is Faustulus's discovery of the twins being nursed by the wolf, a scene that always comprises at least three figures, although Rhea Silvia and her husband, the river god Tiberinus, may also appear, as in Rubens' *Romulus and Remus* (1618, Rome, Musei Capitolini).

Romulus's murder of Remus is sometimes represented, as are other celebrated episodes from the first years of Roman history. Romulus can, for example, appear as the person giving the starting signal in depictions of the rape of the Sabines. A work by Ingres, which depicts an offering in the context of a triumphal scene, alludes to the rape's sequel: after the Sabine men retaliated by attacking Rome, Romulus promised to offer up to Jupiter the arms of the enemy's chieftain, Acron (1812, Paris, École des Beaux-Arts).

Cross-references: Sabines.

Sources: Livy, *History of Rome* I, 4–7. Ovid, *Festivals* II, 381–422. Plutarch, *Life of Romulus*.

ROPE *See* Claudia Quinta.

ROSE *See* Aurora. Graces.

RUDDER *See* Fortune. Venus (celestial).

SABINES

Lat. Sabinae; It. Sabine; Fr. Sabines; Ger. Sabinerin.
Ancient Italian women living northeast of Rome.

HISTORY/MYTHOLOGY

With only a few minor differences, Livy, Plutarch, and Ovid all tell about the same event involved in the founding of Rome: to ensure the growth of their young country's population, the Romans invited the Sabines to a festival during which they abducted the women and chased off the men. The Sabine men retaliated three years later by attacking Rome. When the enemies clashed, however, the Sabine women threw themselves between their Sabine fathers and Roman husbands, whereupon the two peoples made peace and united.

REPRESENTATIONS

The subject has been abundantly represented since the Renaissance and used for crowded confrontation scenes. The two sexes act out antagonistic roles: the violence of the warring men is contrasted with

**The Rape
of the Sabines.**
Nicolas Poussin,
c. 1637–38.
Paris, Louvre.

the grief of the women, who are shown as either victims or opponents of the combatants. In paintings by Poussin, Romulus signals his men to begin the abduction, triggering a range of violent or touching scenes as the Sabine women are torn between the Sabine men, who restrain them, and the Roman abductors (c. 1634–35, New York, Metropolitan Museum of Art and c. 1637–38, Paris, Louvre).

The second conflict between Romans and Sabines is less frequently illustrated, but a version by David (1799, Paris, Louvre) in which the women throw themselves between the combatants has become famous. In the foreground, Hersilia—whom Romulus married and whom Plutarch credits with a speech about peace and harmony—

The Sabine Women.
Jacques-Louis David,
1799.
Paris, Louvre.

separates the Sabine chief, Tatius, shown lowering his sword, from Romulus, who holds his javelin aloft. Other women gather up their nursing children and brandish them like shields, and the weapons are lowered as a result.

Sources: Livy, *Roman History* I, 12–13. Plutarch, *Life of Romulus*, 19. Ovid, *Festivals* III, 167–258.

SACRIFICE

The ancients sacrificed domesticated animals to the gods; Aeneas, for example, sacrificed a sow. In the context of myths, humans were occasionally sacrificed. This was nevertheless exceptional and occurred in response to the demands of either a god, as in the case of Iphigenia, or a dead mortal's spirit, as when the ghost of Achilles demanded the sacrifice of Polyxena; human sacrifice also occurred as part of a barbarian custom, as when Pharoah Busiris tried to sacrifice Hercules.

Cross-references: Aeneas. Busiris. Iphigenia. Laocoön. Polyxena.

The Rape of the Sabines.
Giambologna, bronze, sixteenth century.
New York, Metropolitan Museum of Art.

SAPPHO

Gk., Lat., and Ger. Sappho; Fr. Sapho; It. Saffo.
Greek poetess (late seventh century–early sixth century B.C.).

HISTORY/MYTHOLOGY

Hardly anything is known for certain about the Greek poetess Sappho. She lived on the island of Lesbos from the end of the seventh to the beginning of the sixth centuries B.C. Nevertheless, Herodotus in his *Histories*, Aristotle in his *Rhetoric*, and the Marmor Parium inform us that Sappho was the rival of the poet Alcaeus, whom she refused to marry, and that she was banished from Lesbos for her opposition to Pittacus, the island's ruling tyrant. She then lived in Sicily until about 570 B.C., when she returned to Lesbos, where she remained until her death. From her considerable poetic output there remain only some very brief fragments and two odes: *To a Beloved Woman* and the *Ode to Aphrodite*.

The Greeks greatly esteemed Sappho's poetic talent but appear not to have had more precise biographic details, for legend became widespread by the fifth century B.C., as evidenced especially in Greek drama. One of the most popular legends contends that Sappho fell in love with a shepherd, Phaon, and threw herself from a cliff on Leucas when he scorned her. Sappho's works nevertheless suggest to the contrary that she had a passion for maidens in the community of followers that formed around her.

REPRESENTATIONS

In antiquity, focus is placed mainly on the creative role of Sappho the musician (vase by the Brygos Painter, c. 480 B.C., Munich, Antikensammlungen). Figures of a woman with tablets or a volumen, such as those seen in a wall painting found at Herculaneum and now in the Museo Archeologico in Naples or a sculpture in the Musei Vaticani, can probably be identified as Sappho.

Sappho.
Théodore Chassériau, 1849.
Paris, Louvre.

Sappho, Phaon, and Cupid.
Jacques-Louis David, 1809.
St. Petersburg, Hermitage.

Sappho and Alcaeus.
Attic kalathos, c. 480 B.C.
Munich, Antikensammlungen.

In modern times, Sappho has always had her place in compositions evocative of ancient poetry. She is one of several poets surrounding Apollo in Raphael's *Parnassus* (c. 1509–10, Stanze, Rome, Vatican). Similarly, she appears next to Apelles and Raphael in Ingres' *Apotheosis of Homer* (1827, Paris, Louvre).

Sappho is more frequently represented from the eighteenth century onward when the young woman, accompanied by a lyre and volumen, continued to represent the incarnation of poetic creativity (Fragonard painted several versions of *Sappho Inspired by Cupid*, in which a *putto* whispers into the ear of the semi-nude poet, who is about to write). Sappho's suicide was also frequently depicted. She is shown as a melancholic figure seated on the cliff on Leucas, or she already lies at the bottom of the abyss into which she has hurled herself. Some works attempt to unify the two traditions. Pardier's statue of Sappho (1852, Paris, Musée d'Orsay), for example, explicitly evokes the iconographic tradition centered on her suicide (by creating small waves on the pedestal), but the poet remains essentially a figure of meditation and melancholy, a character trait that is considered a pre-requisite for creativity in the romantic tradition. The same holds true for works by Moreau, who depicted the poet's death several times; Sappho's art here becomes a way of redeeming her unrequited love, and instead of falling into an abyss, she seems almost to ascend, as if she were whisked along by the power of her lyre (Paris, Musée Gustave Moreau).

It is not until the twentieth century and works with erotic overtones that the character's homosexual connotations overpower all other iconographic traditions.

Attributes: Book. Lyre. Rock. Tablets.

Cross-references: Apelles.

Sarpedon Transported by Thanatos and Hypnos. Krater by Euphronius, c. 515–510 B.C. New York, Metropolitan Museum of Art.

SARPEDON

Gk., Lat., and Ger. Sarpedon; Fr. Sarpédon; It. Sarpedone.
Lycian hero.

HISTORY/MYTHOLOGY

Legend records three heroes with this name. In the Cretan cycle, he was the giant son of Poseidon who was killed by Hercules. A son of Europa and Jupiter, also called Sarpedon, left Crete for Asia Minor after a quarrel with his brother, Minos, and became king of Lycia. Finally, in *The Iliad*, Sarpedon, the son of Apollo and Bellerophon's daughter Laodamia, was a Lycian chieftain allied with the Trojans. This last Sarpedon played an important role in the war against the Greeks but was killed by Patroclus, whereupon the gods, who were fond of him, sent Sleep and Death (Hypnos and Thanatos) to carry him back to his homeland and build his tomb there.

REPRESENTATIONS

Ancient vase painters portrayed Sarpedon as a wounded figure who is carried from the battlefield by the winged genies of Sleep and Death. This subject is represented in southern Italy from the end of the sixth until the middle of the fourth centuries B.C.

The same subject appears on a monumental krater by Euphronius which has inscriptions identifying the main characters: under the protection of Hermes, two winged genies bend down to lift Sarpedon's wounded body (515–510 B.C., New York, Metropolitan Museum of Art).

Although modern artists have hardly ever represented the subject, the same scene takes place under the aegis of Apollo in a painting by Berthélémy (1781, Langres, Musée).

Sources: Homer, *The Iliad*, II, 876 ff.; V, 471 ff., 627 ff.; VI, 198 ff.

Jupiter and Saturn. Detail from pediment of the Temple of Artemis at Corfu, end of seventh century B.C. Athens, Archeological Museum.

SATURN

Gk. Cronos (Chronos); Lat. Saturnus; It. and Sp. Saturno; Fr. Saturne; Ger. Saturn.
Father of the gods.

HISTORY/MYTHOLOGY

Saturn was identified with the Greek god Cronos, the youngest of the Titans, and, through an etymological play on words, with Chronos, or

Saturn.
Pieter Bruegel
the Elder.
Engraving, 1574.

**Saturn Devouring
One of His Children.**
Francisco de Goya,
1821–23.
Madrid, Prado.

Time. In Greek mythology, Cronos was the son of Sky (Uranus) and Earth (Gaea), and belonged to the age of the Titans, which preceded that of the Olympians. He helped Gaea avenge herself on Uranus, who killed all her children, by castrating his father with a sickle; Uranus's testicles were thrown into the sea, which consequently gave birth to Venus. Now master of the world, he married his sister, Rhea, and himself devoured his children so that they would not depose him. That resulted in Rhea's losing Hestia (Vesta), Demeter (Ceres), Hera (Juno), Pluto (Hades), and Poseidon (Neptune). She saved Zeus (Jupiter), however, by hiding him and giving Saturn a stone wrapped like a baby to swallow. Jupiter later forced Saturn to regurgitate all the swallowed children and chained him up with the other Titans.

REPRESENTATIONS

Saturn is portrayed as an old man holding a sickle, a scythe, or an armillary sphere (an object symbolizing the universe). Rubens (1636–38, Madrid, Prado) and Goya (1821–23, Madrid, Prado) both produced striking works of Saturn devouring his children. Saturn is also associated with the Golden Age.

Attributes: Sickle. Sphere.

Cross-references: Jupiter.

Sources: Ovid, *Metamorphoses* I, 89–150 (Golden Age).

Bibliography: R. Klibanski, E. Panofsky, and F. Saxl, *Saturn and Melancholy*, Liechtenstein, 1979.

SATYRS

Gk. and Ger. Satyros; Lat. Satyrus; It. and Sp. Satiro; Fr. Satyr.
Mythical creatures.

HISTORY/MYTHOLOGY

Satyrs are the hybrid, half-man, half-animal creatures who most often accompany Dionysus. Their ugliness was as proverbial as their

Satyr and Maenad.
Attic amphora,
c. 500 B.C.
Munich,
Antikensammlungen.

drunkenness, their sexual appetite was insatiable, and their penises were often erect. Forever in quest of a partner—whether animal or human—satyrs relentlessly chased after Bacchantes, whom they surprised in their sleep. They often behaved childishly and unpredictably, a pattern which was set by the eldest of the satyrs, Silenus (also called Papposilenus).

Except for Silenus and Marsyas, satyrs play only secondary roles in Greek legends. Nevertheless, during theatrical competitions, each author presented a satiric drama in which a chorus of satyrs appeared beside the tragic hero to add a comic note to the myths enacted.

REPRESENTATIONS

The satyr's body is part-horse (tail, ears, hooves) or, particularly in Roman iconography, part-goat and therefore similar to Pan. In Greek

Satyr and Peasant.
Jacob Jordaens,
c. 1635.

Satyr.
Attic cup,
c. 500 B.C.
Munich,
Antikensammlungen.

art, satyrs help Dionysus make wine and carry implements for symposia (pitchers, wineskins, drinking vessels), and they are often associated with wine and drunkenness. They are gesticulating and dancing creatures that are forever in motion. Their activities tend to parody those of mortals, whom they can never equal. The satyr's curiosity inspired frontal representations in which the satyr appears as a voyeur.

In modern iconography, satyrs symbolize the raw, untamed side of nature as well as the triumph of paganism. They are bestiality and lust incarnate; their iconography inspired that of the devil, and they have accordingly become comparable to him. The fact that painters have often turned to the theme of voyeurism to portray the female anatomy has resulted in many versions of the *Satyr Surprising a Nymph* and its variant, *Jupiter and Antiope.*

Flemish painters illustrated the *Tale of the Satyr and the Peasant* as a pretext for showing rustic scenes; a satyr is astonished to learn that the same man who blows hot air to thaw his frozen hands can blow cool air to chill his steaming soup.

Attributes: Amphora. Ears of an ass. Flute (*aulos*). Horse (or goat) tail and hooves. Wineskin.

Cross-references: Amymone. Antiope. Bacchantes. Bacchus. Marsyas. Pan. Silenus.

Sources: Aesop, LXXIV (the satyr and the peasant).

Bibliography: F. Brommer, *Satyrspiele*, Berlin, 1959. G. Hedreen, *Silens*, Madison, 1993.

SCEPTER *See* Aegeus. Agamemnon. Cybele. Juno. Jupiter. Pluto.

SCIPIO AFRICANUS

Lat. and Ger. Scipio; It. Scipione; Sp. Escipion; Fr. Scipion.
Roman consul (235–183 B.C.).

HISTORY/MYTHOLOGY

Publius Cornelius Scipio demonstrated exceptional qualities as a warrior at a very young age. He obtained an aedility by the time he was twenty-one—without completing the required ten campaigns—and became proconsul of Spain by the age of twenty-four. The following year, in 210 B.C., he conquered the important stronghold of Carthaginia and demonstrated exceptional kindness by refusing an already betrothed maiden from among the prisoners he enslaved. Scipio's many victories led to the surrender of Spain in 206 B.C. and the end of the Second Punic War in the year 201.

REPRESENTATIONS

Modern painters, especially those of the baroque period, have frequently represented Scipio rejecting the slave from Carthaginia under the title of *The Continence of Scipio.* The subject even held a certain fascination during the reign of Louis XIV. Scipio and the captive constitute the two indispensable characters; the Roman general is seated on a dais while the maiden stands before him; the captive's betrothed, Allucius, is sometimes accompanied by family members as he receives

Scipio.
Giovanni Battista Tiepolo,
1731.
Milan, Palazzo Dugnani.

her from Scipio and demonstrates his gratitude (by touching his hand to his heart in the painting by Poussin, 1643–45, Moscow, Pushkin Museum). Soldiers always figure among secondary characters and express admiration for their leader's exemplary generosity.

The second subject that appears in painting is *The Triumph of Scipio*, which alludes to an event that took place in 204 B.C. during the Second Punic War. When Hannibal disembarked in Italy, an oracle foretold that he would retreat if the bust of Cybele were brought from Pergamum to Rome to be welcomed by the city's worthiest citizen. Scipio, who was designated for this role, is seen receiving the bust.

Cross-references: Cybele.

Sources: Ovid, *Festivals* IV. Livy, *History of Rome* XXVI, 50; XXIX. Valerius Maximus, IV, 3, 1.

SCIRON *See* Theseus.

SCISSORS *See* Fates.

SCORPION *See* Orion.

SCROLL *See* Muses. Sapho. Virgil.

SCYLLA *See* Glaucus.

SEA ANIMALS *See* Amphritite. Arethusa. Neptune. Nereids. Triton. Venus.

SEASONS

Gk. Horai; Lat. Horae; It. Stagioni; Sp. Estaciones; Fr. Saisons; Ger. Horen.
Greek deities.

HISTORY/MYTHOLOGY

In antiquity, there were considered at first to be three Seasons. Hesiod makes them the daughters of Law (Themis) and names them Eunomia, Dike, and Eirene (Good Government, Righteousness, and Peace), names that link them to civic order. In Athens, however, the Seasons were called Thallo, Auxo, and Karpo, names evocative of nature's growth, flowering, and germination. From the Hellenistic period onward, there was considered to be a fourth Season. They guarded the gates to Olympus and guided the chariots of Juno and Minerva. Their influence was always beneficial, and they were associated with fruitfulness. The Seasons were not the subject of any particular myth but were instead often grouped with the gods at festivals and in processions; they attended, for example, the marriage of Thetis and Peleus and were among those who welcomed Hercules to Olympus.

REPRESENTATIONS

The Hours (Seasons) are indistinguishable from each other in archaic Greek art. They appear on the François Vase in the procession of gods coming to pay their respects to Peleus (c. 570 B.C., Florence, Museo Archeologico) and on a cup by the Sosias Painter with Hercules welcomed to Olympus (c. 510 B.C. Berlin, Antikensmuseum). Pausanias specifies that the Hours appeared with the Graces (Charites) on the back of the throne in Phidias's statue of Zeus at Olympia (435 B.C.). In Italiot ceramics, the Seasons hold sheaves of wheat and stand by while Triptolemus prepares to carry wheat to mankind; an inscription collectively names them Horai, a name that associates them more with fertility than with the cycle of time (Apulian krater, c. 370–350 B.C., St. Petersburg, Hermitage).

The four Seasons are frequently represented in the Roman period, when they are differentiated by the kind of vegetation each holds: Spring, flowers; Summer, sheaves of wheat and a sickle; Autumn, grapes and a vase; Winter, reeds and game. The Seasons were a perfect subject for use in square mosaic floor designs, as demonstrated in a second-century A.D. mosaic, where they are full-length figures (Tunis, Bardo Museum). Busts of the Seasons frequently appear in medallions at the four corners of panels. The Seasons are connected to the abstract terms inscribed beside them in a mosaic from Antioch (fourth century A.D., Paris, Louvre): Spring, "ANANEOSIS" (Renovation); Summer, "EUANDRIA" (Virile Force), Autumn, "DYNAMIS" (Power); Winter, "KTISIS" (Foundation). Because of their association with time

Summer.
Detail
from a mosaic,
fourth century A.D.
Paris, Louvre.

and eternity, the Seasons appear on a large number of Roman sarcophagi from the second century A.D. onward; they are sometimes winged adolescents rather than women, as exemplified by the figures that surround Dionysus on a sarcophagus in the Louvre (c. A.D. 250).

The modern iconography of the Seasons may differ from antique models. The subject is frequent in architectural decorations, where it appears in a variety of forms while at the same time preserving the ensemble's unity. The Seasons may be treated as landscapes that evoke rustic life, as in a series of canvases by Francesco Bassano the Younger (c. 1576, Vienna, Kunsthistorisches Museum), and they may even be used to allude to biblical stories, as in a series of paintings by Poussin (1660–64, Paris, Louvre).

Some painters have revived ancient schemas. For example, Tintoretto represented the four Seasons as small, chubby children (1564, Venice, Scuola di San Rocco) and as maidens appropriately accompanied by flowers, wheat, grapes, and reeds (1565–66, New York, priv. coll. and Washington, National Gallery). Contrary to ancient tradition, other artists have linked each Season to a divinity. The most famous example of this is Botticelli's *Primavera* (c. 1480, Florence, Uffizi). Spring and flowers may be associated with Flora and Venus; Summer and the harvest with Ceres; the Autumn and vintages with Bacchus; Winter and fire with Vulcan. Noteworthy is a series of frescoes by Albani (c. 1620, Rome, Palazzo Verospi) and four canvases painted in 1699 by different artists for the King's Pavilion at Marly: *Bacchus and Ariadne* by Charles de La Fosse (Dijon, Musée des Beaux-Arts), *Ceres* by Louis Boullogne (Rouen, Musée des Beaux-Arts), *Springtime, Represented by Zephyr and Flora* by Noel-Nicolas Coypel, and *Winter* by Jouvenet (lost). The Seasons are represented as those same divinities in four oval paintings created by Watteau for the Hôtel de Crozat (1715; known through an engraving, *Summer*, Washington, National Gallery).

Attributes: Flowers. Grapes. Reeds. Wheat.

Cross-references: Bacchus. Ceres. Flora. Venus. Vulcan. Zephyr.

Sources: Hesiod, *Theogony*, 901–3. Pausanias, V, 11, 7. Ovid, *Metmorphoses* II, 1–32. Lucretius, V, 736–47.

Bibliography: G. Hanfmann, *The Season Sarcophagus in Dumbarton Oaks*, 2 vols., Cambridge, Mass., 1951. P. Kranz, *Die Jahreszeiten-sarkophage*, Berlin, 1984. *The Loves of the Gods*, ex. cat., Fort Worth, 1992, no. 6. D. Parrish, *Season Mosaics of Roman North Africa*, 1984.

SELENE *See* Diana. Endymion.

SELEUCUS *See* Antiochos.

SEMELE

Jupiter and Semele (detail).
Gustave Moreau, 1895.
Paris,
Musée Gustave Moreau.

Gk., Lat., and Ger. Semele; Fr. Sémélé.
Theban princess.

HISTORY/MYTHOLOGY

Semele was the daughter of Harmonia and Cadmus, the founder of Thebes. She conceived a son during one of Jupiter's many romantic adventures. Jupiter promised to grant her every wish. Juno, who was jealous, persuaded Semele to ask the god to appear to her in his true splendor. Jupiter reluctantly complied, whereupon Semele was immediately struck dead by the thunderbolts that emanated from his divine countenance. Mercury gathered up the unborn child, Bacchus, and sewed him into Jupiter's thigh until he was ready to be born.

REPRESENTATIONS

Semele's death has captured artists' attention in particular. Ancient representations show Semele sleeping while Mercury carries off the young Bacchus.

Modern artists have treated this same subject as a sort of majestic Epiphany in which Jupiter thunders in the clouds while Semele lies on the ground. The subject is also charged with powerful symbolism in a painting by Moreau (1895, Paris, Musée Gustave Moreau).

Cross-references: Bacchus. Juno. Jupiter. Mercury.

Sources: Ovid, *Metamorphoses* III, 259–309.

SEMIRAMIS

Gk., Lat., and Ger. Semiramis; Fr. Sémiramis; It. Semiramide.
Oriental queen.

HISTORY/MYTHOLOGY

Semiramis, an Assyrian queen as well as a legendary symbol of the female warrior and builder, supposedly lived in the thirteenth century B.C. Like other mythical founders of dynasties (for example, Oedipus and Romulus), she was abandoned as a child and taken in by shepherds. Her name means "dove" in Syrian and alludes to the birds that fed her. She grew up to marry King Ninus and became sole master of the Assyrian Empire after she assassinated her husband. Her brilliant and legendary conquests took her to all parts of Asia until, at the peak of her power, she built and ornamented the fabled city of Babylon, on the banks of the Euphrates. The Hanging Gardens, among other architectural marvels, became one of the seven wonders of the ancient world.

The queen's beauty was also legendary. Indeed, an anecdote claims that when an insurrection erupted in the capital while Semiramis was bathing, she calmed the rebels simply by appearing before them half-naked and with her hair unbound.

REPRESENTATIONS

According to Valerius Maximus, there was a statue in Babylon of a woman with her hair half undone, which would have illustrated the anecdote mentioned above. The story also inspired a modern artist, Raphael Mengs (1728–79), to whom it gave an opportunity to depict a woman at her toilet; here Semiramis's legendary beauty and remarkable self-control are contrasted with the fright manifested by her followers when a soldier comes to inform her of a surrender (Ajaccio, Musée du Palais Fesch). In Alessandro Tiarini's portrayal of the queen at her toilet, Semiramis already grips the pommel of her sword while one servant combs her abundant hair and another brings her armor (seventeenth century, Rome, Galleria Doria Pamphili).

As a warrior-heroine, Semiramis appears alongside Tomyris as one of nine Worthies in many fifteenth-century murals and tapestries. She also appears as a simple character in a Limoges enameled cup by

**Semiramis Building
Babylon.**
Edgar Degas,
c. 1860–62.
Paris, Musée d'Orsay.

Laudin in the Musée de Cluny; Zenobia is seen in a medallion on the
same object. Semiramis is sometimes shown preparing for battle, as in
a work by Guerchino (seventeenth century, Haarlem, Museum Franz
Hals). Another theme surfaces in de Lairesse's etching, *Semiramis at
the Lion Hunt.*

There are still other representations linked to this legend, including
Semiramis Dying at the Entry of the Tomb of Ninus (Lordon and
Dijon, Musée des Beaux-Arts) and a work that is notable for its figure
of Ninus, who lifts a veil to reveal Semiramis (Carlone, Genoa,
Palazzo Reale). In the nineteenth century, Degas was particularly
attracted to the idea of a queen who is both a founder and builder;
drawing inspiration from Assyrian works that had recently entered the
Louvre, he painted *Semiramis Building Babylon* (1860–62, Paris,
Musée d'Orsay).

Attributes: Female warrior. Half-combed hair.

Cross-references: Oedipus. Romulus. Tomyris. Worthies. Zenobia.

SENECA

Lat., It., Sp., and Ger. Seneca; Fr. Sénèque.
Latin philosopher (c. 2 B.C.–A.D. 65).

HISTORY/MYTHOLOGY

Lucius Annaeus Seneca was born in Cordoba in 2 or 4 B.C. and died in
Rome in A.D. 65 or 66. He was a central figure in first-century A.D.
philosophy and literature, and left a body of works on Stoic philosophy
as well as some tragedies. His political role was somewhat ambiguous,
particularly with reference to Nero. If Seneca benefited from favoritism
and excessive wealth, however, he compensated by dying in a way that

The Death of Seneca.
Peter Paul Rubens,
1612–13.
Munich,
Alte Pinakothek.

conformed to Stoic principles in an exemplary way. The circumstances surrounding his forced suicide—imposed by Nero after the Pisonian Conspiracy but perfectly mastered by the philosopher—are reported by Tacitus. Surrounded by friends, he delivered a few Stoic phrases and then cut his veins; his young wife, Paulina, attempted to die too, but survived. Seneca himself endured a long and excruciating agony and had to hasten the flow of blood with a warm bath.

REPRESENTATIONS

Attempts have been made to identify Seneca in several ancient sculptures, including a bronze bust in the museum at Naples and a marble bust in the Musei Vaticani. In all instances, the identifying characteristics are believed to be an aquiline nose, eyebrows furrowed by thought, and the severe look of a Stoic philosopher.

It was Seneca's death, however, that inspired both ancient and modern representations.

Although other iconographic interpretations are now proposed, a statue in dark marble at the Louvre (Roman copy of a Hellenistic original) has been famous since the seventeenth century under the title of *The Dying Seneca* or the *Seneca Borghese*. Seneca here lifts his gazes toward the sky while his upright and prominently veined body sags and wavers as if slowly falling; a red marble vase below alludes to the tub that caught the flowing blood. The statue was sketched by Rubens, whose painting *The Death of Seneca* recalls the "ancient prototype": the philosopher is shown frontally with gaze directed skyward and feet in the tub; in the presence of two of Nero's soldiers, a physician oversees the bleeding while a young disciple takes down his mentor's last words (1612–13, Munich, Alte Pinakothek). The same subject was often painted with relatively little variation; Luca Giordano treated it with brutal realism (seventeenth century, Paris, Louvre). Seneca's death was the subject of the Prix de Rome in 1774, which David failed to win.

Attributes: Blood. Tub for bathing.

Sources: Tacitus, *Annals* XV, 60–64.

Bibliography: A.J.N.W. Prag, *The Oresteia. Iconographic and Narrative Tradition*, Warminster, 1985.

SHADOW *See* Butades.

SHELL *See* Venus.

SHIELD *See* Mars.

SHIP *See* Argonauts. Claudia Quinta.

SHIPWRECK *See* Ajax, son of Oileus. Nero.

SIBYLS

Gk. and Lat. Sibylla; It. Sibilla; Sp. Sibila; Fr. Sibylle; Ger. Sibyll.
Prophetesses.

HISTORY/MYTHOLOGY

Sibyls were prophetesses—often of oriental origin—who pronounced oracles under the inspiration of Apollo. Their prophecies were collected in books that were consulted when necessary and which were preciously preserved, especially at Rome, in the Temple of Jupiter on the Capitoline. Among the most famous Sibyls are one from Erythia in Asia Minor (Erythian Sibyl) and another from Cumaea, near Naples (Cumaean Sibyl). Aeneas consulted the Cumaean Sibyl before he descended into Hades, and Apollo is supposed to have promised her any wish if she would accept him as her lover. She asked to live for as many years as there were grains in a handful of sand, but, having forgotten to ask for continuous youth, in her old age she longed for death.

In the Christian tradition, Sibyls announced the coming of Christ and, for St. Augustine, played a role parallel to that of biblical prophets: the pagan world had a part in announcing the Christian message.

The Delphic Sibyl.
Michelangelo,
1509.
Rome, Sistine Chapel.

REPRESENTATIONS

There is no ancient iconography for Sibyls. As heralds of the coming of Christ in modern and medieval traditions, however, they were later frequently grouped with prophets. They appear in varying numbers; Michelangelo represented five on the ceiling of the Sistine Chapel (1509, Rome, Vatican). In a painting by Antoine Caron, the Tibertine Sibyl foretells the coming of Christ, who appears to Emperor Augustus in a cloud at the top of the painting (c. 1575, Paris, Louvre). In a landscape with a sweeping river, Salvatore Rosa represented Apollo's encounter with the Cumaean Sibyl, who holds out a handful of sand to the god (c. 1650, London, Wallace Collection).

Attributes: Book.

Cross-references: Aeneas. Apollo. Augustus.

Sources: Virgil, *Aeneid* VI, 1–263. Ovid, *Metamorphoses* XIV, 101–53.

SICKLE *See* Hercules. Perseus. Saturn. Seasons.

SILENUS

Gk. and Ger. Silenos; Lat. Silenus; It. and Sp. Sileno; Fr. Silène.
Satyr.

**Silenus before
King Midas.**
Attic stamnos,
c. 460 B.C.
London,
British Museum.

HISTORY/MYTHOLOGY

Silenus is the only satyr other than Marsyas to have been given a personality in mythology. He was older than his companions and was supposed to have held the secret of wisdom. King Midas, who wanted then secret, captured him by using an irresistible fountain of wine as bait.

Silenus.
Peter Paul Rubens,
1616–17.
Kassel, Museum.

REPRESENTATIONS

Greek artists depicted Silenus being captured as well as being brought to King Midas.

In modern painting, a drunk and enormously fat Silenus is often seated on an ass, barely maintaining his balance with help from his companions: satyrs and Bacchantes.

Cross-references: Bacchus. Midas. Satyrs.

Sources: Herodotus, VIII, 138. Virgil, *Eclogues* VI.

SINE BACCHO ET CERER FRIGET VENUS

The translation of this Latin proverb, "Without Bacchus and Ceres, Venus is cold," implies that without food and drink love grows cold. The proverb serves as title for three paintings by Rubens. In one, Venus is curled up all alone (1614, Antwerp); in another, Bacchus, Ceres, and Venus are united in joyful celebration (1612–13, Kassel, Saatliche Kunstsammlungen).

SINIS *See* Theseus.

SIRENS

Gk. and Ger. Seirenes; Lat. Sirenes; Fr. Sirènes; It. Sirene.
Fabled characters.

HISTORY/MYTHOLOGY

Sirens were monstrous women whose enchanting song irresistibly attracted sailors to their deaths on reefs near the Straits of Messina.

Ulysses and the Sirens.
Attic red-figure stamnos,
c. 480 B.C.
London, British Museum.

Ulysses and his companions had to pass near these reefs during their return from Troy. Forewarned by Circe, Ulysses had himself tied to the ship's mast to escape the Sirens' deadly song, and ordered his men to plug their ears with wax and to row as quickly as possible beyond range of the music's magic.

During the voyage of the Argonauts, Orpheus played music to the ship's crew in order to drown out the Sirens' song.

REPRESENTATIONS

Ulysses is shown tied to the mast with hands behind his back to escape the Sirens' song. Homer does not describe the Sirens precisely, but the ancient tradition as a whole portrays them as birdlike creatures with women's heads. Such figures appear in Attic ceramics from the sixth century B.C. onward. There are also many, more ornamental representations of Sirens in the form of shaped vases or images on gems and on the bases of bronze vase handles. Although representations of Ulysses grew much less frequent at the end of the fifth century B.C., the motif became more widespread. Sirens appear in Attic funerary monuments in this period.

The subject of Ulysses and the Sirens reappeared later in Italy, notably in Etruria and in Roman art of the third and second centuries B.C., on Roman and Etruscan sarcophagi, and in important mosaics.

Medieval Sirens often have the bodies of fish, and they correspond to another folk tradition in which they became, like Melusina or Lorelei, genies of rivers and seas. Both iconographic traditions are represented in sculpted Romanesque capitals, where Sirens are either birdlike (Paris, Saint-Julien-le-Pauvre) or fishlike women (Saint Julien de Brioude). Ulysses attached to the mast while Sirens sing was depicted by Annibale Carracci (c. 1596, Rome, Palazzo Farnese, Camerino), and it is also found in a wooden relief from the seventeenth century (Paris, Musée de Cluny).

Attributes: Bird with a woman's head.

Cross-references: Orpheus. Ulysses.

Sources: Homer, *The Odyssey* XII, 154–200.

Bibliography: A.J.N.W. Prag, *The Oresteia. Iconographic and Narrative Tradition*, Warminster, 1985.

SISYPHUS

Gk. and Ger. Sisyphos; Lat. Sisyphus; It. and Sp. Sisifo; Fr. Sisyphe.
Legendary Corinthian king.

HISTORY/MYTHOLOGY

Sisyphus, a Corinthian king and the son of Aeolus, was famous for his wiles and lack of scruples. After Aegina was raped, Sisyphus revealed to the maiden's father that Jupiter was the culprit. Jupiter avenged himself on Sisyphus and ultimately condemned him to Hades, where he must forever push uphill a boulder that rolls backward from its own weight as soon as Sisyphus reaches the top.

Sisyphus.
Attic lekythos,
c. 500 B.C.
Texas,
San Antonio Museum.

REPRESENTATIONS

Sisyphus and his boulder appear in fifth-century B.C. Attic ceramics and, with Tantalus, in Apulian ceramics.
    Inspired by Ovid, modern artists have grouped Sisyphus with Ixion, Tantalus, and Tityus; Sisyphus carries the boulder on his shoulders in Titian's version of the subject (1549, Madrid, Prado).

Cross-references: Ixion. Tantalus. Tityus.

Sources: Homer, *The Odyssey* XI, 593–600. Ovid, *Metamorphoses* IV, 460.

SNAKE

The snake is an animal from the Underworld that was linked to such earthly powers as Ceres or to such children of the Earth as Erichtonius. It was associated with Aesculapius as a symbol of the life force. Snakes were dangerous animals: they wounded Philoctetes and were used by Cleopatra to commit suicide; Bacchantes, on the contrary, handled them without risk. Mercury's caduceus comprises the two intertwined snakes that he tried to separate with a rod. Some mythical snakes are enormous in size, such as the Python of Delphi, which Apollo killed, or the dragon of Thebes, which Cadmus destroyed.

Cross-references: Aesculapius. Apollo. Bacchantes. Cadmus. Ceres. Cleopatra. Erichtonius. Furies. Gorgon (hair). Hercules. Hesperides. Jason. Laocoön. Mercury. Minerva. Ocean. Philoctetes.

SOCRATES

Gk., Lat., and Ger. Socrates; Fr. and It. Socrate.
Greek philosopher (469–399 B.C.).

HISTORY/MYTHOLOGY

Socrates is the most famous of the ancient Greek philosophers. After courageously fighting in the Peloponnesian War, he refrained from becoming involved in the city's politics. He spoke about philosophy and

The Death of Socrates.
Charles-Alphonse
Dufresnoy,
seventeenth century.
Florence, Uffizi.

was followed by many disciples, whom he taught formally but without charge. He had a powerful effect on his audience. He questioned traditional views and maintained that his role consisted less in revealing truth than in helping others discover it for themselves.

Socrates' way of life earned him many enemies, who ultimately accused him of not believing in the revered Athenian gods, of introducing new gods, and of corrupting the youth. He was condemned to die and drank hemlock, the Athenian method of capital punishment.

REPRESENTATIONS

Modern painters predominantly selected two subjects that center on the philosopher: the mirror, which is an allegory for his teaching method ("Know thyself yourself"), and his death, which illustrates the sage's flawless dignity as well as his capacity to maintain his philosophical principles even up to his death. In the first type of representation, the elderly Socrates is surrounded by youths, one of whom looks into a mirror. His death has been a popular subject since the seventeenth century. In this kind of representation, Socrates is shown surrounded by his disciples. Emphasis is given either to the sorrow experienced by his followers as they watch their master breathe his last, as seen in a painting by Giambettino Cignaroli (1706–70, Budapest, Museum für Bildende Künste), or to the superior nature of the sage, who continues to philosophize until the very end, as seen in a work by David (*The Death of Socrates*, 1787, New York, Metropolitan Museum of Art).

Sources: Diogenes Laertius, *History of Philosophy* II, 33. Plato, *Phaedrus*.

Socrates.
Ancient bust.
Naples,
Museo Archeologico.

SOPHONISBA

Gk. Lat., and Ger. Sophonisba; It. and Sp. Sofonisba; Fr. Sophonisbe.
Queen of Numidia (235–203 B.C.).

Sophonisba.
Bartholomeus
Spranger,
c. 1610.
Prague,
Narodni Gallery.

HISTORY/MYTHOLOGY

Sophonisba was the daughter of the Carthaginian general Hasdrubal and lived from 235 to 203 B.C. She was betrothed to Masinissa but married Syphax, who was considered a more certain Numidian ally for Carthage. After Masinissa, who had indeed sided with the Romans, conquered Syphax in the Battle of Utica and crushed the Numidian troops on the plain of Cirta, Sophonisba renewed her original bonds and married him. Scipio, fearing the Numidian queen's intelligence and political skill, then demanded that she be turned over to him as a slave. Masinissa instead had a cup of poison brought to Sophonisba to spare her that humiliation. In an event that marked the end of the Second Punic War, Sophonisba drank the poison after speaking these famous words: "I accept this nuptial gift; it is not distasteful to me, for a husband has never given a more precious gift to a wife. However, tell this to Masinissa: I would die with fewer regrets had I not married so soon before going to my grave."

REPRESENTATIONS

Sophonisba's suicide rarely appears in painting before the baroque period. An exception is a panel painted in cameo by Mantegna, in which the Numidian princess is shown drinking the poison alone near a tree (1500, London, National Gallery). The suicide was often represented in the seventeenth century by Flemish artists (especially in Rembrandt's circle), Italian artists (Guerchino), and French artists (Vouet). The mixture of courage and resignation on the part of the princess who sacrificed her own interests for those of the state made Sophonisba a tragic character who also stimulated the theater in the same period (Mairet, 1629; Crow, 1663; Voltaire, 1774).

Sophonisba is shown as she receives the cup of poison, after Masinissa's letter is read (Rembrandt, 1634, Madrid, Prado; Gerbrand van den Eeckout, 1664, Brunswick, Herzog Anton Ulrich-Museum). She is just as often shown immediately after drinking the poison, as indicated by her ghastly pallor and the clenched hand that she presses to her chest, in a painting by Mattia Preti (seventeenth century, Lyon, Musée des Beaux-Arts). In all cases, Sophonisba's tragic determination is contrasted with the grief expressed by her female attendants.

Attributes: Cup. Letter. Messenger.

Cross-references: Scipio.

Sources: Livy, XXX, 14–15.

SPHINX *See* Oedipus.

SPIDER *See* Arachne.

SPINDLE *See* Fates.

SPRING *See* Arethusa. Narcissus. Niobe.

STAFF *See* Belisarius. Endymion (shepherd's). Homer. Nestor.

STAG *See* Actaeon. Diana. Hercules.

STAR *See* Callisto. Castor and Pollux. Pegasus. Pleiades. Urania.

STATUE

Several legends accord central importance to various divine statues endowed with strong protective powers. During the sack of Troy, Cassandra took refuge beside the statue of Athena when Ajax pursued her; Diomedes seized the *Palladium*, the archaic statue of the same goddess. To escape from the Erinyes' torment, Orestes had to bring the statue of Artemis from Tauris, where his sister Iphigenia served as the goddess's priestess, to Athens.

In other accounts, statues are associated with the idea of creation, whether this involves Prometheus fashioning man or Pygmalion falling in love with his own work of art. Finally, some myths about petrification occasionally involve a metamorphosis into a statue: Perseus used the head of the Gorgon Medusa to change his adversaries into stone, and a grieving Niobe turned herself to stone on the tomb of her children.

Cross-references: Ajax, son of Oileus. Claudia Quinta. Diomedes. Niobe. Orestes. Prometheus. Pygmalion.

STONES *See* Deucalion and Pyrrha.

STRATONICE *See* Antiochos.

STRING *See* Ariadne. Fates.

STYMPHALUS *See* Hercules.

SUN *See* Apollo.

SWAN *See* Apollo. Clio. Hyacinthus. Jupiter. Leda.

SWORD *See* Ajax the Greater. Caeneus. Camillus. Cato. Dido. Hecate. Horatii (broadsword). Mars. Melpomene. Mucius Scaevola.

SYRINX *See* Attis. Faun. Pan. Satyrs.

TAMBOURINE *See* Bacchantes. Erato.

TANTALUS

Gk. and Ger. Tantalos; Lat. Tantalus; It. and Sp. Tantalo; Fr. Tantale. Legendary Lydian king.

HISTORY/MYTHOLOGY

Different and contradictory legends surround Tantalus. He was the son of Jupiter with Saturn's daughter, Pluto, and he reigned in Lydia. He incurred Jupiter's wrath, either by stealing the gods' food, betraying their secrets, or, like Lycaon, by serving his son as dinner. He was condemned to eternal torture in Hades, where he is submerged in water he cannot drink beneath a tree whose fruit he cannot eat.

REPRESENTATIONS

In Apulian ceramics, Tantalus appears with Sisyphus in Hades (krater, c. 300 B.C., Munich, Antikensammlungen).

Modern artists follow Ovid's account and group Tantalus with the other great sinners who were condemned to eternal punishment: Ixion, Tityus, and Sisyphus. Tantalus is usually placed between a tree, toward which he hopelessly reaches, and a river (Titian, 1549, known only through an engraving).

Cross-references: Ixion. Sisyphus. Tityus.

Sources: Homer, *The Odyssey* XI, 582–92. Ovid, *Metamorphoses* IV, 458–9.

TELEMACHUS

Gk. and Ger. Telemachos; Sp. Telemaco; Fr. Télémaque; It. Telemaco. Son of Ulysses and Penelope.

HISTORY/MYTHOLOGY

Telemachus, the son of Ulysses and Penelope, was only a child when his father went off to the Trojan War. Ulysses had done his best not to leave his family by feigning insanity: after yoking a donkey and an ox to his plow, he tilled the soil and seeded it with salt. That sham was exposed, however, when he immediately halted his plow after Palamedes placed the young Telemachus directly in front of it.

Telemachus was actually raised by Ulysses' old friend, Mentor. As a young man, he tried to thwart the ambitions of his mother's suitors, who helped themselves to his father's possessions while trying to force Penelope to remarry. He also traveled in search of his father, and in this context visited Nestor and Menelaus. He returned to Ithaca to find that Ulysses was already there disguised as a stranger.

The story of Telemachus is told in the first four books of *The Odyssey*, which are sometimes called the *Telemachia*. Because Telemachus remains a secondary character in the saga, however, the details of his legend were never really fixed, and this gave rise to a number of additions.

**Telemachus
and Penelope.**
Attic skyphos,
c. 440 B.C.
Chiusi, Museum.

REPRESENTATIONS

Telemachus has a very limited iconography. He appears mostly in the company of Ulysses or Penelope. On an Attic red-figure skyphos in the Museo Archeologica in Florence, for example, he stands next to his mother, who is seated at her loom deep in melancholy (Penelope Painter, c. 440 B.C.).

Two large but lost paintings illustrated Palamedes placing the young Telemachus in the path of Ulysses' plow: one was by Parrhasius, a native of Asia Minor who worked at Athens (fifth–early fourth centuries B.C.), the other was by Euphranor, an Athenian painter and sculptor (fourth century B.C.).

In 1699, Fénelon published his famous novel *The Adventures of Telemachus*, which stimulated the imagination of seventeenth-century painters and engravers, particularly Natoire (1700–77), who devoted five paintings to Telemachus (two in the Musée de Troyes and three in St. Petersburg, Hermitage). A tapestry woven at Brussels after cartoons by van Loo (1719–95) and two works by Angelica Kauffmann (1741–1807) also deal with this subject.

Cross-references: Penelope. Ulysses.

Sources: Homer, *The Odyssey* I, IV. Fénelon, *Les Aventures de Télémaque*, 1699.

TEREUS

Gk., Lat., and Ger. Tereus; Fr. Térée.
Legendary Thracian king.

HISTORY/MYTHOLOGY

Tereus, a Thracian king and the son of Ares, married Procne, the daughter of his ally, Pandion, king of Athens, and with her had a son, Itys. Tereus constantly tried to force his attentions on his sister-in-law,

Philomela, who would have nothing to do with him; he finally raped her and then cut out her tongue so that she could not tell anyone. Philomela told the whole story, however, by embroidering it into cloth, whereupon Procne killed her own son, served him as dinner to his guilty father, and fled with her sister. When Tereus realized what had happened, he hunted the two woman with an ax. He caught up with them in Phocis, but the gods were so moved by pity that they transformed the sisters into a nightingale and a swallow. Tereus himself was transformed into a hoopoe bird.

REPRESENTATIONS

The bloody legend is rare in ancient as well as modern art. It is known on a few vases that show Tereus going off in pursuit of the two women with ax in hand. Discernable on a ceramic fragment is a small bird perched on Tereus' head; he is identified by the remnants of an inscription as a symbol of the king's metamorphosis (Attic red-figure hydria, 460 B.C., Tarentum, Museo Nazionale).

Paintings of the subject are rare and most date from the seventeenth century. Noteworthy is *The Banquet of Tereus* by Rubens (1636, Madrid, Prado): in a palace setting, the two female protagonists are portrayed as half-naked furies who topple everything in their way while Procne presents the young child's head to the visibly horrified king.

Sources: Ovid, *Metamorphoses* VI, 426 ff.

TERPSICHORE *See* Muses.

THALIA *See* Muses.

THANATOS *See* Hypnos.

THESEUS

Gk., Lat., and Ger. Theseus; It. and Sp. Teseo; Fr. Thésée.
Athenian hero.

HISTORY/MYTHOLOGY

Theseus was the most important hero in antiquity. He was the son of Aegeus, king of Athens, and Aethra, according to some traditions; the son of Neptune, according to others. He was raised in secrecy at Troezen and remained ignorant of his true identity until he was an adult. It was then that Aethra told him not only who he was but where he would find his father's sword and sandals, which Aegeus had hidden under a rock after an oracle foretold that Theseus would succeed him when he could lift the rock. Before arriving in Athens, Theseus battled and killed the many monsters and bandits who infested the region: Sinis, who quartered travelers; the sow of Crommyon, a bloodthirsty animal guarded by an old woman; Sciron, who tossed passersby into the sea, where a carnivorous turtle tore them to pieces; Cercyon, who forced everyone to wrestle with him; and finally Procrustes, who made

**The Adventures
of Theseus.**
Attic cup,
c. 420 B.C.
London,
British Museum.

people lie on a bed and adjusted them to its size by either stretching
them or cutting off their feet.

Once Theseus had exterminated those monsters, he purified
himself and entered Athens. By that time, Aegeus had fallen under the
spell of Medea, who considered Theseus a rival to her own son. Hoping
to be rid of Theseus, Medea sent him off to fight the bull of Marathon,
but Theseus overpowered the beast and sacrificed it to Apollo.
According to the most accepted version of the legend, Medea next
tried to poison the young hero at dinner. When Theseus pulled out his
sword as the dinner meat was about to be cut, however, Aegeus
recognized the sword, acknowledged his son, and exiled Medea.

Theseus led one of the expeditions that every nine years paid a
tribute to Crete of seven Athenian youths and seven Athenian maidens. The youths were normally devoured by Crete's Minotaur until
Theseus, with the help of Minos's daughter, Ariadne, slew the monster
and guided himself out of the labyrinth with a string. Theseus stopped
at Naxos on his way home and there abandoned Ariadne in her sleep
(Bacchus later cared for her). As he sailed into Athens, the color of
his sails was to have signaled to his father the outcome of his mission.
However, he forgot to change his sails from black, a sign of defeat.
When Aegeus spotted black sails on the horizon, he threw himself into
the sea that now bears his name.

Theseus subsequently became king of Athens, which he unified.
He accompanied Hercules on his expedition against the Amazons and
brought Antiope back as a captive. He then drove off the Amazons,
who had invaded Attica to rescue her. After Antiope died, Theseus
married Phaedra, whom Venus made fall in love with his son by

**Theseus
and a Centaur.**
Antonio Canova,
1804–19.
Vienna,
Kunsthistorisches
Museum.

Antiope, Hippolyta. When the youth rejected Phaedra's advances, she denounced him to his father, claiming that he had tried to rape her. Theseus then hunted after Hippolytus, who died in a chariot accident.

Theseus's legend includes a number of other episodes. He sailed with the Argonauts, participated in the Calydonian boar hunt, and battled the centaurs when they tried to rape the bride of his friend Pirithoüs, king of the Lapiths, during her wedding. Theseus's death was less than glorious: he was apparently driven out of Athens and sought refuge on Scyros, where he was assassinated or died accidentally, depending on the version of the story. A cult was established in his honor during the classical period. His ashes were brought back to Athens in 475 B.C. by Cimon, who made him a symbol of democracy.

REPRESENTATIONS

Most representations focus on Theseus's adventures in Crete, particularly his defeat of the Minotaur. The subsequent victory dance appears on the neck of the François Vase, along with the battle against the centaurs at the wedding feast for Pirithoüs (c. 570 B.C., Florence, Museo Archeologico). Other adventures appear on red-figure Attic ceramics: the discovery of his father's arms beneath the rock and his battles against different monsters while *en route* to Athens from Troezen. These exploits, which parallel those of Hercules, are treated in cycles, especially on cups. On the interior of one cup, attributed to the Codrus Painter, Theseus leaves the labyrinth with the dead Minotaur; in the continuous frieze that encircles the scene are the Crommyonian sow, Cercyon, the bed of Procrustes, Sciron, the Marathon bull, and Sinis. The same subjects are represented from a different perspective on the underside of the cup (c. 420 B.C., London, British Museum). The parallels between the pan-Hellenic hero Hercules and the Athenian hero Theseus are made explicit in the very fragmentary metopes from the Athenian Treasury at Delphi (after 490 B.C.). Particularly during the classical period, Theseus is again seen abducting Antiope (amphora, c. 490 B.C., Paris, Louvre) or fighting the centaurs (krater by the Achilles Painter, c. 450 B.C., Ferrara, Museo Archeologico). Other subjects are rarer: Theseus abandoning the sleeping Ariadne under the gaze of Minerva (red-figure lekythos, c. 480 B.C., Tarentum, Museo Nazionale) and even Theseus plunging to the bottom of the sea to visit his divine father, Poseidon, who is accompanied by his wife Amphitrite (cup attributed to Onesimos, c. 490 B.C., Paris, Louvre).

Theseus's importance to Attic ceramics is explained by the fact that he was an Athenian hero. Nevertheless, he is found elsewhere. He lifts the rock that hides his father's arms in a Hellenistic relief (second century B.C., Rome, Villa Albani). The Minotaur episode remains popular throughout antiquity. It is found, for example, in an important mosaic discovered near Salzburg, a work in which the artist depicted not only the labyrinth but also its way out; Theseus kills the monster in the middle of the daedalus, and the story of Ariadne figures in three lateral panels (fourth century A.D., Vienna, Kunsthistorisches Museum).

These subjects also appear in modern art. Poussin depicted *Theseus Finding His Father's Shield* (c. 1630–35, Chantilly, Musée Condé); Carpaccio, *The Embassy of Hippolyta to Theseus* (before 1525, Paris, Musée Jacquemart-André); Rubens, the *Battle of the Amazons* (c. 1615, Munich, Alte Pinakothek), in which the presence of the river Thermodon suggests that the subject is the battle led by Theseus rather than the battle fought before Troy. In Carle van Loo's *Theseus Fighting the Bull of Marathon*, an altar at left anticipates the beast's final destiny (1745, Nice, Musée des Beaux-Arts Jules-Chéret). Michallon animated

Theseus and Ariadne (detail).
Jean-Baptiste Regnault.
Rouen,
Musée des Beaux-Arts.

a landscape with *Theseus Pursuing the Centaurs* (1821, Paris, Louvre). In 1832, Hippolyte Flandrin won the Prix de Rome for historical painting with *Theseus Recognized by His Father*, in which the hero stands before a table holding the sword that identified him.

Cross-references: Aegeus. Amazons. Argonauts. Ariadne. Centaurs. Medea. Minotaur. Phaedra.

Sources: *Bacchylide*, 17, 18. Ovid, *Metamorphoses* VII, 404–52. Plutarch, *Life of Theseus*.

Bibliography: J. Neils, *The Youthful Deeds of Theseus*, Rome, 1987. R. Olmos, ed., *Colloquio sobre Teseo y la copa de Aison*, Madrid, 1992. C. Sourvinou-Inwood, *Theseus as Son and Stepson*, London, 1979.

THETIS

It. Teti; Sp. Tetis; Fr. Thétis; Gk., Lat., and Ger. Thetis.
Sea divinity.

HISTORY/MYTHOLOGY

Thetis and Peleus.
Attic cup,
c. 510 B.C.
Berlin, Staatliche
Museen.

Thetis, the daughter of Nereus and Doris, is best known for being Achilles' mother. She was an immortal sea divinity who was raised by Juno, with whom she maintained powerful ties of affection. The gods nevertheless quickly married her off to a mortal, Peleus, when a prophecy foretold that her son would be more powerful than his father.

Thetis tried to get out of the marriage by means of metamorphosis, but was finally seduced by Peleus. She gave birth to Achilles and tried to make him immortal, but was caught by Peleus, who entrusted care of the child to the centaur, Chiron. During the Trojan War and after Patroclus's death, Thetis had Vulcan forge her son a new suit of armor only to end up mourning him with the Nereids when he died in battle.

Jupiter and Thetis (detail).
Jean-Auguste-Dominique Ingres, 1811.
Aix-en-Provence, Musée Granet.

REPRESENTATIONS

Numerous Attic vases show Peleus trying to overtake Thetis during her metamorphosis. On a black-figure amphora, Thetis turns into a unicorn and then into fire (c. 510 B.C., Munich, Antikensammlungen). In several vases, she is seen carrying Achilles' weapons (c. 540 B.C., Boston, Museum of Fine Arts), and she is also seen mourning him while he lies on his deathbed (Corinthian hydria, c. 560 B.C., Paris, Louvre).

In modern painting, Thetis appears in the contexts of her wedding celebration (A. Blomaert, 1638, The Hague, Mauritshuis) and her visit to Vulcan's forge (Rubens, c. 1631, Paris, École des Beaux-Arts). The second subject is, however, rarer than Venus visiting the forge for arms for Aeneas; in contrast to Thetis, the goddess is surrounded by cupids.

Cross-references: Achilles. Chiron. Juno. Nereids. Peleus. Vulcan.

Sources: Hesiod, *Theogony*, 240, 1003. Homer, *The Iliad* XVIII, 368–616 (visit to Vulcan).

Bibliography: X. Krieger, *Der Kampf zwischen Peleus und Thetis in der griechischen Vasenmalerei*, Münster, 1975.

THRONE *See* Juno. Triptolemus.

THUNDERBOLT *See* Jupiter. Semele.

THYRSUS *See* Bacchantes.

TIBERIUS *See* Germanicus.

TIRESIAS

Gk. and Ger. Teiresias; Lat. and Fr. Tiresias.
Theban seer.

HISTORY/MYTHOLOGY

Tiresias is the most famous of the Theban seers. Popular legend tells how he was out walking as a youth and came across two coupled snakes. No sooner had he separated them (or killed the female, according to other versions) than he was changed into a woman. Seven years later, a similar event occurred in exactly the same place and he reverted to male form. Jupiter and Juno later naturally turned to Tiresias, who had experienced both sides of lovemaking, to resolve their argument over whether the male or female partner received more pleasure while making love. Without hesitation, Tiresias asserted that the female's pleasure far exceeded that of her male partner. This disclosure triggered the wrath of Juno, who blinded Tiresias for having revealed such a secret. Jupiter compensated by granting Tiresias long life (some seven times that of other men) and the gift of prophecy, which he was allowed to keep after he died.

Tiresias played an important role in Theban legends. It is he who revealed Jupiter's name to Amphitryon, the god's rival for Alcmena's

Tiresias and Ulysses.
Lucanian krater,
c. 370 B.C.
Paris, Bibliothèque
Nationale de France,
Cabinet des Médailles.

affections, and he again who made Oedipus conscious of his crimes. Beyond the Theban cycle, Tiresias's spirit pointed the way home for Ulysses, who had traveled to the land of the Cimmerians to call forth the spirit on the advice of the sorceress Circe.

REPRESENTATIONS

Tiresias hardly appears in images despite his important role in legend, but two ancient works are most often cited. One is a large Lucanian krater in which the blind and bearded head of Tiresias emerges from the ground near the feet of Ulysses, who sits on a rock flanked by two companions, probably Perimedes and Eurylochus (Dolon Painter, c. 370 B.C., Paris, Bibliothèque Nationale, Cabinet des Médailles); another is a marble Roman relief with the seer dressed in a heavy cloak and leaning on a scepter while facing Ulysses (first or second centuries A.D., Paris, Louvre).

Remarkably, one of the only artists to have portrayed Tiresias in modern painting, Giulio Carpioni (1613–79), did so no less than thirteen times. The episode represented is the seer's prophecy about Narcissus (Besançon, Musée des Beaux-Arts and Vienna, Kunsthistorisches Museum).

Cross-references: Ulysses.

Sources: Homer, *The Odyssey* X, 487 ff; XI, 84 ff. Pausanias, IX, 33 ff. Ovid, *Metamorphoses* III, 320 ff.

Bibliography: L. Brisson, *Le Mythe de Tirésias*, Leiden, 1976.

TITANS

The Titans belonged to the generation of gods that preceded the Olympians. They were the twelve children of Sky (Uranus) and Earth (Gaea): six sons, including Ocean and Cronos (Saturn), and six daughters, including Rhea, Themis (Justice), and Mnemosyne (Memory), mother of the Muses. Some of their own offspring were also considered Titans, notably Prometheus and Atlas. After a bloody battle with the Titans, Jupiter assumed the throne of Olympus and ushered in a reign of order and justice.

Cross-references: Atlas. Jupiter. Ocean. Prometheus.

TITHONUS *See* Aurora.

Tityus.
Cup, c. 460 B.C.
Munich,
Antikensammlungen.

TITYUS

Sp. Ticio; Gk., Lat., Ger. and Fr. Tityos.
Giant.

HISTORY/MYTHOLOGY

Tityus was the Giant who tried to rape Leto and was therefore slain with arrows by Leto's children, Apollo and Diana. He was then condemned to Hades, where two vultures continuously devour his liver.

REPRESENTATIONS

In ancient art, the Giant is beaten to the ground by Apollo (red-figure cup by the Penthesilea Painter, c. 460 B.C., Munich, Antikensamm-lungen).

Inspired by Ovid's text, modern artists have often grouped Tityus with the other great sinners who were condemned to eternal punishment in Hades: Ixion, Tantalus, and Sisyphus (Titian, 1549, Madrid, Prado). Representations of Tityus devoured by vultures are often mistaken for Prometheus, although the latter was chained to the Caucasus and devoured by a single eagle.

Attributes: Apollo. Ixion. Prometheus. Sisyphus. Tantalus.

Sources: Homer, *The Odyssey* XI, 576–81. Ovid, *Metamorphoses* IV, 455–61.

TOMYRIS

It. Tomiri; Sp. Tomiris; Gk., Lat., Ger., and Fr. Tomyris.
Queen of the Massagetae.

HISTORY/MYTHOLOGY

Tomyris ruled over the Massagetae, a warlike people who lived on the shores of the Caspian Sea in the sixth century B.C. Cyrus the Great was determined to conquer the Massagetae, and Croesus suggested a trick: give unlimited food and drink to one part of his own army so that it would be beaten by the Massagetae. Cyrus and the remainder of his army would then score an easy victory over the Massagetae, who would be drunk after having consumed the vanquished portion's remaining drink. Tomyris's son, Spargapises, was captured in that battle and, upon coming to his senses, killed himself out of shame. Tomyris then took command of the army herself and won the next battle. She decapitated Cyrus's corpse when she found it on the field

286

of battle and dipped the head into a wineskin filled with human blood crying, "See now—I fulfil my threat: you have your fill of blood."

REPRESENTATIONS

Tomyris commands an iconography comparable to that of the nine female Worthies, of whom she is one. She appears as a Worthy in many paintings and sculptures, as well as in tapestries. She is seen alongside the Cumaean Sibyl and Esther in Andrea del Castagno's frescoes in the Uffizi, Florence. Tomyris holding the head of Cyrus—a subject easily mistaken for biblical subjects such as Judith and Holofernes or Salome and John the Baptist—was also often represented. In a painting by Rubens, an *aide-de-camp* rather than Tomyris dips the head of the queen's enemy into a blood-filled basin (*Queen Tomyris with the Head of Cyrus*, 1618–19, Boston, Museum of Fine Arts).

Attributes: Head (severed). Wineskin (blood-filled).

Cross-references: Croesus. Cyrus. Worthies.

Sources: Herodotus, I, 201, 205–8, 213, 214.

TOOLS *See* Archimedes (geometric). Urania (geometric). Vulcan (blacksmith's).

TOOTH *See* Graeae (sole tooth).

TORCH *See* Attis. Aurora. Ceres. Cupid. Furies. Hecate.

TOWER *See* Cybele.

TRAJAN

Lat. Trajanus; It. Traiano; Sp. Trajano; Fr. and Ger. Trajan.
Roman emperor (A.D. 52–117).

HISTORY/MYTHOLOGY

The Roman emperor Trajan was successful not only as a military leader who scored victories in Syria, Mesopotamia, Dacia, and Armenia, but also as a peacemaker and modernizer of Roman administration. He abhorred ostentation and flattery, and was renowned for his moderation, affability, and justice.

An anecdote from Trajan's life became legendary and has been singled out by posterity: during one of Trajan's campaigns, his son's rearing horse killed a poor widow's son and, as dictated by Roman law, Trajan compensated by giving the woman his own son. It is said that a relief with that scene moved St. Gregory the Great to tears so that he prayed that Trajan be admitted to Paradise; in the same vein, Cistercian monks in the twelfth century associated Trajan with St. Bernard. Dante recalls this Christianization of the Roman emperor in

**The Justice of Trajan
(detail).**
Eugène Delacroix,
1840.
Rouen,
Musée
des Beaux-Arts.

the *Purgatorio* by evoking Trajan's virtuous deeds alongside those of
David and the Virgin Mary as examples of conduct for the proud.

REPRESENTATIONS

Apart from the many ancient statues, busts, and coins representing
Trajan, one of the most important Imperial Roman monuments is dedicated to the emperor: Trajan's Column (A.D. 113). The monument's
reliefs celebrate the emperor's victories over the Dacians and generally constitute a rich iconographic resource.

Modern artists have pictured not only Trajan's military victories
(*The Triumph of Trajan*) but—in scenes that show him giving public

**Napoleon
in the Guise
of Trajan Distributes
the Scepters of Asia.**
Paul Duqueylar,
c. 1812.
Rome, Quirinal.

The Continence of Scipio.
Niccolò dell'Abbate, c. 1560–70.
Paris, Louvre.

The Death of Seneca.
Peter Paul Rubens, 1612–13.
Munich, Alte Pinakothek.

audiences and helping the poor—also his just character. Their works focus in the main on the episode cited earlier and are generally called *The Justice of Trajan*.

Sources: Pliny the Younger, *Letters* VI, 31; *Panegyricus to Trajan*.

Bibliography: F. Coarelli, *Guida archeologica di Roma*, Rome, 1980.

TREE *See* Adonis. Centaurs. Daphne. Giants. Minerva. Tantalus.

TRIPTOLEMUS

Gk. and Ger. Triptolemos; Lat. Triptolemus; Fr. Triptolème.
Athenian hero.

HISTORY/MYTHOLOGY

Triptolemus was the son of Metaneira and Celeus, king of Eleusis. As a reward for the hospitality which the king showed to her, Demeter gave Triptolemus a chariot drawn by winged dragons and the mission of disseminating throughout the world the secret of growing wheat; she also came to his aid whenever he encountered resistance, most notably from Lynceus, the Scythian king whom she changed into a lynx after he tried to kill Triptolemus. Upon returning to Eleusis, Triptolemus succeeded his father as king and instituted the Thesmophorae, or festivals celebrated in Demeter's honor. He became a judge in Hades after his death.

Triptolemus was linked to Demeter and Persephone in the initiation ceremonies for the Eleusinian Mysteries.

REPRESENTATIONS

There are few representations of Triptolemus, who appears mostly in classical, red-figure Attic ceramics, where he is almost always seated on a throne or in a winged chariot and holding the sheaves of wheat that Demeter has just given him (skyphos by Makron, c. 480 B.C., British Museum, London).

Demeter, Triptolemus, and Persephone. Relief from Eleusis, fourth century B.C.

The most famous classical work, however, consists of a large Eleusinian relief, *The Mission of Triptolemus*, in which the young, nude prince receives the wheat in the presence of Demeter and Persephone (second half of the fifth century B.C., Athens, National Museum). Everything suggests that the relief, in which the figures' deeply expressive faces underscore the serenity of the religious scene, was carried out by a sculptor in the workshop of Phidias.

Ceramists of the fourth century B.C. represented Triptolemus in a context directly related to the celebration of the Eleusinian Mysteries (pelike found at Kerch, c. 375 B.C., St. Petersburg, Hermitage).

There are hardly any modern representations of Triptolemus. One exception is a painting by Giulio Quaglio (1668–1751) in Udine, a work that focuses on Triptolemus's visit to Lynceus, the Scythian king, who is shown trying to kill the sleeping prince.

Cross-references: Ceres. Eleusis. Persephone.

Sources: Pausanias, I, 14, 2 ff.; 38, 6; 41, 2; VII, 18, 3. Ovid, *Metamorphoses* V, 642–61; *Festivals* IV, 549 ff.; *Tristia* III, 8, 1, ff.

Bibliography: G. Schwartz, *Triptolemos*, Graz, 1987.

TRITON

Gk., Lat., Ger., and Fr. Triton; It. Tritone.
Sea divinity.

HISTORY/MYTHOLOGY

Triton, the son of Neptune and Amphitrite, was a sea divinity who was human above the waist and fish-shaped below. He pointed the way home for the Argonauts and was one of the many monsters fought by Hercules. Tritons became a mythical race and, along with Nereids, often formed part of Neptune's cortege of sea creatures.

Triton.
Attic amphora,
c. 530 B.C.
Würzburg,
Martin von Wagner
Museum.

REPRESENTATIONS

Triton—straddled and locked in a bear hug by Hercules—appears frequently in Attic black-figure ceramics (Attic cup, c. 560 B.C., Tarquinia, Museo Nazionale). He is bearded and has a human torso, but the rest of the monster's body, which ends in a fish tail, is covered with scales; Nereus is sometimes a spectator to the struggle. Triton's physical peculiarities and his long, undulating body made him popular in Roman decorative arts, where his form is repeated many times with Nereids in sea processions (sarcophagus from the beginning of the third century A.D., Rome, Musei Vaticani).

In modern art, Tritons have often been used as decorative motifs for basins and fountains; Giambologna's model for a bronze fountain is one example (1562–65, cast in 1598, New York, Metropolitan Museum of Art). Sculpted examples include Bernini's marble *Triton Fountain* for the Piazza Barberini in Rome (1643) and Rodin's marble *Triton and Nereid on a Dolphin* (c. 1900, Paris, Musée Rodin). Triton has been equally frequently painted; in a work by Böcklin, he is seen from behind as he blows his conch while a Nereid lies on a rock holding a sea serpent (1873–74, Munich, Schack Galerie).

Attributes: Fish tail. Sea horn.

Cross-references: Hercules. Neptune.

Bibliography: G. Ahlberg-Cornell, *Heracles and the Sea Monster in Attic Black-figure Vase Painting*, Stockholm, 1984.

TROILUS *See* Achilles.

TROY

Gk. Ilion; Lat. and Ger. Troja; Sp. Troya; Fr. Troie; It. Troia.

HISTORY/MYTHOLOGY

Troy, the city of Priam, was the setting for a long war between Greeks, led by Agamemnon, and Trojans, fighting under the aegis of Hector. The gods were divided: Venus and Jupiter favored the Trojans while Juno, Minerva, and Neptune sided with the Greeks.

Homer's poem *The Iliad* (whose title comes from another name for Troy, Ilium) tells about only one year of the ten-year war. The most memorable of *The Iliad*'s principal episodes are: the wrath of Achilles (directed at Agamemnon), Briseïs leaving Achilles' tent, Venus wounded by Diomedes, Hector bidding Andromache farewell, Achilles dragging Hector's body behind his chariot, Priam visiting Achilles, the grief of Andromache, and the funeral of Patroclus.

After a ten-year siege, the Greeks finally won the war by making believe they set sail for home and leaving ashore a wooden horse that purported to be a sacred offering to Minerva but was in fact filled with Greek warriors ready to attack as soon as the gift was brought into the city. The Trojans were suspicious but ultimately pulled the gift-horse past their ramparts into the city, whereupon the warriors lying in ambush jumped out and opened Troy's gates to their fellow soldiers, who then began the *Ilioupersis*, or destruction of Troy. Several violent episodes followed: the rape of Cassandra by Ajax, son of Oileus; Diomedes' abduction of the *Palladium*; the slaughter of children

**The Siege of Troy
(detail).**
Biagio de Antonio,
fifteenth century.
Cambridge,
Fitzwilliam
Museum.

(including Astyanax), and the burning of Troy. Aeneas succeeded in fleeing while carrying his elderly father, Anchises, on his back.

REPRESENTATIONS

The Trojan horse appears in relief on a pithos at Mykonos (c. 675 B.C., Archeological Museum): the Greek warriors inside are visible through small apertures. In a Pompeian fresco, the Trojans drag the horse into the city (first century B.C., Naples, Museo Archeologico).

Scenes from the *Ilioupersis* appear on Attic black-figure ceramics, as well as on early red-figure ceramics. On a hydria attributed to the Kleophrades Painter, the following scenes appear in succession: Aeneas carrying Anchises, the rape of Cassandra, the death of Priam and Astyanax, Andromache (?) attacking a Greek, Demophon and Acamas saving Aethra.

Ancient cycles of the Trojan War exist. Several scenes from *The Iliad* appear in the Iliac Tables—small, portable tablets from Hellenistic or Roman times whose reliefs and inscriptions summarize each verse of the poem and serve as a mnemonic device. *The Iliad*'s oldest manuscripts are similarly illustrated with images that reflect an ancient pictorial tradition (for example, the so-called *Ilias Ambrosiana* manuscript in Milan from the fifth century A.D.).

The Homeric epic also inspired modern artists. Giulio Romano and his workshop used it to decorate the Sala de Troia at Mantua (1538, Palazzo Ducale), as did Tiepolo two centuries later in the Stanza dell'Iliade at Vicenza (c. 1757, Villa Valmarana). Illustrators of *The Iliad* increased the number of scenes, with Flaxman, for example, providing a series of thirty-nine drawings in 1792. In 1757, the Comte de Caylus published a small pattern-book for painters entitled *Tableaux tirés de l'Iliade, de l'Odyssée d'Homère et de l'Énéide de Virgile.*

In a very rich and complex image, Matthias Gerung (1540, Paris, Louvre) grouped *The Destruction of Troy and the Judgement of Paris* in a single work by juxtaposing the end of the war with its beginning. Adam Elsheimer turned the sack of Troy into a dramatic nocturnal scene lit by the glow from the fire; in the center is the Trojan horse, and Aeneas carries Anchises in the foreground. Rochegrosse accentuated the horror of the scene by having the Trojans drown in a pool of blood, at the foot of a staircase marked with a curious swastika (*Andromache*, 1883, Rouen, Musée des Beaux-Arts).

Cross-references: Achilles. Aeneas. Agamemnon. Ajax. Anchises. Andromache. Astyanax. Diomedes. Hector. Helen. Homer. Laocoön. Memnon. Nestor. Paris. Patroclus. Philoctetes. Polyxena. Priam.

Sources: Homer, *The Iliad.* Quintus Smyrnaeus, *Posthomeric.* Virgil, *Aeneid* II.

Bibliography: R. Bianchi Bandinelli, *Hellenistic Byzantine Miniatures of The Iliad,* Olten, 1955. K. Friis Johansen, *The Iliad in Early Greek Art,* Copenhagen, 1968. J.-M. Moret, *L'Ilioupersis dans la céramique Italiote,* Rome and Geneva, 1975. A. Sadurska, *Les Tables iliaques,* Warsaw, 1964. D. Wiebenson, "Subjects from Homer's *Iliad* in Neo-Classical Art," *Art Bulletin* 46 (1964): 23–37.

TRUMPET *See* Muses. Venus. Victory.

TUB *See* Diogenes. Seneca.

TYNDAREUS *See* Castor and Polllux.

ULYSSES

Gk. and Ger. Odysseus; Lat. Ulixes; It. Ulisse; Sp. Ulises; Fr. Ulysse. Greek hero.

HISTORY/MYTHOLOGY

Ulysses, king of Ithaca, was the son of Anticlea and Laertes; he married Penelope, with whom he had a child, Telemachus. He was perhaps one of the most popular Greek heroes and he played a principal role in the Trojan War. He took ten years to return to Ithaca after the fall of Troy and his journey was rife with difficulties because he aroused Poseidon's wrath; the epic account of this voyage is the subject of Homer's *Odyssey.* Renowned for his courage and wiles, Ulysses was also an excellent negotiator and for this reason was assigned such tasks as tempting Achilles away from Lycomedes' court, returning Chryseis to her father, and retrieving Hercules' bow from Philoctetes.

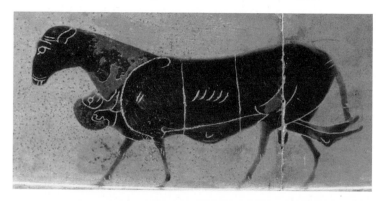

Ulysses Escaping from the Lair of Polyphemus. Attic cup, c. 530 B.C. London, British Museum.

**Ulysses,
with His Companions
Transformed
into Pigs.**
Attic lekythos,
c. 500 B.C.
Tarentum,
Museo Nazionale.

REPRESENTATIONS

The different phases of the Ithacan hero's voyage home are the principal sources of inspiration for ancient and modern artists: Ulysses and Polyphemus (one of the Cyclops), Ulysses and Circe, Ulysses and the Sirens, Ulysses on the island of Calypso, Ulysses and Penelope, Ulysses and Penelope's suitors. Throughout different periods of ancient art, these subjects appeared in all media: coins, gem carvings, sculptures, reliefs, sarcophagi, toreutics, and goldsmiths' work.

Ulysses may appear alone; in such cases he is shown seated, sometimes on a rock, with a pensive air and wearing a conical cap, the *pilos*. He is always bearded and may be dressed as a beggar.

Episodes from his journey were also illustrated by Italian (Allori) and French Renaissance painters (Galerie d'Ulysse, formerly Château de Fontainebleau; destroyed in the eighteenth century, this cycle had an enormous influences through copies and engravings), as well as by seventeenth-century Flemish artists (Schubert van Ehrenberg, J. Paul Getty Museum, Malibu).

Attributes: Beard. *Pilos.*

Cross-references: Calypso. Circe. Cyclops. Nausicaä. Penelope. Philoctetes. Polyphemus. Sirens. Telemachus.

Sources: Homer, *The Odyssey.*

Bibliography: B. Andreae, *L'immagine di Ulisse*, Milan, 1983. O. Touchefeu-Meynier, *Thèmes odysséens dans l'art antique*, Paris, 1968.

URANIA *See* Muses.

URANUS *See* Saturn.

URN *See* Alpheus.

VEIL *See* Fortune. Iphigenia.

VENUS

Gk. Aphrodite; Lat., Sp., and Ger. Venus; It. Venere; Fr. Vénus. Goddess of love.

HISTORY/MYTHOLOGY

Venus was one of the twelve great Olympian divinities and was the subject of various legends. According to Homer, she was the daughter of Zeus and Dione; according to Hesiod, she sprang from the foam of waves after Uranus's genitals were cut off by Cronos and fell into the sea.

The goddess plays a fundamental role in *The Iliad*. It is she who promised the Trojan shepherd, Paris, the hand of Helen, wife of King

The Birth of Venus.
Detail from the Ludovisi
Throne,
c. 460 B.C.
Rome,
Museo delle Terme.

Menelaus, after he awarded her the apple that confirmed her as the
most beautiful goddess. The Judgement of Paris triggered the Trojan
War, during which Venus continuously sided with the Trojans.
Although her allies were defeated, Venus succeeded in saving her son,
Aeneas, whom she supported in his one-on-one combat with Diomedes,
by whom she herself was wounded. She ultimately enabled Aeneas to
flee the burning city and to carry Troy's penates across the seas to Italy.
Thus, Venus ensured the descent of Aeneas, particularly the *gens Julia*
(the family of Julius Caesar), and accordingly occupied an important
position in Rome from the beginning of the first century B.C.

The Odyssey evokes Venus's infidelity to Vulcan, the limping
husband whom Jupiter assigned her as punishment for rejecting his
own affections. The goddess was in fact in love with Mars, with whom
she was caught and displayed for ridicule to all the Olympian gods;
their daughter was Harmonia. With Hermes, Aphrodite conceived
Eros (Cupid) and Hermaphroditus; with Bacchus, Priapus. Venus also
loved various mortals, particularly Adonis, whose death she could not
prevent, and Anchises, with whom she had Aeneas.

Venus was above all the goddess of love and beauty. Ancient
authors celebrated different features: her "loveable" smile, her "tender
and voluptuous" appearance, "the gold of her hair" and, more intimately,
her feet "white as silver," the small of her back, etc. Venus was also
the protectress of marriage and fertility: she "loved engaged couples,"
"prepared marriages," "stood watch at bridal chambers," and "presided
over births." Her paradoxical nature—both legitimate wives and
courtesans established cults for her—may be the reason why ancient
authors distinguished between several Aphrodite-Venuses. Plato in
fact contrasted Aphrodite Urania (celestial), goddess of chaste and
pure love, with Aphrodite Pandemos (popular), patroness of carnal
love. Pausanias spoke of yet a third Aphrodite, *apostrophia*, who
detested impurity.

Ancient literature also attributed a number of secondary functions
to Venus: as the marine Venus, she protected the sea and navigators;
as the victorious Venus, she was invoked in combat, and so on. In
Rome, Venus was both goddess of charm (*venia*) and of the magical
power to subdue (*venenum*). Protectress of Aeneas and therefore the
Romans, Venus is invoked by the poet Lucretius in the prelude to *De*

The Cnidian Venus.
Marble,
second century A.D.
Rome,
Musei Vaticani.

Capitoline Venus
Marble,
second century A.D.
Rome,
Musei Capitolini.

Venus de Milo.
Marble,
end of second
century B.C.
Paris, Louvre.

Medici Venus.
Marble,
first century B.C.
Florence, Uffizi.

**The Crouching
Venus.**
Marble,
second century A.D.
Paris, Louvre.

natura rerum. She had the inseparable functions of presiding over sexual impulses as well as over the city's political prosperity.

Venus is probably the most often evoked ancient deity in literature, especially in Western poetry from the Renaissance through the romantic period.

REPRESENTATIONS

The iconography of Venus is immense in both its quantity and variety. The goddess inspired artists from antiquity up to the twentieth century, when representational art was abandoned; these artists include those who illustrated the episodes of her legend and those for whom Venus, with no narrative context, simply served as a reason to portray the ideal female nude.

Celestial Venus

Ancient descriptions inform us that Venus was represented with such attributes as an apple, a poppy, and the evening star. The goddess, who is sometimes winged, also appears with scepter and stars. In a Pompeian panel in the Museo Archeologico at Naples, she is crowned, leans on a rudder, and holds a shaft that terminates in a ship's mast (first century B.C.).

Popular Venus (pandemia)

The goddess of carnal love is sometimes accompanied by a goat, which she straddles or holds by the horns (bronze Corinthian mirror, c. 370 B.C., Paris, Louvre).

Venus on a Seashell.
Fresco,
first century B.C.
Pompeii.

Venus Victrix

Venus victrix was the war cry that Caesar used to rally his soldiers during the Battle of Pharsalus (48 B.C.). There are many Victorious Venuses in ancient sculpture and coins; winged or helmeted and generally partially clothed, they may hold a crown or even a trumpet. Venus is represented in this form more widely than just in her ancient iconography; more particularly, representations of her take on the facial characteristics of European sovereigns, as demonstrated in Canova's sculpted portrait of the Princess Pauline Bonaparte (1804–08, Rome, Galleria Borghese).

The Toilet of Venus

In this category are representations of the goddess coming out of her bath, drying herself, and modestly covering or, on the other hand, exposing different parts of her body. One example is the famous *Capitoline Venus*, in which the goddess tries to hide her left breast with her right hand and her genitals with her left hand, a prototypic gesture that is reflected in many later works (second century A.D., Rome, Musei Capitolini). The subject of Venus at her toilet also gave artists the opportunity to explore highly contorted and propitious poses in an effort to highlight their models' charms; two equally celebrated examples of the goddess unveiling her curves are *The Crouching Venus* in the Uffizi, Florence, and the *Callipygian Venus* in the Museo Nazionale, Naples. Ancient marbles such as these often derive from bronze Greek originals and are buttressed by accessories appropriate to bathing, including towels, vases, and drapery. In modern painting, the number of props increased with additions such as the mirror in Titian's *Venus with a Mirror*, a work in which cupids play supporting roles to the goddess as she grooms herself (1555, Washington, National Gallery).

Venus Marina

Hesiod's account of the legend links the goddess to the sea, where he says she is born. Under the epithet of Venus Anadyomene, an entire series of representations illustrates this birth, including the famous Ludovisi throne (c. 460 B.C., Rome, Museo delle Terme). Other representations dramatize the *Triumph of Venus* over the waves, while still others simply surround the goddess with symbols of the sea. One example is the *Medici Venus*, a work similar in pose to the *Capitoline Venus* but which otherwise adds a dolphin and a shell to the composition (Roman copy of a third-century B.C. bronze original, Florence, Uffizi).

Venus and a Cupid.
Lucas Cranach
the Elder, c. 1530.
Munich,
Alte Pinakothek.

Rokeby Venus.
Diego Velásquez,
1650.
London,
National Gallery.

In the most widespread iconographic type concerning the birth of Venus, the goddess rises nude from the waves, and she often stands on a shell; cupids, Naiads, Tritons, or other sea divinities may preside at this birth. The ancients situated the birth on the island of Cyprus, and the goddess was consequently particularly important there. The motif of the marine Venus is successfully celebrated in all periods of art with occasional variations; in an ancient silver medallion dating from Imperial Roman times, for example, the goddess sits on the shell of a bivalve supported by sea centaurs (Paris, Louvre).

In Botticelli's famous *Birth of Venus*, she stands on a shell, and her long hair is animated by the breath of Zephyr and Flora (1482, Florence, Uffizi); by contrast, in Cabanel's *Birth of Venus*, a much later work from the time when reclining female nudes were legion, the

The Venus of Urbino.
Titian, 1538.
Florence, Uffizi.

The Birth of Venus.
Sandro Botticelli,
1482.
Florence, Uffizi.

goddess stretches herself along the crest of a foamy wave (1863, Paris, Musée d'Orsay).

Sleeping or Resting Venus
Reclining figures of Venus began to appear only in the Renaissance. The role of the mythical figure here is clearly to justify the representation of the female nude in a position of repose. This is the subject *par excellence* that served as the basis for the purely formal exploration of ideal beauty. Giorgione's *Sleeping Venus* (early sixteenth century, Dresden, Staatliche Kunstsammlungen) and Titian's *Venus of Urbino* (1538, Florence, Uffizi) respectively illustrate the two symbolic poles that the goddess incarnates: spiritual love and carnal love. Any ambiguity about which of the two dominated later representations is dispelled by the provocatively posed and well-endowed reclining Venuses of the eighteenth and nineteenth centuries.

Cross-references: Adonis. Aeneas. Cupid. Diomedes. Mars. Psyche. Vulcan.

Sources: Hesiod, *Theogony*, 190–206. Homer, *The Iliad* V, 311–430. *Homeric Hymn to Aphrodite*. Lucretius, I, 1–43.

Bibliography: C. Barbillon, *Vénus et l'Amour*, Carnet-parcours du Musée d'Orsay no. 8, Paris, 1988. K. Clark, *The Nude*, London, 1956. A. Pasquier, *La Vénus de Milo*, Paris, 1991. E. Simon, *Die Geburt der Aphrodite*, Berlin, 1959.

VESTA

Gk. and Ger. Hestia; Lat., Fr., and It. Vesta.
Goddess of the hearth.

HISTORY/MYTHOLOGY

Vesta, the daughter of Saturn, was a virgin goddess. She was connected with the home, but her permanent dwelling place was on Mount Olympus. Ovid tells how the braying of a donkey awakened her just as Priapus was about to seduce her in her sleep.

In Roman religion, Vesta's priestesses, or Vestals, were guardians of the city's fire and had to remain virgins. One of these Vestals, Claudia Quinta, was accused of adultery but proved her innocence by miraculously pulling ashore the ship that was carrying the statue of Cybele to Rome.

REPRESENTATIONS

Hestia (Vesta) has hardly any distinguishing characteristics in ancient art and therefore inscriptions usually identify her in divine assemblies. She appears beside Demeter at the head of a procession on its way to congratulate Peleus on the François Vase (c. 570 B.C., Florence, Museo Archeologico); in a cup by Oltos, she sits opposite Zeus, a position normally reserved for Hera (c. 510 B.C., Tarquinia, Museo Archeologico). In Rome, Vesta was not portrayed until Imperial times, when she is shown as a veiled matron who is seated while preparing a libation (first century B.C. Sorrento, Museo Correale). Vesta is flanked by the Lar gods in several Pompeian frescoes (first century B.C.).

Vesta has rarely been represented in modern art. She is thought to be one of the figures in Bellini's *Feast of the Gods* (1513, Washington, National Gallery).

Cross-references: Claudia Quinta. Priapus.

Sources: Ovid, *Festivals* VI, 249–472.

VESTAL *See* Claudia Quinta.

VICTORY

Gk. and Ger. Nike; Lat. and Sp. Victoria; It. Vittoria; Fr. Victoire. Allegorical figure.

REPRESENTATIONS

Victory is often shown as a winged female figure posed on a vanquished foe. One of the most famous examples is the Victory of Samothrace, which was placed on the prow of a ship in commemoration of a naval battle (second century B.C., Paris, Louvre). In numerous Attic vases, Victory performs ritual acts of offerings and libations, which are indicative more of a successful undertaking—such as a marriage or a competition—than of a military triumph. Winged Victory was also a common motif on Roman coins.

In modern art, Victory is assigned military significance and is found mainly in historical paintings, on triumphal arches, or in allegories (Le Nain, c. 1635, Paris, Louvre).

The Victory of Samothrace.
c. 190 B.C.
Paris, Louvre.

Attributes: Palm. Trumpet. Wings.

Bibliography: C. Isler-Kerényi, *Nike*, Zurich, 1969.

VINE *See* Bacchantes (grapevine). Bacchus (grapevine). Pomona (vine shoot).

VIOL, VIOLIN *See* Apollo. Arion. Erato. Terpsichore.

VIRGIL
Lat. Vergilius; It. and Sp. Virgilio; Fr. Virgile; Ger. Vergil.
Latin poet (c. 70–19 B.C.).

HISTORY/MYTHOLOGY
Publius Vergilius Maro, the most famous of the Latin poets, was born
around 70 B.C. in the city of Mantua. He grew up in a turbulent period
of Roman history, one that witnessed the civil war between Caesar
and Pompey and the subsequent struggle between Caesar's inheritors
and supporters of the Republic. Those events left their mark on the
imagination of the young poet, whose works are characterized by a
disdain for discord and a love for peace and order. Virgil's provincial
origins moreover gave him an attachment to rural society and to
nature itself that was in some ways religious.

Virgil's first collection of verse, the *Eclogues*, dates from 37 B.C.
The natural world occupies an important place, but the shepherds
evolve into characters who express opinions on all the political and
literary questions of the day. The *Georgics* were composed ten years
later, when Virgil befriended Maecenas, an advisor to the young
Octavius, the future Emperor Augustus. The *Georgics* are poetry
about nature and celebrate an ideal way of a life, one that is closely
connected to the earth. Virgil devoted the end of his own life to writing
the *Aeneid*, a poem about the strong and peaceful Rome that he
envisioned. Linked to Homer's *Iliad* through the Trojan origin of its

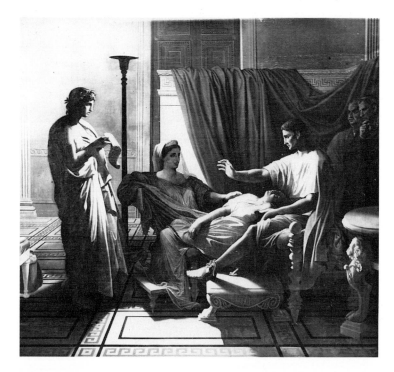

Tu Marcellis eris.
Jean-Auguste-
Dominique Ingres,
1812.
Toulouse,
Musée des Augustins.

301

hero Aeneas, the *Aeneid* is a masterpiece of epic Roman poetry, although Virgil died in 19 B.C. before completing it.

The Middle Ages considered Virgil a sage as well as a poet. He served as Dante's guide for the journey to the world beyond in the *Divine Comedy* (written between 1306 and 1316). Significantly, the Latin poet comes to Dante's aid during the descent into Hades, where he guides Dante through different "circles"—corresponding to different degrees of moral transgression—encountered during the infernal journey.

REPRESENTATIONS

A few ancient sculptures, notably a statue in his native city of Mantua, are identified as portraits of Virgil. The poet also appears in a mosaic found at Sousse, in which he is flanked by two muses and holds an open scroll inscribed with the first words of the *Aeneid* (beginning of the third century A.D., Tunis, Musée du Bardo). From miniatures of the Middle Ages to Delacroix's celebrated *Bark of Dante* (1822, Paris, Louvre), representations of the Latin poet have been linked to those of Dante, and they are entirely faithful to the *Divine Comedy*. In addition, Virgil figured among the numerous philosophers, intellectuals, poets, and doctors of the church in the highly prized portrait galleries of noble Italian Renaissance dwellings.

With respect to the *Georgics* and the *Aeneid*, the tradition that evokes Virgil's attachment to Octavius Augustus provided the subject of *Virgil Reading the Aeneid before Augustus*, as exemplified by Pieter Verhagen's canvas (Paris, Louvre) as well as by Ingres' *Tu Marcellis eris* (1812, Toulouse, Musée des Augustins).

Bibliography: J.-F. Crome, *Das Bildnis Vergils*, Mantua, 1935.

The Return of Vulcan to Olympus.
Attic krater,
c. 490 B.C.
Paris, Louvre.

VULCAN

Gk. Hephaistos; Lat. Vulcanus; It. and Sp. Vulcano; Fr. Vulcain; Ger. Vulcan.
God of the forge.

HISTORY/MYTHOLOGY

Vulcan was the son of Jupiter and Juno, according to some accounts; the son of only Juno, according to others. He was god of the forge, master of fire, and, along with Minerva, protector of artisans. He had a characteristic limp, for which several explanations have been offered. Some say the god was lame from birth and that Juno threw him from Mount Olympus for this reason; he then avenged himself on his mother by making her a throne that was impossible to get up from once seated, and only Bacchus was able to bring him back to Olympus to free the goddess. By contrast, others say that Vulcan angered Jupiter by trying to protect Juno, that it was Jupiter who threw him from Olympus, and that he was subsequently cared for at Lemnos by nymphs.

Vulcan resembles an artisan: he wears a round cap (*pilos*) and a short tunic, and he often holds or shoulders blacksmith's tools.

REPRESENTATIONS

One of the most common subjects, especially in archaic art, is Hephaestus's return to Olympus in the company of Dionysus (François Vase, c. 570 B.C., Florence, Museo Archeologico); Hephaestus is sometimes drunk and supported by either a satyr or Dionysus. His assistance at the birth of Athena, who popped fully armed out of Jupiter's head after Hephaestus hit it with a hatchet, is generally represented by having him quickly retreat from the Olympian king's presence with the hatchet over his shoulder (Attic pyxis, c. 560 B.C., Paris, Louvre). He may also be shown forging Achilles' weapons for Thetis (cup, c. 490 B.C., Berlin, Antikensammlungen), a subject that also appears in Pompeian painting (first century B.C., Naples, Museo Archeologico). Hephaestus is also seen assisting at the birth of Pandora (Attic cup, c. 460 B.C., London, British Museum) and at the punishment of Ixion, whom he attaches to the wheel with Minerva's help (metope, first century B.C., Pompeii).

Vulcan's forge has been depicted many times in modern art. Sometimes Thetis is seen coming there in search of new arms for her son, Achilles; usually, however, it is Aeneas's mother, Venus, who visits the divine blacksmith. The cupids who accompany Venus distinguish one scene from the other (Louis Le Nain, 1641, Reims, Musée Saint-Denis). As the unfortunate husband of Venus, who herself preferred Mars, Vulcan trapped his wife and her lover together in a net he made and exhibited them for ridicule to the other Olympian gods. The Dutch painter Martin Van Heemskerck devoted a triptych to Vulcan (c. 1540, Prague, Narodni Galeri). In the central panel, Venus is in Vulcan's forge; in one lateral panel, Vulcan gives Thetis Achilles' shield. Vulcan surprises Venus and Mars in the second lateral panel: the blacksmith is seen from behind in the foreground, and the couple is trapped in an enormous net while, in the upper right corner, the other gods burst out laughing (Vienna, Kunsthistorisches Museum). Van Heemskerck's use of the triptych format to tell Vulcan's story

Venus at the Forge of Vulcan.
Louis Le Nain, 1641.
Reims,
Musée Saint-Denis.

The Forge of Vulcan.
Jacopo Tintoretto, 1576.
Venice, Palazzo Ducale.

gave the myth a moral value equal to that of Christian subjects. Vulcan also assisted at Pandora's birth, and it was he who chained Prometheus to the Caucasus.

Attributes: Cap. Tools (blacksmith's).

Cross-references: Achilles. Aeneas. Bacchus. Jupiter. Minerva. Pandora. Prometheus. Thetis. Venus.

Sources: Homer, *The Iliad* XVIII, 369 (arms of Achilles). Virgil, *Aeneid* VIII, 370–453 (arms of Aeneas).

Bibliography: F. Brommer, *Hephaistos*, Mayence, 1972. M. Delcourt, *Héphaïstos ou la légende du magicien*, Paris, 1982. *The Loves of the Gods*, ex. cat., Fort Worth, 1992, nos. 38, 43.

WALLET *See* Perseus.

WHEAT *See* Augustus. Ceres. Triptolemus.

WHEEL *See* Fortune. Ixion.

WHIP *See* Camillus. Furies. Hecate.

WINESKIN *See* Aeolus. Satyrs. Tomyris (blood-filled).

WINGED SANDALS *See* Mercury. Perseus.

WINGS

Wings characterize a number of divine powers, most often secondary ones who, like Iris and Victory, act as intermediaries between gods and mortals or, like Hypnos and Thanatos (Sleep and Death), between mortals and the Underworld. Certain gods associated with celestial phenomena are also winged; these include Aurora (Eos) and the Winds (Boreas and his sons, the Boreads, as well as Aeolus and Zephyr). As a cosmic power and a divine force circulating among mortals, Eros (Cupid) is also winged.

Moreover, wings are a sign of monstrosity on some beings, including the Harpies and the Gorgons, as well as certain animals, including griffins, the Sphinx, and the horse Pegasus, who was the offspring of the Gorgon Medusa.

Finally, wings indicate their bearer's speed, especially when they appear on feet, as in representations of Mercury and Perseus.

Cross-references: Aurora. Boreas. Cupid. Daedalus. Gorgon. Griffin. Harpies. Hypnos. Icarus. Iris. Mercury. Pegasus. Perseus. Venus.

VENVS

Venus.
Detail from a mural by Perugino (Pietro Vanucci), 1496.
Perugia, Collegio del Cambio.

The Birth of Venus.
Odilon Redon, c. 1912.
Paris, Petit Palais.

WOLF *See* Romulus and Remus.

WORTHIES

HISTORY/MYTHOLOGY

In the Middle Ages, poets and authors of romances established a list of heroes who were related to each other through shared qualities of valor and bravery. The number of heroes varied, but it was usually fixed at nine and included three characters from antiquity (Hector, Alexander, and Caesar), three biblical figures (Joshua, David, and Judas Maccabee), and three legendary Christian heroes (Arthur, Charlemagne, and Godefroi de Bouillon). These figures are often called the Worthies. Noble knights traditionally traced their descent back to them and paid tribute to them in medieval festivals and court ceremonies.

Some romances centering on chivalry add the names of nine female Worthies, all of whom are heroines and warriors from antiquity: Tomyris, Deifemme, Lampredo, Hippolyta, Semiramis, Penthesilea, Tancqua, Desilla, and Menelippa.

REPRESENTATIONS

Whether or not a Worthy was individually represented depended on how celebrated his or her exploits were. Serial portraits of the Worthies have been used on playing cards since the fifteenth century, but this principle was applied on a wider scale during the vogue for portrait galleries establishing in noble and royal residences. At the Château de Pierrefonds, for example, nine statues of the female Worthies decorate the chimney mantel in the reception hall known as the Hall of the Preuses, a hall that echoes the Hall of the Preux (male Worthies) in the nearby Château de Coucy.

Cross-references: Alexander. Caesar. Hector. Penthesilea. Semiramis. Tomyris.

ZALEUCUS

Gk. and Ger. Zaleukos; Lat. Zaleucus; Fr. Zaleucos.
Lawmaker (eighth century B.C.).

HISTORY/MYTHOLOGY

Zaleucus was lawmaker for the Locrians (Magna Graecia). Although the texts of his laws have not survived, it is known that he supported a severe and rigorous moral code. An anecdote tells that, according to one of Zaleucus's edicts, the punishment for any man convicted of adultery was to have both eyes plucked out. As it happened, the lawmaker's own son was caught committing adultery and, although the public favored clemency, Zaleucus remained steadfast. Torn between paternal love and his duties as a magistrate, however, he sacrificed one of his own eyes to save one of his son's.

Zaleucus.
Antonio Fantuzzi.
Engraving, c. 1542.

REPRESENTATIONS

Most often, the father's sacrifice is represented. The purpose of such images was to exemplify political virtue, and they fulfill this function in the Palazzo Publico in Siena (Beccafumi, c. 1530) and the Town Hall in Haarlem (Jan de Bray, 1676).

ZENOBIA

Gk., Lat., Ger., and It. Zenobie; Fr. Zénobie.
Queen of Armenia.

HISTORY/MYTHOLOGY

A mass uprising drove the king of Armenia, Radamistus, and his wife, Zenobia, from their capital of Artaxata. Zenobia, who was about to have a child, was seized by contractions and begged her husband to kill her rather than let her fall into enemy hands. Radamistus stabbed her with his dagger and then threw her into the river Araxes. Zenobia, still alive, was rescued by shepherds.

REPRESENTATIONS

Artists have represented the shepherds discovering the wounded young queen. A drawing by Poussin illustrates the episode (Windsor Castle, Royal Library), which also inspired a painting by Dufresnoy (seventeenth century, St. Petersburg, Hermitage). *Zenobia Found by the Shepherds on the Banks of the Araxes* was the subject for the 1855 Prix de Rome, for which one of the prizewinners was Bouguereau (Paris, École des Beaux-Arts).

Sources: Tacitus, *Annals* XII, 51.

Zenobia.
Detail from Adolphe
William Bouguereau,
*Zenobia Found
on the Banks of the
Araxes*, 1850.
Paris,
École des Beaux-Arts.

ZEPHYR

Gk. Zephros; It. Zafiro; Sp. Céfiro; Fr. Zéphyr; Ger. Zephyr; Lat.
Zephyrus.
God of the wind.

HISTORY/MYTHOLOGY

Zephyr personified the breeze (west wind). In antiquity, the Winds
played an important role in navigation. They lived in caves and were
commanded by the great Olympian divinities as well as by magicians
and nymphs (Circe, Calypso, and so on). In Homeric tradition they
also acted as intermediaries between Hades and the Upperworld.
According to Ovid, Zephyr saw the nymph Chloris one day, fell hopelessly in love with her, and then pursued, raped, and finally married
her. He made Chloris ruler over the kingdom of flowers as a gift, and
she became Flora as a result.

REPRESENTATIONS

Few ancient representations of the god of the wind survive. Attic ceramists were more interested in Boreas's abduction of Orithyia, and
sculpted representations are rare. Pausanias (I, 37, 1) speaks of an
Altar of Zephyr at Athens, but nothing remains.

    On each of the eight sides of the Tower of the Winds at Athens,
each Wind appears in human form; four are evil and four, including
Zephyr, who holds a flower, are good (first century B.C.).

    Another, somewhat late monument (first–second centuries A.D.)
is also dedicated to the Winds. It was found at Carnuntum (an ancient
Celtic city and the first fixed Roman camp, established on the Danube,
not far from Vienna) and has four nude figures that have wings in
their hair and which blow trumpets. As a light and beneficial wind,
Zephyr is represented as a young man who half kneels on a rocky crag
and points the bell of his trumpet toward the sky.

Zephyr Leading His Sisters to Pysche.
Tapestry, seventeenth century.

In the Middle Ages, the personification of wind was often reduced to only a puff-cheeked head that blows through its mouth or a shell.

From the fifteenth century onward, artists highlighted the legend, particularly the episode involving the meeting of Zephyr and Chloris/Flora.

The Winds appear at the extreme right of Botticelli's highly celebrated painting, *Primavera* (c. 1482, Florence, Uffizi). There Zephyr has long flowing hair and large wings, and his bluish-pink color distinguishes him from the other characters; he bursts upon the scene through flowering orange trees just as he catches hold of the fleeing figure of Chloris, from whose mouth comes a flowering branch as she turns into Flora, the third person in the group.

Artists involved in the seventeenth-century decorative programs for the Palace of Versailles were particularly fond of the subject, as demonstrated in works by Noël Coypel, painter of the Grand Trianon, Louis Lecomet, author of the stone group at the entrance of the Orangerie, Léonard Roger, responsible for the stone statues for the façade near the south parterre, and Philippe Bertrand and René Frémin, who created a marble group for the park at Trianon.

Finally, Clodion made a superb terracotta group, now in the Frick Collection, New York, which dates from 1799. Here the kissing figures of Zephyr and Flora intertwine and turn in a balletic movement. Zephyr, who is represented as a young god with butterfly wings, supports a crown of flowers above Flora with one hand and clasps her with the other; the nymph herself is barely older than an adolescent and wears a garland of flowers; three cupids accompany the couple.

Cross-references: Aeolus. Boreas. Flora.

Sources: Homer, *The Iliad* XXIII, 194 ff. Hesiod, *Theogony*. Ovid, *Festivals* V, 200–206. Pausanias, I, 37, 1.

Bibliography: A. Warburg, *Sandro Botticellis "Geburt der Venus" und "Frühling": Eine Untersuchung der Antike in der Italienischen Frührenaissance*, Hamburg and Leipzig, 1893.

ZEUS *Greek name for* Jupiter.

ZEUXIS

Gk., Lat., Ger., and Fr. Zeuxis; It. Zeusi.
Greek painter (late fifth–early fourth centuries B.C.).

HISTORY/MYTHOLOGY

Zeuxis was one of fifth-century B.C. Greece's greatest painters. He is known largely because of three anecdotes that make a point about aesthetic values. The first of these anecdotes tells how, in preparation for his portrayal of Helen of Troy, Zeuxis had the citizens of Croton parade their five most beautiful maidens nude through the gymnasium. Finding that no single model met his expectations, he decided to combine the most beautiful features of each one in a single, ideal figure.

The second anecdote introduces another celebrated artist, Parrhasius. Zeuxis painted a cluster of grapes so perfectly that birds came to peck at them. Parrhasius responded with a painting covered by a curtain; after Zeuxis reached to draw aside the curtain, which was also painted, Parrhasius judged himself the better artist. The third anecdote, which reinforces the preceding one, concerns a painting by Zeuxis of a child carrying grapes: after the work attracted birds, the artist pointed out that the birds would not have approached had the child been as well-rendered as the grapes.

REPRESENTATIONS

Zeuxis's surprise upon discovering that Parrhasius's curtain was rendered in *trompe l'oeil* is the subject of one of a series of several grisailles painted by Vasari for his home in Arezzo. Nevertheless, the maidens of Croton was the most popular anecdote among artists of the Middle Ages, the Renaissance, and subsequent centuries.

The story of the maidens of Croton has been depicted since the eighteenth century, notably in Gothic illuminations for Cicero's

Zeuxis.
Gerhard de Jode.
Engraving,
sixteenth century.

309

Rhetoric. In the early fifteenth century, French and Flemish illuminators picked up on the same subject and depicted five maidens facing the artist at work. In the case of a manuscript from the end of the 1480s in the university library at Ghent, the painter altered the ancient account: the maidens are no longer nude and the debate seems to focus on which of them is the most elegant and best dressed.

The tale of Zeuxis at Croton is recounted in Jean de Meung's *The Romance of the Rose*, where it is illustrated with the five nude virgins, although some illuminators betray a poor understanding of the anecdote by depicting five paintings.

A painting by Vincent focuses on the maidens' modesty and the seriousness of the painter's mission (*Zeuxis Choosing the Five Most Beautiful Maidens of Croton as Models*, 1789, Paris, Louvre). Zeuxis appears not to have been painted in the nineteenth and twentieth centuries.

Attributes: Curtain. Grapes. Nude or undressing maidens. Painting.

Sources: Cicero, *Rhetoric* II. Pliny the Younger, *Natural History* XXXV, 64. Jean de Meung, *The Romance of the Rose*, 1665 ff.

Bibliography: P. Georgel and A.-M. Lecoq, *La Peinture dans la peinture*, Paris, 1987, ch. II: "Fables et héros."

SELECT BIBLIOGRAPHY

Sources

Only authors cited several times are listed.

Greek Authors

Apollodorus (first century A.D.), *The Library* (3 books).
Apollonius of Rhodes (c. 295–215 B.C.), *Argonautica* (4 songs).
Athenaeus (c. A.D. 200), *The Deipnosophists* (15 books).
Diodorus Siculus (first century B.C.), *Library of History* (40 books).
Dion Cassius (c. A.D. 150–235), *Roman History* (80 books).
Herodotus (c. 490–425 B.C.), *The Histories* (9 books).
Hesiod (c. 700 B.C.), *Theogony* (poem).
Homer (eighth century B.C.), *The Iliad* (24 songs); *The Odyssey* (24 songs).
Homeric Hymns (eighth–sixth century B.C.; 23 poems).
Nonnus of Panopolis (fifth century A.D.), *Dionysiaca* (48 books).
Pausanias (c. A.D. 160), *Description of Greece* (10 books).
Philostratus (second century A.D.), *Imagines* (2 books).
Plutarch (c. A.D. 46–120), *Parallel Lives* (50 books).
Quintus Smyrnaeus (fourth century A.D.), *Posthomerica* (14 songs).
Strabo (64 B.C.–c. A.D. 24), *Geography* (17 books).

Latin Authors

Aulus Gellius (c. A.D. 130–180), *Attic Nights* (20 books).
Cornelius Nepos (c. 100–25 B.C.), *Famous Men* (1 book).
Hyginus (c. 64 B.C.–A.D. 17), *Fabulae* (1 book).
Livy (59 B.C.–A.D. 17), *History of Rome* (142 books).
Ovid (43 B.C.–A.D. 17), *Metamorphoses* (15 songs); *Festivals* (6 songs).
Pliny the Elder (A.D. 24–79), *Natural History* (37 books).
Statius (c. A.D. 45–96), *Achilleide* (2 songs, incomplete).
Suetonius (c. A.D. 70–122), *The Twelve Caesars* (12 books).
Tacitus (c. A.D. 56–117), *Annals* (16 books).
Valerius Maximus (first century A.D.), *The Book of Memorable Deeds and Words* (8 books).
Virgil (70–19 B.C.), *Aeneid* (12 songs).

General Works

Dictionnaire des mythologies, sous la direction de Y. Bonnefoy, Paris, 1981.
Enciclopedia dell'Arte Antica, Rome, 1958–66, 7 vols.
Grimal, P., *Dictionnaire de la mythologie grecque et romaine,* Paris, 1951.
Lexicon Iconographicum Mythologiae Classicae (LIMC), Zurich and Munich, beginning in 1981, 6 vols published (A–O).
Roscher, W., *Ausführliches Lexikon der greichischen und römischen Mythologie,* Leipzig, 1884–1934, 10 vols.

Antiquity

Brommer, F., *Denkmälerlisten zur greichischen Heldensage*, Marburg, 1971–6, 4 vols.

Brommer, F., *Vasenlisten zur greichischen Heldensage*, 3rd ed., Marburg, 1973.

Carpenter, T., *Art and Myth in Ancient Greece*, London, 1991.

Schefold, K., *Götter- und Heldensagen der Greichen und der spätarchaischen Kunst*, Munich, 1978.

Schefold, K., *Die Göttersage in der klassichen und hellenistischen Kunst*, Munich, 1981.

Schefold, K. and Jung, F., *Die Urkönige Perseus, Bellerophon, Herakles und Theseus in der klassischen und hellenistischen Kunst*, Munich, 1988.

Schefold, K., *Myth and Legend in Early Greek Art*, London, 1991.

Shapiro, A., *Myth into Art; Poet and Painter in Classical Greece*, London, 1994.

Modern Works

Alpers, S., *The Decoration of the Torre de la Prada. Corpus Rubenianum Ludwig Burchard*, London, 1971, vol. IX.

Bosque, A. de, *Mythologie et Maniérisme*, Paris, 1985.

Grabar, A., *Les Voies de la création en iconographie chrétienne. Antiquité et Moyen Age*, Paris, 1979.

Grunchec, P., *Les Concours de prix de Rome: 1797–1863*, Paris, 1986.

Hall, J., *Dictionary of Subjects and Symbols in Art*, London, 1974.

Kestner, J., *Mythology and Misogyny. The Social Discourse of XIXth Century British Classical-Subject Painting*, Madison, 1993.

Moormann, E. M. and Uitterhoeve, W., *Van Alexandros tot Zenobia*, Nimègue, 1989.

Panofsky, E., *Studies in Iconology*, New York, 1939.

Pigler, A., *Barrockthemen*, Budapest, 1956.

Reid, J.D., *The Oxford Guide to Classical Mythology in the Arts 1300–1990s*, 2 vols., Oxford and New York, 1993.

Seznec, J., *The Survival of the Pagan Gods*, Princeton, 1972.

Tervarent, G. de, *Attributs et symboles dans l'art profane (1450–1600)*, Geneva, 1958.

Van Marle, R., *Iconographie de l'art profane au Moyen-Âge et à la Renaissance*, The Hague, 1931.

Weitzmann, K., *Greek Mythology in Byzantine Art*, Princeton, 1951.

Wethey, H.E., *The Paintings of Titian*, vol. 3: *The Mythological and Historical Paintings*, London, 1975.

Wind, E., *Pagan Mysteries in the Renaissance*, New York, 1972.

Exhibitions

L'École de Fontainebleau, Paris, 1972.

Kilinski, K., *Classical Myth in Western Art*, Dallas, 1985.

Bailey, C.B., *The Loves of the Gods*, Fort Worth, 1992.

The Odyssey and Ancient Art, Bard College, New York, 1992.

INDEX OF PEOPLE, AUTHORS, AND PLACES

The names of places are in capital letters. Italic numbers refer to pages with illustrations.
Numbers in bold refer to individual entries.

PICTURE CREDITS

Black and white illustrations: A.C.L. Brussels, 46; Agraci, Paris, 96; Alinari-Giraudon, Paris 12, 15, 39 top, 45 top, 50 top, 105, 112 bottom, 113 top, 128, 134, 138, 177, 207, 211 top, 229, 231 top, 242; Anderson-Giraudon, Paris 19, 45 bottom, 63, 76, 90, 91, 119, 148, 175; Bibliothèque nationale, Paris, 60 bottom, 135, 143 bottom, 196 top, 243, 285; Boiron, Paris 186 top; Boudot-Lamotte, Paris 65, 133, 193 top, 215 bottom, 125, 222 bottom, 297 top; Bulloz, Paris 113 bottom, 237 top, 266; École nationale supérieure des Beaux-Arts, Paris, 73; Flammarion, 11, 12, 17, 26, 27 bottom, 41, 61, 90 top, 95, 103 top, 108, 112 bottom, 113 top, 114, 156, 173, 197, 198, 200, 248 top right, 258, 259; Gerondal, Lille, 44; Giraudon, Paris, 51, 60 top, 83, 84, 100, 110, 159 top, 252; Lauros-Giraudon, Paris 111 top; Réunion des musées nationaux, Paris 20, 21, 52, 62 bottom, 67, 75 top, 80, 86, 98, 121, 126 bottom, 137, 146, 152, 153 bottom, 168 top, 177, 188, 204, 206, 211 bottom, 216 top, 223 top, 251, 267; Savio, Rome 256; Tavanti, Arezzo, 32.

Color plates: Artothek, Preissenberg, II, VII, XXX; Bibliothèque nationale, Paris, XXVII; Bulloz, Paris, IV, XIV, XXII, XXV, XXXII; Dagli Orti, Paris, XI, XXIII; Giraudon, Paris, I, VI, XXI, XXVI, XXXI; Metropolitan Museum, New York, XIX; Réunion des musées nationaux, Paris, III, V, VIII, IX, X, XII, XIII, XV, XVI, XVII, XVIII, XX, XXIV, XXVIII, XXIX.

Jacket front and back: Réunion des musées nationaux, Paris.
© Photo RMN - René Gabriel Ojeda.

ACKNOWLEDGEMENTS

The authors would like to express their deep gratitude to Claire Lagarde without whose «heroic» competence and patience this book would never have seen the light. They are also extremely grateful to: Christine Claudon, Colette Malandain, Aurélien Moline, Daphné Pappers, Yves Raynaud, Séverine Roscot, Marion Tezenas du Montcel and Murielle Vaux.

Printed in Italy by G. Canale, Turin